APPROACHES TO BOOTSTRAPPING
VOLUME 2

LANGUAGE ACQUISITION & LANGUAGE DISORDERS

EDITORS

Harald Clahsen
University of Essex

Lydia White
McGill University

EDITORIAL BOARD

Melissa Bowerman (Max Planck Institut für Psycholinguistik, Nijmegen)
Katherine Demuth (Brown University)
Nina Hyams (University of California at Los Angeles)
William O'Grady (University of Hawaii)
Jürgen Meisel (Universität Hamburg)
Mabel Rice (University of Kansas)
Luigi Rizzi (University of Siena)
Bonnie Schwartz (University of Durham)
Antonella Sorace (University of Edinburgh)
Karin Stromswold (Rutgers University)
Jürgen Weissenborn (Universität Potsdam)
Frank Wijnen (Utrecht University)

Volume 24

Jürgen Weissenborn and Barbara Höhle (eds.)

Approaches to Bootstrapping.
Phonological, lexical, syntactic and neurophysiological
aspects of early language acquisition. Volume 2.

APPROACHES TO BOOTSTRAPPING

PHONOLOGICAL, LEXICAL, SYNTACTIC
AND NEUROPHYSIOLOGICAL ASPECTS OF
EARLY LANGUAGE ACQUISITION

VOLUME 2

Edited by

JÜRGEN WEISSENBORN

BARBARA HÖHLE

University of Potsdam

JOHN BENJAMINS PUBLISHING COMPANY
AMSTERDAM/PHILADELPHIA

The paper used in this publication meets the minimum requirements of American National Standard for Information Sciences — Permanence of Paper for Printed Library Materials, ANSI Z39.48-1984.

Library of Congress Cataloging-in-Publication Data

Approaches to bootstrapping : phonological, lexical, syntactic and neurophysiological aspects of early language acquisition / edited by Jürgen Weissenborn, Barbara Höhle.
    p.   cm. -- (Language acquisition & language disorders : ISSN 0925-0123; v. 23-24)
Includes bibliographical references and index.
    1. Language acquisition. 2. Language awareness in children. I. Weissenborn, Jürgen.
II. Höhle, Barbara. III. Series.
P118.A66.   2000
401'.93--dc21   00-058560
ISBN 90 272 2491 9 (Eur.) / 1 55619 992 9 (US) (v. 1. – alk. paper)
ISBN 90 272 2492 7 (Eur.) / 1 55619 993 7 (US) (v. 2. – alk. paper)

© Copyright 2001 - John Benjamins B.V.
No part of this book may be reproduced in any form, by print, photoprint, microfilm, or any other means, without written permission from the publisher.

John Benjamins Publishing Co. • P.O.Box 36224 • 1020 ME Amsterdam • The Netherlands
John Benjamins North America • P.O.Box 27519 • Philadelphia PA 19118-0519 • USA

Table of Contents

PART III
Interactions of Prosodic and Morphosyntactic Knowledge in Early Language Production

Prosodic Constraints on Morphological Development   3
  Katherine Demuth

The Interface of Phonology and Syntax: The emergence of the article in the early acquisition of Spanish and German   23
  Conxita Lleó

Interaction between Prosody and Morphosyntax: Plurals within codas in the acquisition of European Portuguese   45
  M. João Freitas, Matilde Miguel & Isabel Hub Faria

Compounds Triggering Prosodic Development   59
  Paula Fikkert

Prosodic Form, Syntactic Form, Phonological Bootstrapping, and Telegraphic Speech   87
  David Lebeaux

From Prosody to Grammar in English: The differentiation of catenatives, modals, and auxiliaries from a single protomorpheme   121
  Ann M. Peters

Input and production in the early development of function words   157
  Sven Strömqvist, Hrafnhildur Ragnarsdóttir & Ulla Richthoff

PART IV
Neurophysiological Aspects of Language Acquisition

Language Development during Infancy and Early Childhood:
Electrophysiological correlates   181
    Dennis L. Molfese, Dana B. Narter, Amy J. Van Matre,
    Michelle R. Ellefson & Arlene Modglin

Development Patterns of Brain Activity: Reflecting semantic and
syntactic processes   231
    Angela D. Friederici & Anja Hahne

Electrophysiological Studies of Language Development   247
    Marie St. George & Debra L. Mills

PART V
Additional Perspectives on Language Acquisition

Interactionist Approaches to Early Language Acquisition   263
    Kim Plunkett

Repertoires of Primitive Elements: Prerequisite or result of
acquisition?   281
    Manfred Bierwisch

Developmental Trajectories of Complex Signal Systems in Animals:
The model of bird song   309
    H. Hultsch & D. Todt

Index   333

PART III

Interactions of Prosodic and Morphosyntactic Knowledge in Early Language Production

Part III

Prosodic Constraints on Morphological Development

Katherine Demuth
Brown University

1. The acquisition of grammatical morphology

Since Roger Brown's (1973) influential work on the acquisition of grammatical morphology by Adam, Eve, and Sarah, the issue of how and when children come to acquire grammatical morphemes has presented a challenge to the field. Since that time there have been several proposals for how and why grammatical morphology might be missing from children's early speech. These proposals have ranged from the primacy of semantics in early grammars (e.g. Braine 1971; Bowerman 1973) to the impoverishment of early syntax (e.g. Guilfoyle & Noonan 1988; Lebeaux 1989; Radford 1990). Yet many syntacticians note that children seem to 'know' that grammatical morphemes exist even if they don't produce them (e.g. Demuth 1992, 1994; Hyams 1992). If this is true, then there needs to be an explanation for this phenomenon.

It has recently been proposed that children's early omission of grammatical morphology is due to *rhythmic production constraints* (e.g. Gerken, Landau & Remez 1990; Gerken 1991; Gerken & McIntosh 1993; Demuth 1994). Under this proposal stressed or strong (S) syllables and the unstressed, or weak (w) syllables that follow them form *trochaic feet* — structures which are seen as playing an important role in determining which syllables will be retained or omitted in children's early speech. Given a wSw sequence of syllables such as in the word *banana*, the *rhythmic production constraints* approach would predict that the second and third syllables — i.e. the Sw trochaic foot *nana*, would surface, the initial weak syllable being deleted unless it could combine with a stressed syllable from a preceding word to form a trochaic foot. This approach seems to account for much of the data around the ages of 2;6–3;6, especially in stress-timed languages like English and Dutch. It is unclear, however, how it generalizes to earlier stages of acquisition, and how it accounts for the acquisition of grammatical morphology crosslinguistically. To address these issues Demuth (1995, 1996a) and Demuth & Fee (1995) have developed a model of *Prosodic Constraints* which appeals to higher-level prosodic structures such as phonological words and phonological phrases, and shows how early words may be constrained at these different levels of structure. This approach provides a framework for examining earlier stages of prosodic word development not only in stress-timed languages like English, but also in morphologically rich languages where 'stress' or 'syllable prominence' is represented at higher levels of prosodic structure such as the phonological phrase (e.g. French, Sesotho). Furthermore, a theory of *Prosodic Constraints* offers a developmental account of how children eventually move to a more adult-like phonological and morphological grammar.

The purpose of this paper is to account for syllable omission and the emergence of grammatical morphology in early Spanish. The data are drawn from spontaneous productions of Sofía, a child learning Argentinean Spanish, between the ages of 1;8 and 1;9 (Gennari & Demuth 1997). Interestingly, we find that a *rhythmic production constraints* approach makes the wrong predictions about where grammatical morphology should be included or omitted in early speech productions. However, if we determine the prosodic shape of the child's early monomorphemic words, we find that the inclusion of certain grammatical morphemes is actually predicted, providing further support for the presence of *prosodic constraints*.

The paper is organized as follows: After briefly outlining the theory of *Prosodic Constraints* and how it applies in acquisition, we report on the shapes of Sofía's early monomorphemic words and multimorphemic words and phrases, focusing on the emergence of articles, negation, and prepositions. The results of this study are interesting for several reasons. First, they demonstrate how the *Prosodic Constraints* approach to early acquisition can be extended to account for syllable/morpheme omissions in multimorphemic utterances. Second, they indicate that the *prosodic constraints* operating in early Spanish are somewhat different from those found in English. And finally, they provide an explanation for why certain types of grammatical morphology may appear earlier in the speech of Spanish-speaking children than in that of their English-speaking peers. The paper concludes with a discussion of how a theory of *Prosodic Constraints* contributes to a more general *Constraint-based Approach to Language Acquisition*.

2. Prosodic constraints in children's early words

Demuth & Fee (1995) develop a prosodic approach to early phonological word development, showing how English- and Dutch-speaking children gradually learn to exploit units of the Prosodic Hierarchy (Selkirk 1984; Nespor & Vogel 1986), focusing initially on the levels of structure at and below the Phonological Word (e.g. the mora, syllable, Foot, and Phonological Word). These and higher levels of the Prosodic Hierarchy are illustrated in (1) below, along with sample pieces of phrase structure.

(1)   The Prosodic Hierarchy
      Utt   (Phonological Utterance)   *I think Sue likes bananas*
      |
      IP   (Intonational Phrase)   *Sue likes bananas*
      |
      PP   (Phonological Phrase)   *likes bananas*
      |
      PW   (Phonological Word)   *bananas*
      |
      Ft   (Foot)   *nanas*
      |
      σ   (Syllable)   *nas*
      |
      μ   (Mora)   *na*

Demuth & Fee (1995) identify four major stages of prosodic word development below (see Fikkert 1994 for similar proposals). Interestingly, epenthetic syllables are sometimes found with trisyllabic targets during later stages of development, resulting in prosodic words composed of two feet.

(2)   Stages in the Development of Phonological Words
      (e.g. for target = *banana*)
      Stage I   Core (CV) Syllables   ba, na
      Stage II   Minimal Words   nana, bana
      Stage III 1 Stress-Foot   nana, nanas
      Stage IV   2 Stress-Feet   babanana

Many children seem to spend several months at the Minimal Word stage, where the majority of their early Phonological Words take the shape of binary feet, either disyllabic feet like /'dagi/ 'doggie' (3a), or monosyllabic bimoraic feet like /dag/ 'dog' (3b), where the first mora is the nucleus (vowel) of the syllable, and the second mora either a vowel or coda consonant.

(3) a. Disyllabic Foot   b. Monosyllabic foot

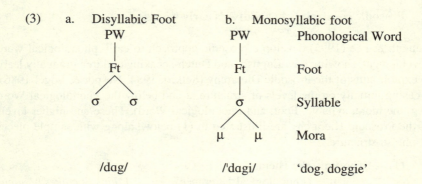

Some children seem to permit Minimal Words of type (3a) first, and then begin to permit Minimal Words of type (3b), allowing for increased complexity at the sub-syllabic level. That is, it appears that children's use of prosodic structure becomes more complex over time. This is outlined in (4), where children's earliest Phonological Words (PWs) are often formed of Core (CV) Syllables, then disyllabic feet, then bimoraic feet, and finally two feet. It is at this later 'stage' that children's utterances become prosodically more complex, being composed of more than one word, and forming a larger Phonological Phrase (PP). We illustrate the development of such structure with the examples /bəˈnænə/ *banana* and /ˈɛləfənt/ *elephant*, showing how these words, which have different structures, develop over time (see Fikkert 1994; Demuth & Fee 1995; and Demuth 1996b for specific examples from children's speech).

(4) Development of Prosodic Structure

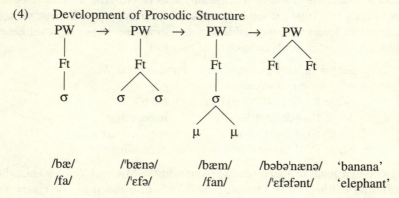

It would therefore appear that children's early words are *prosodically constrained*, with only a certain amount of prosodic structure permitted. This may be due to the fact that syllable structure in languages like English and Dutch is especially complex — taking some time to learn, and that keeping words to a Minimal Word length provides the learner with the opportunity to explore the nature of that syllable structure more fully. Alternatively, it may be that Minimal Words are especially prominent in the acquisition of languages like English and Dutch because many of the high frequency words in both these languages tend to be monosyllabic. That is, the presence of a Minimal Word stage of development may have something to do with learnability and language planning factors (e.g. start with small syllables/words — cf. Elman 1991, 1993; Newport 1990) and/or it may reflect children's awareness of the frequency effects of the prosodic structures present in the ambient language.

The identification of these prosodic structures in the early development of languages like English and Dutch raises several questions. First, are these patterns of prosodic development universal? That is, are they found in all children and in all languages? Peters (1983, 1985) has suggested that some English-speaking children do not follow this pattern at all, but begin to speak in larger prosodic chunks where the identification of individual words is difficult at best. We suggest that some children may approach the acquisition of prosodic structure by focusing initially on higher levels such as the Phonological Phrase or the Phonological Utterance. Furthermore, we predict that such a strategy will have serious implications for the acquisition of grammatical morphemes. To test these hypotheses we turn to early words in Sofía's speech, examining the prosodic structure of both monomorphemic and multimorphemic utterances.

The data are drawn from Gennari & Demuth (1997) who report on the longitudinal development of Sofía's early words and utterances between the ages of 1;8 and 2;3 years. Sofía had already begun speaking a few months earlier, so the data do not include her earliest words. In this paper we examine the structure of Sofía's monomorphemic and multimorphemic words and utterances at 1;8 and 1;9 years, focusing specifically on the structure of her Phonological Words (PW) and Phonological Phrases (PP). In so doing we follow Hayes (1995) in determining the nature of Feet and Phonological Words.

3. Prosodic constraints in Early Spanish

Spanish is a language which permits stress on any of the last three syllables of a word (Harris 1983). The default (and most frequent) position for stress is the penultimate syllable of a word. At the lexical level there is no secondary stress: This arises only at the level of the Phonological Phrase, where unstressed syllables can assume secondary stress, with an alternating SwSw pattern emerging. Given that Spanish exhibits high frequency of trochaic feet, we might expect young Spanish-speaking children to show evidence of trochaic feet in their early utterances.

At 1;8 years Sofía uses both trochaic (5) and iambic (6) words.

(5) Trochaic Feet
		Child	Adult target		
	a.	[óto]	/róto/	'broken'	(1;8)
	b.	[káxa]	/káxa/	'box	
	c.	[néne]	/néne/	'kid'	
	d.	[éta]	/ésta/	'this'	

(6) Iambic Feet
		Child	Adult target		
	a.	[papá]	/papá/	'daddy'	(1;8)
	b.	[mamá]	/mamá/	'mommy'	
	c.	[aká]	/aká/	'here'	
	d.	[así]	/así/	'in this way'	

Although trochaic words are much more frequent in Spanish than iambic words, it would appear that Sofía has available to her the following prosodic structures.

(7) a. Troachaic Feet   b. Iambic Feet

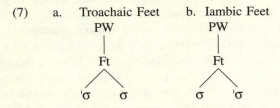

Alternatively, it could be that the 'iambic' forms are actually more prosodically complex structures which encompass a monosyllabic trochaic foot and a preceding syllable represented at a higher level of structure — i.e. at the level of the PW (8).

(8)

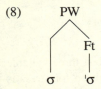

Further support for the presence of PW structures like that in (8) come from Sofía's trisyllabic word targets (9).

(9) Trisyllabic Targets: wSw > Sw ~ (wSw)

	Child	Adult target		
a.	[máka]	/amáka/	'hammock'	(1;8)
b.	[manθána]	/mansána/	'apple'	
c.	[méka]	/muɲéka/	'doll'	(1;9)
d.	[tána]	/bentána/	'window'	
e.	[ríba]	/aríba/	'above'	

Many of the trisyllabic wSw targets are reduced to a Sw trochaic foot, but a few are realized in their full wSw form. Thus, though there seems to be a tendency to omit pre-tonic syllables, as predicted by the *rhythmic production constraint* approach, and to produce only a binary foot (or Minimal Word), Sofía is apparently capable of representing PWs at 1;8 years with the structure given in (10).[1]

(10)
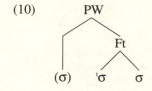

Note that this structure has an initial weak syllable: Lexical items with this type of structure are infrequent in languages like English and Dutch until after the age of two (cf. Smith 1973; Fikkert 1994; Wijnen, Kirkhaar & den Os 1994; Demuth & Fee 1995). Thus, although Sofía at 1;8 years frequently reduces her words to a disyllabic trochaic foot (9), she is also able to produce prosodically more complex structures similar to those found in English- and Dutch-speaking children after the age of 2. It is therefore possible that Sofía uses similar structures, such as that in (8), for representing so-called 'iambic' words rather than having two types of feet — trochaic and iambic.

There are few examples in Sofía's spontaneous speech corpus of trisyllabic targets. However, if she is capable of representing PWs that are larger than a Foot, this should be evidenced in larger PWs as well. Harris (1983) notes that Spanish lexical items undergo 'restructuring at the level of the Phonological Phrase, introducing secondary stress on alternating syllables'. This means that PWs with the lexical structure wwSw become SwSw when embedded in a larger PP, or as the only word in an utterance. Consider the following quadrisyllabic targets, where secondary stress falls on the first syllable of the target word.

(11) Quadrisyllabic Targets: SwSw > wSw ~ (Sw)
       Child   *Adult target*
  a. [dóro]   /inodóro/   'lavatory'   (1;8)
  b. [kaléra]   /èskaléra/   'stairs'
  c. [maléra]   /màmadéra/ 'feeding bottle'

Here we see that either the initial Sw foot of the word, or the initial S (secondarily stressed) syllable of the word, has been omitted. Under the *rhythmic production constraints* approach the omission of the initial Sw Foot would be completely unexpected, as would the omission of the initial S syllable. Under the *prosodic constraints* account, however, the forms in (11) are expected given what we have already seen with disyllabic and trisyllabic targets in (9) and (10). That is, PWs with the structure in (12a) are allowed, whereas PWs composed of two (binary) feet are not yet permitted (12b).

(12) a. PW   b. * PW

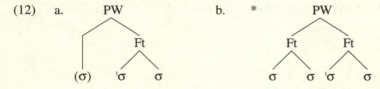

Thus, we see that Sofía's PWs are *prosodically constrained*, where the upper bound on prosodic structure permitted is a Foot optionally preceded by an unfooted syllable. The prosodic structure in (12b) is therefore apparently prohibited in Sofía's monomorphemic words at this stage of development.[2]

In this section we have shown that Sofía's monomorphemic PWs at 1;8–1;9 years are generally composed of an optional (unstressed and unfooted) syllable followed by a trochaic foot. Sofía has therefore gone beyond the Minimal Word stage by the age of 1;8 years — a time when the maximal structure found in the speech of many of her English- and Dutch-speaking peers is only a binary foot (Demuth & Fee 1995). There are (at least) two possible explanations for this apparently precocious behavior: First, it could be that Sofía is more advanced than her other Spanish-speaking peers, though Lleó (1997, 1998) reports similar findings of early trisyllabic wSw lexical items from several Spanish-speaking children of around the same age. It therefore appears that Sofía's prosodic word development is typical of other Spanish-speaking children of the same age. Alternatively, then, it may be that the prosodic structure of Spanish differs sufficiently from that of English and Dutch such that the development of Spanish PWs will take a different course. Note that this prosodic difference would need to prevail despite the fact that the default and most frequent position of stress in Spanish creates a word-final trochaic foot. The data from Sofía are inadequate for fully addressing this hypothesis as they were not collected from the onset of her first words. However, given the higher frequency of polysyllabic words in Spanish, we predict that Spanish-speaking children will begin to represent more complex prosodic word structures at an earlier stage of development than their English- and Dutch-speaking peers. That is, we expect that *all* children will exhibit *prosodic constraints* in the development of their early words, but also that the prosodic characteristics of the target language will have a major influence in determining the nature of those *prosodic constraints* (cf. Demuth 1996a).

In the following section we explore the implications of the theory *Prosodic Constraints* for the emergence of grammatical morphology.

4. Prosodic constraints and multimorphemic words and phrases

In their theory of prosodic structure Selkirk (1984, 1996) and Nespor & Vogel (1986) show how grammatical morphemes and lexical items within an utterance are prosodically organized into Phonological Words and Phonological Phrases. Selkirk (1996) provides a 'typology' of prosodic structures that grammatical morphemes (or function categories) may assume within a larger Phonological Phrase. These are outlined below, where fnc = (closed class grammatical) functional item and lex = (open class) lexical item.

(13) The prosodic status of grammatical function morphemes
  Prosodic Word $((fnc)_{PW} \, (lex)_{PW} \,)_{PP}$
  Prosodic Clitics
  a. free clitic $(fnc \, (lex)_{PW} \,)_{PP}$
  b. internal clitic $((fnc \, lex)_{PW} \,)_{PP}$
  c. affixal clitic $((fnc \, (lex)_{PW} \,)_{PW} \,)_{PP}$

These structures can be schematized as follows.

(14) Prosodic Words   Prosodic Clitics

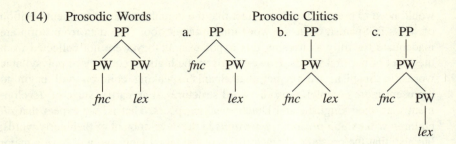

Selkirk (1996) shows that the prosodic structures permitted will vary both from language to language, as well as within a language, depending on the nature of the prosodic characteristics of the grammatical morpheme. For example, *unstressed* English function words such as prepositions, articles, auxiliaries, and pronouns take the structure in (14a), where the function word is prosodified at the level of the PP (e.g. *to Boston, a message, can cook, his picture*). In contrast, *stressed* auxiliaries and pronouns (e.g. *we CAN, HE knows*) are themselves PWs, and combine with lexical items at the level of the PP (14). The structures in (14b) and (14c) occur in other languages, but not in English. We use the above as a starting point for examining the shape of Sofía's multimorphemic Phonological Phrases, and show that she has both the structures in (14a) and (14b) (where function words are prosodified along with the lexical item as a PW), albeit for different grammatical morphemes.

Consider Sofía's quadrisyllabic multimorphemic forms in (15). These consist of either a trisyllabic lexical item plus a grammatical morpheme such as a determiner (/la muɲéka/ 'the doll'), or a disyllabic lexical item plus a disyllabic determiner (/una móto/ 'a motorbike'). These quadrisyllabic targets are prosodified in Spanish as SwSw at the level of the Phonological Phrase. Under the *rhythmic constraints* account we would expect such forms to be produced in full, with the determiner included. However, given what we now know about the prosodic constraints operating on Sofía's monomorphemic PWs, the *prosodic constraints* account would predict a trisyllabic wSw form to be produced, and this is exactly what we find.

(15) Prosodic Clitics (Det): SwSw > wSw

	Child	Adult target		
a.	[namáka]	/una:amáka/	'a hammock'	(1;8)
b.	[eméka]	/la muɲéka/	'the doll'	(1;9)
c.	[amwéka]	/la muɲéka/	'the doll'	
d.	[namóto]	/una móto/	'a motorbike'	

MORPHOLOGICAL DEVELOPMENT: PROSODIC CONSTRAINTS

In all cases a maximum of three syllables was produced. When the indefinite article /una/ is used, the initial vowel/syllable is dropped (15a, d). In contrast, the vowel (or an approximation thereof) of the definite feminine article is maintained in (15b, c) and a syllable from the trisyllabic word /muɲéka/ 'doll' is omitted. Neither of these scenarios is expected under the *rhythmic constraints* account, whereas both are possible and expected under a *prosodic constraints* account. The structure that appears to be operative is that in (16a), a structure similar to that seen above in the discussion of monomorphemic PWs (cf. (10) and (12a)).

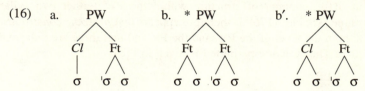

(16)

Cl refers to a *prosodic clitic*, equivalent to Selkirk's *fnc*. Note that the clitic appears to be limited to one syllable — it cannot have the phonological content of a foot. That is, the structure in (16b) is disallowed, as already shown in (12b) above, and its prosodic clitic equivalent in (16b′) is no better. It therefore appears that the determiner is prosodified as part of the PW, but it is prosodically limited to one syllable. This is exactly what was found in Sofía's multisyllabic monomorphemic word targets (cf. (12a)).

In addition to noun phrases consisting of Det + Noun, Sofía uses some more complex structures involving either verbs and their complements (e.g. V + N, (Neg +) V (+ Adv)), or prepositions and their complements (e.g. Prep + Det + N). These structures are no longer merely Phonological Words but higher level Phonological Phrases. We might therefore expect more grammatical morphology to be represented. The data are presented in (17).

(17) Phonological Phrases (V, Neg, Prep): (w)SwSw > (S)wSw

	Child	Adult target		
a.	[elakása]	/en la kása/	'in the house'	(1;8)
b.	[akaása]	/a la kása/	'to the house'	
c.	[enóno]	/ase nóno/	'to go to sleep'	
d.	[nonáda]	/no ai náda/	'there isn't anything'	
e.	[egwardáda]	/está gwardáda/	'it is put away'	

Here we see some variation in the shape of the forms actually produced, yet there is also some regularity. In all cases there are two types of constraints that must be satisfied: First, we have already seen that there is an upper bound on the amount of structure that can be represented as part of a PW, and this is a maximum of three syllables (a foot with a preceding syllable). Determiners are prosodic clitics which prosodify along with the following noun as part of a PW, as seen in (17a, b). In both these cases the Preposition is also prosodified, providing evidence of access to higher-level PP. The second constraint appears to operate on the amount of structure that can be represented at the level of the PP. This also appears to be one syllable. This is seen in examples (17c, d, and e) where disyllabic verbs and/or negation and a verb are reduced to one syllable independent of the amount of structure within the PW (either two syllables (17c, d) or three syllables (17e). It therefore appears that *prosodic constraints* are operating at both the level of the PW and the PP, and that these are independent of one another. The structure permitted is given in (18).

(18)
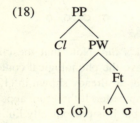

Note that the preservation of either three or four syllables (depending on the grammatical structure involved) falls out naturally from the theory of *prosodic constraints*. In contrast, the *rhythmic constraints* account would predict that four syllables should surface. It therefore appears that Sofía must be sensitive to the hierarchical nature of the prosodic representations, and must be operating at this level rather than at the level of surface rhythmic constraints.

In this section we have seen that Sofía treats Det + Noun sequences as PWs, where the determiner can take the form of one syllable, and the maximum amount of structure permitted is a Foot preceded by a syllable. This is the same structure permitted for monomorphemic words. On the other hand, Sofía is also capable of producing quadrisyllabic PPs, where a monosyllabic Verb, Preposition, or Negation can precede the PW. Thus, Sofía can produce an increased number of surface syllables (and grammatical morphemes) only if they are represented at the higher level of a Phonological Phrase. These facts are difficult to deal with under a surface level *rhythmic production constraints* account. They fall out naturally, however, from a theory of *Prosodic Constraints* (Demuth 1995; Demuth & Fee 1995).

5. Implications for the emergence of English grammatical morphology

In the foregoing discussion of Spanish grammatical morphology we have shown that different types of grammatical morphology are prosodified at different levels of structure. We have also shown that Sofía's early utterances are prosodically constrained, even though she apparently has access to several different levels of prosodic structure (including Ft, PW, PP). If we know the level at which different grammatical morphemes are prosodified in a language, and the nature of the prosodic constraints operative within a child's grammar at a given point in development, we should be able to make strong predictions regarding the types of grammatical morphemes that are likely to appear. Consider the case of English stressed and unstressed object pronouns as in 'LIKE 'im' versus 'like HIM'. When the pronoun is stressed it functions as an independent PW that would combine with a verb at the level of the Phonological Phrase. This is illustrated in (19a). In contrast, the unstressed pronoun functions as a *free prosodic clitic* with the structure shown in (19b).³

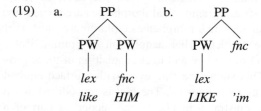

(19) a.   PP   b.   PP

If the prosodic constraints in a child's grammar permit Phonological Phrases that contain only a PW and not other prosodic material, then both of the structures in (19) will be ruled out. This would be typical of what is found at the one-word stage of development that many children exhibit. On the other hand, if two PWs are permitted within a PP, the structure in (19a) would be expected. Alternatively, it could be that two PWs are disallowed, but that a PW is permitted with some accompanying material that is not itself a PW. In this case a structure like that in (19b) would be permitted. Matthei (1989: 47) provides an interesting example of a case like that in (19a). Here we see that two lexical items can be produced in isolation, each a disyllabic PW (constituted of a binary (probably trochaic) foot) (20a, b). But when the two are combined into a possessive construction both items are phonologically reduced (20c), again yielding a binary foot.

(20) Child   Adult target
 a. [beˈbi]   /beˈbi/   'baby'   (1;5)
 b. [bʊkɔ]   /bʊk/   'book'
 c. [beˈbʊ]   /beˈbiz bʊk/ 'baby's book'

It would appear that, at 1;5 years, this child does not have access to the higher level of the PP, or at least does not differentiate it from the level of the PW. Thus, the PW constraints apply, yielding a binary foot, as illustrated below.

(21) PW/PP

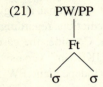

The *prosodic constraints* approach can also be extended to non-syllabic grammatical morphemes like those found in English. Given the different levels of prosodic structure at which different grammatical morphemes are prosodified we can again make predictions about which morphemes children are most likely to acquire first. Specifically, we predict earlier acquisition of grammatical morphemes prosodified at the level of the PW and later acquisition of those prosodified at the level of the PP. This should be true even with 'surface equivalent' structures such as *plural* versus *possessive* /s/: The first is prosodified as part of a PW (Selkirk's affixal clitic illustrated in (14c)), the second as part of a PP (Selkirk's free clitic illustrated in (14a)).

(22)

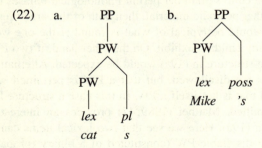

Interestingly, these predictions are supported by the findings reported in Brown (1973), where all three children studied exhibited earlier acquisition of the plural morpheme than the possessive counterpart. Thus, it would appear that, in addition to whatever semantic or syntactic constraints might be operating on children's early grammars, the prosodic realization of different grammatical function morphemes may play a role in determining the rate and relative order in which they are acquired.

6. Discussion

This paper has shown that certain types of grammatical morphology were either included or excluded from Sofía's early words depending on (1) the level of structure at which the particular grammatical morpheme is prosodified, and (2) the *prosodic constraints* operating within the child's grammar at a given point in development. The nature of these *prosodic constraints* may vary to some extent from child to child and from language to language. Once these were determined for Sofía, it was possible, given a new target utterance, to predict which syllables and/or morphemes would be included or omitted.

The Spanish data are extremely interesting for a number of reasons. First, they demonstrate an *early awareness of different levels of prosodic structure*, and these are reflected in the shape of the child's early multimorphemic utterances. Interestingly, studies of infant speech perception indicate that there may be an awareness of 'phrase boundaries' (i.e. Phonological Phrases) even as young as 4;5 months (cf. Jusczyk 1989; Jusczyk, Kemler Nelson, Hirsh-Pasek, Kennedy, Woodward & Piwoz 1992; see also Hirsh-Pasek, Kemler Nelson, Jusczyk, Wright Cassidy, Druss & Kennedy 1987). It should not be surprising, then, that we find early production evidence for such structures. What has been unclear until now is how and when children begin to represent aspects of this higher-level hierarchical structure in their own productions, and the role this may play in shaping early multimorphemic utterances.

Second, results from this study indicate that Spanish-speaking children may begin to represent larger and higher-level units of prosodic structure earlier than children learning English or Dutch. This hypothesis will need to be tested over larger groups of children with longitudinal data from 1–3 years, however preliminary reports on other Spanish-speaking children from Lleó (1997, 1998), plus studies of children learning Italian grammatical function morphology (Guasti 1993/1994; Bottari, Cipriani & Chilosi 1993/1994) indicate that this may be the case. It therefore seems reasonable to expect that the nature of prosodic constraints will vary to some extent from language to language, and that learning these constraints represents one of several early steps toward learning the grammatical structure of the target language (Demuth 1996a).

Third, if all children exhibit prosodic constraints in the acquisition of phonological and morphological structure, we might expect that children with language delay might also exhibit less developed prosodic structures than their peers. Interestingly Fikkert & Penner (1998), in their study of two language-impaired children learning Swiss German, report that this is precisely the case. The theory of *Prosodic Constraints* may therefore be useful for investigating individual differences of children learning the same language and in the early identification of children at risk for language delay.

Several scholars have recently begun to explore an Optimality-theoretic approach to the acquisition of prosodic, segmental, phonotactic, and stress systems (e.g. Demuth 1995, 1996b, 1997; Gnanadesikan 1995; Paradis 1995; Pater 1997; Bernhart & Stemberger 1998; see also papers in Bernhardt, Gilbert & Ingram 1996). The study presented here lays the groundwork needed for exploring the acquisition of larger prosodic structures along similar lines (see also Gerken 1996). Ultimately, I suggest that a fuller understanding of the course of language development will need to be couched within a more general *Constraint-based Approach to Language Acquisition*, where phonological constraints of various types, along with memory, planning, and other grammatical constraints, will all be found to play a role in determining the shape of children's early utterances and how these develop over time. The acquisition of grammatical morphology at the higher-level Phonological Phrases examined here provides a step in that direction.

Acknowledgments

An earlier version of this paper was presented at the 21th Conference on Language Development, Boston University. I thank that audience as well as Silvia Gennari, Barbara Höhle, and Jürgen Weissenborn for comments and discussion.

Notes

1. I follow Hayes (1995) in treating this pretonic syllable as unfooted, though this has no larger theoretical implications here. Interestingly, many English- and Dutch-speaking children seem to produce SwSw words prior to allowing wSw words — even to the extent of adding epenthetic vowels (Fikkert 1994; Demuth & Fee 1995). This indicates that unfooted syllables may be dispreferred in the early grammars of these children.
2. We know little of when and how Spanish-speaking children learn about secondary stress. It is therefore possible that the forms in (11) are actually wwSw targets for children, where the initial weak syllable or syllables are omitted. However, even if this were the case, these forms would still be problematic for the *rhythmic production constraint* account which would predict only disyllabic Sw forms to surface.

3. Studies of the acquisition of English grammatical morphology rarely document the prosodic (stressed vs. unstressed) status of pronouns, yet such details are critical to developing a more sophisticated understanding of how and when children will omit certain types of grammatical morphology.

References

Bernhardt, B., Gilbert, J. & Ingram, D. (eds.) 1996. *Proceedings of the International Conference on Phonological Acquisition.* Somerville, MA: Cascadilla Press.
Bernhardt, B. & Stemberger, J. 1998. *Handbook of phonological development from the perspective of constraint-based nonlinear phonology.* New York: Academic Press.
Bottari, P., Cipriani, P. & Chilosi, A. M. 1993/1994. "Protosyntactic Devices in the Acquisition of Italian Free Morphology." *Language Acquisition* 3(4): 327–369.
Bowerman, M. 1973. *Early syntactic development: A crosslinguistic study, with special reference to Finnish.* Cambridge: Cambridge University Press.
Brown, R. 1973. *A first language: The early stages.* Cambridge, MA: Harvard University Press.
Braine, M. 1971. "On two types of models in the internalization of grammars." In *The ontogenesis of grammar*, D. I. Slobin (ed.). New York: Academic Press.
Demuth, K. 1992. "Accessing functional categories in Sesotho: Interactions at the morpho-syntax interface." In *The Acquisition of Verb Placement: Functional Categories and V2 Phenomena in Language Development*, J. Meisel (ed.). Dordrecht: Kluwer Academic Publishers.
Demuth, K. 1994. "On the 'Underspecification' of Functional Categories in Early Grammars." In *Syntactic Theory and First Language Acquisition: Cross-Linguistic Perspectives*, B. Lust, M. Suñer & J. Whitman (eds.). Hillsdale, N.J.: Lawrence Erlbaum Associates.
Demuth, K. 1995. "Markedness and the development of prosodic structure." In *Proceedings of the North East Linguistic Society* 25, J. Beckman (ed.). Amherst, MA: GLSA, University of Massachusetts.
Demuth, K. 1996a. "The Prosodic Structure of Early Words." In *Signal to Syntax: Bootstrapping from Speech to Grammar in Early Acquisition*, J. Morgan & K. Demuth (eds.). Mahwah, N.J.: Lawrence Erlbaum Associates.
Demuth, K. 1996b. "Alignment, stress and parsing in early phonological words." In *Proceedings of the International Conference on Phonological Acquisition*, B. Bernhardt, J. Gilbert & D. Ingram (eds.). Somerville, MA: Cascadilla Press.
Demuth, K. 1997. "Multiple optimal outputs in acquisition." *University of Maryland Working Papers in Linguistics* 5: 53–71.
Demuth, K. & Fee, E. J. 1995. "Minimal Prosodic Words in Early Phonological Development." Ms., Brown University and Dalhousie University.
Dinnsen, D. & Barlow, J. 1998. "Root and manner feature faithfulness in acquisition." In *Proceedings of the 22nd Annual Boston University Conference on Language Develop-*

ment, A. Greenhill, M. Hughes, H. Littlefield & H. Walsh (eds.). Somerville, MA: Cascadilla Press.

Elman, J. 1991. "Incremental learning, or the importance of starting small." *Proceedings of the 13th annual conference of the Cognitive Science Society*. Hillsdale, N.J.: Lawrence Erlbaum Associates.

Elman, J. 1993. "Learning and development in neural networks: The importance of starting small." *Cognition* 48: 71–99.

Fikkert, P. 1994. *On the acquisition of prosodic structure*. Leiden, The Netherlands: University of Leiden Dissertation.

Fikkert, P. & Penner, Z. 1998. "Stagnation in Prosodic Development of Language-Disordered Children." In *Proceedings of the 22nd Annual Boston University Conference on Language Development 1*, A. Greenhill, M. Hughes, H. Littlefield & H. Walsh (eds.). Somerville, MA: Cascadilla Press.

Gnanadesikan, A. 1995. "Markedness and faithfulness constraints in child phonology." Ms., University of Massachusetts, Amherst. ROA.

Gennari, S. & Demuth, K. 1997. "Syllable omission in Spanish." *Proceedings of the 21st Annual Boston University Conference on Language Development*. Somerville, MA: Cascadilla Press.

Gerken, L. 1991. "The metrical basis of children's subjectless sentences." *Journal of Memory and Language* 30: 431–451.

Gerken, L. 1996. "Prosodic structure in young children's language production." *Language* 72: 683–712.

Gerken, L., Landau B. & Remez, R. E. 1990. "Function morphemes in young children's speech perception and production." *Developmental Psychology* 27: 204–216.

Gerken, L. & McIntosh, B. 1993. "The interplay of function morphemes and prosody in early language." *Developmental Psychology* 29: 448–457.

Guasti, M. T. 1993/1994. "Verb syntax in Italian child grammar: Finite and non-finite verbs." *Language Acquisition* 3: 1–40.

Guilfoyle, E. & Noonan, M. 1988. "Functional categories and language acquisition." Paper presented at the Conference on Language Development, Boston University.

Harris, J. 1983. *Syllable structure and stress in Spanish*. Cambridge, MA: MIT Press.

Hayes, B. 1995. *Metrical stress theory: Principles and case studies*. Chicago: University of Chicago Press.

Hirsh-Pasek, K., Kemler Nelson, D., Jusczyk, P., Wright Cassidy, K., Druss, B. & Kennedy, L. 1987. "Clauses are perceptual units for young infants." *Cognition* 26: 269–286.

Hyams, N. 1992. "The genesis of clausal structure." In *The Acquisition of Verb Placement: Functional Categories and V2 Phenomena in Language Development*, J. Meisel (ed.). Dordrecht: Kluwer Academic Publishers.

Jusczyk, P. 1989. "Perception of cues to clausal units in native and non-native languages." Paper presented at the biennial meeting of the Society for Research in Child Development, Kansas City, Missouri.

Jusczyk, P., Kemler Nelson, D., Hirsh-Pasek, K., Kennedy, L., Woodward, A. & Piwoz, J. 1992. "Perception of acoustic correlates of major phrasal units by young infants." *Cognitive Psychology* 24: 252–293.
Lebeaux, D. 1988. *Language acquisition and the form of grammar*. Ph. D. dissertation, Amherst, MA: University of Massachusetts.
Lleó, C. 1997. "Filler syllables, Proto-articles and early prosodic constraints in Spanish and German." In *Language Acquisition: Knowledge, Representation and Processing. Proceedings of GALA '97*, A. Sorace, C. Heycock & R. Shillcock (eds.). Edinburgh: Edinburgh University Press.
Lleó, C. 1998. "Proto-articles in the acquisition of Spanish: Interface between Phonology and Morphology." In *Modelle der Flexion: 18. Jahrestagung der Deutschen Gesellschaft für Sprachwissenschaf*, R. Fabri, A. Ortmann & T. Parodi (eds.). Tübingen: Niemeyer Verlag.
Matthei, E. 1989. "Crossing boundaries: More evidence for phonological constraints on early multi-word utterances." *Journal of Child Language* 16: 41–54.
Newport, E. 1990. "Maturational constrains on language learning." *Cognitive Science* 14: 11–28.
Nespor, M. & Vogel, I. 1986. *Prosodic phonology*. Dordrecht: Foris Publications.
Paradis, J. 1995. "Prosodic development and differentiation in bilingual first language acquisition." Cognitive Science Center Technical Report #2295, McGill University, Montreal.
Pater, J. 1997. "Minimal violation and phonological development." *Language Acquisition* 6(3): 201–253.
Peters, A. 1983. *The units of language acquisition*. Cambridge: Cambridge University Press.
Peters, A. 1985. "Language segmentation: Operating principles for the perception and analysis of language." In *The Cross-Linguistic Study of Language Acquisition*, Vol. 2, D. I. Slobin (ed.). Hillsdale, N.J.: Lawrence Erlbaum Associates.
Radford, A. 1990. *Syntactic Theory and the Acquisition of English Syntax*. Oxford: Basil Blackwell.
Selkirk, E. 1984. *Phonology and syntax: The relation between sound and structure*. Cambridge, MA: MIT Press.
Selkirk, E. 1996. "The prosodic structure of function words." In *Signal to Syntax: Bootstrapping from Speech to Grammar in Early Acquisition*, J. Morgan & K. Demuth (eds.). Mahwah, N.J.: Lawrence Erlbaum Associates.
Smith, N. V. 1973. *The Acquisition of Phonology*. Cambridge: Cambridge University Press.
Wijnen, F., Krikhaar, E. & den Os, E. 1994. "The (non)realization of unstressed elements in children's utterances: Evidence for a rhythmic constraint." *Journal of Child Language* 21(1): 59–83.

The Interface of Phonology and Syntax
The emergence of the article in the early acquisition of Spanish and German

Conxita Lleó
University of Hamburg

1. Introduction

It has been shown (see Lleó 1997 and 1998) that Spanish children begin to develop proto-articles at about 1;4, a few months earlier than German children, whose first articles make their appearance towards the end of the second year, at about 1;10. In this paper, the two different courses of development between 1;5 and 2;3 are studied on the basis of the data of three Spanish and four German children. Whereas Spanish children begin to produce proto-articles at the one-word stage, German children produce most of their early articles within longer utterances. In search of an explanation for the two different developments, the prosodic structures of the articles in the respective target languages are compared. In German, articles may have a reduced and an unreduced form. If unreduced, they constitute a prosodic word on their own, and if reduced, they are produced as clitics with the host to the left, i.e. as enclitics. In Spanish it has been shown that definite articles are proclitic, prosodically attached to the following noun (Harris 1989). It will further be argued that indefinite articles, too, are generally pronounced as proclitics to the noun to their right. The different prosodic characteristics of the articles in the two target languages can be captured by an OT analysis. This yields different rankings of the relevant constraints in the target languages, resulting in different constraint ranking in the child grammars of the two language groups, thereby providing an explanation for the different acquisition phenomena. The data presented here show that children are especially sensitive to the prosodic units of the target language and that their early grammars are primarily built upon such prosodic units.

2. Theoretical issues

Analyses of early productions from a prosodic perspective have shown some differences in the development of basic prosodic structures, and in the development of certain function words, which might be due to prosodic differences as well. In Fikkert (1994), Demuth & Fee (1995), Demuth (1996) and Demuth (this volume), it is argued that children acquiring English or Dutch go through a stage of two-feet (Figure 1a) before allowing unfooted syllables, i.e., syllables which skip the level of foot and are directly attached to the next higher level, the prosodic word or the phonological phrase (Figure 1b). On the other hand, Lleó (1998) argues that children acquiring Spanish take a reverse path, producing unfooted syllables before the two-foot stage.[1]

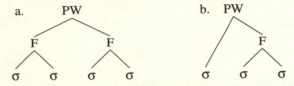

Figure 1.

This developmental prosodic difference has its correlate in an important difference related to the acquisition of certain morphemes, i.e. function words like the articles. In Lleó (1998) it has been shown that a pretonic syllable, often consisting of a laryngeal consonant and an open vowel, generally produced before a trochee appears as soon as 1;4 within the data of children acquiring Spanish, at the one-word stage, when the majority of utterances are nouns. Pretonic syllables manifest two different functions in Spanish child data. They either are a reduced form of the initial target unstressed syllable of a trisyllabic noun or they precede a disyllabic or monosyllabic noun, filling the position of an article. These latter syllables, observed in the acquisition of various languages, have been dubbed "filler" syllables and have been attributed the purpose of "holding the place" for the article (Peters & Menn 1993). They are thus proto-articles or articles in "embryonic stage". The production of such unfooted syllables in the acquisition of Spanish has been also confirmed for the age of 1;8 by Gennari & Demuth (1997) and Demuth (this volume). From a syntactic perspective, López-Ornat (1997) has reported production of such fillers for Spanish and Bottari, Cipriani & Chilosi (1993/1994) for Italian, beginning at about 1;7 in both cases.

In Lleó (1997) it has been shown that until 1;10 German children do not generally produce filler syllables or proto-articles. Fillers have also been attested in the acquisition of languages like English, but they appear much more sporadically than in Spanish and at a later age (Peters & Menn 1993). Given this initial difference in the acquisition of Spanish and German, the question is how long the difference holds and what happens thereafter. This poses some interesting questions:

a. In the first place, the end-point has to be carefully compared: When can articles be said to have been acquired? Are articles acquired earlier in one language than in the other? Or are Spanish and German articles acquired by the same time?
b. Assuming that they are acquired at the same time in both languages, for instance at 2;2 or 2;3, and taking into consideration that the production of proto-articles at about 1;4 up to 2;3 is much more advanced in Spanish than in German, why does their acquisition run at such different rates in the two languages, starting later in German, but then showing a steeper increase in German than in Spanish?
c. What are the theoretical implications of the earlier appearance of proto-articles in Spanish and of their later appearance in German?
d. Are the formal (i.e. linguistic) contexts of appearance of the first articles or proto-articles the same in the two languages?

To answer some of these questions, the developmental paths regarding the acquisition of the articles in each language, Spanish and German, will be closely analyzed and compared.

3. Acquisition data and results

3.1 *Acquisition data*

The data analyzed in this paper are drawn from a longitudinal research project involving four monolingual children acquiring Spanish in Madrid and five monolingual children acquiring German in Hamburg.[2] Their productions began to be recorded at about nine months of age, in the pre-word stage. The Spanish recording sessions took place on a monthly basis. The German recordings were conducted twice a month up to ca. 1;8 and once a month thereafter. Both sets of data were collected in naturalistic settings, using toys, infant books and a few props for object naming. The Spanish data were video and audiotaped; the German data were audiotaped and supplemented by careful notation of the linguistic as well as situational context. The recordings were made by means of a high-fidelity Sony TCD-D10 PRO cassette recorder and a portable Beyerdynamic microphone concealed in a vest worn by the children. Both data sets were phonetically transcribed by two trained phoneticians, who made a narrow transcription of the recordings using IPA symbols, supplemented by additional diacritics designed for child language (Bush et al. 1973).

For the purpose of the present study the data of three of the Spanish children (José, María and Miguel) and four of the German children (Britta, Johannes, Marion and Thomas) from 1;5 to 2;3 have been selected.[3] They have been analyzed with respect to noun production, and the presence vs. absence of articles and proto-articles preceding nouns. In Lleó (1998) it was shown that the first proto-articles made their appearance at about 1;4 in Spanish and according to Lleó (1997) the first proto-articles in German appear at about 1;8, their frequency being very low during the first two or three months. At 1;6 there are only three proto-articles registered, produced by one child, and after this point their number increases slowly, showing eight appearances at 1;8 for the whole German group. Given these differences in the development of articles in the two languages, 1;5 thus appears to be an appropriate starting point for comparison, since up to that point the German (proto-)articles are absolutely non-existent. The analysis stopped at 2;3, when all Spanish children had already reached more than 90% of (proto-)article production in obligatory contexts.

3.2 *Results: Production of (proto-)articles in Spanish and German child language*

All spontaneous utterances produced by each child were analyzed with respect to nouns, in order to know the frequency of appearance of articles or proto-articles. In Lleó (1997) articles and proto-articles were calculated in relation to all produced nouns not preceded by another determiner like possessives or demonstratives. As noted there, this calculation is conservative, in the sense that it results in lower percentages than real, since not all nouns are equally eligible for article production. Here, the percentages of nouns preceded by (proto-)articles have been calculated out of the obligatory contexts, i.e. out of all nouns for which an article should be expected because of the lexical and contextual properties of the noun. That is, the calculation has excluded generic nouns, most of proper nouns, for which in Spanish as well as in German article use is optional, and nouns used as vocatives. In the Spanish data target trisyllabic nouns in general have been also excluded, because as shown in Lleó (1998) it is often difficult to decide whether an initial reduced syllable in the child production corresponds to the initial syllable of the target noun or to the proto-article. Only a few cases like *muñeca* have been included for the following reasons: This noun is usually produced as a disyllable [ˈkeka] not only by the child, María, but also by her mother, when talking to the child. Besides, the "filler" syllable preceding it generally is [ha], [ʔa] or [hə], phonetically quite remote from the target initial syllable [mu]. Cases in which the (proto-)article preceded a trisyllabic noun procuded with all of its syllables were counted, as well.

Table 1 shows the percentages (%) and raw numbers (N) of nouns preceded by a "filler" syllable or a (proto-)article out of all nouns that should have been preceded by an article, given their lexico-syntactic and contextual properties. Each column presents the values for each particular child and for the whole language group on a monthly basis.[4] The table does not distinguish full-fledged articles from proto-articles. A striking difference between the two sets of data, Spanish and German, can be noticed. At 1;6 one of the Spanish children, María, has more than 50% of proto-articles in obligatory contexts, and another Spanish child, Miguel, reaches 61% at 1;7. Although the third child, José, has lower values, e.g. 27% at 1;7, he still shows much higher values than the German children, already reaching 94% at 1;11, when the mean percentage of the German group is just 20%. The initial marks for the German children are very low, the highest one being Britta's 5% at 1;9. The development of the two groups with regard to percentages of (proto-)articles is very different, as well. The Spanish children exhibit continuous increases, Miguel reaching 86% at 1;10, José 94% at 1;11 and María 92% at 2;0. The German group shows a steep increase between 2;0 and 2;1, and it reaches 51% much later than the Spanish group, namely at 2;1. Only one child, Britta, arrives at the 50% mark one month earlier, at 2;0.

Table 1. *Number and Percentage of nouns preceded by articles and proto-articles produced by the German and the Spanish children out of all eligible nouns, in obligatory contexts*

Age	Britta		Johan		Marion		Thomas		German	José		María		Miguel		Spanish
	%	N	%	N	%	N	%	N	%	%	N	%	N	%	N	%
1;5	–	–	–	–	–	–	–	–	–	14	1	36	10	19	5	26
1;6	–	–	–	–	8	3	–	–	–	17	1	54	15	13	5	29
1;7	0	0	0	0	–	–	0	0	–	27	9	45	33	61	67	50
1;8	3	4	0	0	3	2	3	2	2	–	–	–	–	77	69	77
1;9	5	2	0	0	–	–	–	–	3	44	7	–	–	–	–	44
1;10	19	18	8	9	5	3	4	2	10	36	22	66	51	86	91	67
1;11	42	24	11	11	36	20	4	3	20	94	98	–	–	–	–	94
2;0	50	15	12	12	49	32	6	4	24	93	138	92	25	85	47	91
2;1	64	14	52	58	–	–	48	49	51	–	–	92	33	–	–	92
2;2	80	40	68	74	67	40	66	75	69	–	–	75	38	98	119	91
2;3	81	54	–	–	–	–	81	75	81	–	–	86	32	–	–	86

The different development of the two groups is shown in Figure 2 by two comparative curves, one for Spanish and one for German. The values at each point in time represent the mean percentage for the whole group in a cumulative fashion for every two months, except for the last point, which corresponds to one single month, 2;3. The curves summarize in a graphic way the partly parallel development of the (proto-)articles in Spanish and German. In Spanish, after a steep increase from 1;6 to 1;7–1;8, growth is rather constant, whereas in German between 1;9 and 2;2 it is practically exponential (3%, 10%, 20%, 24% and 51%). The most important difference that arises from the comparison of the two curves is the temporal displacement of the two developments, in German always taking place almost half a year later than in Spanish. The two language groups only meet at 2;3, with almost identical numerical values.

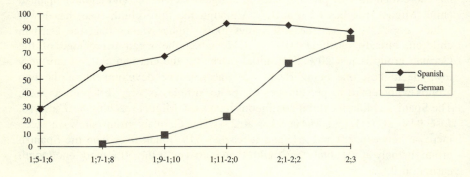

Figure 2. *Development of (**proto**)**art** + **noun** in Spanish and German (mean percentages)*

A further difference between the two groups relates to the position of the (proto-)articles in the utterance: German children begin to produce higher percentages of nouns preceded by an article within sentences or longer utterances, but not when nouns are uttered in isolation. On the contrary, Spanish children tend to produce higher percentages of nouns preceded by an article when these are in isolation. It is also important to notice that (proto-)articles manifest different prosodic characteristics in the two language groups. In the Spanish data, the article is always produced as a syllable before the noun, which serves as its prosodic host, either in isolation at the one-word stage, or within longer utterances later on. The syllable corresponding to the article is prosodically weak or unstressed, and phonetically unspecified, often constituted by a laryngeal and an open vowel. If (proto-)article plus noun are produced within a longer utterance, they are often preceded by disyllabic words like *mira* 'look!', *quiero* '(I) want' or *tiene* '(he/she) has' and the (proto-)article plus noun constitute a new intonation curve. In the German data, on the other hand, the (proto-)article appears in three different shapes. It is produced as: (a) an unstressed syllable, attached to the previous word as an enclitic, (b) a targetlike nasal, also cliticized to the previous word, often a monosyllabic verb or a particle, and (c) as an independent foot preceding the foot of the noun. Table 2 illustrates (proto-)article production and some of its contexts with representative examples in the two languages.[5]

Table 2. *Examples of* art + noun *and* proto-art + noun *produced within longer utterances by the German and the Spanish children*

sitzt *ein* (sch)warzer Mann	'a black man is sitting'	Britta (1;11,29)
sitzt *ein* Mann	'a man is sitting'	
Hat *der* Papa gesagt	'Daddy has said'	Britta (2;3,23)
Ha(t) *die* Kerze angemacht	'has lighted the candle'	
noch *der* Mann	'still the man'	
hier[dɐ] Feuer	'here the fire'	Johannes (2;0,11)
Hier[də] Kuh	'here the cow'	
Noch *ein* Kipper	'one more dumper'	Johannes (2;1,9)
noch[ajm] Waggon	'one more waggon'	
Das *ein* 'Teddy	'that (is) a teddy bear'	
[nɔvə dotə] "noch ein Vogel"	'one more bird'	Marion (1;10,5)
Noch [ʔn̩]Toilette	'one more W.C.'	Marion (2;0,19)
Noch[ɐnt]Hun(d)	'one more dog'	
mira *un* patito	'look a little duck'	José (1;10,3)
mira *una* guitarra	'look a guitar'	José (2;0,3)
toca [ʔɛ]ce(r)dito	'the piggy plays'	
mi[ð]a [rɔ] "los" cerdito(s)'	look the piggies'	
mira [ɛh]guau guau	'look the dog'	María (1;10,17)
(D)éjame [ɐ]queca	'give me the doll'	María (2;2,11)
mi(r)a [ʔo](te)léfono	'look a phone'	Miguel (1;10,18)
tiene *una* (es)trellita	'has a little star'	
mira *una* tele grande	'look a big TV'	
y yo quie(ro) [um] bizcocho	'and I want a cake'	Miguel (2;0,20)
quiero [u]bizcocho	'(I) want a cake'	

As a result of these different prosodic shapes of (proto-)articles in the two language groups, filler syllables are more frequent in Spanish than in German, that is, targetlike full-fledged articles begin sooner to be more frequent in German than in Spanish, in spite of the later first appearances of filler syllables in German. Table 3 shows the proportion of filler syllables to targetlike or (quasi-)targetlike articles in the data of the two language groups. The data are shown beginning at 1;7, because as mentioned above there is almost no (proto-)article production before that point in German. As this table shows, at first both language groups exhibit a high percentage of fillers, but the German percentage of fillers is reduced sooner than the Spanish percentage, in favor of full-fledged articles. For instance, at 2;3, when according to Table 1 German children produce 81% and Spanish children 86% of articles and/or proto-articles in obligatory contexts, fillers constitute only 2% of German article production, whereas it still reaches 45% in the case of one Spanish child, María. Notice that this result cannot be attributed to a more developed phonological system in the German data, because the data being compared correspond to the same age in both language groups, and there is no evidence for a more advanced phonology in German than in Spanish.

Table 3. *Number and Percentage of filler syllables out of all articles and proto-articles produced by the German and the Spanish children*

	Britta		Johann		Marion		Thomas		German	José		María		Miguel		Spanish
Age	%	N	%	N	%	N	%	N	%	%	N	%	N	%	N	%
1;7	50	2	–	–	–	–	–	–	50	89	8	88	29	40	27	59
1;8	100	2	–	–	100	2	100	2	100	–	–	–	–	41	28	28
1;9	0	0	–	–	–	–	–	–	–	100	7	–	–	–	–	100
1;10	8	1	33	3	67	2	50	1	27	68	15	86	42	14	3	43
1;11	13	3	36	4	0	0	33	2	16	29	28	–	–	–	–	29
2;0	13	2	42	5	38	12	0	0	30	13	7	70	16	11	5	23
2;1	–	–	21	12	–	–	35	17	24	–	–	79	26	–	–	79
2;2	5	2	12	9	16	6	39	29	20	–	–	71	27	2	2	18
2;3	2	1	–	–	–	–	3	2	2	–	–	45	14	–	–	45

This development is summarized in Diagram 3, where the values for every three months have been added up at each point. The comparison has been done on the time axis, and the values are shown for the same ages in both groups. The difference in phonetic realization can only be attributed to the prosodic make-up of the (proto-)articles: in Spanish they are reduced because of their proclitic status as unstressed unfooted syllables, whereas in German they are phonetically better realized, because they either constitute independent feet, and are thus stressed, or they correspond to the target reduced form of the article.

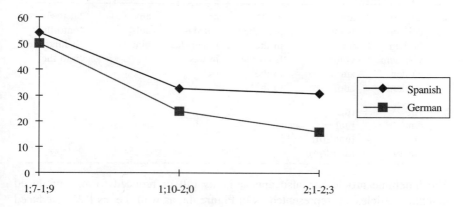

Figure 3. *Percentage of filler syllables in Spanish and German*

4. The prosodic structure of target articles: Implications for acquisition

Possible explanations for the differences in the developmental paths followed by the two groups of children in the acquisition of articles will now be looked for in the prosodic structure of the articles in the respective target languages, and in the way the target structures are reflected in the children's grammars.

In German, articles may have both a full and a reduced form. In this respect we have to distinguish definite from indefinite articles. Definite articles usually appear in their full form and are reduced when preceded by a preposition, as shown in Table 4a.[6] The definite unreduced article has been analyzed as a phonological word on its own by Wiese (1996: 75 and 250 f.). When it is reduced after a preposition it is a clitic and constitutes a single phonological word with the preposition that serves as its host, i.e. it is enclitic. The representation of the definite article in German is shown in Figure 4a, where it appears as a PW according to Selkirk (1996): the PW on the left can either correspond to the unreduced article or to the merger of preposition plus reduced article.[7]

Table 4. *Reduced articles in target German: (a) preposition + definite article and (b) indefinite article (from Wiese 1996: 250)*

	Full form	reduced form		full form	reduced form	
a.	an dem	am	'at the'	an das	ans	'at the'
	bei dem	beim	'near the'	auf das	aufs	'onto the'
	in dem	im	'in the'	hinter das	hinters	'behind the'
	von dem	vom	'from the'	in das	ins	'into the
	zu der	zur	'to the'	...		
	zu dem	zum	'to the'			
b.	ein	[n̩]				
	eine	[nə]				
	einen	[nən]/[n̩]				
	einem	[nəm]/[n̩]				

The indefinite article can also appear in its full or reduced form. Unreduced indefinite articles are represented as in Figure 4a, as well, i.e. as PWs. Reduced indefinite articles are constituted by a single syllable, either a syllabic nasal, or the nasal consonants as onset and coda, respectively, and a schwa [ə] between both consonants, as shown in Table 4b. Indefinite articles are phonetically represented there in their reduced forms. As in the case of the definite article, the reduced indefinite article is cliticized to the word to its left, which serves as the host. This is often a verb, but any word type may do. As far as the prosodic representation of reduced indefinite as well as definite articles in German, Wiese (1996: 251) claims that they "lose their status as phonological words", and that as clitics, "they must therefore be subsumed under the phonological word of the host". According to this view, if the host and the clitic constitute a PW, they should be represented as the mirror image of Figure 1b, that is, as an unfooted syllable to the right, as shown in Figure 4d. On the other hand, if we were to attribute them the status of Selkirk (1996)'s free clitics, they would directly attach to the PPh, as in Figure 4b. Representing them as an unfooted syllable dominated by the PW, as in Figure 4d, offers a more unified account for the following reason. Under the assumption that feet should be binary, in the case of a monosyllabic host, as in *kommt ein Mann* 'a man is coming', the reduced article can attach to the previous monosyllabic foot, as shown in Figure 4c.[8] But if the host is disyllabic, as in *Hans malte einen Mann* 'Hans has drawn a man', where the verb *malte* being disyllabic already fills the whole binary foot, the enclitic article cannot be part of the previous foot, and thus should be directly attached to the higher node. If we were to attach it to the PPh, we would be claiming two radically different descriptions for the article, just depending on the monosyllabicity or disyllabicity of the host, i.e. after monosyllables it would be represented as in Figure 4c, and after disyllables as in Figure 4b. Since there is no compelling reason for skipping the PW level in the representation, Figure 4d is assumed to be a more appropriate representation than Figure 4b.

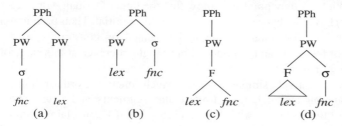

Figure 4.

According to this description, cliticized articles can never be initial in German, but must belong to a previous phonological constituent. They are always preceded by at least one F, or part of an F, in some PW, and are not dominated by their own PW. Only unreduced articles can constitute a foot and a PW of their own. In this respect an interesting asymmetry has been observed in the productions of a German child studied by Schönenberger, Penner & Weissenborn (1997: 541). They report that at 1;9 up to 2;0 "while determiners are not attested at all in the object position, they are never absent in the subject position of interrogatives and existential declaratives." Illustrative examples of articles in subject position are shown in (1)–(2), and examples for lack of articles in the object are shown in (3):

(1)	a.	wo 's de lala	'where is the pacifier'	(1;10,20)
	b.	wo 's der saft	'where is the juice'	(1;10,20)
(2)	a.	da is der lala	'that is the pacifier'	(1;9,11)
	b.	da is de maus	'that is the mouse'	(1;9,11)
(3)	a.	bilderbuch holen	'picture book fetch'	(2;0,1)
	b.	hose ausziehn	'trousers off-take'	(1;10,21)

Schönenberger, Penner & Weissenborn (1997: 545) try to give a syntactic explanation for this asymmetry, because "in the case of object nouns the child resorts to a minimal lexical projection as a default setting, avoiding maximal phrasal projections", which "accounts for the asymmetrical distribution of the definite article in early grammar: the child expands nouns to full-fledged noun phrases in the subject position (hence, [+determiner]), but not in the object position." This is a mere restatement of the facts. An alternative, more adequate, explanation for this asymmetry could be proposed in prosodic terms. Accordingly, articles preceding the subjects of such interrogative and existential sentences can be cliticized to the previous word, whereas article production with objects like those in (3) — which, as they point out, show that the target German word order OV (object + verb) has already been acquired — would be initial. Their production would require an extra-foot, and this might be banned by constraints on the maximal amount of feet that can be produced in a single utterance at this stage of development (see §4 below).

In German it is relatively simple to decide which function words are clitics, given vowel reduction and deletion of particular segments and even whole syllables within clitics. This is why Wiese (1996: 249 ff.) can claim without difficulty that "the most obvious clitics in German are the *reduced forms* of personal pronouns and articles." (Emphasis mine). In Spanish, on the other hand, there is no vowel reduction and no deletion in the crucial contexts, so that the conclusion is unavoidable that "Spanish clitics seem to constitute an idiosyncratic class, whose membership can be specified only by lexical listing." (Harris 1989: 355). We could try to consider prosodic criteria for cliticity, as proposed by Nespor & Vogel (1986), who following Zwicky (1984) tried to define some tests for cliticity: (a) clitics cannot appear by themselves, (b) clitics cannot get contrastive stress, and (c) they do not affect the stress of the host, as in *dando* [which with clitic *nos* becomes ['dandonos] and with clitics *nos* and *lo* becomes ['dandonoslo], maintaining the stress on the same (initial) syllable.

Under these three criteria, Harris' (1989) decision to attribute clitic status to the Spanish definite article but not to the indefinite one is not entirely convincing. Certainly, the definite article consists of monosyllables, whereas all forms of the indefinite article except the masc. sing. (*un*) are disyllabic, but so are many prepositions (*bajo*, *contra*, *hasta*, *sobre*, etc.), which nevertheless are analyzed as clitics. That is, monosyllabicity is not a necessary condition for cliticity. Harris (1989) as well as Halle, Harris & Vergnaud (1991: 151 f.) present an additional criterion to support the cliticity of the definite article. Sketched roughly, the relevant evidence concerns the necessity for the article and the following N, not the whole NP, to form a constituent. This is achieved by a process of *Restructuring*, which converts the syntactic NP represented in Figure 5a to the prosodic phrase of Figure 5c through previous *Cliticization* (Figure 5b). It is claimed that the constituent structure of Figure 5c, which is directly tied to the clitic status of the definite article, offers a basis for the explanation of the data in Table 5, i.e. for the application of *la-el* replacement, which substitutes the form *el* for the fem. sing. form *la* under certain conditions. Basically, *el* replaces *la* when the following noun begins with stressed [a], but Table 5b shows that the substitution takes place in compounds and diminutives, too, in spite of the lack of stress on the initial [a].[9] Halle, Harris & Vergnaud (1991) make the substitution in Table 5b vs. the non-substitution in Table 5c dependent on the cyclic status of stems and suffixes like *-ad-* in *aguada* vs. the non-cyclicity of the diminutive *-it-* in *agüita*. "In *el agwíta* [...] there is no cyclic constituent other than the stem. Thus, the S[tress] E[rasure] C[onvention] has no chance to erase the stress assigned to stem-initial *a-* in the first cycle. The stem then enters S3 as *ágw-*, whose stressed [á] provides the context in which *la-el* replacement applies."

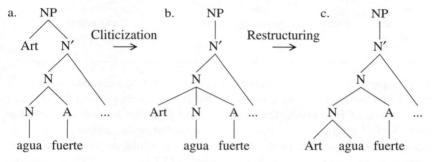

Figure 5.

Table 5. *Examples of definite article allomorphy in target Spanish (Harris 1989: 347)*[a]

a.	el#a	b.	el+noun	c.	la#...'V
	el 'agua		el aguaf'uerte		la ag'uada
	el 'arma		el aguam'ala		la armad'ura
	el 'alma		el aguan'ieve		la alm'eja
	el águila		el agü'ita		la angu'ila
	el área		el am'ita		la ar'ena
	el 'ama		el alm'ita		la am'iga

[a] For the sake of clarity, stressed vowels (and diphthongs) have been marked with " ' ", if they are not graphically accented in Spanish.

Certainly, this treatment of the Spanish data is only reasonable within a derivational model that takes cyclicity for granted. The assumptions of this type of model pose some difficulties for learnability, though: not only the concept of cyclicity as a whole is dubious, but the distinction between cyclic constituents (e.g. stems, suffix *-ad-*) and non-cyclic ones (e.g. suffix *-it-*) is difficult to substantiate. But even granting the logic of the analysis, if *la-el* replacement offers the crucial evidence for the prosodic constituency of art + noun, a parallel argument can be constructed to analyze the indefinite article as a clitic, because there is also *una-un* optional replacement, as shown in Table 6. Certainly, the phenomena characterized in Table 6 are subject to dialectal variation, but so are those of Table 5, too.

Table 6. *Examples of indefinite article allomorphy in target Spanish*

a.	un#a	b.	un+noun	c.	una#a...'V
	un agua		un aguafuerte		una aguada
	un arma		un aguamala		una armadura
	un alma (en pena)		un aguanieve		una almeja
	un área		un agüita		una amiga
	...		...		...

Paraphrasing Halle, Harris & Vergnaud (1991: 151 f.), we can thus say that in Spanish indefinite articles are proclitics. That is, though they "have the syntactic independence of free words, their phonological behavior is identical to that of morphological prefixes" and "must form a single prosodic constituent with the stem on their immediate right, regardless of the syntactic or morphological category of the latter." And as Harris (1989: 352 f.) puts it, "Clitic-host strings are 'phonological words', not phrases, although their syntactic structure is phrasal." The effects of the prosodic structure of target articles for acquisition are obvious. Spanish children treat both, definite as well as indefinite articles as proclitics, i.e. as clitics attached to the following noun. The prosodic transparency of articles in the target language stimulates their production at a very early age, during the one-word stage.

5. OT analysis of the acquisition data

The child language data presented in §3 will now be analyzed within Optimality Theory (see e.g. Prince & Smolensky 1993), in order to establish the ranking of constraints in the child's grammar and its relationship to constraint ranking in the adult grammar. Some of the relevant constraints for the present analysis are:

(4) Prosodic constraints
FTBIN: Feet must be binary at some level of analysis (σ, μ)
1FOOT: utterances cannot consist of more than one foot
EXHAUST: No C^i immediately dominates a constituent C^j, $j < i-1$, e.g. no PW immediately dominates a σ (Selkirk 1996: 190).

(5) Faithfulness constraints
MAX(σ)-IO: Every syllable in the Input has a correspondent in the Output: no syllable deletion is allowed

At the one-word stage, a single prosodic word is allowed, and each word can only consist of one foot. Thus some constraints limiting production to one PW and limiting the length of the PW to one foot are necessary for the earliest stages. Here, these constraints are just formulated in a shortcut way by means of 1FOOT. Such a constraint is only relevant at the one-word stage and will soon be demoted.

The data described in §3 have shown that at the one-word stage German children do not produce any articles, neither in full nor in reduced form. This suggests that for these function words German children adopt the prosodic structure that the target language attributes to them. As we have seen in §4, unreduced articles are PWs in their own right in German, which entails that they cannot be produced at a stage in which children are limited to producing a single PW and a single F per utterance. In a parallel fashion, Spanish children adopt the target prosodic structure for this function word, and attribute the status of a clitic to it, i.e. proclitic status. This is why Spanish children are ready to produce (proto-)articles as soon as at the one-word stage. Certainly, article production in Spanish entails violating the Strict Layered Hypothesis, specifically, the constraint on EXHAUSTIVITY.[10] This constraint requires that the prosodic hierarchy be respected at each step, i.e. that syllables attach to feet, that feet attach to the prosodic word, etc.

In German, EXHAUSTIVITY could be considered as not relevant at this stage, because the prosodic status of the article as a prosodic word in German prevents its adjunction to the next PW and seems to render EXHAUSTIVITY inert. Nevertheless, violations of EXHAUSTIVITY in German begin to happen at the level of the lexical word, in those cases in which the unfooted syllable of a trisyllabic word is produced by the child, either at the beginning of the PW (*Trom'pete* 'trumpet') or at the end of the PW ('*Schmetterling* 'butterfly'). As shown in Lleó (1998) the early lexicon of German children does not contain many trisyllables and these are truncated in the children's productions for a relatively long time. On the other hand, as also shown there, the target language Spanish offers many trisyllabic nouns that are adopted by the Spanish children in their early lexicon and produced as such. This can be interpreted in the present terms as making them familiar with violations of EXHAUSTIVITY. Spanish children are able to extend their experience with EXHAUSTIVITY to function words, allowing for their integration in the prosodic tree as unfooted syllables (see Figure 1b above). Notice that according to this analysis, Spanish children are claimed to go through the stage of unfooted syllables (Figure 1b) previously to the two-foot stage (Figure 1a). EXHAUSTIVITY is more highly ranked in German than in Spanish, and its violation enters the German grammar at a later stage. Tableaux 1 and 2 illustrate this discussion of the constraints in a simple way.

Tableau 1. die Klappe *'the lid'* (Thomas 1;10,4)

[die]$_F$ [Klappe]$_F$	EXHAUST	IFOOT	MAX-IO
[die]$_F$ [Klappe]$_F$		*!	
[die [Klappe]$_F$]$_{PW}$	*!		
☞ [[Klappe]$_F$]$_{PW}$			*

Tableau 2. el pato *'the duck'* (María 1;7,24)

[el [pato]$_F$]$_{PW}$	MAX-IO	IFOOT	EXHAUST
[el]$_F$ [pato]$_F$		*!	
[pato]$_F$	*!		
☞ [el [pato]$_F$]$_{PW}$			*

The relevant difference between Spanish and German at this stage concerns the prosodic structure of the article, which constitutes both a PW and an F in German, but not in Spanish. Spanish children can produce articles by violating EXHAUSTIVITY, whereas German children do not have this option. But notice that EXHAUSTIVITY is also responsible for the lack of (proto-)articles in the German data. EXHAUSTIVITY must be higher up in the German children's hierarchy than in the Spanish children's hierarchy of constraints, given the longer lasting reluctance of German children to produce trisyllables. This fact has an indirect influence on the earlier appearance of the article in Spanish than in German, too. The difficulty for the German children to produce art+noun in isolation is directly explained by the fact that they would have to violate the high-ranked constraint that disallows more than one PW and F. Once this constraint is demoted, German children produce articles in a targetlike way. On the other hand, assuming that EXHAUSTIVITY is higher up in the German hierarchy than in the Spanish one can also explain the impossibility for the German children to reanalyze articles as proclitics and produce them in the way that the Spanish children do.

As far as medial articles are concerned, they are preferred in this position by the German children over initial position, whereas in the Spanish group there is no such preference. On the other hand, as the data in Table 2 illustrate, most of the words produced before medial articles in German are monosyllabic at first, whereas they are not limited in this way in the Spanish data, often being disyllables. This entails that most of medial articles in German can be described as the right branch of the F, being dominated together with the lexeme by PW, as in Figure 4c.[11] That is, they do not require a violation of EXHAUSTIVITY, but rather a violation of another constraint, PROS-SYNT, as displayed in Tableau 3. This latter constraint requires identity of mapping between the syntactic and the prosodic structure, and it implies the presence of at least two lexical words, in order to go from the syntactic to the prosodic mapping. In Spanish, on the other hand, production of medial articles is arrived at by the same mechanism that allows initial articles, i.e., violation of EXHAUSTIVITY (see Tableau 4). This entails that different rankings between German and Spanish have to be postulated: The constraint on PROSODY-SYNTAX mapping can be violated in German, i.e., it is dominated, whereas EXHAUSTIVITY is not, since articles can appear if they can be attached to a monosyllabic host to their left, with which they constitute a disyllabic foot. This constraint ranking coincides with that of the respective adult grammars. The proclitic status of articles in Spanish implies a constant violation of EXHAUSTIVITY, since the syllable belonging to the function word is immediately dominated by PW (Figure 1b). On the other hand, the enclitic status of many articles in German implies violation of PROS-SYNT, since prosodically the function word is not parsed together with the following prosodic constituent, to which it syntactically belongs, but is parsed together with the previous lexical word (see Figures 4c and 4d above).

Tableau 3. Noch ein Kipper *'one more dumper'* *(Johannes 2;1,9)*

[noch ein]$_F$ [Kipper]$_F$	MAX-IO	EXHAUST	PROS-SYNT
[noch]$_F$ [Kipper]$_F$	*!		
[noch]$_F$ [ein[Kipper]$_F$]$_{PW}$		*!	
☞ [noch ein]$_F$ [Kipper]$_F$			*

Tableau 4. Mira un perro *'look a dog'* *(José 2;0,3)*

	Max-IO	Pros-synt	Exhaust
[[mira]$_F$]$_{PW}$ [un [perro]$_F$]$_{PW}$			
[[mira]$_F$]$_{PW}$ [[perro]$_F$]$_{PW}$	*!		
☞ [[mira]$_F$]$_{PW}$ [un[perro]$_F$]$_{PW}$			*
[[mira]$_F$]$_{PW}$ un]$_{PPh}$ [perro]$_F$]$_{PW}$		*!	

Although, as discussed in §4, the clitic status of Spanish articles requires some restructuring, too, because the clitic article is prosodically attached to the following N and not to the whole NP, this restructuring is not as radical as the restructuring done in German, since the article in Spanish prosodically remains part of the following NP to which it syntactically belongs. In German, the article switches phrases, from its syntactic to its prosodic representation. The different prosodic analyses of the article in the corresponding target languages point to a more highly ranked Pros-Synt mapping constraint in Spanish than in German.

Later on, when articles are produced after disyllabic words in German, not only Pros-Synt is violated, but also Exhaustivity, because the enclitic article is attached directly to the previous PW, skipping the level of the foot, i.e., the enclitic reduced article is an unfooted syllable (as in Figure 4d above). The Exhaustivity constraint is a constraint internal to the prosodic theory, in the sense that it regulates prosodic structure in an internal way: it predicts what form the organization of prosodic nodes must take.

The analysis done here in terms of the Pros-Synt constraint can be related to Align, and in fact in Lleó (1997) the analysis of Spanish data similar to those described in Tableau 4 was done on the basis of Align:

(6) ALIGN(F, L, PW, L): Align the left edge of the foot with the left edge of the PW.

That is, any prosodic word that contains an unfooted syllable to the left, with the structure of Figure 1b, entails a violation of AlignLeft, because the left edge of the foot does not coincide with the left edge of the prosodic word. Here Align is formulated in purely prosodic terms, by matching only prosodic categories. In order to account for the German data, as for instance those represented by Figure 4c above, this constraint is too weak, since an article preceded by a monosyllabic word would accordingly not violate it. Align should thus be formulated as a more general constraint, regulating the alignment of syntactic constituents with prosodic constituents, i.e., at the interface of Phonology and Syntax. In terms of this type of generalized Align constraint, the unfooted syllable of the reduced articles in German could be accounted for by means of the following constraint:

(7)　　ALIGN(LEX, R, PW, R):　　Align the right edge of the lex with the right edge of the PW.

This constraint is violated in those cases in which the PW is constituted by a foot and the article (Figure 4d), as well as in those cases where the lexical word is monosyllabic and the function word is footed (Figure 4c). This entails that both descriptions, either by means of PROS-SYNT as well as by means of ALIGNRIGHT, exhibit a violation of the relevant constraint, and seem to account for the data equally well. Here, I leave the question open of which solution is more adequate. The constraint PROS-SYNT makes explicit that in German radical mismatches between syntactic and prosodic parsing are allowed, and it can be extended to other cases of mismatch along the prosodic hierarchy. As regards the relationship of this constraint to acquisition, it can be argued that mastering such a radical constraint (in the sense of allowing violations to it) may take longer than mastering violations to constraints that are more straightforward, such as ALIGNLEFT just formulated in purely prosodic terms, as above, or EXHAUSTIVITY.

The comparison of the phenomena of cliticization in the Spanish and German data can help us to assess some of the constraints discussed in the literature and can lead to interesting proposals in this respect. At present, the decisive point relates to the different interaction of the constraints in the different target languages and their reflection in the children's grammars and thus in their courses of acquisition. Prima facie, the differences between the acquisition of articles by the Spanish and the German children are impressive. Furthermore, syntactic or pragmatic differences between the two target languages do not provide an explanation, since Spanish and German have huge areas of overlap with respect to syntax and use of articles. Only prosodic differences between target articles can offer a convincing explanation. At the same time, the prosodic explanation for the lack of (proto-)articles in German — and in other languages often mentioned in the acquisition literature, like English — renders the postulation of a pre-functional stage (as in Radford 1990) fully unnecessary.

6. Conclusion

A comparison of article production by Spanish and German children between the ages of 1;5 and 2;3 has manifested impressive differences. Whereas at 1;7, Spanish children reach about 50% of proto-article production, out of all expected articles, German children produce almost no articles at all. In general, the development of (proto-)articles in German takes place about half a year later than in Spanish, so that Spanish children produce many proto-articles with single nouns, at the one-word stage, whereas German children are more prone to include articles within sentences or longer utterances. The explanation for these different behaviors has been traced back to the different prosodic structures of articles in the respective target languages. These prosodic differences in the target language influence the early grammars of the two groups of children with respect to the ranking of constraints that control the prosody-syntax interface and the internal structure of the prosodic word.

At 2;3 both groups of children have reached comparable levels of article production, that is, German children have caught up with the acquisition of articles. This development weakens the necessity of a prefunctional stage, as proposed for instance by Radford (1990). It offers support to the idea that functional categories are innate, but that they are more readily expressed depending on their prosodic characteristics and on the prosodic make-up of the language to be acquired. In order to arrive to these results, the sensitivity of children to prosodic units has to be acknowledged. These are the basic units upon which early child grammar is built.

Acknowledgments

I thank Katherine Demuth, Paula Fikkert, Barbara Höhle, Ann Peters and Jürgen Weissenborn, who read an early version of the paper and made valuable suggestions.

Notes

1. The symbols used in Figure 1 correspond to the standard usage in prosodic phonology: PW = prosodic word, F = foot, σ = syllable.
2. The data were collected with the financial support of the Deutsche Forschungsgemeinschaft, to which I want to express my gratitude. I want to thank the research assistants of the project, Dr. Christliebe El Mogharbel and Dr. Michael Prinz, as well as the students who made the transcriptions, Marianne Brockman, Thorsten Framm, Isabel Jiménez, Beate Klemt, Fatima Marinho, Henny Metzendorf, Susann Oberacker, Rolf Oechsler and Cristina Trujillo.
3. The fifth German child, Bernd, shows a slightly different pattern than the other four German children. He has been partially described in Lleó (1997) and will be omitted from the present description. The data of the fourth Spanish child has also been excluded from examination, because it contains many gaps and data collection stopped at 2;1.
4. Although as mentioned above, data were collected monthly (and bimonthly in some cases), there are gaps due to several reasons (family vacation, child's illness, etc.). These are marked

with a dash "–" in the corresponding boxes. Counting for a particular child has stopped as soon as (proto-)article production reached a 90% mark for more than one session; this explains some of the dashes corresponding to the last sessions in the Spanish group.

5. The articles pronounced targetlike by the child have been written in standard orthography and italicized. Proto-articles have been transcribed phonetically and placed between brackets. Sounds omitted in the child's pronunciation have been placed in parentheses. The symbol [n̩] corresponds to a syllabic nasal.
6. The description adopted here corresponds to Wiese (1996), and limits itself to the standard language. In spoken German, there are more cases of cliticization than the ones described by Wiese (1996). So, for instance, in colloquial speech the definite article can be reduced after a verb, and not only when preceded by a preposition.
7. Besides the standard symbols used in Figure 1, Figure 4 contains the following: PPh = phonological phrase, fnc = function word and lex = lexical word.
8. For very enlightening experiments drawing on the differential number of syllables of the host and the different behavior of footed and unfooted syllables in child production in English, see Gerken (1996).
9. For the sake of clarity, in Table 5 stressed vowels (and diphthongs) have been marked with "ˈ", if they are not graphically accented in Spanish.
10. See Demuth (this volume) for a similar claim, as well as Selkirk (1996) and Gerken (1996) for discussions of EXHAUSTIVITY in English.
11. Nevertheless, if the syllable preceding the function word is closed, it might not accept a further syllable within the foot it belongs to, since a closed syllable already complies with foot binarity at the level of the mora and fills the whole foot. In that case, the article must be represented as in Figure 4d.

References

Bottari, P., Cipriani, P. & Chilosi, A. M. 1993/94. "Protosyntactic Devices in the Acquisition of Italian Free Morphology." *Language Acquisition* 3: 327–369.
Bush, C. N., Edwards, M. L., Luckau, J. M., Stoel, C. M., Macken, M. A. & Petersen, J. D. 1973. "On Specifying a System for Transcribing Consonants in Child Language. A Working Paper with Examples from American English and Mexican Spanish." Stanford: *Child Language Project*.
Demuth, K. 1996. "Stages in the Development of Prosodic Words." In *Proceedings from the 27th Child Language Research Forum*, E. Clark (ed.). Stanford University: CSLI.
Demuth, K. (this volume). "Prosodic Constraints and Morphological Development."
Demuth, K. & Fee, J. 1995. "Minimal Prosodic Words in Early Phonological Development." Manuscript.
Fikkert, P. 1994. *On the Acquisition of Prosodic Structure*. Leiden, The Netherlands: University of Leiden Dissertation.
Gennari, S. & Demuth, K. 1997. "Syllable Omission in the Acquisition of Spanish." In *BUCLD 21 Proceedings,* E. M. Hughes & A. Green (eds.). Somerville: Cascadilla Press.

Gerken, L. 1996. "Prosodic Structure in Young Children's Language Production." *Language* 72: 683–712.

Harris, J.W. 1989. "The Stress Erasure Convention and Cliticization in Spanish." *Linguistic Inquiry* 20: 339–363.

Halle, M., Harris, J.W. & Vergnaud, J.-R. 1991. "A Reexamination of the Stress Erasure Convention and Spanish Stress." *Linguistic Inquiry* 22: 141–159.

Lleó, C. 1997. "Filler Syllables, Proto-Articles and Early Prosodic Constraints in Spanish and German." In *Language Acquisition: Knowledge, Representation and Processing. Proceedings of GALA '97.*

Lleó, C. 1998. "Proto-Articles in the Acquisition of Spanish: Interface between Phonology and Morphology." In *Modelle der Flexion: 18. Jahrestagung der Deutschen Gesellschaft für Sprachwissenschaft,* R. Fabri, A. Ortmann & T. Parodi (eds.). Niemeyer: Tübingen.

López-Ornat, S. 1997. "What Lies in between a Pre-Grammatical and a Grammatical Representation? Evidence on Nominal and Verbal Form-Function Mappings in Spanish from 1;7 to 2;1." In *Contemporary perspectives on the Acquisition of Spanish,* A.T. Pérez-Leroux & W.R. Glass (eds.). Somerville: Cascadilla Press.

Nespor, M. & Vogel, I. 1986. *Prosodic Phonology.* Dordrecht: Foris.

Peters, A.M. & Menn, L. 1993. "False Starts and Filler Syllables: Ways to Learn Grammatical Morphemes." *Language* 69: 742–777.

Prince, A. & Smolensky, P. 1993. *Optimality Theory.* Rutgers University.

Radford, A. 1990. *Syntactic Theory and the Acquisition of English Syntax.* London: Blackwell.

Schönenberger, M., Penner, Z. & Weissenborn, J. 1997. "Object Placement and Early German Grammar." In *Proceedings of the 21st Annual Boston Conference on Language Development,* E. Hughes & A. Green (eds.). Somerville: Cascadilla Press.

Selkirk, E. 1996. "The Prosodic Structure of Function Words." In *Signal to Syntax: Bootstrapping from Speech to Grammar in Early Acquisition,* J.L. Morgan & K. Demuth (eds.). Mahwah, NJ: Lawrence Erlbaum Associates.

Wiese, R. 1996. *The Phonology of German.* Oxford: Clarendon Press.

Zwicky, A. 1984. "Clitics and particles." *Language* 61: 283–305.

Interaction between Prosody and Morphosyntax
Plurals within codas in the acquisition of European Portuguese

M. João Freitas, Matilde Miguel & Isabel Hub Faria
Universidade de Lisboa

1. Introduction

Our main purpose is to show that when linguistic information from more than one module of the grammar interacts with a particular prosodic structure, acquisition may not follow the expected patterns of prosodic development. The general hypothesis is that information external to the prosodic level can lead to the emergence of a prosodic structure earlier than one would expect it to occur based on purely prosodic factors. The specific hypothesis is that in European Portuguese (EP), the coda associated with fricatives disrupts the regular pattern of coda development by the interference of morpho-syntactic information with the setting of this syllabic constituent. In this paper, we will follow the interaction between the early acquisition of plural features (number) and the acquisition of syllables with codas in the process of emergence of the $V(G)C_{fricative}$ (Vowel + Optional Glide + Fricative) rhyme, in order to test the hypothesis above.

2. Methodology

The data considered for analysis are part of a larger *corpus* of longitudinal cross-sectional data from seven portuguese children aged 0;10 to 3;7 years. The children have been videotaped monthly for one year, at home, with their mother and the researcher, in sessions during 30 to 60 minutes (one of the children has been videotaped for two years). The *corpus* has been treated within the CHILD-PHON Wordbase, an application of the '4th Dimension' software for Macintosh, developed at the Max Planck Institut for Psycholinguistics — Nijmegen — and first used by Levelt (1994) and by Fikkert (1994).

We will analyze data from four of the seven children, namely Inês (0;11.14 to 1;10.29), Marta (1;02.00 to 2;02.17) Luís (1;09.29 to 2;11.02) and Laura (2;02.30 to 3;03.10). The utterances considered for analysis consist of (1) isolated words or (2) sequences of words where *sandhi* phenomena occur.

3. Domain of investigation: The coda

As mentioned above, we will focus on the acquisition of the coda constituent. Segmental material in this syllabic position is not obligatory in all natural languages; languages differ in the number and the quality of the segments associated with this position. Within an 'Onset-Rhyme' approach, from the constituents considered in the hierarchical structure of the syllable, the coda position is the most problematic one for language acquisition (Fikkert 1994; Stemberger 1996).

The status of the core syllable assigned to the CV structure presupposes that the absence of the coda within the rhyme, i.e. a non-branching rhyme, represents the unmarked, universal structure. Therefore, within the theoretical framework of Principles and Parameters, a rhyme with a coda, i.e. a branching rhyme, would constitute the marked value of the Branching Rhyme Parameter. This fact allows us to predict that branching rhymes are acquired later than non-branching rhymes.

3.1 *Codas in European Portuguese*

It is assumed for EP that /l/, produced as [ɫ], /r/ and the postalveolar fricative, with the allophones [ʃ, ʒ, z], are the only segments associated with the coda position (Mateus & Andrade 1998):

(1)   *Codas in EP*

mel	['mɛɫ]	'honey'
salto	['saɫtu]	'jump'
soldado	[soɫ'dadu]	'soldier'
mar	['maɾ]	'sea'
porta	['pɔɾtɐ]	'door'
portão	[puɾ'tẽw̃]	'gate'
paz	['paʃ]	'peace'
frasco	['fɾaʃku]	'bottle'
assustado	[ɐsuʃ'tadu]	'frightened'

INTERACTION BETWEEN PROSODY AND MORPHOSYNTAX

papéis   [pɐ'pɛjʃ]   'papers'
fausto   ['fawʃtu]   'luxury'

The coda associated with a liquid obligatorily follows a non-branching nucleus; the coda associated with a fricative follows either a non-branching or a branching nucleus, although the first structure — a non-branching nucleus followed by a coda fricative — is more frequent. According to the previous description, the phonological rhyme in EP has the following possible shapes:

(2) *Target rhymes*
    a. V   casa   ['kazɐ]   'house'
    b. VG   caixa   ['kajʃɐ]   'box'
    c. VC$_{fricative}$ frasco   ['fraʃku]   'bottle'
    d. VC$_{liquid}$ salto   ['saɫtu]   'jump'
    e. VGC$_{fricative}$ fausto   ['fawʃtu] 'luxury'

Therefore, in order to describe the EP rhyme, we have to assume the marked value [Yes] of the BRANCHING RHYME PARAMETER and the marked value [Yes] of the BRANCHING NUCLEUS PARAMETER:

(3) a. BRANCHING RHYME PARAMETER (Fikkert 1994: 150)
       Rhymes can branch into a nucleus and a coda   [No/<u>Yes</u>]
    b. BRANCHING NUCLEUS PARAMETER (Fikkert 1994: 152)
       The nucleus can be branching   [No/<u>Yes</u>]

The possible structures at the rhyme level in EP are then the ones represented in (4):

(4) *Rhyme structures*

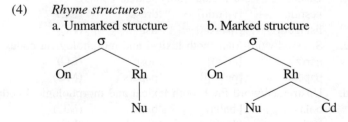

Focussing now on coda fricatives in EP, they can be either lexical or morphological, as shown in the examples in (5):

(5) *Nature of fricatives within codas*
    a. Lexical codas (LC)
          nariz   [nɐ'ɾiʃ]   'nose'
          luz   ['luʃ]   'light'
          costa   ['kɔʃtɐ]   'coast'
    b. Morphological codas (MC)
          bolas   ['bɔlɐʃ]   'balls'
          papéis   [pɐ'pɛjʃ]   'papers'
          falas   ['falɐʃ]   '(you) speak'

A morphological fricative obligatorily occurs in word-final position and it can be either a nominal plural morpheme (as in *bolas* ['bɔlɐʃ]) or a verbal person morpheme (as in *falas* ['falɐʃ]). In the case of morphological codas, we will focus on the NP functional projections, therefore, we will be strictly concerned with the plural morpheme.

Let us now consider the distribution of coda fricatives within the noun. Morphological coda fricatives only occur in word-final position, as mentioned above, within stressed or unstressed syllables, whereas lexical coda fricatives occur both in word-medial or word-final positions, within stressed or unstressed syllables, as shown in the examples in (6):

(6) *Distribution of coda fricatives in EP*
    a. Stressed/word-medial (only lexical codas)
          cesto   ['seʃtu]   'basket'   (LC)
          fausto   ['fawʃtu]   'luxury'   (LC)
    b. Unstressed/word-medial (only lexical codas)
          vestido [vɨʃ'tidu]   'dress'   (LC)
          listagem [liʃ'taʒẽj]   'list'   (LC)
    c. Stressed/word-final (both lexical and morphological codas)
          nariz   [nɐ'ɾiʃ]   'nose'   (LC)
          papéis   [pɐ'pɛjʃ]   'papers'   (MC)
    d. Unstressed/word-final (both lexical and morphological codas)
          bolas   ['bɔlɐʃ]   'balls'   (MC)
          lápis   ['lapiʃ]   'pencil'   (LC)

3.2 Acquisition of codas in EP: Assumptions and predictions

Thus, Portuguese children have to set, at some point in the process of language acquisition, the BRANCHING RHYME PARAMETER to the marked value [Yes]. Fikkert (1994) proposes the following stages for the acquisition of rhymes in

Dutch, where the setting of the marked value for the BRANCHING RHYME PARAMETER takes place during Stage II (Stage IV in Fikkert's scale concerns word-finally syllables with extra-rhymal positions; the extra-rhymal parameter is set to its unmarked value in EP, therefore Portuguese children do not provide empirical evidence for Stage IV):

(7) *Acquisition of rhymes (Fikkert 1994)*
    Stage I: No syllable parameters are set. All parameters have the default value.
    Stage II: The branching rhyme parameter (rhymes can branch into a nucleus and a coda) has been set to the marked value: [Yes].
    Stage III: Branching nucleus parameter (nuclei can branch) is set to the marked value: [Yes].

Fikkert's scale is confirmed by Portuguese children's data: (i) At Stage I, only V rhymes are produced (see examples from Inês, in (10a1)); (ii) At Stage II, coda fricatives ermerge (see examples from Inês, in (10a2)); (iii) Syllable-final liquids emerge much later both in Dutch and in Portuguese children's productions, at Stage III. Although this is not the question under discussion in this paper, note that syllable-final liquids emerge much later than coda fricatives as a result of their syllabic status: syllable-final liquids are represented within a branching nucleus, which explains their later emergence at Stage III, when the Branching Nucleus Parameter is set to its marked value (for the presentation of arguments supporting this analysis, see Fikkert 1994 and Freitas 1997). The examples in (8) show that the emergence of coda fricatives precedes the emergence of syllable-final liquids:

(8) *Syllable-final consonants in EP (data from Marta)*
    a. Fricatives

	isto	/'iʃtu/	→ ['iʃtu]	(2;01.19)	'this one'
	esta é	/'ɛʃtɐ 'ɛ/	→ ['ɛʃtɛ]	(2;01.19)	'this is'
	asneiras	/ɐʒ'nɐjɾɐʃ/	→ [ɐʒ'nɐɾɐʃ]	(2;01.19)	'foolish thing'
	buscar	/buʃ'kaɾ/	→ [vʃ'kɐ]	(2;01.19)	'to get'
	bolinhas	/bɔ'liɲɐʃ/	→ [pɔ'liɲiʃ]	(2;02.17)	'balls'
	meias	/'mɐjɐʃ/	→ ['mɐjɐʃ]	(2;02.17)	'socks'
b.	Liquids				
	urso	/'uɾsu/	→ ['usu]/['uθu]	(2;02.17)	'bear'
	porco	/'poɾku/	→ ['pʰoku]	(2;02.17)	'pig'
	árvore	/'aɾvuɾi/	→ ['afɨ]	(2;02.17)	'tree'
	calçar	/kaɫ'saɾ/	→ [kɐ'sɐ]	(2;02.17)	'to put shoes on'
	Marta	/'maɾtɐ/	→ ['matɐ]	(2;02.17)	

Let us assume the following facts on the distribution of codas based on stress and on word position:

a. The combination of stress and word position determine whether a syllable is prominent or not: it is traditionally assumed that [+stress; −word-final] syllables are the most prominent, while [−stress; +word-final] syllables are the least prominent.
b. Stressed syllables are prominent prosodic structures, both for acquisition and for language processing; information within unstressed syllables is traditionally considered to be less prominent (Segui et al. 1990; Treiman et al. 1991). Stressed syllables protect phonological information from the effects of phonetic processes of segmental deletion or reduction in colloquial speech. Unstressed word-final syllables frequently allow phonetic rules to reduce or delete segmental material in colloquial EP (Delgado-Martins 1994).
c. Word-initial and word-medial positions, like stressed syllables, tend to preserve both segmental and prosodic properties. However, the status of the word-final unstressed position is controversial: some authors claim that this is a weak position, therefore, less prominent in the language processing, while others argue that word-final structures are prone to be preserved (see, among others, Echols & Newport 1992 and Morais et al. 1993).
d. In EP, lexical coda fricatives occur both in word-medial and in word-final position, while morphological coda fricatives only occur in word-final position. Most morphological coda fricatives occur in unstressed syllables since stress in EP is generally assigned to the penultimate syllable.

The assumptions (a–c), and leaving (d) aside for the moment, allow us to formulate the predictions in (9), concerning the order of acquisition of the coda fricative in EP:

(9) *Predictions for the emergence of the coda fricatives in EP*
The emergence of coda fricatives in the path of acquisition of the syllable structure in EP will follow the order:
a. coda fricatives within stressed syllables, in word-medial position;
b. coda fricatives within stressed syllables, in word-final position;
c. coda fricatives within unstressed syllables, in word-medial position;
d. coda fricatives within unstressed syllables, in word-final position.

According to these predictions, morphological fricatives used for plural marking should be among the last segments to emerge, since they occur only in word-final position, generally within an unstressed syllable, due to the general rule of stress assignment in EP. However, this is not the case, as we will see in the data

INTERACTION BETWEEN PROSODY AND MORPHOSYNTAX 51

analysis: plural marking is, in fact, the first coda fricative to emerge in the acquisition of EP.

3.3 *The data*

The examples in (10) illustrate the emergence of the V(G)C$_{fricative}$ rhyme in Portuguese children's productions:

(10) V(G)C$_{fricative}$ *rhyme in Portuguese children's data*
a. **Inês**
1.

Inês	/iˈneʃ/	→	[neˈne]	(0;11.14)	
não presta	/ˈnẽw̃ ˈprɛstɐ/	→	[ɐˈbɛ]	(0;11.14)	'it is not good'
mais	/ˈmajʃ/	→	[ˈma]/[ˈmɐ]/[ˈmaj]	(1;1.30)	'more'

2.
Stressed/word-medial

gosta	/ˈgɔstɐ/	→	[ˈgɔ]	(1;8.2)	'likes'(3^{d}SG)
festa	/ˈfɛstɐ/	→	[ˈtɛtɐ]	(1;9.19)	'party'
estas	/ˈɛstɐʃ/	→	[ˈɛtɐʃ]	(1;10.29)	'these'

Unstressed/word-medial

| buscar | /buʃˈkaɾ/ | → | [βuˈka] | (1;10.29) | 'to get' |
| escuro | /iʃˈkuɾu/ | → | [ˈkulu] | (1;10.29) | 'dark' |

Stressed/word-final

nariz	/nɐˈɾiʃ/	→	[ɐˈgiɐ]	(1;8.2)	'nose'
Inês	/iˈneʃ/	→	[neˈne]	(1;9.19)	
meus	/ˈmewʃ/	→	[ˈmewʃ]	(1;9.19)	'my/mine'
nariz	/nɐˈɾiʃ/	→	[ðɨˈɾiʃ]	(1;10.29)	'nose'

Unstressed/word-final

lápis	/ˈlapiʃ/	→	[ˈpatu]/[ˈpato]/[ɐˈpatu]	(1;8.2)	'pencil'
bonecas	/buˈnɛkɐʃ/	→	[mɨˈɲɛkɐʃ]	(1;9.19)	'dolls'
bolos	/ˈboluʃ/	→	[ˈboloʃ]	(1;9.19)	'cakes'

b. **Marta**
Stressed/word-medial

estes	/ˈeʃtiʃ/	→	[ˈetiʃ]	(1;5.17)	'these'
presta	/ˈprɛstɐ/	→	[ˈpeti]	(1;5.17)	'it is good'
gosta	/ˈgɔstɐ/	→	[ˈkɔtɨ]	(1;6.23)	'likes'(3^{d}SG)

Unstressed/word-medial

| história | /iʃˈtɔɾjɐ/ | → | [ˈtɔjɐ] | (1;6.23) | 'story' |

Stressed/word-final

nariz	/nɐˈɾiʃ/	→	[niˈi]	(1;3.8)	'nose'
mais	/ˈmajʃ/	→	[ˈmaj]	(1;4.8)	'more'
pés	/ˈpɛʃ/	→	[ˈpɛʃ]	(1;5.17)	'feet'
nariz	/nɐˈɾiʃ/	→	[uˈdiʃ]	(1;6.23)	'nose'

Unstressed/word-final
flores	/ˈflorɨʃ/	→	[ˈfːojʃ]	(1;2.0)	'flowers'
flores	/ˈflorɨʃ/	→	[ˈʃoːʃ]	(1;4.8)	'flowers'
bananas	/bɐˈnɐnɐʃ/	→	[ɐˈmɐnɐʃ]	(1;4.8)	'bananas'
maçãs	/mɐˈsẽʃ/	→	[mɨˈʃaʃ]	(1;4.8)	'apples'

c. Luís
Stressed/word-medial
isto	/ˈiʃtu/	→	[ˈitu]	(1;9.29)	'this one'
cesto	/ˈseʃtu/	→	[ˈʃjetu]	(1;11.20)	'bag'
festa	/ˈfɛʃtɐ/	→	[ˈfɛtɐ]	(2;0.27)	'party'
Crespo	/ˈkrɛʃpu/	→	[ˈkɛpu]	(2;0.27)	

Unstressed/word-medial
buscar	/buʃˈkar/	→	[ũˈkari]	(1;11.20)	'to get'

Stressed/word-final
Luís	/luˈiʃ/	→	[ˈwi]	(1;9.29)	
Luís	/luˈiʃ/	→	[ˈwi]	(1;11.20)	
Luís	/luˈiʃ/	→	[ˈwi]/[ˈiʃ]/[ˈwiʃ]	(2;0.27)	
uns	/ˈũʃ/	→	[ˈũʃ]	(2;0.27)	'some'
jornais	/ʒurˈnajʃ/	→	[ʒurˈnajʃ]	(2;0.27)	'newspapers'

Unstressed/word-final
Carlos	/ˈkarluʃ/	→	[ˈkaɫu]	(1;9.29)	
Becas	/ˈbɛkɐʃ/	→	[ˈmɛkɐ]	(1;11.20)	
Poupas	/ˈpopɐʃ/	→	[ˈpupɐ]	(1;11.20)	
bolachas	/buˈlaʃɐʃ/	→	[ˈlaʃɐʃ]	(1;11.20)	'cookies'
papagaios	/pɐpɐˈgajuʃ/	→	[pɐkɐˈkajɨʃ]	(2;0.27)	'parrots'
motas	/ˈmɔtɐʃ/	→	[ˈmɔtɐʃ]	(2;0.27)	'bicycles'
Poupas	/ˈpopɐʃ/	→	[ˈpopɐ]	(2;0.27)	
Egas	/ˈɛgɐʃ/	→	[ˈɛkɐ]/[ˈɛgɐ]	(2;0.27)	

d. Laura
Stressed/word-medial
este	/ˈeʃtɨ/	→	[ˈeʃtɨ]	(2;2.30)	'this'
testa	/ˈtɛʃtɐ/	→	[ˈtɛʃtɐ]	(2;2.30)	'forehead'

Unstressed/word-medial
buscar	/buʃˈkar/	→	[buʃˈkarɨ]	(2;3.20)	'to get'
estranho	/iʃˈtrɐɲu/	→	[sˈtɐɲu]	(2;6.17)	'strange'
pescoço	/piʃˈkosu/	→	[pɨˈkos]	(2;6.17)	'neck'

Stressed/word-final
três	/ˈtreʃ/	→	[tɨˈreʃ]	(2;2.30)	'three'
feliz	/fɨˈliʃ/	→	[fɨˈliːʃ]	(2;2.30)	'happy'

Unstressed/word-final
bolinhas	/bɔˈliɲɐʃ/	→	[bɔˈliɲɐʃ]	(2;2.30)	'small balls'
bichos	/ˈbiʃuʃ/	→	[ˈbiʃuʃ]	(2;2.30)	'animals'

From the analysis of the data in (10), we can conclude that:

a. At the first stage, Inês does not produce coda fricatives, at all (cf. Inês (10.1)); at the second stage (cf. Inês (10.2)), she starts producing morphological coda fricatives both in stressed and unstressed word-final position. This means that at this stage, stress is irrelevant for the emergence of the V(G)C$_{fricative}$ rhyme, while word position is not. Afterwards, lexical word-final coda fricatives appear in stressed position.
b. Marta starts producing only morphological coda fricatives, both in stressed and in unstressed word-final syllables; afterwards, she produces morphological and lexical coda fricatives but only in stressed and unstressed word-final position. Once more, in the early stages, stress is irrelevant for the emergence of the V(G)C$_{fricative}$ rhyme, while word position is relevant.
c. Data from Luís confirm the behavior attested for Inês and Marta: the first coda fricatives to emerge are morphological ones, both in stressed and in unstressed word-final syllables. Word-final lexical coda fricatives occur later but prior to lexical coda fricatives in word-medial position.
d. Data from Laura shows that the unstressed word-medial position is the last one to stabilize, in the acquisition of the V(G)C$_{fricative}$ rhyme in EP, which means that, at later stages, stress seems to become relevant for the setting of this syllabic structure.

3.4 *Discussion*

As shown in (8) and in (10), fricatives are the first consonantal segments to appear in syllable-final position. According to our predictions in (9), one would expect stress to be a crucial prosodic fact for the emergence of the V(G)C$_{fricative}$ rhyme, that is, coda fricatives should first emerge in stressed syllables and only afterwards in unstressed ones. Moreover, we predicted that word position should also be crucial but secondary in relation to stress, that is, coda fricatives should emerge in stressed syllables, first in word-medial and only after, in word-final position. Contrary to our predictions in (9), according to which we expected morphological coda fricatives to be the last type of codas to develop, what we find instead is the following order of acquisition for V(G)C$_{fricative}$ rhymes in EP:

(11) *Actual order of acquisition for V(G)C$_{fricative}$ rhymes in EP*
    a. morphological coda fricatives in stressed and in unstressed word-final syllables;
    b. lexical coda fricatives in stressed and in unstressed word-final syllables;

c.   lexical coda fricatives in stressed word-medial syllables;
d.   lexical coda fricatives in unstressed word-medial syllables;

Thus, we have to explain why, contrary to our predictions in (9), morphological coda fricatives in unstressed word-final syllables are not the last but rather the first type of coda fricatives to emerge, along with morphological coda fricatives in stressed word-final syllables. Our predictions in (9) were based on two factors: syllable position and stress. These two factors alone do not explain the children's behavior in respect to the emergence of coda fricatives:

(i)   First, the relevant issue for the emergence of coda fricatives seems to be the syllable position in the word and not stress — coda fricatives first emerge in word-final position, both in stressed and in unstressed syllables.
(ii) Only later does stress become relevant: within the same word-medial position, first they set stressed syllables and only after unstressed ones will be stable.

Considering that the word-final position in EP is generally associated with morpho-syntactic information, both within the NP and the VP, our proposal is that the early acquisition of morphological coda fricatives in unstressed word-final syllables is due to their morphematic status in the target system. Höhle & Weissenborn (1998) show that unstressed function words seem to be perceived much earlier than expected, which allows us to predict that some unstressed prosodic structures may be prominent in perception in specific grammatical contexts.

As shown in Freitas & Miguel (1998), the plural marker in the acquisition of EP first emerges on nouns, possesives and demonstratives (as shown in (12)) and only later on articles (see examples in (13)):

(12)   *Data from Marta*

a.

meu	/'mew/	→ ['mew]	(1;5.17)	'my/mine' (MASC.SG)
isto	/'iʃtu/	→ ['itu]	(1;5.17)	'this' (NEUT)
estes	/'eʃtiʃ/	→ ['etiʃ]	(1;5.17)	'these' (MASC.PL)
outro	/'otru/	→ ['atu]	(1;5.17)	'another one' (MASC.SG)
outra	/'otrɐ/	→ ['otɐ]	(1;5.17)	'another one' (FEM.SG)

b.

rato	/'ʀatu/	→ ['ʀatu]	(1;5.17)	'mouse' (MASC.SG)
ratos	/'ʀatuʃ/	→ ['ʀatuʃ]	(1;5.17)	'mice' (MASC.PL)
pés	/'pɛʃ/	→ ['pɛʃ]	(1;5.17)	'feet' (MASC.PL)
o coelho	/uku'ɐʎu/	→ [ukɨ'ʎɛʎu]	(1;5.17)	'the rabbit' (MASC.SG)
a caneta	/ɐkɐ'netɐ/	→ [ɐkɐ'lɛlɐ]	(1;5.17)	'the pen' (FEM.SG)

c.

as flores	/ɐʃ'floriʃ/	→ [ɨ'ʃo·jʃ]	(1;4.8)	'the flowers'

as bananas	/ɐzbɐˈnɐnɐʃ/	→ [ɐˈmɐnɐʃ]	(1;4.8)	'the bananas'
as flores	/ɐʃˈfloɾiʃ/	→ [oˈʃoʃ]	(1;5.17)	'the flowers' (FEM.PL)
os óculos	/uzˈɔkuluʃ/	→ [udɨsˈkɔtsˑ]	(1;6.23)	'the glasses' (MASC.PL)

(13)   Data from Marta

| as canetas | /ɐʃkɐˈnetɐʃ/ | → [ɐʃkɐˈketɐʃ] | (1;11.10) | 'the pens' (FEM.PL) |
| as fraldas | /ɐʃˈfɾaɫdɐʃ/ | → [iʃˈfadɐʃ] | (1;11.10) | 'the diapers' (FEM.PL) |

Marta's and Inês' development of number features seem to be parallel and show the following steps: (i) first, number features emerge in noun heads; (ii) afterwards, agreement between determiners and noun heads occurs (see Freitas & Miguel 1998 for further information on the acquisition of NP functional projections in EP).

The early emergence of the plural marker on nouns, demonstratives and possessives and its later production on articles may be due to the different prosodic structure of the two types of words at the prosodic level (see Demuth 1996 and Lleó, this volume). For the moment, let us stress the following: the fact that this emergence first occurs on noun heads and only later on articles and the fact that morphological coda fricatives in both stressed and unstressed word-final syllables are acquired before other coda fricatives indicate that the children are able to isolate the word-final fricative and interpret it as a separate constituent — a morpheme — at the word level.

Summarizing, the early emergence of the word-final coda fricative is a consequence of its prominent status in EP. This status can be derived from two factors: (1) its word-final position; (2) its morphological content. Our proposal is that this status is strictly derived from its morphological nature — a plural marker — once word-final morphological coda fricatives emerge before word-final lexical coda fricatives (see examples from Luís in (10), where by the age of 1;11.20 *Becas* [ˈmɛkɐ] and *Luís* [ˈwi] are produced without the lexical coda fricative, while *bolachas* [ˈlaʃɐʃ] is produced with the morphological coda fricative). The fact that lexical coda fricatives in word-final syllables (as in *nariz*) emerge before lexical coda fricatives in word-medial syllables (as in *festa*) can be interpreted as a consequence of the frequency of the plural marker in the input or as the result of a prominence status assigned to word-edges (see, among others, Echols & Newport 1992 and Morais et al. 1993).

4.   Conclusion

In this paper, we presented empirical evidence from the acquisition of EP to show that the development of the coda fricative can not be explained by purely prosodic factors like stress and syllable position within the word. Our proposal is that coda fricatives in EP are bootstrapped by morphological markers. In order to account for the acquisition data in EP on target syllables with coda fricatives, morphosyntactic information must then be considered and an interaction between two modules of the grammar — prosody and morphology — has to be assumed. Moreover, this interaction may have consequences on the order of acquisition: in the case of the coda fricatives, we observed that morphosyntactic information assists in the acquisition of a prosodic structure. In other words, our findings suggest that the morphematic nature of the plural marker has a facilitating effect on the acquisition of the branching rhyme structure in EP.

Within the Principles and Parameters approach, it is assumed that the process of parameter setting is instantaneous, i.e. once it is set no variation is expected. Our results contribute to this discussion of the process of parameter setting: it seems that, in some cases, one has to assume that parameter setting is not instantaneous but gradual in the course of acquisition. In the case of the Branching Rhyme Parameter, parameter setting first takes place locally, in syllables with morphological coda fricatives, and then spreads to other types of codas, depending on stress and on syllable position within the word. We hope to have contributed to the discussion of which factors play a role in the gradual process of parameter setting and how they interact, in the cases where children are submitted to interface structures.

Acknowledgments

We wish to thank P. Fikkert, B. Höhle, J. Weissenborn and the participants at the The TROPICS Conference for the comments on this paper.

This research was part of a larger project on the acquisition of European Portuguese supported by JNICT (PCSH/C/LIN/524/93).

References

Delgado-Martins, M. R. 1994. "Relação fonética/fonologia: a propósito do sistema vocálico do Português." *Actas do CIP,* Vol. I. Lisbon: APL.

Demuth, K. 1992. "Accessing functional categories in Sesotho: Interactions at the morpho-syntactic interface." In *The Acquisition of Verb Placement,* J. Meisel (ed.), Dordrecht: Kluwer.

Demuth, K. 1996. "The prosodic structure of early words." In *Signal to Syntax: Bootstrapping from Speech to Grammar in Early Acquisition*, J. L. Morgan & K. Demuth (eds.). Mahwah: LEA Publishers.

Echols, C. & Newport, E. 1992. "The role of stress and position in determining first words." *Language Acquisition* 2: 189–220.
Fikkert, P. 1994. *On the Acquisition of Prosodic Structure*. Leiden: HIL.
Freitas, M. J. 1997. *Aquisição da Estrutura Silábica do Português Europeu*. PhD Dissertation, Lisbon: University of Lisbon.
Freitas, M. J. & Miguel, M. 1998. "Prosodic and syntactic interaction: the acquisition of NP functional projections in European Portuguese." *Proceedings of ConSOLE VI*. Leiden: SOLE.
Höhle, B. & Weissenborn, J. 1998. "Sensitivity to closed-class elements in preverbal children." In *Proceedings of the 22nd Annual Boston Conference on Language Development*, A. Greenwich, M. Hughes, H. Littlefield & H. Walsh (eds.). Somerville: Cascadilla Press.
Levelt, C. 1994. *On the Acquisition of Place*. Leiden: HIL.
Mateus, M. H. & Andrade, E. 1998. "The syllable structure in European Portuguese." D.E.L.T.A., Vol. 14, N° 1.
Morais, J., Kolinsky, R., Cluytens & Pasdeloup, V. 1993. "Unidades no reconhecimento da fala em Português." *1° Encontro de Processamento da Língua Portuguesa*. Lisboa.
Müller, N. 1994. "Gender and number agreement within DP." In *Bilingual First Language Acquisition: French and German Grammatical Development*, J. Meisel (ed.). Amsterdam: John Benjamins.
Peters, A. M. 1996. "Language typology, prosody and the acquisition of grammatical morphemes." In *The Crosslinguistic Study of Language Acquisition*, Slobin, D. (ed.). Hillsdale, NJ: LEA Publishers.
Segui, J., Dupoux, E. & Mehler, J. 1990. "The role of the syllable in speech segmentation, phoneme identification and lexical access." In *Cognitive Models of Speech Processing*, G. Altmann (ed.). Cambridge: MIT Press.
Stemberger, J. 1996. "Syllable structure in English, with emphasis on codas." In *Proceedings of the UBC International Conference on Phonological Acquisition*, B. Bernhardt, J. Gilbert & D. Ingram (eds.). Somerville: Cascadilla Press.
Treiman, R. & Zukowski, A. 1991. "Levels of phonological awareness." In *Phonological Processes in Literacy*, S. Brady & D. Shankweiler (eds.). Hillsdale: LEA Publishers.

Compounds Triggering Prosodic Development

Paula Fikkert
University of Nijmegen

1. Introduction

This paper argues against the commonly held view that structures that are less complex are easier to learn than more complex structures. Instead, it argues that the structures that are learned more easily are those for which the evidence is particularly clear to the language learner, independent of their grammatical complexity. To show this I will consider the acquisition of prosodic structure of both monomorphemic words and compounds restricting myself to nouns and nominal compounds in Dutch.

I will only use evidence from production data. The data come from a large database, currently available also through CHILDES (MacWhinney 1995), which contains spontaneous longitudinal data from 12 children acquiring Dutch as a first language (Fikkert 1994; Levelt 1994). The children were between 1 and 2 years old at the start of a one-year period of data collection. In addition, I will use some data from my oldest daughter Hilde.

Compounds are usually regarded as more complex than monomorphemic words, simply because they consist of at least two monomorphemic words. But are compounds consisting of two feet also more complex than monomorphemic words consisting of two feet? Often, such compounds are prosodically more complex than monomorphemic words, since they may, for instance, have intervocalic consonant clusters not allowed in monomorphemic words. In, for instance, the Dutch words *brand.slang* ['bʀɑnt‚slɑŋ] 'fire hose' and *vlieg.tuig* ['vli:χ‚tœyχ] 'airplane' the underlined consonant clusters could never arise in a monomorphemic word, since in the latter no more than three consonants (a coda and an onset cluster) can occur after a short vowel, and no more than two (which must form an acceptable onset cluster) after a long vowel, as in *cen.trum* ['sɛn.tʀʉm] 'centre' and *ze.bra* ['ze:.bʀɑ:] 'zebra'. Word-internal syllables always contain two positions in the rhyme: a long vowel or a short vowel plus a consonant. Therefore, the syllable boundary in such monomorphemic words invariably falls after the vowel if it is long, otherwise after the first consonant of a sequence of consonants. Consequently, the consonants after the syllable boundary must form a possible onset of Dutch. Therefore, the *gt* cluster, as in for example *vliegtuig* ['vliːχˌtœyχ] 'airplane', cannot arise in monomorphemic words, and indicates a compound. The constraints on possible word-internal consonant clusters are dictated by constraints on syllable structure; in particular, those determining well-formed onsets, and those determining possible rhymes.

On the basis of these structural prosodic observations one could argue that since compounds often contain more complex structures they will be learned later than monomorphemic words of the same length. It will be shown that this hypothesis is not borne out by the data. Rather, the acquisition of compounds guides the child in acquiring monomorphemic words consisting of more than one foot.

In this paper we will look at how children's systems develop in the course of acquisition; and what kind of information or evidence in the input children use to build up their phonological (or, more general, their grammatical) system. I will show that children's developmental stages can be well described in terms of parameter setting: if children discover particular cues in the input data, they use this information to set parameters from the unmarked (default) to the marked value; children do not necessarily use the whole input word from the start for their production forms, but they only use the segmental content contained in a prosodic category of the target (often smaller than a word); and children build upon their own systems, which gradually become more like the system of the adult.

In other words, the child's grammar is never dramatically different from the adult's (the same principles and parameters are at stake), but may differ in the sense that not all parameters are set, i.e. all or some may still have the default value or may still be irrelevant. Parameters are not all set simultaneously (as would have been done by the ideal (instantaneous) learner (cf. Dresher & Kaye 1990; Gillis et al. 1992), but are set when they become relevant and only after the required evidence for the marked setting is encountered.

The paper is organized as follows. § 2 gives a short description of the target grammar that children learning Dutch are to acquire. § 3 summarizes the main findings of Fikkert (1994), which describes the intermediate stages found in the acquisition of monomorphemic words. § 4 accounts for the first acquisition stages, based on Fikkert (1994). In § 5 it will be discussed how the acquisition of compounds fits into the developmental pattern. § 6 argues that the complex prosodic structure of compounds helps the child in learning to analyze the prosodic patterns of target words.

2. Background: The prosodic system of Dutch in a nutshell

Without going into details of the stress system of Dutch (see Kager 1989 or Booij 1995 for overviews) the main parameters that I assume to be relevant for describing the Dutch (both adult and child) stress patterns are given in (1). (1a) gives the parameters that determine the foot shape, (1b) those that determine the parsing of feet, (1c) those relevant for distinguishing between main and secondary stressed feet, and (1d) gives the parameter for compound stress.

(1) *Stress parameters with settings for Dutch*[1]
    a. FOOT-SHAPE PARAMETERS
        headedness parameter: Feet are strong on the LEFT/right
        quantity-sensitivity (QS) parameter: Feet are <u>quantity-sensitive</u>/QUANTITY-INSENSITIVE
        weight parameter: Feet are QS to <u>closed syllables</u>/nucleus/rhyme
    b. PARAMETERS OF FOOT CONSTRUCTION
        directionality parameter: Feet are built from the <u>right</u>/left
        iterativity parameter: Feet are built iteratively [<u>yes</u>/NO]
    c. WORD TREE DOMINANCE PARAMETERS
        main stress parameter: The word-tree is strong on the <u>right</u>/left
        extrametricality parameter: There is an extrametrical unit [<u>yes</u>/NO]
        unit of extrametricality (EM) parameter: The unit of EM is a [consonant C, a mora μ, a syllable σ, a foot F, a <u>monosyllabic foot</u>, etc.]
    d. COMPOUND STRESS PARAMETER
        compound stress parameter: Stress the [<u>left</u>/right] prosodic word of a compound.

        _{The underlined value is the value required for Dutch. The parameters for which a universal default value[2] can be assumed are in capitals.}

In other words, Dutch has quantity-sensitive (QS) trochaic feet built iteratively from right to left. Closed syllables count as heavy for stress. Although vowel length is contrastive in Dutch, long vowels do not count as heavy. Main stress is on the last foot, unless this foot consists of a heavy syllable. In that case the final foot would be extrametrical, and main stress would be on the pre-final foot. Superheavy syllables (-VVC and -VCC) are not made extrametrical, and receive stress in the unmarked case. Compounds have stress on the main stressed syllable of the first prosodic word.

With regard to syllable structure it is important to mention that although Dutch has a vowel length contrast in closed syllables, this contrast mainly manifests itself in word-final position where superheavy syllables are allowed. Word-internal superheavy syllables are rare; in general, word-internal rhymes either consist of a long vowel or of a short vowel plus a consonant. Thus, usually only -VC or -VV rhymes occur word-internally, whereas in word-final position -VVC and -VCC rhymes can also be found.

Given the default values in (1), children acquiring Dutch have to learn that Dutch is a QS language. They also have to learn what determines quantity. Furthermore, they have to learn that feet are built iteratively, that main stress is right, and that final feet consisting of a heavy syllable are extrametrical, i.e. they cannot receive main stress. Let us now review the earlier findings regarding the acquisition of prosodic structure in monomorphemic words.

3. Acquiring the prosodic structure of monomorphemic words: A description

All early production forms of children are monosyllabic, and they usually correspond to adult monosyllabic forms, showing that children are able to select those input forms for production that match their phonological system (Schwartz & Leonard 1982; Schwartz et al. 1987). Hilde, for example, for a long time had no disyllabic forms (other than 'papa' and 'mama'), and most of her forms corresponded to monosyllabic targets. Shortly before she produced disyllabic forms, she had monosyllabic forms corresponding to disyllabic targets (2a), and barely two weeks later, she produced them as disyllabic (2b). Crucially, if disyllabic targets are reduced, it is always the stressed syllable of the adult target that surfaces in the child's production form. (2c) shows that at this stage monosyllabic target words are sometimes produced as disyllabic. Thus, at stage 1, words can be both monosyllabic or disyllabic, as long as they form a single foot.

(2) *Monosyllabic Stage* (STAGE 0)
    a. vakantie 'vacation' /vaːˈkɑnsiː/ → [kat͡s] Hilde (1;4.15)
        zitten 'to sit' /ˈzɪtən/ → [tɪt͡s]
        appel 'apple' /ˈɑpəl/ → [ɑp]
    One Foot Stage (STAGE 1)
    b. vakantie 'vacation' /vaːˈkɑnsiː/ → [ˈkat͡siː] Hilde (1;4.30)
        zitten 'to sit' /ˈzɪtən/ → [ˈtiːtaː]
        appel 'apple' /ˈɑpəl/ → [ˈɑpaː]
    c. koek 'cookie' /kuːk/ → [ˈkuːka] Hilde (1;4.30)
        kop 'cup' /kɔp/ → [ˈkuːpa]

Insofar as stress and number of syllables is concerned, disyllabic adult words with initial stress are produced correctly from a very early stage by most children. Disyllabic words with final stress are not only significantly more often truncated, but also show significantly more stress errors (Fikkert 1994; Archibald 1995). This is in line with observations brought up in the literature on the acquisition of stress: namely, that children seem to have a bias for a trochaic pattern, and are most likely to retain stressed and final syllables in their own production of target words (cf. Allen & Hawkins 1978, 1980; Echols 1987, 1988; Echols & Newport 1992; Gerken 1994a, b, 1996; Fikkert 1994, 1995; Demuth 1995, 1996a, b; Demuth & Fee 1995; Wijnen et al. 1994; Lohuis-Weber & Zonneveld 1996).

On further inspection the disyllabic target words with final stress show a clear pattern of development, as shown in (3a–d).

(3) *Stages of development (all data from Robin)*
    a. STAGE 1

ballon[3] 'balloon' /bɑˈlɔn/	→	[ˈmɔmə], [ˈbɔmə]	(1;7.13)
konijn 'rabbit' /koːˈnɛin/	→	[ˈtɛin], [ˈtœin]	(1;7.27)
trompet 'trumpet' /ˌtrɔmˈpɛt/	→	[ˈpɪt]	(1;9.4)
banaan 'banana' /baːˈnaːn/	→	[ˈpaːn]	(1;10.7)
muziek 'music' /myːˈsiːk/	→	[ˈsiːk]	(2;0.4)
banaan 'banana' /baːˈnaːn/	→	[ˈbaːn]	(2;1.7)

    b. STAGE 2

ballon 'balloon' /bɑˈlɔn/	→	[ˈbuːɔn]	(2;1.7)
gitaar 'guitar' /χiːˈtaːr/	→	[ˈsiːtaː]	(2;1.7)
giraf 'giraffe' /ʃiːˈraf/	→	[ˈʃiːaf]	(2;1.26)

    c. STAGE 3

ballon 'balloon' /bɑˈlɔn/	→	[ˈbanˈdɔn]	(2;1.26)
kasteel 'castel' /ˌkasˈteːl/	→	[ˈtaːsˈteːu]	(2;1.26)
banaan 'banana' /baːˈnaːn/	→	[ˈmaːˈnaːn]	(2;2.27)
misschien 'maybe' /ˌmɪsˈχiːn/	→	[ˈpɪˈziːn], [ˈmɪˈziːn]	(2;3.10)

    d. STAGE 4

meneer 'sir' /məˈneːr/	→	[məˈneːɹ]	(2;2.22)
misschien 'maybe' /ˌmɪsˈχiːn/	→	[ˌmɪˈsiːn]	(2;3.10)
konijn 'rabbit' /koːˈnɛin/	→	[kɔˈnɛin]	(2;4.8)
kameel 'camel' /kaːˈmeːl/	→	[ˌkaˈmeːw]	(2;4.29)
muziek 'music' /myːˈsiːk/	→	[ˌmyːˈsiːk]	(2;4.29)

As is clear from these data, the transitions from stage to stage are always gradual. There will be forms from both the previous and following stage, which may obscure the developmental pattern. Nevertheless, these four stages can be clearly distinguished. They are also attested in the data of other children (cf. Fikkert 1994). The developmental pattern for disyllabic words with final stress that can be detected from the data can (albeit in a simplified fashion) be summarized as in (4):

(4) *Summary of developmental pattern for disyllabic targets with final stress*
STAGE 1: Adult disyllables with final stress are truncated to monosyllables. The final syllable — the stressed one — is kept in the child's realization. An extra syllable is sometimes added.
STAGE 2: Both syllables of the adult target word are realized. However, contrary to the adult pattern, they are produced with initial stress.
STAGE 3: Again both syllables of the adult target word are realized, but receive an equal amount of stress, resulting in level stressed forms.
STAGE 4: In respect to the number of syllables and stress patterns, the child produces the word in an adult-like manner.

For disyllabic target words with initial stress, no developmental pattern can be detected. They are produced correctly insofar as the stress pattern and the number of syllables is concerned. In other words: $(\sigma_s\ \sigma_w)_{Wd} \rightarrow (\sigma_s\ \sigma_w)_{Wd}$ during all stages, except the first monosyllabic stage.

Two observations about the data are crucial. First, the stressed syllable of the adult word is always maintained, and second, the stressed syllable of the adult word is not necessarily stressed in the child's form. These observations indicate that stress in the adult target is important, since it guides the child in selecting material from the adult target. Furthermore, the child could not be picking out a prosodic constituent from the adult target with its segmental material, because then the attested stress errors would not be expected. That is, foot structure is not copied along with the segmental material: stress and segmental structure are largely independent. If we look at the child's production of trisyllabic adult words, the pattern in (5) surfaces:

(5) *Adult target*   *Stage 1*   *Stage 2*   *Stage 3*   *Stage 4*
a. Trisyllabic words with penultimate stress
pantoffels 'slippers' ['tɔfhiːs] ['tɔfɔs] ['panˈtɔfɔls] [ˌpanˈtɔfɔls]
/ˌpanˈtɔfəls/
spaghetti 'spaghetti' ['hɛta] ['hɛta] ['paːˈhɛta] [paːˈhɛta]
/spaːˈχetiː/

b. *Trisyllabic words with final stress*
   telefoon 'telephone' ['fɔm]   ['tɪfoːm]   ['teːnə'ʃaõn]   ['teːləˌfoːm]
   /ˌteːlə'foːn/
   krokodil[4] 'crocodile' ['diːw]   ['koːwɪ]   ['kɛkɛ'kɪw]   ['koːkəˌdɪw]
   /ˌkroːkoː'dɪl/
c. *Trisyllabic words with initial stress*
   olifant[4] 'elephant'   ['fan]   ['oːfan]   ['oːfiː'fan]   ['oːɸiːˌfant]
   /'oːliːˌfant/
   kangoeroe 'kangaroo' ['kɑu]   ['kaːku]   ['kaːkə'ʀuːŋ]   ['kɑkuːˌjuː]
   /'kɑŋgəˌruː/

At the first two stages one trochaic foot is produced. At the third stage a second foot is produced, where both feet receive an equal amount of stress. The forms in (5b) and (5c) show a similar developmental pattern, although the adult forms differ in the location of main stress: in (5b) main stress is final and the antepenultimate syllable has secondary stress; in (5c) main stress is on the antepenultimate syllable and the final syllable has secondary stress. At the first stage, the rightmost foot is produced, or rather the segmental material of the rightmost foot is selected for production, *independent of the stress level in the adult word*. It is not the main stressed foot, but the rightmost foot (bearing at least secondary stress) that is selected. At stage 2, the initial syllable is adjoined to the monosyllabic form of stage 1, and the resulting string of segments is produced as a trochee. At stage 3 two feet are produced, both with an equal amount of stress. At stage 4 main stress is assigned; it is, however, not assigned to the rightmost foot (the normal location for main stress in Dutch), but to the leftmost foot.

For the data in (5b) there is a fifth stage in which the stress pattern is as in the adult words: final main stress and antepenultimate secondary stress. Some more data are given in (6), (7), and (8).

(6) *Tirza: trisyllabic words with penultimate stress*
   a. STAGE 1 AND 2
      vakantie 'vacation' /vaː'kɑnsi/   →   ['tasiː]   (1;8.5)
      kabouter 'gnome' /kaː'bɑutər/   →   ['bɑutə]   (2;1.7)
   b. STAGE 3
      tracteren 'to treat' /ˌtrɑk'teːrə/   →   ['tɑk'teːʀə]   (2;5.21)
      kabouter 'gnome' /kaː'bɑutər/   →   ['kaː'bɑutə]   (2;5.21)
   c. STAGE 4
      tracteren 'to treat' /ˌtrɑk'teːrə/   →   [ˌtɑk'teːʀə]   (2;5.21)

(7) *Tirza: trisyllabic words with final stress*
   a. STAGE 1
      telefoon 'telephone' /ˌteːlə'foːn/   →   ['χoːn]   (1;9.11)
      paraplu 'umbrella' /ˌpaːraː'plyː/   →   ['pyːtʃ]   (1;10.22)

b.	STAGE 2			
	boerderij 'farm' /ˌbuːrdəˈrɛi/	→	[ˈpɔdɛi]	(1;11.19)
c.	STAGE 3′			
	muzikant 'musician' /ˌmyːziːˈkɑnt/	→	[ˈtiːkˈtʊnt]	(1;11.19)
	boerderij 'farm' /ˌbuːrdəˈrɛi/	→	[ˈpyːˈhaːj]	(2;0.18)
	boerderij 'farm' /ˌbuːrdəˈrɛi/	→	[ˈbuːˈdɛi]	(2;1.17)
d.	STAGE 3			
	papegaai 'parrot' /ˌpaːpəˈχaːj/	→	[ˈpapaˈχaːj]	(2;2.12)
	koningin 'queen' /ˌkoːnɪˈŋɪn/	→	[ˈkoːnɪŋˈɪŋ]	(2;5.5)
	indiaan 'Indian' /ˌɪndiːˈjaːn/	→	[ˈɪndiːˈjaːnə]	(2;5.5)
	telefoon 'telephone' /ˌteːləˈfoːn/	→	[ˈteːnəˈʃoːn]	(2;5.21)
e.	STAGE 4			
	Amsterdam idem /ˌɑmstərˈdɑm/	→	[ˈɛmstəˌdɛm]	(2;3.27)
	koningin 'queen' /ˌkoːnɪˈŋɪn/	→	[ˈkoːnɪˌŋɪŋ]	(2;5.5)

(8) *Tirza: trisyllabic words with initial stress*

a.	STAGE 1			
	olifant 'elephant' /ˈoːliːˌfɑnt/	→	[ˈɑnt], [ˈɑunt]	(1;11.19)
b.	STAGE 2			
	Gideon *name* /ˈχiːdeˌjɔn/	→	[ˈχiːja]	(2;0.5)
	olifant 'elephant' /ˈoːliːˌfɑnt/	→	[ˈoːt͡sɑnt]	(2;0.18)
	kangoeroe 'kangaroo' /ˈkɑŋɡəˌruː/	→	[ˈkɑntuː]	(2;1.17)
	ooievaar 'stork' /ˈoːjəˌvaːr/	→	[ˈoːʃaː]	(2;2.12)
c.	STAGE 3′			
	olifant 'elephant' /ˈoːliːˌfɑnt/	→	[ˈoːnˈt͡sʌnt]	(2;0.18)
d.	STAGE 3			
	goochelaar 'conjurer' /ˈχoːχəˌlaːr/	→	[ˈsoːχəˈlaːɹ]	(2;2.12)
	olifant 'elephant' /ˈoːliːˌfɑnt/	→	[ˈoːləˈsɑnt]	(2;2.25)
e.	STAGE 4			
	allemaal 'all' /ˈɑləˌmaːl/	→	[ˈɑnəˌsaː]	(2;1.17)
	olifant 'elephant' /ˈoːliːˌfɑnt/	→	[ˈoːləˌlɑmp]	(2;3.12)
		→	[ˈɔliːˌfɑnt]	(2;6.12)
	ooievaar 'stork' /ˈoːjəˌvaːr/	→	[ˈoːjəˌfaːɹ]	(2;6.12)

These data also show an intermediate stage 3′. This stage can only be accounted for by assuming that the child's own output forms at each stage play a crucial role in further development. The data in (7c) and (8c) typically precede stage 3, but already have the level stress, which is characteristic of stage 3. Apparently the child's segmental structure of the word does not change dramatically from stage 2 to 3′, but the prosodic structure does, whereas the difference between stage 3′ and 3 is not in prosodic but in segmental structure.

How can we explain the developmental patterns? What triggers the transition from one stage to the next? I claim that the transitions from one stage to the next can be understood as (a) the setting of one or more parameters from the default (unmarked) value to the marked, and/or (b) the extension of the child's template.

4. Accounting for the developmental patterns: Part one

At the stage (stage 0) at which children only have monosyllabic words (mostly corresponding to monosyllabic targets) none of the stress parameters need to be set, since they simply are irrelevant. However, as we saw, disyllabic words (with initial stress) enter their active vocabularies relatively early; and then, some of the stress parameters become relevant. When the child compares his/her monosyllabic production forms with the disyllabic target forms, i.e. comparing ['ɑp] with target apple 'apple' /'ɑpəl/, s/he may detect a mismatch in the number of syllables and produce an extra syllable, and it is in this way that the foot-shape parameters (1a) need to be considered.[5]

On the hypothesis that the child expands his/her system in a systematic way by making use of the basic prosodic constituents, the prediction is that when the child adds a syllable to the monosyllabic template, it could either be added to the right or to the left of this template, thus creating a disyllabic foot, which could in principle be either left- or right-headed. When the input contains both trochaic $(\sigma_s\ \sigma_w)_{Wd}$ words, like *baby* /'beːbiː/ 'baby' and iambic $(\sigma_w\ \sigma_s)_{Wd}$ words, like *banaan* /baːˈnaːn/ 'banana', the child knows that one of these forms contains more than one foot. At this point a decision has to be made about headedness and direction of parsing. If the child starts parsing from a word edge until the parse includes a stressed syllable, the possibilities in (9) arise, where right-to-left parsing results in a left-headed foot, and left-to-right parsing in a right-headed foot:

(9) *Target words*: $(\sigma_s\ \sigma_w)_{Wd}$ ['beːbiː] $(\sigma_w\ \sigma_s)_{Wd}$ [baːˈnaːn]
   a. D:RL, H:L $(\sigma_s\ \sigma_w)$ ['beːbiː] (σ_s) ['naːn]
   b. D:LR, H:R (σ_s) ['beː] $(\sigma_w\ \sigma_s)$ [baːˈnaːn]

D = Directionality, H = Headedness, L = Left-headed, R = Right-headed

Only the settings of (9a) explain the observed pattern characterizing stage 1 in child language. The child seems to have left-headed feet parsed from the right, or from the word's *ending*. Biases towards word endings and stressed syllables are commonly found in the literature on child language (cf. Slobin 1973; Echols 1987, 1988; Echols & Newport 1992). They are often viewed as performance properties. In Fikkert (1994) I hypothesized that this performance property is reflected in the universal default value for directionality as [right-to-left]; but research from language change shows that it is more likely that the default value is [left-to-right] for trochees (Lahiri et al. 1999). Under this hypothesis the child has already discovered an important feature of the Dutch stress system: directionality of foot parsing. It also indicates that the child has already learned that not all target words have initial stress, even though the child's output forms all have initial stress (because they contain only one foot). The existence of target $(\sigma_s\sigma_w)$ and $(\sigma_w\sigma_s)$ words is therefore not yet used for the QS parameter (see below), but is used to determine the directionality of footification. Stress[6] in the adult target guides the child in the acquisition process. The child seems to know that stress in the adult target word indicates the boundary (the strong branch) of a foot.

The literature on acquisition of phonology also frequently mentions biases towards trochaic feet. Some assume that the basis for this bias lies in UG, where the trochee is viewed as universally unmarked or default. Typologically the only quantity-insensitive feet are trochaic. Others argue that this bias reflects the much higher frequency of trochaic forms in the target language — an argument that surely holds for the Germanic languages. It is therefore important to look at data from other languages that either have trochees parsed from left to right, or have an iambic stress pattern; for these may give us more clues about default values.

The fact that the child's template consists of minimally one and maximally two syllables, which form exactly one initially-stressed foot, indicates that s/he has a binary left-headed (trochaic) foot, of which at least the head is filled. That a foot maximally contains two syllables is clear from the following data, which are invariably reduced to disyllabic forms with initial stress:

(10) *Trisyllabic target words with initial stress only (data from Elke)*
tekenen 'to draw' /ˈteːkənə[n]/ → [ˈkaːkə]   (1;8.13)
                                 → [ˈkɛkiː]   (1;8.31)
                                 → [ˈkɛikɛi]   (1;9.24)
andere 'others' /ˈandərə/   → [ˈaːnə]   (2;0.25)

The fact that exactly one foot is produced suggests that the iterativity parameter (1b) — 'Are feet built iteratively? [yes/no]' — has a default value [no].[7] The child seems to take the segmental material from the rightmost foot of the adult target word and map this onto his/her own trochaic foot template. If the target word consists of more than one foot, the remainder of the adult target word is not realized, because it does not fit into the child's template. If the target foot consists of two syllables, both syllables are realized in the child's output form (explaining why disyllabic target words with initial stress are produced correctly). If the target foot consists of one syllable, the child's realization can be either monosyllabic or disyllabic. In the latter case (as in (2c)), a syllable can be added to the right of the selected material to fill both positions in the foot. The child does not copy the foot structure of the adult word, since this extra syllable is not present in the adult target foot.[8]

This does not mean that children cannot sometimes incorporate more material into their template than just the segmental material of the final stressed foot: As shown in Fikkert (1994) and Levelt (1994), children build up representations, which initially are largely underspecified: only those features that are necessary to discriminate different words in the child's lexicon are represented. When the final target foot begins with a coronal consonant, but the target word with a labial or dorsal consonant, the child often produces the word with an initial labial or dorsal place of articulation. On the assumption that coronal is underspecified (cf. Paradis & Prunet 1991) the child is able to incorporate a place specification from elsewhere in the target word, because there then is an empty slot for a place feature to dock on to. Some data are given in (11):

(11) a. *Elke*
konijn 'rabbit' /koːˈnɛin/ → [ˈkɛin] (2;3.27)
banaan 'banana' /baːˈnaːn/ → [ˈmaŋ] (1;8.13)
konijn 'rabbit' /koːˈnɛin/ → [ˈŋɑɲ] (1;8.31)
fornuis 'stove' /ˌfɔrˈnpœs/ → [ˈmpœs] (2;2.6)
konijn 'rabbit' /koːˈnɛin/ → [ˈkɛ] (1;10.21)

b. *Noortje*
banaan 'banana' /baːˈnaːn/ → [ˈmaːm] (2;2.22)
konijn 'rabbit' /koːˈnɛin/ → [ˈŋɛiç] (2;2.22)
meneer 'sir' /məˈneːr/ → [ˈmɪ] (2;3.7)
konijn 'rabbit' /koːˈnɛin/ → [ˈkaː], [ˈkɛin], [ˈkɛi] (2;3.21)
bananen 'bananas' /baːˈnaːnən/ → [ˈmaːmə], [ˈmaːnə] (2;7.17)
meneer 'sir' /məˈneːr/ → [ˈmeːə] (2;8.29)

c. *Jarmo*
ballonnen 'balloons' /baˈlɔnən/ → [ˈpɔma] (2;0.28)
kadootje 'gift' *dim* /kaːˈdoːtjə/ → [ˈkoːχjə], [ˈkoːʃə] (2;1.8)
kadootje 'gift' *dim* /kaːˈdoːtjə/ → [ˈkoːχjə], [ˈkoːʃə] (2;1.8)
gitaar 'guitar' /χiːˈtaːr/ → [ˈkaː] (2;1.22)
meneer 'sir' /məˈneːr/ → [ˈbeːə], [ˈmeːə] (2;3.9)

On the assumption that the default value for the quantity sensitivity (QS) parameter is that feet are quantity-insensitive (QI), the child seems to have default values for all stress parameters that are relevant at this stage, except perhaps for the directionality parameter. The motivation for the QI default value comes from several facts. First, whereas both rhyme structure and the number of syllables are important for QS languages, QI languages only consider the number of syllables, and therefore require less knowledge from the learner. Second, if we look at the data from stage 2 we see that there are 'heavy' and 'superheavy' stressless syllables, clearly indicating that the system is QI. If QS were the default value, the parameter would be set to the marked value QI at stage 2. However, on the assumption that learning is deterministic, children would never again arrive at the required value QS. Third, there is a strong positive cue to detect QS, namely, the existence of words in the input with an equal number of syllables but different stress patterns.

It is important to note that, although the cue for QS is available at stage 1, quantity does not seem to play a role yet. This illustrates how children are incremental mode learners: although the relevant cues are in principle available from the start of the acquisition process, the cues are only used to determine parameter values when the child is 'ready' to use the cues. That is, children build up the stress system incrementally, rather than focusing on all parameters simultaneously.

Another important point is the following. Suppose that the child is building metrical structure on the segmental strings of the *input* (= target) forms to test the current settings of the parameters. We then expect that disyllabic target words with final stress will be realized as disyllabic words with initial stress, given the default values of the parameters. Although there is a stage at which this prediction is borne out (namely stage 2), this is not the first stage in the development. Rather, the first stage is the stage at which these words are typically reduced to the stressed (monosyllabic) foot of the adult target. Only when metrical trees are not built on the whole string of segments of the adult target with final stress, but on the segments in the final foot of the adult word, do we expect the forms typical of stage 1. Only if the final foot is considered as input to the learning system, do the output forms created on the basis of the parameter settings match the input forms with respect to stress; and thus, the child will not change any stress parameters, there being no evidence for the marked settings.

The child may not have detected any stress errors in his/her output as compared with the input at stage 1, but s/he has discovered that his/her output forms and the target forms do not always match in the number of syllables. To solve this mismatch between input and output, the next step in the development is to produce an extra syllable in words that have one syllable in the output form, and two (or more) in the adult target form (stage 2). If the child's form at stage 1 consists of one syllable the child takes another syllable of the target word — if available the (secondary) stressed syllable; otherwise, the leftmost one. The segmental content of that syllable is adjoined to the child's previously monosyllabic form. This segmental material is mapped onto the same foot template of the previous stage: a quantity-insensitive (QI) trochaic foot, resulting in an initial-stressed disyllabic foot.[9] Interestingly, sometimes the segmental material of the leftmost syllable is adjoined to the right of the child's previous template resulting in metathesis, as in (12a). A second syllable can also be produced by reduplication, as in (12b). This shows that the child builds on his/her own previous representation of the word.

(12) a. *Metathesis*
papier 'paper' /paːˈpiːr/ → [ˈpiːpaː] Catootje (1;10.25)
→ [ˈpiːˈpaːj] Catootje (1;11.10)
b. *Reduplication*
ballon 'balloon' /bɑˈlɔn/ → [ˈpɔpɔm] Noortje (2;5.23)
konijn 'rabbit' /koːˈnɛin/ → [ˈkɛˈkɛin] Noortje (2;7.2)
ballon 'balloon' /bɑˈlɔn/ → [ˈpaːˈboːn] Catootje (1;11.10)

So far, there has been no evidence that any of the stress parameters are inappropriately set. Therefore, the parameter values at stage 2 still have the same values as at stage 1.

If the output forms of stage 2 are compared with the target forms, two things may be detected: (a) disyllabic and trisyllabic targets with final (main or secondary) stress are produced with the wrong stress pattern at stage 2, while disyllabic and trisyllabic target forms with penultimate stress have the right stress pattern; and/or (b) the number of syllables is lower in the output forms than in the trisyllabic target forms. If the child focuses on the number of syllables first, the prediction is that all trisyllabic target forms are produced as trisyllabic at the next stage (stage 3), where the (unchanged) parameter settings create the following stress pattern: $\sigma\ (\sigma_s\ \sigma_w)_F$. However, this is not borne out. We have seen that sometimes the child keeps a disyllabic realization, but with two stressed feet, clearly showing that the number of syllables has not changed, but the prosodic system has (stage 3'). Moreover, we saw above that children first focus on feet, and only later on the number of syllables. This is not different at this stage. Since disyllabic and trisyllabic target words with penultimate stress are not changed, let us focus on the types with final stress, starting with the disyllabic ones.

The child now has encountered words with an equal number of syllables (two) but a different stress pattern ($(\sigma_s\ \sigma_w)_{Wd}$ and $(\sigma_w\ \sigma_s)_{Wd}$, and thus has access to the cue for quantity-sensitivity. Although at stage 1 the child's input (the adult forms) already contained both types of words, only one type of disyllabic word was completely selected by the child then. Of the other type only the segmental material of the final stressed monosyllabic foot was realized in the child's output. At stage 3 the child has discovered that the difference between the two types of disyllabic words — those with initial stress and those with final stress — is linguistically significant. Therefore, the child now is able to use the cue for the

QS parameter and set it to its marked setting [QS]. Now, the child also has to determine what counts as a heavy syllable (weight parameter of (1a)). Children seem to regard any closed syllable as heavy, independent of the length of the vowel and independent of the nature of the final consonant(s), since all closed syllables, whether heavy (-VC) or superheavy (-VCC and -VVC), are now stressed in the child's output forms.

Besides setting the QS parameter to the marked value the child also has to make a decision about the value of the iterativity parameter at this stage, since s/he now knows that some target words consist of more than one foot. Moreover, the produced forms at stage 3 can contain two feet, whereas previously the child's production forms all consisted of exactly one foot. It seems that the iterativity parameter is set to its marked value [yes] at stage 3. Although now the main stress parameter is relevant, it is still not set. The fact that the child produces forms with two feet where both feet receive an equal amount of stress indicates that the parameter is simply not yet considered.

Thus, all foot-shape parameters and all parameters of foot construction have been set at stage 3. Only the word-tree dominance parameter(s) (1c) and compound parameter (1d) still have to be fixed. The account for the transitions from stage 3 to further stages differs from that given in Fikkert (1994). We will therefore postpone further discussion and first look at the acquisition of nominal compounds.

5. The acquisition of compounds

On the hypothesis that simple structures are acquired before complex structures one could hypothesize that children first learn monomorphemic words and that compounds are at first treated like monomorphemic words. At first sight, compound words seem to show essentially the same pattern as bipedal monomorphemic words, as shown in the data in (13), where for each stage an example of bipedal monomorphemic words with final and initial main stress is given, followed by an example of a compound. This seems to confirm the hypothesis that compounds and monomorphemic words are treated alike.

(13) *All data from Tirza*
    a. STAGE 1
        telefoon 'telephone' /ˌteːləˈfoːn/ → [ˈχoːn] (1;11)
        olifant 'elephant' /ˈoːliːˌfɑnt/ → [ˈɑnt] (1;11)
        hobbelpaard 'rocking horse' /ˈhɔbəlˌpaːrt/ → [ˈpɑnt] (1;11)

b. STAGE 2
    telefoon 'telephone' /ˌteːləˈfoːn/ → ['pɪfɔm]   (2;0)
    olifant 'elephant' /ˈoːliːˌfɑnt/   → ['oːt͡sɑnt]   (2;0)
    schildpad 'tortoise' /ˈsχɪl[t]ˌpɑt/ → ['sɪpɑt]   (2;0)
c. STAGE 3
    papegaai 'parrot' /ˌpɑːpəˈχaːj/   → ['pɑpɑˈχaːj]   (2;1)
    ooievaar 'stork' /ˈoːjəˌvaːr/   → ['oːjəˈsaːɪ]   (2;1)
    hobbelpaard 'rocking horse' /ˈhɔbəlˌpaːrt/ → ['hʌbəlˈpaːt] (2;1)
d. STAGE 4
    krokodil 'crocodile' /ˌkʀoːkoːˈdɪl/ → ['koːkuːˌdiːw] (2;2)
    olifant 'elephant' /ˈoːliːˌfɑnt/   → ['oːləˌlɑmp]   (2;3)
    hobbelpaard 'rocking horse' /ˈhɔbəlˌpaːrt/ → ['ɔpəˌpaːt] (2;2)

Thus, children who truncate (almost) all final stressed words should, under this hypothesis, do the same with compound forms. Remember that words like *olifant*, with initial main stress and secondary stress on the final syllable (which look very similar to compound stressed forms) were truncated to the final foot by most children. If compounds and monomorphemic words are treated in the same way by children, the question arises: How and when do children treat them differently? After all, they have, among others things, different prosodic structures.

On closer inspection there are two striking observations to be made concerning compounds. First, not all children who do truncate monomorphemic words also truncate compounds. Second, compound words appear relatively late in children's productive vocabulary, though they appear before bipedal monomorphemic words and are produced as such. Let us consider both observations in more detail.

Although some children only realize the final foot of compounds at the early stages, as shown by the data from Noortje in (14), this is not true for all children.

(14) *Noortje's realization of target compounds (in early production forms)*
     vliegtuig 'airplane' /ˈvliːχˌtœyχ / → ['hɑuχ] (2;3.20)
     sneeuwpop 'snow man' /ˈsneːwˌpɔp/   → ['pɔp]   (2;4.4)
     theepot 'tea pot' /ˈteːˌpɔt/   → ['pɔt]   (2;4.4)
     vliegtuig 'airplane' /ˈvliːχˌtœyχ/ → ['hœyχ] (2;4.4)

Eva, Elke, Jarmo and Tirza are among the children that truncate almost all final stressed words. However, none of these children seem to truncate compounds systematically to the final stressed foot. Some examples of Eva are given in (15):

(15)   Eva's production of target compounds
a.   kraanwagen 'crane' /'kraːnˌʋaːχən/ → ['taːŋ 'laːχə] (1;6.1)
     schildpad 'tortoise' /'sχɪl[t]ˌpat/ → ['sɑu 'pɑt] (1;9.8)
                                       → ['tɛupə 'paːt] (1;9.8)
     heerbeestje 'ladybird' /'heːrˌbeːsjə/ → ['fɯ 'beːsə] (1;9.8)
     boodschappen 'shopping' /'boːtˌsχapən/ → ['boːtə 'zapə] (1;9.8)
     vliegtuig 'airplane' /'vliːχˌtœyχ/ → ['fiːʔ 'tœyχ] (1;9.22)
     zakdoek 'handkerchief' /'zɑgˌduːk/ → ['sak 'duːt] (1;11.8)
     draaimolen 'merry-go-round' /'draːjˌmoːlən/ → ['taim 'boːjə] (1;11.8)
b.   glijbaan 'slide' /'χlɛiˌbaːn/ → ['dɛibaːn] (1;9.8)
     zandbak 'sand box' /'zɑmˌbak/ → ['sɑmbɑ] (1;9.8)
c.   olifant 'elephant' /'oːliːˌfɑnt/ → ['oːʋat] (1;7.22)

One immediate question is whether Eva perhaps already knows one or both of the members of the compound, in which case she simply realizes both words. In the forms of (15a) Eva may have known some of the members of the compounds as separate words, like *wagen* /'ʋaːχən/ 'wagon', *molen* /'moːlən/ 'mill' etc., but this is certainly not the case for all compounds in (15a), some of which are, certainly for children, not entirely transparent, like *vliegtuig* /'vliːχˌtœyχ/ 'airplane'. Tirza's data from the early stages of the production of compounds show that semantic factors may play a role in determining which part of the compound is realized. At the early stages she only realizes one part of the compound, as shown in (16). Interestingly, she realizes the word that is known to her (*tuin* /'tœyn/ 'garden', *zee* /'zeː/ 'sea', *zak* /'zɑk/ 'bag', *paard* /'paːrt/ 'horse' and *glijden* /'χlɛidə[n]/ 'slide' are all part of her active vocabulary); it does not seem to matter whether the word is in head or in complement position.

(16)   Tirza's earliest realizations of target compounds
     dierentuin 'zoo' /'diːrəˌtœyn/ → [tœyn] (1;8.5)
     zeehond 'seal' /'zeːˌhɔnt/ → [seː] (1;10.22)
     zakdoek 'handkerchief' /'zɑgˌduːk/ → [sɑːk] (1;11.8)
     hobbelpaard 'rocking horse' /'hɔbəlˌpaːrt/ → [pɑnt] (1;11.19)
     glijbaan 'slide' /'χlɛiˌbaːn/ → [χei] (1;11.19)

Although semantic factors thus may play a role, the data in (15) cannot be explained this way. Of interest is the fact that Eva distinguishes between words in (15a) and (15b), the former being treated as two prosodic words, the latter as one. Interestingly, words like *olifant* 'elephant', which she unfortunately has only a very little of, are realized like those in (15b), as shown in (15c). Apparently, Eva is able to distinguish some, but not all, compounds from monomorphemic words with more than one stress. The difference between the targets in (15a) and (15b) is that the latter could have been monomorphemic with regard to syllable phonotactics[10] — i.e. they look similar to words like *olifant* 'elephant', whereas the former could not: the first word of the compound forms a superheavy syllable which is only found at word edges. However, the difference between heavy and superheavy syllables is learned very late. Moreover, in the word *zakdoek* /'zɑɡˌduːk/ 'handkerchief' the first word does not contain a superheavy syllable, but it nevertheless patterns with the compounds that do have a superheavy first syllable. However, there is another prosodic difference between the forms in (15a) and (15b): they all contain medial clusters in which the consonants differ in place of articulation. Such clusters are usually not found word medially in monomorphemic words. Apparently, Eva is able to use this kind of prosodic information in the input. It therefore seems that the forms in (15a) are treated as two prosodic words each consisting of a single foot on the basis of syllable phonotactics, rather than on the basis of prosodic factors like syllable quantity.

Elke and Jarmo realize all disyllabic compounds as disyllabic monomorphemic words with initial stress, regardless of the syllable make-up of the target words, as shown in (17). However, words like *olifant* /'oːliːˌfɑnt/ 'elephant' are also treated like that, as is shown in (18).

(17)   a.   *Elke's productions of target compounds*
                     schildpad 'tortoise' /'sχɪlˌpɑt/ → ['χɪpɑt] (2;3.26)
                     vliegtuig 'airplane' /'vliːχˌtœyχ/ → ['fiːtœy] (2;4.15)
                     kauwgom 'chewing gum' /'kɑuˌχɔm/ → ['kɑuχəm] (2;4.15)
                     zandbak 'sand box' /'zɑmˌbɑk/ → ['sɑmbɑk] (2;4.29)
    b.   *Jarmo's productions of target compounds*
                     vliegtuig 'airplane' /'vliːχˌtœyχ/ → ['tiːtɑ] (1;7.29)
                                                                       → ['titœyf] (2;1.8)
                     wipwap 'seesaw' /'ʋɪpˌʋɑp/ → ['piːpaː] (1;8.12)
                                                                       → ['ʋiːpɑ] (1;9.9)
                     kauwgom 'chewing gum' /'kɑuˌχɔm/ → ['kɑuχɔ] (1;11.20)
                     schildpad 'tortoise' /'sχɪl[t]ˌpɑt/ → ['tiːtɑːt] (1;11.20)
                     dierentuin 'zoo' /'diːrəˌtœyn/ → ['tiːtœy] (2;4.1)
(18)   a.   *Elke*
                     olifant 'elephant' /'oːliːˌfɑnt/ → ['oːfɑnt] (2;3.26)
                                                          → ['oːflɑnt] (2;4.29)
    b.   *Jarmo*
                     olifant 'elephant' /'oːliːˌfɑnt/ → [fɑut] (2;1.22)
                                                          → ['toːtɑut] (2;1.22)
                                                          → ['hoːtɑ] (2;2.6)
                                                          → ['hɔntəˌflɑŋ] (2;4.1)

Apparently, these children tend to focus on the main stress in the word, rather than on just any stress. All final stressed words are realized as typical for stage 1 and/or stage 2 in § 2, but words with initial main stress and final secondary stress behave differently as soon as the child has a foot template: both stressed syllables are mapped onto a trochaic template, as in (18a). The same happens with compounds in (17).[11] Words of the type *olifant* /ˈoːliːˌfɑnt/ 'elephant' and compounds therefore seem to behave similarly. Since the child clearly produces only one foot it must be a monomorphemic word.[12] Elke and Jarmo truncated most words that contain more than one foot,[13] and did not show the whole range of developmental stages; i.e. at the end of the recording period they still produced mostly words consisting of a single foot. It should therefore not surprise us that compounds are also still realized as one foot and one word.

What about the children that showed a clear developmental pattern for monomorphemic larger words? Robin showed the full range of developmental stages in the period he was recorded, as shown in § 2. The data in (19) represent his developmental stages in the acquisition of compounds. As with Elke and Jarmo, the predicted first stage — the stage at which only the final foot is realized — is not attested in his data. This could be an accidental gap, but it could also reflect the strong bias to attend to main-stressed syllables. Children do seem to differ in whether a final foot with secondary stress is selected at stage 1 (cf. (5c) and (8a)), or whether the selection should at least include the main-stressed syllable (cf. 18a).

(19) *Robin's production of target compounds*
    a. STAGE 2
        sesamstraat 'Sesame street' /ˈseːsɑmˌstraːt/ → [ˈseːsaː] (1;7.13)
        autobus 'bus' /ˈoːtoːˌbʉs/ → [ˈɔbɪs] (1;8.10)
        vliegtuig 'airplane' /ˈvliːχˌtœyχ/ → [ˈtiːtaː] (1;8.24)
    b. STAGE 3
        speeltuin 'play ground' /ˈspeːlˌtœyn/ → [ˈdyːnˈdœyn] (1;9.3)
        vliegtuig 'airplane' /ˈvliːχˌtœyχ/ → [ˈfiːχəˈdaχ] (1;8.24)
        tankauto 'tanker' /ˈtɛŋkˌoːtoː/ → [ˈtiːnəˈʔoːtoː] (1;10.7)
        zandbak 'sand box' /ˈzɑmˌbɑk/ → [ˈsɑntəˈbɑk] (1;10.21)
        brandweer 'fire brigade' /ˈbrɑntˌʋeːr/ → [ˈhɑntəˈfʉ] (1;10.21)
    c. STAGE 4
        zandbak 'sand box' /ˈzɑmˌbɑk/ → [ˈʊɪmˌpaːt] (1;11.7)
        zandbak 'sand box' /ˈzɑmˌbɑk/ → [ˈfaːˌpɑk] (1;11.7)
        vliegtuig 'airplane' /ˈvliːχˌtœyχ/ → [ˈfɪsˌhɑχ] (1;11.7)

Robin's data do however show the other three stages in development that correspond to the stages 2–4 for monomorphemic words.

What is striking about these data in comparison to the monomorphemic ones is that stage 3 with the two equally stressed feet occurs much earlier in compounds (see § 2). This brings us to the second observation that at the early stages of acquisition compound targets are rarely attempted by children, yet they nonetheless occur earlier than bipedal monomorphemic ones. If we look at when compound targets are attested more frequently in the child's productive vocabulary, it seems that they start appearing *before* the child produces level stressed monomorphemic words; or, to put it differently: compounds are attempted before children start producing monomorphemic words consisting of two feet. Those compounds usually appear with level stress at first. Tirza's data show this nicely. If Tirza realizes both words, they are realized with level stress, as shown in (20a):

(20) Tirza's realizations of target compounds

a.
slaapzak 'sleeping bag' /ˈslaːpˌzɑk/	→	[ˈsɑps ˈsɑk]	(1;11.8)
windzak 'wind sack' /ˈʋɪntˌzɑk/	→	[ˈnɪnt ˈtɑk]	(1;11.19)
boterham 'slice of bread' /ˈboːtərˌhɑm/	→	[ˈboːdʉˈlʉm]	(2;0.5)
graafmachine 'excavator' /ˈχraːfmaʃiːnə/	→	[ˈaːfχˈtiːnə]	(2;0.5)
klimrek 'climbing frame' /ˈklɪmˌrɛk/	→	[ˈpɛm ˈpɛk]	(2;0.5)
vliegtuig 'airplane' /ˈvliːχˌtœyχ/	→	[ˈtiːχ ˈtœχ]	(2;0.5)
vrachtwagen 'truck' /ˈvrɑχtˌʋaːχən/	→	[ˈhɑχ ˈtaːkə]	(2;0.5)
appelmoes 'apple sauce' /ˈɑpəlˌmuːs/	→	[ˈaːpəˈmuːs]	(2;0.18)

b.
olifant 'elephant' /ˈoːliːˌfɑnt/	I	→	[ˈaunt]	(1;11.19)
ooievaar 'stork' /ˈoːjəˌvaːr/	II	→	[ˈoːʃaː]	(2;2.12)
olifant 'elephant' /ˈoːliːˌfɑnt/	III	→	[ˈoːloːˈjɑn]	(2;2.25)
	III	→	[ˈoːloːˈsɑnt]	(2;2.25)
	IV	→	[ˈoːliːˌfɑnt]	(2;6.12)
ooievaar 'stork' /ˈoːjəˌvaːr/	IV	→	[ˈoːjəˌfaːɪ]	(2;6.12)

Tirza realizes compounds differently from monomorphemic words with two stresses, which are produced much later (2-3 months), as can be seen in (20b). Although words like *olifant* /ˈoːliːˌfɑnt/ 'elephant' and *ooievaar* /ˈoːjəˌvaːr/ 'stork' seem to have exactly the same stress pattern as words like *appelmoes* /ˈɑpəlˌmuːs/ 'apple sauce' and *boterham* /ˈboːtərˌhɑm/ 'slice of bread' they are apparently treated differently. Since all monomorphemic words form still one foot, the data in (20a) should be interpreted as forming two separate words.

Thus, compounds seem in fact to have triggered the development of monomorphemic words with multiple stress. As shown above, compounds often have a syllabic structure that differs from monomorphemic words in that far more types of consonant clusters are found in the former than in the latter, and far more superheavy syllables occur word medially in compounds than in monomorphemic words. This evidence in the input probably helps the child in deciding that compounds contain two prosodic words, when a prosodic word still maximally is a single foot.

The data in (20a), which are typical of stage 3, thus show that the word is a central notion in acquisition. It seems therefore that the crucial question is not 'how and when do children know that word-like units can be combined into compounds?' but rather 'when do children learn that words can contain more than one foot'? A stage 3 they realize two prosodic words, each consisting of one foot, rather than one prosodic word made up of two feet. That is, most forms that are analyzed as level stress forms by the children at stage 3 represent compounds or rather compound-like structures; i.e. the concatenation of two monopedal monomorphemic words. They do not have compound stress. How do we know? Crucial evidence comes from the next stage in children's development, where initial stress is prevalent. This is typical for compound stress, since in the unmarked case stress is on the final foot in monomorphemic words.

6. Accounting for the developmental patterns: Part two

Stage 3 can be characterized as the stage in which children start combining two prosodic words, where both words have an equal amount of stress and each word contains maximally one foot.[14] When the level stress forms of stage 3 are compared with the target forms, the child may discover that there is a difference between main stress and secondary stress in the adult forms; therefore s/he may focus on the location of main stress. Since the monomorphemic disyllabic target words with final stress are now produced correctly, we could conclude that children have learned that main stress is assigned to the rightmost foot. However, we would expect to find main stress on the rightmost syllable in longer words, too. This prediction is not borne out by the data. Rather, it looks as if the children have discovered that the first foot from the left receives main stress.

The fact that there are many more longer forms with main stress on the left than on the right if we not only consider monomorphemic words but also consider compounds and compound-like structures (like Noun Verb phrases) may provide evidence for initial stress to the child.[15] In any event, the acquisition data clearly indicate that stress is on the left-most foot for words with more than two feet. The question is whether this is accomplished by setting the main stress parameter or the compound stress parameter. It seems to be the latter, since the notion of the word is a central one. Those forms that clearly form two separate words, based on syllable structure or semantic transparency, do receive compound stress at stage 4: the initial foot/word is stressed.

Thus, we have seen that words that are compounds or words that could have been compounds (like *olifant* /'o:li:ˌfɑnt/ 'elephant'), receive stress on the first foot. Moreover, **all** monomorphemic target words that have two feet in the adult target language now receive stress on the first foot, as this rule also applies to words like *krokodil* /ˌkʀo:ko:'dɪl/ 'crocodile'. On the other hand, those words that cannot with certainty be analyzed as two words on the basis of their prosodic structure will be reanalyzed: *konijn* /ko:'nɛin/ 'rabbit', which has only one stress in the adult form (and therefore cannot be a compound) is realized as one foot with an adjoined syllable at the left. These forms therefore undergo destressing and defooting at stage 4.

Thus, children acquire the compound stress rule at stage 4, as well as destressing of degenerate feet in the disyllabic final-stressed words. It should be noticed, however, that all words are still at most one foot (although now sometimes realized loosely, since it can have adjoined syllables). The main stress parameter, however, is still not set.

The question is when does the child learn that there are also monomorphemic words with more than one foot? Clearly, when the child is comparing targets like *telefoon* /ˌte:lə'fo:n/ 'telephone' with his/her own output s/he may discover that stress is different. Now, words that are incorrectly analyzed as compounds, that is, those that have final stress in the target language, have to be reanalyzed as monomorphemic words with two feet. At this point, i.e. at stage 5, the child seems to have discovered that main stress is not left, but right in monomorphemic words.

In conclusion, at stage 4 the parameters determining compound stress and destressing parameters are set and only at stage 5 is the main stress rule set.[16] In other words, children learn compounds before they acquire longer monomorphemic words. Based on frequency in the input this is not surprising: compound and compound-like structures outnumber the bipedal monomorphemic words with final stress. Although compounds may be regarded as prosodically more complex than monomorphemic words, there is no *a priori* reason why this should be so for the child. Rather, it seems that it is precisely due to the prosodic structure of compounds being more complex than that of monomorphemic words that guides the child in analyzing the prosodic structure of target words.[17]

Notes

1. There are a number of differences in comparison with Fikkert (1994, 1995), the most important one being that the obligatory branching parameter is made redundant. But the cases where this parameter was needed in Fikkert (1994, 1995) can all be accounted for by the compound stress parameter in (1d), which was therefore added to the list of parameters.

2. There is a strong relationship between the default value and the Subset Principle (Berwick 1986; Dell 1981; Wexler & Manzini 1987). The default value is the value for which positive evidence is least available to the language learner. However, sometimes other criteria are used as well. For example, the default value for the QS parameter is feet being QI; and this requires less knowledge from the learner, in the sense that the details of syllable structure need not be acquired yet. There also is a strong cue for detecting QS: the existence of two groups of words with an equal number of syllables but a different stress pattern indicates that the language must be QS. Typologically, the only QI feet are trochaic (cf. Hayes 1995). All points together suggest that children start with QI trochaic feet, which is supported by the data, as we will see. For some of the other parameters it is hard to define a default value *a priori*.

3. Notice that the input contains many forms that show a different (exceptional) stress pattern than expected based on the parameter values for Dutch given in (1). However, since the child has to make his/her hypotheses on the basis of the input data, these forms will (have to) be considered. In Fikkert (1994) I argue that, contrary to the standard analyses, the regular stress pattern for words ending in a — VC rhyme is final and that words like *robot* /ˈroːbɔt/ 'robot' are the exception. Crucial evidence comes from acquisition data (Fikkert 1994: 287 ff.).

4. *Krokodil* /ˌkroːkoːˈdɪl/ 'crocodile' and *olifant* /ˈoːliːˌfɑnt/ 'elephant' are exceptional according to the normal stress rules given in (1). In *krokodil* the final heavy syllable bears main stress, but it should have been extrametrical and therefore not bear main stress. In *olifant* main stress is initial, but should have been on the superheavy final syllable. The final syllable only has secondary stress, as if the form had compound stress. See also note 6.

5. It is common knowledge that children's perception is ahead of their production. Moreover, it has usually been assumed in the linguistic literature that perception is adult-like, and therefore children store an accurate representation of the input form. However, there is also ample evidence (see Waterson 1971, 1987, and the discussion in Macken 1980 and Smith 1989) that this assumption is far too strong. Although perception is ahead of production, it is not yet perfect. One has to bear in mind that the 'fish'-phenomenon (Smith 1973), where the child is aware of his incapability of producing the correct form, typically occurs with older children, and usually involves 'difficult' sounds. Moreover, although research into perception shows that even very small babies are already able to distinguish many phonetic details (cf. Jusczyk 1997), one has to separate acoustic phonetic discrimination from linguistic identification. The child may well hear many distinctions, but s/he still has to learn which of these distinctions are linguistically relevant, and how to represent the relevant linguistic distinctions in the lexicon. This issue has so far hardly received any attention in the literature on acquisition (but see Lahiri & Marslen-Wilson (1991) for psycholinguistic arguments for a similar distinction in adult language). A second point that bears on this issue is the exact form of a lexical representation. I assume that the mental representation of lexical items is underspecified as much as possible. This is true not only for children, but also for adults. In comparing input and output, only linguistic mismatches lead to learning. 'No mismatch' (i.e. no match and no mismatch) and 'perfect match' do not lead to revision of either the lexical representation, or the lexical phonology.

6. Most children do not distinguish between main and secondary stress and therefore take the final secondary-stressed syllable of the target *olifant* 'elephant' /ˈoːliːˌfɑnt/, as shown in (5c) and (8a).

7. In an OT account, the one foot stage would be accounted for by a high ranking of Alignment constraints (cf. Prince & Smolensky 1993; McCarthy & Prince 1993; Demuth 1996b).

8. Also, stress in the child's output forms does not always conform to that in the adult's target form, indicating a different prosodic structure for target (input) and output forms (i.e. stages 2 and 3).

9. Thus, words are not stored in the child's lexicon with prosodic information. Only unpredictable segmental (or prosodic) content is stored (cf. for similar conclusions Lahiri & Marslen-Wilson 1991; Wheeldon & Lahiri 1997, among others.)

10. The word *zandbak* 'sand box' /'zɑmˌbɑk/ is usually produced with an initial CVC syllable, since the final coronal stop is seldom realized.

11. The same is reported for English children (Kehoe & Stoel-Gammon 1997), although English and Dutch differ significantly in their prosodic system in that final secondary stress is less common in English nouns due to final syllable extrametricality.

12. It should be noted that Jarmo and Elke have been followed from a stage earlier than, for instance, Tirza and Eva, and have not been followed through all stages. So it might very well be the case that Jarmo and Elke, too, would have shown the same pattern as the latter two in the later stages, if only we had followed them long enough.

13. Of the disyllabic target words with final stress, Elke truncated 94% and Jarmo 92%. They invariably realized the final foot.

14. This has interesting consequences for the acquisition of syntactic structures. One could hypothesize that only at stage 3 are children able to acquire more complex syntactic phrases, consisting of a head and a complement (or vice versa), since only now are they able to realize these structures prosodically.

   The input to the child contains not only many compounds where the phonological head is morphologically the complement, and the phonological non-head is the morphological head (the right-hand head rule). Many syntactic phrases have the same structure: the syntactic complement in a noun-verb phrase is the phonological head of the phrase, i.e. *boekje* in *boekje lezen* ('read a book' *dim.*) and *koekje* in *koekje eten* ('eat a biscuit' *dim.*) and bears more stress than the verb, which is the syntactic head. If not only nominal compounds, but also these syntactic constituents are regarded as compounds (see Penner, Wymann & Weissenborn, this volume, for an analysis along these lines), the number of compounds is so overwhelming that it is bound to trigger an early setting of the compound stress parameter.

15. Alternatively, stress is on the first foot because of the default value [main stress is initial] of the main stress parameter. However, the child's input does contain words where stress is not initial. These words could have triggered the setting of the parameter to the marked value.

16. Demuth & Fee (1995) and Demuth (this volume) have a somewhat different analysis in terms of stages. They call the first stage in acquisition the 'CV stage'. This does not correspond exactly with my monosyllabic stage, which also contains CVC words. The stage in which CVC syllables occur is preceded by a stage in which no closed syllables occur: the core syllable stage (Fikkert 1994, Chapter 4). In this sense, there is no disagreement as to the existence of such a stage. However, according to Demuth & Fee the next stage is the minimal word stage and is characterized by CVC, CVV and CVCV words, which form exactly one moraic (i.e. QS) trochee. This stage does not correspond to any stage in my description; and, although Demuth uses my data to confirm this stage, I could not find any evidence for it. I also think that the name of this stage is misleading. Although in a sense the child has a minimal word (at *my* stage 1/one foot stage) which equals a disyllabic foot, the foot is not a moraic trochee, as in the target languages, but a syllabic trochee. In other words, in the child's system a CVC word would be a degenerate foot, since it only consists of one syllable, whereas a foot would have two syllables. That is not to say that they are not allowed; we have seen that they occur abundantly. At my stage 1, CVCV and CVC both are one single foot, but at stage 2 a weak member of a foot can consist of a (super)heavy syllable, clearly indicating that weight or mora counting is simply irrelevant at this stage and that the child-forms exceed the minimal foot template of the adult.

After a minimal word stage, children enter — according to Demuth & Fee — a stress foot stage. This stage roughly coincides with my stage 1 and stage 2. My stage 3 and 4 roughly correspond to Demuth & Fee's '2 Stress Feet' stage. I would like to maintain that children go from a monosyllabic stage to a stage characterized by the fact that all forms consist of exactly one foot (my stage 1 and stage 2). It is true that at stage 3 more than one feet are allowed, but this is mostly a consequence of the changing of the foot type from QI to QS. Thus, whereas I explain transitions as the setting of the QS parameter, which results in a change from QI to QS feet, Demuth characterizes the same change (transition from stage 1, 2 to 3, 4) as one from one foot to two feet, without explaining what triggers this, and why children did not have words consisting of two feet before.

A further point which is not considered in depth and is very much oversimplified in Demuth's analysis is the fact that she considers CVV and CVC both as bimoraic. Though true for English, it is not true for Dutch, where open syllables with long vowels invariably behave as light for purposes of stress. But Dutch does have words made up of exactly one CVV syllable (for example koe /kuː/ 'cow', zee /zeː/ 'sea', sla /slaː/ 'salade', etc.). Apparently Dutch allows subminimal words, but that is not to say that CVV is a heavy syllable: normally CVV would never make a foot on its own.

17. A similar conclusion is reached in Fikkert & Freitas (1997). There, the acquisition of syllable structure constraints in Dutch and Portuguese is compared. Although Dutch has a far more complex rhyme structure than Portuguese, Dutch children acquire the intricate details of the Dutch system much quicker than the Portuguese children. We argue that this is due to the evidence for the Dutch language learner being far more salient than that for the Portuguese language learner. Stated differently: As long as the evidence is not entirely clear, children hold on to unmarked structures. It is only after receiving enough transparent evidence that they will set parameter values to marked settings. The complexity of the structures to be acquired is not at issue; it is the evidence for those structures that counts for 'ease' of learnability that is at issue.

References

Allen, G. D. & Hawkins, S. 1978. "The Development of Phonological Rhythm." In *Syllables and Segments*, A. Bell & J. B. Hooper (eds.). New York: Elsevier-North Holland.

Allen, G. D. & Hawkins, S. 1980. "Phonological Rhythm: Definition and Development." In *Child Phonology: Production*, G. H. Yeni-Komshian, J. F. Kavanagh & C. A. Ferguson (eds.). New York: Academic Press.

Archibald, J. 1995. Review of "On the Acquisition of Prosodic Structure". *Glot International* 4.

Berwick, R. 1986. *The Acquisition of Syntactic Knowledge*. Cambridge, MA: MIT Press.

Booij, G. E. 1995. *The Phonology of Dutch*. Oxford: Oxford University Press.

Dell, F. 1981. "On the Learnability of Optional Phonological Rules." *Linguistic Inquiry* 12: 31–37.

Demuth, K. 1995. "Markedness and the Development of Prosodic Structure." In *Proceedings of the North East Linguistic Society 25, Volume II*, J. Beckman (ed.). Amherst, MA: GLSA, Univ. of Mass.

Demuth, K. 1996a. "The Prosodic Structure of Early Words." In *From Signal to Syntax: Bootstrapping from Speech to Grammar in Early Acquisition*, J. Morgan & K. Demuth (eds.). Hillsdale, N.J.: Lawrence Erlbaum Associates.

Demuth, K. 1996b. "Alignment, Stress, and Parsing in the Construction of Early Prosodic Words." In *Proceedings of the UBC International Conference on Phonological Acquisition*, B. Bernardt, J. Gilbert & D. Ingram (eds.). Somerville, MA.: Cascadilla Press.

Demuth, K. *This volume*. "Prosodic Constraints and Morphological Development."

Demuth, K. & Fee, J. 1995. "Minimal Words in Early Phonological Development." Ms. Brown University and Dalhousie University.

Dresher, B. E. & Kaye, J. D. 1990. "A Computational Learning Model for Metrical Theory." *Cognition* 34: 137–195.

Echols, C. H. 1987. *A Perceptually-based Model of Children's First Words*. Doctoral Dissertation, University of Illinois.

Echols, C. H. 1988. "The Role of Stress, Position and Intonation in the Representation and Identification of Early Words." *Papers and Reports on Child Language Development* 27: 39–46.

Echols, C. H. & Newport, E. 1992. "The Role of Stress and Position in Determining First Words." *Language Acquisition* 3: 189–220.

Fikkert, P. 1994. *On the Acquisition of Prosodic Structure*. Doctoral Dissertation, Holland Institute of Generative Linguistics, Diss. 6, Leiden University.

Fikkert, P. 1995. "Models of Acquisition: How to Acquire Stress." In *Proceedings of the North East Linguistic Society 25, Volume II*, J. Beckman (ed.). Amherst, MA: GLSA, Univ. of Mass.

Fikkert, P. & Freitas, M. J. 1997. "Acquisition of Syllable Structure Constraints: Evidence from Dutch and Portuguese." In *Proceedings of the GALA '97 Conference on Language Acquisition*, A. Sorace, C. Heycock & R. Shillcock (eds.). Edinburgh: Edinburgh University Press.

Gerken, L. A. 1994a. "A Metrical Template Account of Children's Weak Syllable Omissions from Multisyllabic Words." *Journal of Child Language* 21: 565–584.

Gerken, L. A. 1994b. "Young Children's Representation of Prosodic Phonology: Evidence from English-Speakers' Weak Syllable Productions." *Journal of Memory and Language* 33: 19–38.

Gerken, L. A. 1996. "Prosodic Structure in Young Children's Language Production." *Language* 72: 683–712.

Gillis, S., Durieux, G., Daelemans, W. & van den Bosch, A. 1992. "Exploring Artificial Learning Algorithms: Learning to Stress Dutch Simplex Words." *Antwerp Papers in Linguistics* 71.

Hayes, B. 1995. *Metrical Stress Theory: Principles and Case Studies*. Chicago: Chicago University Press.

Jusczyk, P. W. 1997. *The Discovery of Spoken Language*. Cambridge, MA: MIT Press.

Kager, R. 1989. *A Metrical Theory of Stress and Destressing in English and Dutch*. Dordrecht: Foris.

Kehoe, M. & Stoel-Gammon, C. 1997. "The Acquisition of Prosodic Structure: An Investigation of Current Accounts of Children's Prosodic Development." *Language* 73: 113–144.
Lahiri, A. & Marslen-Wilson, W. 1991. "The Mental Representation of Lexical Form: A Phonological Approach to the Recognition Lexicon." *Cognition* 38: 245–294.
Lahiri, A., Riad, T. & Jacobs, H. 1999. "Diachronic Prosody." In *Word Prosodic Systems in the Languages of Europe*, H. van der Hulst (ed.). Berlin: Mouton de Gruyter.
Levelt, C. C. 1994. *On the Acquisition of Place*. Doctoral Dissertation, Holland Institute of Generative Linguistics, Diss. 8, Leiden University.
Lohuis-Weber, H. & Zonneveld, W. 1996. "Phonological Acquisition and Dutch Word Prosody." *Language Acquisition* 4: 245–284.
McCarthy, J. & Prince, A. 1993. "Generalized Alignment." In *Yearbook of Morphology 1993*, G. Booij & J. van Marle (eds.).
Macken, M. 1980. "The Child's Lexical Representation: The Puzzle-Puddle-Pickle Evidence." *Journal of Linguistics* 16: 1–17.
MacWhinney, B. 1995. *The CHILDES Project: Tools for Analyzing Talk*. Hillsdale, N.J.: Lawrence Erlbaum Associates.
Paradis, C. & Prunet, J. F. (eds.). 1991. *The Special Status of Coronals. Internal and External Evidence*. San Diego: Academic Press.
Penner, Z., Wymann, K. & Weissenborn, J. *This volume*. "On the Prosody/Lexicon Interface in Learning Word Order. A Study of Normally Developing and Language Impaired Children."
Prince, A. & Smolensky, P. 1993. "Optimality: Constraint Interaction in Generative Grammar." Ms. Rutgers University and University of Colorado.
Schwartz, R. & Leonard, L. B. 1982. "Do Children Pick and Choose? An Examination of Phonological Selection and Avoidance in Early Lexical Acquisition." *Journal of Child Language* 9: 319–336.
Schwartz, R., Leonard, L. B., Frome Loeb, D. M. & Swanson, L. 1987. "Attempted Sounds are Sometimes Not: An Expanded View of Phonological Selection and Avoidance." *Journal of Child Language* 14: 411–418.
Slobin, D. I. 1973. "Cognitive Prerequisites for the Development of Grammar." In *Studies of Child Language Development*, C. A. Ferguson & D. I. Slobin (eds.). New York: Holt, Rinehart, and Winston.
Smith, N. V. 1973. *The Acquisition of Phonology: A Case Study*. London: Cambridge University Press.
Smith, N. V. 1989. *The Twitter Machine. Reflections on Language*. Oxford: Basil Blackwell.
Waterson, N. 1971. "Child Phonology: A Prosodic View." *Journal of Linguistics* 7: 179–211.
Waterson, N. 1987. *Prosodic Phonology: The Theory and its Application to Language Acquisition and Speech Processing*. Newcastle upon Tyne: Grevatt & Grevatt.
Wexler, K. & Manzini, R. 1987. "Parameters and Learnability in Binding Theory." In *Parameter Setting*, T. Roeper & E. Williams (eds.). Dordrecht: Reidel.

Wheeldon, L. & Lahiri, A. 1997. "Prosodic Units in Speech Production." *Journal of Memory and Language* 37: 356–381.
Wijnen, F., Krikhaar, E. & den Os, E. 1994. "The (Non)realization of Unstressed Elements in Children's Utterances: Evidence for a Rhythmic Constraint." *Journal of Child Language* 21: 59–83.

Prosodic Form, Syntactic Form, Phonological Bootstrapping, and Telegraphic Speech

David Lebeaux
NEC Research Institute

1. Introduction

This paper concerns questions at the interface between phonology and syntax, and the syntactic-prosodic tree mapping. I am interested in particular in deriving the discrepancies between the prosodic tree and the syntactic tree (Nespor & Vogel 1986) in some interesting way. In more detail, from the point of view of language acquisition, I am interested in deriving the form of telegraphic or simplified speech, as a consequence of how the prosodic-syntactic system works. This is the acquisition part of the problem. The generative part of the problem is as follows: to derive syntax/prosodic discrepancies - the discrepancies between the syntactic and prosodic trees - as a consequence of how these trees are put together.[1]

The outline of the paper is as follows:

First, I will demonstrate the differences in structure between the syntactic and prosodic trees, for a number of different types of structures.

Second, I will derive telegraphic or kernel speech (by the child) as a consequence of the child computing structure with two representations: the syntactic one and the prosodic one. The child attempts to find the maximal alignment of these two structures (Lebeaux 1996, 1997) by factoring out their discrepancies, i.e. their discrepancies in structure. This is done by removing the same discrepant elements, one-by-one from the syntactic and prosodic trees. The resultant, the maximal alignment, is called the kernel or telegraphic speech (Lebeaux 1996, 1997).

Third, I attempt to derive the syntactic/prosodic differences in a model of the adult grammar (i.e. the differences in the syntactic and prosodic trees in general).

I rely here on the original work by Chomsky on Generalized Transformations (Chomsky 1955, 1957), as well as more recent work which relies on this early work, especially in the Tree-Adjoining Grammar (TAG) tradition (Kroch & Joshi 1985, 1988; Kroch 1989; Frank 1992, 1997, and many others), work by Bach (1977), who resurrected the generalized transformation, and Partee, and my own work (Lebeaux 1988, 1991, 1997). The view of generalized transformations adopted here is in line with that of Lebeaux (1988, 1991), as well as the TAG tradition, as well (I think) with Chomsky's original conception (1955, 1957), and differs from his more recent, interesting, conception (Chomsky 1995), which only uses GTs as a way of building up the phrase structure bottom-up. I argue in addition that the syntactic and prosodic trees are computed in a quasi-parallel fashion, as in the form of the grammar of Montague (1974), Kroch & Joshi (1985), Jackendoff (1972, 1995), and Lebeaux (1991), as well as work in the Montague, and Tree-Adjoining Grammar traditions. The way that the derivation for the prosodic and syntactic trees proceeds is as follows. Both syntactic and prosodic components start off with structurally identical elements, the kernel structures. Thus far the prosodic and syntactic bracketings are identical. How they differ is in the generalized transformations joining the kernel structures. They have different effects in the syntactic and prosodic trees (which are computed in parallel). That is, the Generalized Transformations attach structurally identical elements together in structurally different ways in the two components. Thus the differences in the phonological and the syntactic bracketing are precisely the evidence that a generalized transformation has taken place. This explanation depends on GTs not simply initially putting together words, as in Chomsky (1995), but rather structures in fairly complex ways, as in Lebeaux (1988). Thus the discrepancies come in the putting together of these structures. This will become clearer in the discussion below. This system accounts for the similarities and differences in structure between the syntactic and prosodic trees: the similarities because both components start off with structurally identical kernel structures, the differences because of the distinct ways that the Generalized Transformations apply in the syntactic and prosodic trees. Finally, the use of generalized transformations allows for the claim to be made that the initial grammar is simpler, as argued for in a remarkable series of papers by Vainikka (1985, 1986, 1993) and Roeper (1995).[2]

The fourth question, which I do not have the space to discuss here, is the question of how the child arrives at the syntactic tree, if all s/he is given is the prosodic tree? This is an extremely difficult question which gets to the very root of the grammar.

2. The discrepancies

In this section, I will catalog four differences between the prosodic form and the syntactic form. For a complete listing of differences, see Lebeaux (1997). These will form the basis for the further discussion of how to derive these differences, and how precisely these differences are principled.

2.1 *Prehead Specifiers of NP are grouped with the head in the Prosodic Structure, but separated from it in the Syntax (Nespor & Vogel 1986)*

The first example of the differing structure of the NP is given below. The syntax is given in (1a).

(1)   a.

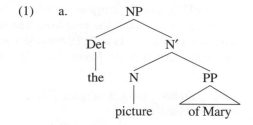

The phonology is given in (1b).

(1)   b.   Phonology: (the picture)$_{cg}$ or $_\phi$ (of Mary)$_{cg}$ or $_\phi$
                    (cg = clitic group; ϕ = phonological phrase)

Similarly for the more complex example in (2).

(2)   a.   Syntax: (the (tall (cousin of Jeff)))
       b.   Phonology: (the tall cousin)$_\phi$ (of Jeff)$_\phi$

As can be seen, while the syntactic representation is right branching, the phonological representation "clumps" into two constituents (the tall cousin) and (of Jeff). The crucial fact about this phonological "clumping" is that the elements on the left-hand side of the head noun are grouped with it in a phonological constituent, as if these elements, starting with the closed class *the*, were more closely associated with the head noun than the head noun is with its complement. More exactly, the phonological representations are given by an extremely important generalization by Nespor & Vogel (1986).

(3) Nespor & Vogel (1986)
Elements on the nonrecursive side of a head C are grouped with C in a phonological phrase.

For Nespor & Vogel, C simply denotes the head of a phrase. Recall, that at the time that Nespor & Vogel were writing this, the NP node was assumed rather than the DP. The elements on the nonrecursive side would therefore be the elements on the left-hand side of the noun phrase: namely, the determiner and adjectives. Similarly, they adopted a recursive VP structure, where the auxiliary verbs would be on the left-hand, nonrecursive, side of the main verb. It is these verbs which are grouped with the main verb, as a sort of verb cluster. See the discussion in Section 2.2.

Similar data can be seen in the timing data from Abney (1991), who in turn draws from Grosjean, Grosjean & Lane (1979), Gee & Grosjean (1983). In the numbers below the text, 0 represents the least juncture, 1, the next least, and so on. (I do not use exactly the same formalism here as in (1) and (2), because I am quoting from work by Abney; Grosjean, Grosjean & Lane; and Gee & Grosjean.)[3]

(4) show $_0$ me $_1$ the $_0$ nonstop $_0$ flights $_2$ on $_0$ American $_0$ Airlines $_2$ from $_0$ Denver $_2$ to $_0$ San $_0$ Francisco $_2$
(note junctural 'clumping' of nonrecursive elements with the head in "the nonstop flights on American Airlines")

(5) after $_0$ the $_0$ cold $_0$ winter $_1$ of $_0$ that $_0$ year $_2$ most $_0$ people $_1$ were $_0$ totally $_0$ fed-up
(note junctural 'clumping' of nonrecursive elements with the head in "after the cold winter of that year")

The entire prosodic structure of the sentence can be seen in (6). This is taken from Abney (1991) who attributes the bracketing to Selkirk. Aside from the structuring of the Noun Phrase, please note the bracketing of the auxiliary verb, that it is a unit with the verb prosodically, though it is right-branching syntactically.

(6)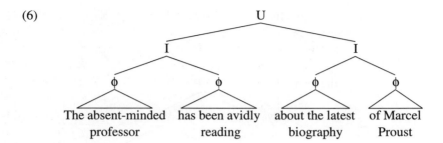

U: Utterance
I: Intonational Phrase
φ: Phonological Phrase

The prepositional phrase groups just as Nespor & Vogel (and I) have suggested. In addition, the auxiliary together with the main verb forms a single phrase.

2.2 The structure of the auxiliary

Consider now the second construction under investigation, the structure of the auxiliary. In the sentence given directly below (7), the syntax of the auxiliary, with respect to bracketing is given in (7a), the usual right-branching structure. The phonological bracketing given in (7b) is radically different.

(7) a. Syntax: (has (been (avidly (reading (about NP)))))
b. Phonology: (has been avidly reading)$_\phi$ (about NP)$_\phi$

I claim that these correspond in general to the two different bracketings shown in (8a, b). The syntax is right-branching; while in the phonology, the auxiliary verb forms a sort of complex verb with the main verb.

(8) a.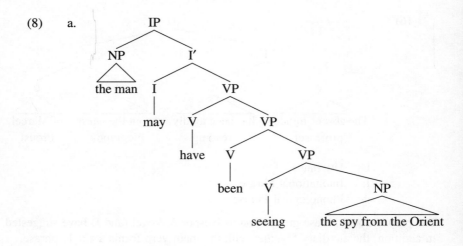

b.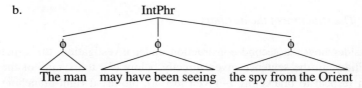

The sequence of auxiliaries and the verb forms a kind of complex verb phonologically. This can also be seen in the timing data from Abney (1995). Note the (lack of) juncture between the auxiliary and the main verb. For many more examples, see Abney (1995).

(9) a. the $_0$ expert, $_3$ who $_0$ couldn't $_0$ see $_1$ what $_0$ to $_0$ criticize $_3$ sat $_0$ back $_2$ in $_0$ despair
(Note lack of juncture in *couldn't see* and *what to criticize*)
b. that $_0$ a $_0$ solution $_1$ couldn't $_0$ be $_0$ found $_3$ seemed $_0$ quite $_0$ clear $_3$ to $_0$ them
(Note lack of juncture in *couldn't be found*)

There are additional complexities in this situation. As examples (10a, b) show, the first element of the auxiliary may cliticize backwards onto the subject (Kaisse 1985; Selkirk 1984; Nespor & Vogel 1986, and many others).

(10) a. John's leaving.
b. Bill's left.

I return to this below; but from the Abney data, the Selkirk example, and other data in the literature, it does appear that it is reasonable to group the auxiliary verb cluster as a unit with the verb. That is, there is a sort of phonological verb cluster.

2.3 The structure of the relative clause

We turn now to the third structure, that of the relative clause. In cases where it is recursive, i.e. there are two of them, and perhaps more generally than that, they tend to break into individual intonational units (Chomsky & Halle 1968; Nespor & Vogel 1986). Thus the following common example:

(11) a. Syntax: This is the cat (that ate the rat (that ate the cheese))
b. Phonology: (This is the cat)$_I$ (that ate the rat)$_I$ (that ate the cheese)$_I$

Here, the right branching structure in the syntax breaks into three co-ordinated units in the phonology. This is the third discrepancy between the phonological and syntactic bracketing.

(12)

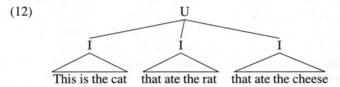

2.4 Cliticization of closed class head onto preceding specifier

A fourth type of discrepancy, actually a cluster of three such discrepancies, seems quite systematic in English. This is the cliticization of a closed class head onto a preceding specifier, even though it is grouped syntactically with the following complement. That is, the general structure in (13).

(13) a. Syntax: ($_{XP}$ NP ($_{X'}$ H YP))
b. Phonology: ((NP H) YP)

There are actually three distinct cases in which this occurs: at the level of the DP, at the level of the IP, and at the level of the CP. These are given below.

(14) Syntax
    a. level of IP: (John) (is going)
    b. level of CP: (What) (is that)
    c. level of DP: (John) ('s book) assuming the DP analysis

(15) Phonology
    a. level of IP: John's going
    b. level of CP: What's that?
    c. level of DP: John's book

That is, for all the categories, the closed class head is cliticized backward, though it forms a syntactic category with the forward element. This is the fourth (or fourth through sixth) discrepancy.[4]

2.5 Conclusion

The above constitutes 4 (or 6) discrepancies between the phonological and syntactic tree, taken mostly from Nespor & Vogel (1986). These data should be exploited in two ways. First, why are there these remarkable differences between the phonological and syntactic forms? How does one generate them in an explanatory theory? Second, do they have any bearing on language acquisition? It is the contention of this paper that, first, a remarkable generalization holds with respect to the difference in the phonological and syntactic forms, informing an understanding of telegraphic speech. Namely: telegraphic speech is the result of trying to align these two forms in a maximal way "throwing out" the elements that are divergent. That is, telegraphic speech forms a **greatest** common denominator of the prosodic and the syntactic tree, throwing out discrepant bracketings. The second contention of this paper is that formally the differences between the phonological and syntactic representations fall out if a theory of generalized transformations (of the types suggested in Chomsky 1955, 1957; Lebeaux 1988, 1991, 1996, 1997; Kroch & Joshi 1985, 1988, and Frank 1992, 1997) is adopted. This version of generalized transformations is very different from the interesting version adopted in Chomsky (1995), which uses GTs just as a means of building up the phrase marker bottom-up. In the version of generalized transformations suggested in the present paper (and also originally in Chomsky 1955, 1957), the operations had a far richer set of structural descriptions and structural changes, involving substitution (Chomsky 1957), adjunct–adjunction (Lebeaux 1988), a splicing operation called adjunction (Kroch & Joshi 1985), and projection into a closed class frame (Lebeaux 1988). It is precisely this set that is needed, I argue, to meaningfully describe the prosodic/syntactic discrepancies listed above.

3. The construction of telegraphic speech

In this section, I would like, in a sense, to tell an "as-if" story. We have established a set of prosodic-syntactic discrepancies. The "as-if" story is that if we take the prosodic form for a given structure, and we take the syntactic form (for that same structure), and we remove the discrepant elements — i.e. those producing discrepant bracketing — then we arrive at precisely the sort of kernel or telegraphic speech that children actually use. That is, there is an exceedingly simple function from the dual inputs (Prosodic Structure, Syntactic Structure), which arrives at telegraphic speech.

(16)   f(Prosodic Structure, Syntactic Structure) → telegraphic speech

The reasoning underlying why such a function might exist is the following. The child is given a prosodic tree (presumably from input). The child is also, by hypothesis, given a syntactic tree (whose genesis I leave to further research). These two trees differ in structure. Therefore, the child cannot simply adopt one of these trees as his/her representation. I will assume that there is no movement to bridge the relation between these two structures, both because these structures are of differing types, and because movement itself does not arise until later (in development). So what does the child do, given a prosodic and a syntactic tree, with differences between them? The child chooses precisely the minimal way: s/he tries to find the structure which retains the maximal amount of structure common to the two structures which s/he is trying to mesh, by aligning the two structures and throwing out the discrepant elements. This is called the Maximal Alignment of the two structures (Lebeaux 1996, 1997). This leads to the following conjecture:

(17)   Telegraphic speech is the maximal alignment of trees from prosodic representation and the syntactic representation.

I show now how this is done, for the 4 (or 6) structures above. Each time, the maximal alignment produces telegraphic speech.

3.1 *Prehead specifiers of NP*

Suppose that the child is handed two structures, those in 18 a) and b):

(18) a. Syntax:

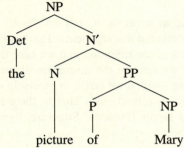

b. Prosody:

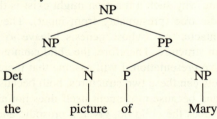

The "phonological" structure given in (18b) isn't the actual phonological structure, which would be given in terms of phonological categories. It is the bracketing of the phonological structure, treated as if it were a syntactic structure, with *the* and *picture* bracketed together. Suppose now that the child were trying to mutually satisfy both structures. Since the geometries of the structures are different, the only way to do so is to remove elements. The elements to be removed are those elements which introduce discrepancies into the two representations. The element in this case is the word *the*. In Nespor & Vogel's terms, it is the element on the non-recursive side of the head. With *the* removed, we arrive at a single representation, which is the same:

(19)   NP

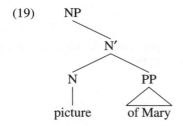

That is, the grammar looks at the following two bracketings, and removes the element so that they may be brought into congruence.

(20)   a.   structure 1:   (the (picture of Mary))
       b.   structure 2:   (the picture)(of Mary)

The same holds for the more complex nominal in (21):

(21)   a.   structure 1:   (the (tall (cousin (of Jeff))))
       b.   structure 2:   (the tall cousin)(of Jeff)

Something must be said to remove the (counter-intuitive) possibility that in the removal process in (20), the phonologically strong element *picture* is not removed, and the phonologically weak element *the* is, since in both cases a common geometry would be retained:

(22)   a.   maximal alignment 1:   (picture (of Mary))
       b.   maximal alignment 2:   (the (of Mary))

For the moment, I will assume that there is simply a constraint which prevents the removal of a strong element at this level, or possibly that all removal operations begin from an edge; space considerations prevent further discussion.

(23)   a.   *Possibility A*
            Constraint: To construct a maximal alignment, never remove a phonologically strong element.
       b.   *Possibility B*
            Constraint: To construct a maximal alignment, begin by removing elements from a particular edge.

Note that the maximal alignment *picture of Mary* precisely drops the determiner, and elements on the nonrecursive side. This dropping of the determiner is a particular characteristic of telegraphic speech.[5]

3.2 *The structure of the auxiliary*

Consider now the structure of the auxiliary. The syntactic form is shown in (24a), while the phonological form is given in (24b).

(24) a. Syntactic Form

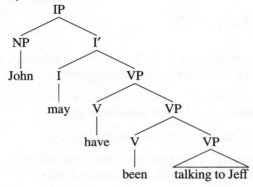

b. Prosodic Form:

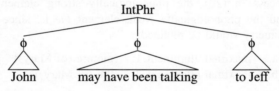

The kernel representation, gotten by removing the discrepant elements from these two representations, is given in (25).

(25)

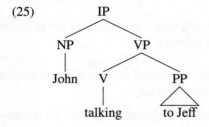

This simplification is again precisely the sort that children do. For example, instead of saying *John may have been talking to Jeff*, children would say *John*

talking to Jeff (I leave aside the additional simplification of *to* which would occur, since that is irrelevant to the discussion of the simplification of the auxiliaries.)

3.3 *The structure of the relative clause (Chomsky & Halle 1968; Tavakolian 1978; Nespor & Vogel 1986)*

The situation with the relative clause is similar, but not precisely so, perhaps because we are dealing with (i) intonational phrases instead of phonological phrases, and (ii) recursive structures. The phonological bracketing of the relative clause in (26a) is (26b), creating a discrepant bracketing.

(26) a. Syntax: (This is the cat (that ate the rat (that ate the cheese)))
     b. Phonology: (This is the cat)(that ate the rat)(that ate the cheese)

To be fair, this type of discrepant bracketing appears to show up only when the relative clause is recursive, i.e. under two layers of embedding (Nespor & Vogel 1986). There is no such clear division into intonational phrases when one relative clause is attached off a noun phrase in a simple sentence.

Let us nonetheless take the possibility of the intonation break, i.e. the breaking into intonational phrases, in (26a,b), as central. If so, the child is handed two discrepant representations. From this, s/he must create a single representation which is in accord with the geometry of both. The only way of doing this is by preserving exactly one of the clauses.

(27) This is the cat that ate the rat that ate the cheese
     (Maximal alignment) This is the cat, or
                         that ate the rat, or
                         that ate the cheese

This is again precisely the sort of simplification that children do, preserving one clause in relative clause constructions. Let us consider the construction in more detail. In her landmark study of relative clauses, Tavakolian (1978) discovered the following acquisition sequence:

(28) Stage I: Children drop relative clauses entirely
     Stage II: Conjoined clause analysis (high attachment)
     Stage III: Correct analysis

The first stage, of dropping the relative clause entirely, has already been predicted by our maximal alignment hypothesis in (27) above. What is the high attachment analysis? Here, Tavakolian had a particularly intriguing result. She noted that relative clauses had a different analysis depending on whether they were subject or object relatives. Relatives off of a subject (with a subject position relativized) were interpreted as if they were predicated of the subject (i.e. the correct interpretation). But relatives off of an object (with a subject position relativized) were interpreted incorrectly, as if they also were predicated of the subject of the sentence. That is, the example sentences were (29a–d).

(29)   a.   The sheep that hit the rabbit kisses the lion.
      b.   The sheep that the lion hit kisses the rabbit.
      c.   The sheep kisses the rabbit that hit the lion.
      d.   The sheep kisses the rabbit that the lion hit.

Of these, the two that gave particularly interesting results are (29a, c). (29a) had the interpretation in (30a), and (29c) had the interpretation in (30b).

(30)   a.   the sheep hit the rabbit ∧ the sheep kisses the lion.
      b.   the sheep kisses the rabbit ∧ the sheep hit the lion.

The interpretation of (30a) is expected, but that of (30b) is not, and is erroneous. Why should this be? Tavakolian had a brilliant explanation for this. She suggested that in neither case was the relative clause being structurally represented correctly by the child, but rather in both (29a) and (29c), the relative clause was attached high in the tree by the child. That is, the structure for (29c), with the reading (30b), was that in (31):

(31)   High attachment (conjoined clause analysis)

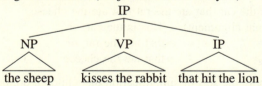

Now, predication operates roughly on sisters (Williams 1980) (I modernize her analysis a slight amount.) This means that the IP *that hit the lion* must be predicated of *the sheep*, not *the rabbit*, since *the rabbit* does not c-command the IP. But this then means that children get the wrong analysis. Thus Tavakolian explains the wrong analysis with the high attachment structure.

What about the structure where children get the right interpretation: *the sheep that hit the rabbit kisses the lion*? Here, according to Tavakolian, they get the right interpretation, but for the wrong reasons. The structure that children adopt for this sentence is again one in which the relative clause is hanging off the matrix IP — i.e. the wrong structure. This is shown in 32).

(32) (the sheep)(that hit the rabbit)(kisses the lion).

However, given that predication applies between sisters, this wrong structure will still give the right predication-interpretive structure, with *that hit the rabbit* being predicated of *the sheep*, since *the sheep* minimally c-commands it. Thus the data set is brilliantly accounted for by the Tavakolian analysis. Why, however, should the child adopt the high attachment analysis in the first place? While there is some syntactic literature on this (Tavakolian 1978; Matthei 1979; Solan & Roeper 1978 ; Lebeaux 1988; Frank 1992, 1997), one thing that is clear is that the child is adopting an analysis that is precisely that which the phonology would give. That is, the following holds:

(33) a. The High Attachment analysis is the phonological bracketing — intonational phrase bracketing of the sentence. (That is, (b) and (c) are identical.)
  b. High Attachment Analysis:

  c. Prosodic Analysis:

This suggests that the child has direct recourse to the phonological phrasing, in coming up with an analysis. The full set of stages that the child adopts, (28) above, has children first using a maximal alignment analysis, then using solely the intonational phrase analysis as a guide to the syntax, and finally adopting the correct syntactic tree. This analysis is slightly different than our maximal alignment analysis above, but still very similar to it (perhaps because we are dealing with full intonational phrases here, instead of phonological phrases or clitic groups).

3.4 *Cliticization of closed class head onto preceding specifier*

The fourth, or fourth through sixth, phenomenon in which the maximal alignment hypothesis predicts child speech is the cluster of phenomena associated with the cliticization of a closed class head onto the preceding specifier. This occurs even though the head is more closely associated syntactically with the following complement. The abstract structure is given in (34).

(34) a. Syntax: ($_{XP}$ NP ($_{X'}$ H YP)) H associated with YP
     b. Phonology: (NP H) (YP) H associated with preceding NP

There are three distinct levels at which this occurs: DP, IP, and CP. The specific cases are shown below.

(35) Syntax:
  a. level of IP: (John)(I′ is going)
  b. level of CP: (What (C′ is that))
  c. level of DP: (John (D′ 's book)) assuming the DP analysis

(36) Phonology:
  a. level of IP: John's going   (cliticize onto the preceding NP)
  b. level of CP: What's that $^?$(″)
  c. level of DP: John's book   (″)

What is again striking is that the maximal alignment may be determined by removing the closed class element — which introduces a discrepancy into the bracketing — leaning in one case to the right, and in one case to the left. When this closed class element is eliminated, what is left is precisely the sort of simplifications that children use, for these structures. These are also what the child produces in a repetition task.

(37) a. IP. Simplification: John going   (John's going)
     b. CP. Simplification: What that   (What's that?)
     c. DP. Simplitification: John book   (John's book)

The simplifications in (37) are precisely those that the child uses, and they are what is predicted by the maximal alignment hypothesis. They would also be those that the child would produce in a repetition task. A sample simplification is given in (38).

(38) Syntax: John (is going) | Determine Kernel
     Phonology: John's going |——————→
     Output: John going

In fact, the data are even more convincing than this would suggest. Brown (1973) noted that in some cases, the closed class head is not cliticizeable in adult speech: for example, in (39) with an *it* subject.

(39) What is it?
     Who is it?

*What's it?
*Who's it?
(adult speech)

He went on to note the following:

> Between III and IV, Adam used the following questions 36 times and never omitted a copula.
> What is it?
> Who is it?
> Where is it?
> In the same samples, there were 34 sentences of a set of closely related questions, but here the copula was omitted 17 times:
> What's that? or What that?
> What's this? or What this?
> Who's that? or Who that?
> Wherever SE [Standard English, D.L.] can contract, child English can delete (whether "is", "am", or "are"), and vice versa...

In other words, the structures like *What is it* (the first set of structures) do not have a cliticizeable auxiliary in adult speech; these same structures do not allow the omission of the auxiliary in child speech. However, the structures like *What's that* (the second set of structures) do have a cliticizeable auxiliary in adult speech; and these same structures **do** allow the omission of the auxiliary in child speech. Exactly the environments in which auxiliaries can be cliticized (in the adult grammar) are the contexts where the child omits auxiliaries altogether. But the cliticizeable constructions are precisely the constructions, according to the present paper, in which the closed class head is bracketing differently in the phonology and the syntax.

4. Generalized transformations, simplicity, and the discrepancies

Above, I have argued that by creating the maximal alignment of the syntactic and prosodic trees, telegraphic speech is created. (I have put aside the question of exactly how the syntactic tree is created.) There is therefore a very simple function which creates telegraphic speech. Suppose now that generalized transformations, i.e. transformations putting together two trees, put together the phrase marker. These will be discussed in more detail below. Suppose that of the full set of generalized transformations, some subset, say t1, t3, t7, and t8, put together a particular phrase marker. Suppose that these generalized transformations operated with a set of four kernel structures, k1, k2, k3, and k4, putting them together with these transformations. Then the full complexity of the set would be:

(40) Complexity of derivation: k1, k2, k3, k4, t1, t3, t7, t8

In general, we might expect that the supersets of transformations (assuming the same kernel structures) would appear after their subsets.

(41) Derivational Theory of Complexity (revisited):
Supersets of transformations constructing phrase markers always follow their subsets.

The claim in (41) gives us a simple, and indeed, powerful way of indicating the complexity of the grammar. In effect, it once again brings the notion of simplicity to the fore in evaluating possible child grammars, and allows the acquisition sequence to make sense in terms of the simplicity of the system. In more detail, we might expect the following:

(42) a. A particular generalized transformation would appear across-the-board in the grammar — i.e. at the same time in a number of different constructions.
b. Structures with zero generalized transformations should appear before those with one, structures with one generalized transformation should appear before those with two, and so on.

Very detailed argumentation for point (42b) is made in Frank (1992), for the particular Tree Adjoining Grammar transformation of "Adjoin", which is a sort of splicing. See also Lebeaux (1988, 1997), and Powers & Lebeaux (1998), for argumentation about the point in (42a). For extensive, brilliant work on the notion of simplicity in the grammar, see Vainikka (1985, 1986, 1993).

The second type of argument that can be made for generalized transformations is that made in the current paper: that while kernel structures are identical across the syntax and phonology, the generalized transformations actually act somewhat differently in the two components, and precisely this gives rise systematically to the prosodic/syntactic discrepancies. There are thus two types of arguments for GTs, of which this paper is focussing on the second (see Lebeaux 1988, 1997; Vainikka 1993, and Frank 1992 for more argumentation about the first).

(43) Arguments for GTs
a. simplicity arguments
b. arguments on discrepancy between syntactic and prosodic forms

Finally, it should be noted that the type of generalized transformations used here are similar to those of Chomsky (1955, 1957), Bach (1977), Lebeaux (1988,

1991, 1997), Kroch & Joshi (1985, 1988), Frank (1992, 1996), and very different than those interestingly used by Chomsky in Chomsky (1995). In Chomsky (1995) the generalized transformation used just builds phrase markers bottom-up, and does nothing more complex than that. Thus, starting with *see*, *the*, and *ball*, it would first place together *the* and *ball*, and then place together the resultant with *see*. In contrast, the set of generalized transformations assumed here, like that in Chomsky's original work, has a much richer set of structural descriptions and structural changes.

In the following, I will quickly catalogue the set of generalized transformations used, which are culled from Chomsky (1957), Lebeaux (1988), Kroch & Joshi (1985, 1988), and Frank (1992). I will then show how from identical kernel structures in the syntax and the phonology, the generalized transformation itself introduces the discrepancy in the representation consistently.[7] Thus the heretofore remarkable and unexplained differences between the syntactic and prosodic bracketing are introduced precisely by the generalized transformations, and are thus explained.

4.1 *The transformations*

I catalog here four of the generalized transformations used. (These are actually used to describe a wider set of data in Lebeaux (1997), which deals with ten discrepancies.)

I. Substitution (Chomsky 1957)
s1: I believe it
s2: that John likes Mary   Substitute ⟶

Output: I believe that John likes Mary.

II. Adjoin-α (Lebeaux 1988): takes two well formed structures, each obeying the Projection Principle, and with an adjunct-of relation between them, and adjoins the second into the first.
s1: the man met the woman   Adjoin-α ⟶
s2: who loved him

Output: The man met the woman who loved him

(Note that this is not bottom-up, but takes two well formed structures, and creates a so-called "segmented" structure.)

III. Splicing Operation, called *Adjunction* in the Tree Adjoining Grammar (TAG) tradition (Kroch & Joshi 1985; Frank 1992, and many others)

This is a more complex operation, in which one tree is spliced into another tree. The tree which is spliced in has two representations of the same node type (e.g. I′, VP) as its root and "frontier" nodes (one of its open terminals), and in essence stretches the "splicee". Splicing is an exact description of what occurs.

This is used to describe Raising, Comp-to-Comp movement, and many other traditional operations.

(a) For Raising:

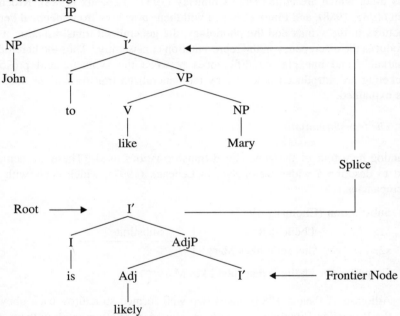

Here, the I′ node in the top tree is "cut into two", and the material in the bottom tree spliced into its position.

Output: John is likely to like Mary.

(b) For *wh*-movement:

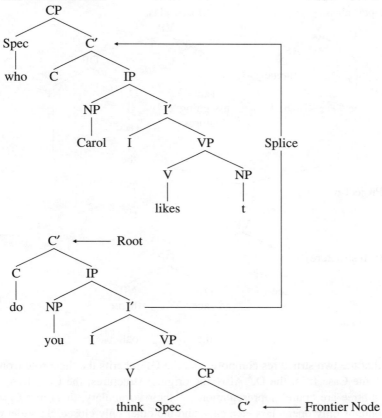

Output: Who do you think Carol likes t?
The root and the frontier node must be identical in this transformation.

IV. Project-α (Lebeaux 1988). This is somewhat similar to the splicing (adjunction) operation of TAG, but motivated by work on idioms, and by Garrett's and Shattuck-Hufnagel's work on speech errors (Garrett 1975; Shattuck 1974; Fromkin 1971). This operation projects open class elements into a closed class frame, or projects a theta subtree into a Case frame. (There are at least two other distinct notions of projection in the literature: Speas 1990 and Powers 1996).

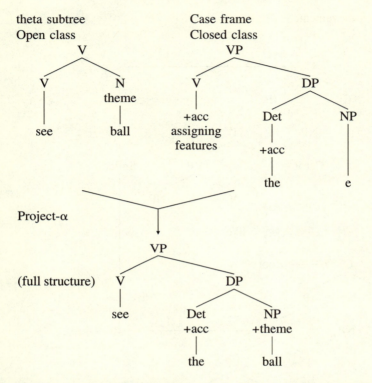

Note that the two structures compose, and the DP inherits the theta role from the N, and the Case from the D.[8] Also, the original structures, the Case frame and theta subtree are "pure" representations of their vocabulary, theta and Case, so one contains only open class elements, and the other only closed class elements.

4.2 Using the transformations

Assuming that these transformations are part of the grammar, the full set of phonological/syntactic discrepancies can be accounted for by assuming that they operate differently in the phonology and the syntax. That is, the discrepancies are introduced by the GTs, assuming the kernel structures are the same.

4.2.1 The structure of the auxiliary

With respect to the structure of the auxiliary, I will assume the splicing (adjunction) operation of TAG. The sentence is *John may have been seeing Mary*. The operation would proceed as follows.

(44) s1: John seeing Mary
      s2: been
      s3: have
      s4: may

These should all compose to get *John may have been seeing Mary*. Structurally, this would occur in the following derivation, successively splicing in *been*, *have*, *may* (as in the derivations given above).

(45) ((John)(seeing Mary)) →
      ((John)(been (seeing Mary))) →
      ((John)(have (been (seeing Mary)))) →
      ((John) (may (have (been (seeing Mary)))))

The auxiliary has been successively spliced in, in the syntax. What occurs in the phonology? Here we will assume low daughter adjunction, a different type of operation. The daughter adjunction will be to the verb. Here, continued low daughter adjunction will give the following tree:

(46)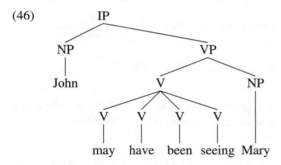

Note that the discrepancies have been introduced by the generalized transformation. The differing attachments are as follows:

(47) Syntax: Splicing (TAG Adjunction)
      Phonology: Low Daughter adjunction

Why should there be this difference in the operations in the syntax and the phonology? A complete answer goes beyond the scope of this paper, but Robert Frank (personal communication) suggests the possibility that the syntax is recursive, while the phonology is not, the latter obeying the "Strict Layer Hypothesis" (intonational phrases dominating phonological phrases, phonological phrases dominating clitic groups, clitic groups dominating feet, and so on, with nothing of the lower category dominating a higher category). If so, a recursive operation like the splicing operation might be expected to not be available in the phonology, and in its place some sort of default operation, such as low daughter adjunction or high daughter adjunction, would be expected to occur. In fact, this is precisely what happens.

4.2.2 *Prehead specifiers of DP*
I have suggested earlier that the structure of the noun phrase in the syntax is (48a), while the structure in the phonology is (48b).

(48) a. Syntax: see (the (picture of Mary))
      b. Phonology: see ((the picture)(of Mary))

How can this be accounted for? There are two ways of doing the syntax, which have similar effects. Using a TAG-type approach, we might assume that the nominal exists as a simple NP (together with the verb — recall that we are adopting the DP hypothesis), and the *the* is spliced into that, in the syntax.

(49) Syntax:
    s1: (see (picture of Mary)) |⎯⎯ Splice ⎯⎯→
    s2: the

    Output: see (the (picture of Mary))

In the paired phonological representation, the *the* is low daughter adjoined directly to the head noun, just as in the auxiliary structure above.

(50) Phonology:
    s1: (see (picture of Mary)) |⎯⎯ Low daughter adjunction ⎯⎯→
    s2: the

    Output: see (the picture)(of Mary)

In this case too, the generalized transformation introduces the discrepancy in the representation. Note that if the generalized transformation does not apply, then in a simple V-NP structure, the resultant is just the simple, s1 structure.

(51)   Simpler Structure
   s1:   see ball   ⎮   No generalized
   s2:   the   ⎮   transformation   ⟶

   Output: see ball

This simpler structure is precisely the sort that children speak. This suggests that a generalized transformation may simply be lacking in early speech. As a reviewer points out, this comment depends on adopting my notion of GTs, in which structures are merged, not Chomsky's, which starts out with simple lexical items. Of course, in Chomsky's system, anything larger than one lexical item would require a GT (but not in mine, because of the theta tree, Lebeaux 1988). The other, fairly similar way of composing with the determiner is with the Project-α transformation of Lebeaux (1988, 1991, 1997). In this transformation, an open class theta subtree is projected into a closed class Case frame. The syntactic way of doing this transformation would be that in (52)).

(52)   Project-α (Lebeaux 1988)
   s1:   see picture Mary
   s2:   INFL __ the __((of) __)

Here *see* goes into the first open slot, and *picture* into the second (and *Mary* into the third). I have included the material *Mary* and *of* in the above representation, even though it makes it less like telegraphic speech, because it is only in this case that the difference in bracketing between the prosody and the syntax is actually visible. I.e.: (the (picture of Mary)) vs. ((the picture) (of Mary)). If the transformation succeeds, we syntactically get the correct form. If it fails, as in early speech, we get *see picture Mary*, i.e. telegraphic speech. The paired phonological derivation presumably attaches *the* differently, leading to the distinct bracketing. The *the* is higher up in the syntactic bracketing, (the (picture of Mary)), and lower down in the phonological bracketing ((the picture)(of Mary)). Note that there are different operations in the syntax and the prosody.
To summarize, if elements of the nonrecursive side of the noun phrase (DP) are introduced by generalized transformations, then the distinct bracketings between the phonology and the syntax can be predicted.

4.2.3 *Relative clauses*
Given two clausal structures, the syntactic attachment of the relative clause is to the NP. The quasi-parallel phonological attachment of the relative clause is to the dominating S, or intonational phrase. This creates precisely the discrepant

bracketing in the two cases, where the relative clause is syntactically part of the NP, but may prosodically be in a separate intonational phrase (especially if the relative clause is recursive, as in: *This is the cat that ate the rat that ate the cheese*). Note that while the relative clause is a separate intonational phrase, the relative clause itself, and the clause to which it is attached, have the same form in the prosodic tree and the syntactic tree (that is, the kernel structures are the same; only the generalized transformation introduces a discrepancy).

(53) Relative clauses
  a. Syntactic attachment (Adjoin-α, Lebeaux 1988).

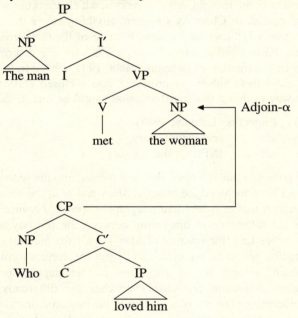

Output structure: the man (met (the woman (who loved him)))
  b. Phonological Attachment:

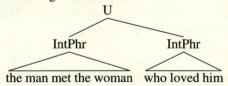

The two attachments are given below.

(54) a. Syntax: Chomsky-adjunction to NP (since the terminology "Chomsky-adjunction" has fallen into disuse, it means the structure of repeated nodes, as in relative clauses.)
      b. Phonology: Daughter adjunction to the highest node

Note that once again, the two kernel structures are the same. Only the generalized transformation introduces the discrepancy, because the two types of GTs are different (between the syntax and the prosody). Again, it seems likely that the "flatter" set of operations in the phonology can be traced to its non-recursive nature. While the syntax has recourse to the recursive Chomsky-adjunction operation, the phonology just has the possibility of high daughter adjunction. Presumably, it is high daughter adjunction, rather than the low daughter adjunction of the other two examples, because of the difference in the type of phrases involved (intonational phrases vs. phonological phrases).

4.2.4 *Cliticization of closed class head*

The final case of a syntax/prosody discrepancy is in the cliticization of the closed class head. As noted above, this is the discrepancy in the syntactic and phonologyical representations between the following forms:

(55) a. Syntax: $(_{XP}$ NP $(_{X'}$ X YP$))$
      b. Phonology: (NP X) (YP)

This discrepancy occurs at the CP, IP, and DP levels. We may account for this by a splicing operation in the syntax, and the operation of low daughter adjunction (to the left) in the phonology. Examples are shown below. Note that in all the examples, e.g. 57), the adjunction really is low daughter adjunction, and is not structurally sensitive, because of examples like *the man who I met's hat*, where *'s* attaches to *meet* phonologically, in contrast to its syntactic structure. Note that there are different operations operating in the syntax and the prosody.

(56) a. Syntax
          s1:   John going
          s2:   is
          Output: John (is going)

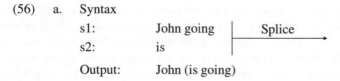

        b. Phonology
           s1:   John going | Low daughter adjunction
           s2:   is | (to left)
           Output: (John's) going

(57) a. Syntax
           s1:   Who that | Splice
           s2:   is |
           Output: Who (is that)

        b. Phonology
           s1:   Who that | Low daughter adjunction
           s2:   is | (to left)
           Output: Who's that?

(58) a. Syntax
           s1:   John hat | Splice
           s2:   's |
           Output: John ('s hat)

        b. Phonology
           s1:   John hat | Low daughter adjunction
           s2:   's | (to left)
           Output: John's hat

Note that it is low daughter adjunction that is shown by examples like *the man who I met's hat*.

In all the cases above, the discrepancy between the syntactic and the prosodic forms is handled by allowing for a generalized transformation which splices in the syntax, and low daughter-adjoins in the phonology. Once again, the kernel structures are the same, and the difference in bracketing is introduced just by the generalized transformation. Note that if the generalized transformation fails, we are left with the simpler structures of early speech:

(59) a. John going.
  b. Who that?
  c. John hat

To conclude this section, the generalized transformations introduce the discrepancies in bracketing in all six of the constructions above. The kernel structures are the same, only the generalized transformations introduce the discrepancies — thus a prosodic/syntactic discrepancy is a sign that a generalized transformation has taken place. Second, when the generalized transformation fails to take place in the derivation, we are left with the simpler kernel structures of telegraphic speech (Lebeaux 1988).

5. Conclusion

In this paper I have tried to argue for a particular theory of the grammar, both in terms of how telegraphic speech is generated, and in terms of the prosodic/syntactic discrepancies which exist in adult speech. Telegraphic speech (or kernel speech) by the child is derived as a consequence of the child computing structure with two representations: the syntactic one and the prosodic one. The child attempts to find the maximal alignment of these two structures (Lebeaux 1996, 1997) by factoring out their discrepancies. The resultant is telegraphic speech. One might ask how the child could find a maximal alignment of two structures if the syntactic structure does not yet exist. This is again the question of directionality. I have three responses to that. First, it is a remarkable fact that time after time, the maximal alignment of the syntactic and prosodic trees arrives at telegraphic speech. This generalization must be leading to some insight over the derivation. Second, as noted above, directionality problems must sometimes simply be accepted for intermediate results. Third, directionality problems have in fact been endemic to (and accepted by) the generative tradition for the last 40 years. For example, GB and its successors have always had a mapping from DS to SS. Yet, from the point of view of language comprehension, the mapping must go from SS to LF. But this has not stopped 40 years of fruitful work. In further work, I have attempted to reverse the direction.[9]

The prosodic/syntactic discrepancies of the adult are derived from a theory of grammar which: (i) has the syntactic and phonological derivations proceeding in quasi-parallel, and (ii) has generalized transformations applying to put together pairs of structures. For similar theories, see Chomsky's original work (1955, 1957), Bach (1977), who resurrected the embedding transformation, my own work (Lebeaux 1988, 1991, 1996), and work in the Tree-Adjoining Grammar tradition

(Kroch & Joshi 1985, 1988), as well as Montague (1974) and Jackendoff (1972, 1995). Here I argue that the generalized transformations introduce the prosodic/syntactic discrepancies into the representation, by putting together the kernel structures in different ways in the two components. Thus the kernel structures are structurally identical in the phonology and the syntax, but the generalized transformations introduce their differences.

Acknowledgments

I would like to thank Susan Powers, Alan Munn, Cristina Schmitt, and Juan Uriagereka for constant encouragement, Jürgen Weissenborn and Barbara Höhle for their kind invitation, Robert Frank for great interest and animated discussion about these matters, Kiyoshi Yamabana for a careful reading of this paper, and Anne Vainikka for leading the way in simplicity descriptions of the early grammar. I would also like to particularly thank Jürgen Weissenborn, Susan Powers, Barbara Höhle, and the Potsdam group for the opportunity to present this material at the September, 1996 conference, "How to Get into Language: Approaches to Bootstrapping in Early Language Development", and for a wonderful time at that conference, and Tom Roeper for a like opportunity at the conference "New Perspectives in Language Acquisition: Minimalism and Pragmatics". Thanks to Steve Abney, whose work on performance structures triggered this one. I would like to thank Linda Lombardi and Irene Vogel for phonological guidance, and Emmon Bach for deep syntactic thought. I would also like to thank Noam Chomsky, all of whose work forms the basis of what I have to say, though I disagree with him substantially here. Also, particular thanks to Sandiway Fong and the NEC Research Institute, for providing the opportunity to do this research.

Notes

1. This paper is culled from a much longer paper of the same intent and subject, entitled "Determining the Kernel II: Prosodic Form, Syntactic Form, and Phonological Bootstrapping, currently published as Lebeaux (1997). While I give six divergencies in the paper here, I give ten in Lebeaux (1997).
2. Of course, as a reviewer points out, for this to be the case a formal notion of simplicity, and some notion of a simplicity metric is necessary. For discussion, see Lebeaux (1997) or Chomsky (1965).
3. The work in (4)–(6) is pure timing data, i.e. from the speech signal. Rather remarkably, this gives almost exactly the same junctural properties as the pure linguistic work.
4. In Lebeaux (1997), 10 discrepancies are given and discussed.
5. It may be that the constraint is against that of removing the head element of a semantic phrase.
6. This constitutes a slightly different way for the genesis of the early phrase marker than is discussed in the bulk of the paper, which is the maximal alignment algorithm. There is no conflict between these proposals; the notion of complexity of a derivation is discussed at length in other work by myself (e.g. Lebeaux 1988, 1997). This paper, however, concentrates on the maximal alignment procedure as the mode of simplification.

7. The generalized transformations themselves are argued for on purely syntactic, as well as language acquisition grounds, in the above works.
8. The Case frame might instead be just as below, with just a slot for the NP, instead of an NP node. This possibility was pointed out to me by Susan Powers.

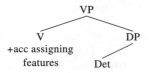

9. There is one further comment to make, an example. Given that two structures, A and B, produce a third structure C, one can often reverse the directionality, and use A and C to produce a possible set of structures B (which have helped to produce C). For example, suppose A and B unify to produce C. Then, knowing A and C, one can determine almost everything about B: namely, that it is the material that is in C that is not in A, plus optionally any of the overlap with A — it is this last part which is optional, and so not fully known. Even simpler, suppose two sets A and B union to make C. Then, given A and C, we know almost everything about B: namely, that it is the set difference of C — A, plus optionally any of the elements in A.

References

Abney, S. 1991. "Parsing By Chunks." In *Principle-Based Parsing*, R. Berwick, S. Abney & C. Tenny (eds.). Dordrecht: Kluwer.
Abney, S. 1995. "Chunks and Dependencies: Bringing Processing Evidence to Bear on Syntax." In *Linguistics and Computation*, J. Cole, G. Green & J. Morgan (eds.). Stanford, CA.: Center for the Study of Language and Information.
Bach, E. 1977. "The Position of the Embedding Transformation in the Grammar Revisited." In *Linguistics Structures Processing*, A. Zampoli (ed.). New York: North-Holland.
Brown, R. 1973. *A First Language*. Cambridge, Mass.: Harvard University Press.
Chomsky, N. 1957. *Syntactic Structures*. The Hague: Mouton.
Chomsky, N. 1975–1955. *The Logical Structure of Linguistic Theory*. Chicago, Ill. : University of Chicago Press.
Chomsky, N. 1965. *Aspects of the Theory of Syntax*. Cambridge, Mass.: MIT Press.
Chomsky, N. 1995. *The Minimalist Program*. Cambridge, Mass.: MIT Press.
Chomsky, N. & Halle, M. 1968. *The Sound Pattern of English*. New York: Harper and Row.
Frank, R. 1992. *Syntactic Locality and Tree Adjoining Grammar: Grammatical, Acquisition, and Processing Perspectives*. Univ. of Pennsylvania PhD. Dissertation.
Frank, R. 1997. "Structural Complexity and the Time Course of Grammatical Development." Manuscript, Baltimore: MD: Johns Hopkins University.

Fromkin, V. 1971. "The Nonanomalous Nature of Anomalous Utterances." *Language* 47, 27–52.
Garrett, M. 1975. "The Analysis of Sentence Production." In *The Psychology of Learning and Motivation*, Vol. 9, G. H. Bower (ed.). New York: Academic Press.
Gee, J. & Grosjean, L. 1983. "Performance Structures: A Psycholinguistic and Linguistic Appraisal." *Cognitive Psychology* 15, 411–458.
Grosjean, F., Grosjean, L. & Lane, H. 1979. "The Patterns of Silence: Performance Structures in Sentence Production." *Cognitive Psychology* 11, 58–81.
Jackendoff, R. 1972. *Semantic Interpretation in Generative Grammar*. Cambridge, Mass.: MIT Press.
Jackendoff, R. 1997. *The Architecture of the Language Faculty*. Cambridge, Mass.: MIT-Press.
Kaisse, E. 1985. *Connected Speech*. New York: Academic Press.
Kroch, A. & Joshi, A. 1985. "The Linguistic Relevance of Tree-Adjoining Grammars." MS-CS-85-16, Dept. of Computer and Information Science, University of Pennsylvania.
Kroch, A. & Joshi, A. 1988. "Analyzing Extraposition in a Tree Adjoining Grammar." In *Syntax and Semantics 20*, G. Huck & A. Ojeda (eds.). New York: Academic Press.
Kroch, A. 1989. "Asymmetries in Long Distance Extraction in a Tree Adjoining Grammar." In *Alternative Conceptions of Phrase Structure*, M. Baltin & A. Kroch (eds.). Chicago, Ill.: University of Chicago Press.
Lebeaux, D. 1988. *Language Acquisition and the Form of the Grammar*. University of Massachusetts, PhD. Dissertation.
Lebeaux, D. 1991. "Relative Clauses, Licensing, and the Nature of the Derivation." In *Syntax and Semantics 25, Perspectives on Phrase Structure: Heads and Licensing*, S. Rothstein (ed.). New York: Academic Press.
Lebeaux, D. 1996. "Determining the Kernel." In *Phrase Structure and the Lexicon*, J. Rooryck & L. Zaring (eds.). Dordrecht: Kluwer.
Lebeaux, D. 1997. "Determining the Kernel II: Prosodic Form, Syntactic Form, and Phonological Bootstrapping." Tech Report 97–094, NEC Research Institute.
Matthei, E. 1979. *Stalking the Second Green Ball*. University of Massachusetts PhD. Dissertation.
Montague, R. 1974. In *Formal Philosophy*, R. Thomason (ed.). New Haven, Conn.: Yale University Press.
Nespor, M. & Vogel, I. 1986. *Prosodic Phonology*. Dordrecht: Foris.
Powers, S. 1996. *The Growth of the Phrase Marker: Evidence from Subjects*. University of Maryland PhD. Dissertation.
Powers, S. & Lebeaux, D. 1998. "More Data on DP Acquisition." In *Issues in the Theory of Languae Acquisition: Essays in Honor of Jürgen Weissenborn*, N. Dittmar & Z. Penner (eds.). Berlin: Peter Lang.
Roeper, T. 1995. "The Role of Merger Theory and Formal Features in Acquisition." In *Generative Approaches in Language Acquisition*, H. Clahsen (ed.). Amsterdam: John Benjamins.

Selkirk, E. 1984. *Phonology and Syntax*. Cambridge, Mass.: MIT Press.
Shattuck, S. 1974. *Speech Errors: An Analysis*. MIT PhD. dissertation.
Solan, L. & Roeper, T. 1978. "Children's Use of Syntactic Structure in Interpreting Relative Clauses." In *University of Massachusetts Occassional Papers in Linguistics* 4, H. Goodluck & L. Solan (eds.). Amherst, Mass.: University of Massachusetts.
Speas, M. 1990. *Phrase Structure in Natural Language*. Dordrecht: Kluwer.
Tavakolian, S. 1978. *Structural Principles in the Acquisition of Complex Sentences*. University of Massachusetts PhD. Dissertation.
Vainikka, A. 1985. "The Acquisition of English Case." Paper presented at the 10th Boston University Conference on Language Development, Boston, Mass.: Boston University.
Vainikka, A. 1986. "Case in Acquisition and Finnish." Manuscript, University of Massachusetts.
Vainikka, A. 1993. "Case in the Development of English Syntax." *Language Acquisition* 3, 257–324.
Williams, E. 1980. "Predication." *Linguistic Inquiry* 11, 203–238.

From Prosody to Grammar in English
The differentiation of catenatives, modals, and auxiliaries from a single protomorpheme

Ann M. Peters
University of Hawai'i

1. Introduction

One goal of the study of language acquisition is to seek an understanding of the developmental process, focussing on how the less universal aspects of language are acquired (Braine 1994). While agreeing that human children are endowed with abilities that make possible certain kinds of linguistic knowledge not demonstrable in other species, the focus is less on innate abilities and more on the process of acquisition of the whole of a language. On this view, the child is initially endowed with a range of abilities (motor, sensory, affective, social) which develop over time, and is propelled by functional and social needs to learn ever more about language structure and use. Viewing language acquisition as but a part of a more complex developmental picture leads away from the assumption that language acquisition and analysis are all-or-none states (either you know it or you don't); in fact, if one looks for it, there is much evidence that PARTIAL ANALYSIS and PARTIAL ACQUISITION are pervasive — even for native-speaking adults (Peters & Menn 1993).

Starting with as few assumptions as possible about innate availability of linguistic categories and knowledge of linguistic structure, one approach to early syntactic development is to see how much of it can be described with a series of frame-and-slot grammars, each successive one of which has a larger number of linguistic categories and a larger number of positions to be filled or expanded.[1] The working assumption is that the child gradually discovers that he needs not only to include more open-class lexical items (nouns and adjectives with each verb), but that there are more and more closed class POSITIONS that he must fill.

And it seems to be an awareness of grammatical positions, which may be perceptible primarily because of their prosodic characteristics, that leads some children to produce them initially as filler syllables which eventually develop into identifiable grammatical morphemes.

How well is such a scenario supported by evidence? As a demonstration I will describe the development of auxiliaries, modals, and catenative verbs in an English-speaking child. We will see that they initially emerge as fillers which subsequently evolve into protomodals and amalgams, and, finally to fully differentiated adult grammatical categories.

1.1 *English modals and auxiliaries*

Stromswold (1995) argues that the complexities of English modals and auxiliaries are so great that children must be equipped with a good deal of innate knowledge in order to acquire them at all. She identifies two major potential problems (p. 858), the first of which is: **How can a child distinguish auxiliaries such as *be*, *have*, *do* from their lexical homonyms?** Examples are given in (1). The problem is also relevant for some modals (2) and catenatives (3).

(1) a. He **is** sleeping.   vs. He **is** sleepy.
     b. He **has** eaten cookies.   vs. He **has** cookies.
     c. He **does** not wash windows. vs. He **does** windows.

(2)   She **can** eat peaches.   vs. She **cans** peaches.

(3) a. Do you **wanna** get down? vs. Do you **want** a cookie?
     b. Do you **need to** go?   vs. Do you **need** some food?
     c. I'd **like to** eat it.   vs. I **like** cookies.

Stromswold proposes that to deal with this ambiguity children must be predisposed to distinguish between two kinds of linguistic categories: **lexical** categories (nouns, verbs, adjectives) and **functional** categories (auxiliaries, modals, articles, etc.). Some such ability seems quite plausible, if only because lexical categories carry so much more semantic information than functional ones that they are more likely to attract a young child's attention. My detailed study of a longitudinal corpus (e.g. Peters & Menn 1993), coupled with my review of the acquisition of grammatical morphemes (aka "functional categories") in languages with differing morphological and phonological structures (Peters 1997) suggests that many children initially become aware of functional categories through their phonological presence and distributional predictability (as unstressed syllables that have no immediately obvious function in an utterance).

Stromswold estimates that there are only some 100 unique sequences of auxiliaries that are acceptable in English, out of a potential population of 10^{18} (1990, p. 857). The second problem which she poses is therefore: **How can a child learn all the co-occurrence privileges and restrictions on modal and auxiliary verbs in English?** Is it necessary to sift through the billions of possibilities?

1.2 *English catenative constructions*

In addition to modals and auxiliaries, English has a class of verbs with modal-like functions but a distinct set of syntactic properties. This class, which includes *want to, have to*, and *like to*, is variously labelled CATENATIVES (i.e. "chaining" verbs, Brown 1973, p. 54; Limber 1973, p. 176) or MATRIX VERBS (Bloom 1991, p. 57). I will use CATENATIVE to refer to the subset of English complement-taking verbs that use the infinitive-marker *to* to introduce the next verb. Although they are modal-like in that they are used to express notions such as desire, need, or intention, catenatives are technically main verbs, since any verb they introduce belongs to an embedded clause.[2] Examples are:

(4) I **want to** read that book.
     I'm **going to** read that book.
     I **have to** read that book.

Despite the descriptive grammarian's view that the second verb (along with its infinitive-marker *to*) is subordinate to the catenative (5), there is evidence that, at least in American English, the **processing unit** is actually *catenative + to* (6). This latter clustering is also marked in the prosody and suggests that *to* may have been (at least partially) reanalyzed as a part of the catenative rather than as associated with the verb it introduces.[3]

(5) I want [to + read that book].
(6) I want + to read that book.

One kind of evidence supporting this sort of reanalysis is heard in the frequent phonological assimilations made by adults, such as *gonna* for *going to* or *wanna* for *want to*. Further evidence comes from Lois Bloom's investigation of the acquisition of verb + *to* constructions; she concludes that her children learned *to* in association with the preceding catenative (6) rather than with the complement (5) (1991, p. 290).

The intuition that *catenative + to* constructions have a modal-like quality is contributed to by two properties: they modify the meaning of the following verb and the subjects of the two verbs must be the same.

(7) I ought to [I] read that book.
John is going to [John] read that book.
We will try to [we] read that book.
John wants to [John] read that book.

For at least three catenatives, however, (*want, like, need*), it is also possible for the introduced verb to have a distinct subject, as in (8).

(8) **John** wants **you** to come.
Would **you** like **me** to come?
Do **you** need **me** to come?

How, then, do children discover the syntax of these constructions which involve two verbs (the first finite, the second not) and a possibility of two subjects?

Evidence that learners create partial and increasing analyses of grammatical forms, coupled with observation of their "filler syllables" lead me to the following proposal:

> Learners may create an undifferentiated pre-verbal protomodal class which serves as a "holding tank",[4] affording a place for the accumulation of enough information about the members of the class to enable its subsequent analysis into a more adult-like set of classes.

On this view, the emergence of catenatives may be intertwined with the development of auxiliaries and modals; all of these may first appear as simple fillers that have at most a protomodal function, but which subsequently differentiate into syntactically distinct classes.

Thus, although it is possible that some children control two-clause constructions before producing sentences with *wanna* or *liketa* (as claimed by Limber 1973), the data I will present demonstrate that this is not necessary. For some children the origins seem to lie in a very simple construction, namely a single-subject sentence in which the main verb is preceded and modified by one of a single class of **protomodals**:

(9) SUBJ PM VP

At first this protomodal position is occupied by **filler syllables**, but they gradually become better defined both phonologically and syntactically until it is possible to claim that they have differentiated into three classes: **auxiliaries, modals**, and **catenatives**. Table 1 lists the forms I have been investigating, with their approximate ages of emergence. They include fillers, protomodals, a phonologically defined class of frequent modal-subject amalgams, as well as catenatives, auxiliaries and modals. Where possible the layout is intended to help the reader see which earlier forms might have developed into which later forms.

Table 1. *Target forms under investigation with approximate ages of emergence*

Fillers		Protomodals		Amalgams[a]	
N	1;7.2	want/wanna	1;8.0	want-Da(dd)y	2;3.1
				wan(t)-me-ta	2;4.2
ə	1;8.0			whats-(th)at	1;9.0
				where-d	2;2.0
		əm(mə)	2;3.1	I-(a)m-(g)on(na)	2;4.2
				wouldja	2;4
		əyə	2;4.0	whatta/whicha	2;4.0
				whatcha	2;6.3
IZ	1;10.2	IZ(a)	2;4.0	lets	2;1.0
		lemme	(2;1)	le(t)-Da(dd)y	2;3.1
da	1;11.0	dya	2;4.0	didja	2;0.0
				Da(dd)y-(i)s	2;4
				dontcha	2;0.0
əŋ(ə)	1;11.0	gon/gonna	2;1.0	canya	2;1.2
		can	2;1.2	c(a)n-Da(dd)y	2;6.0
		ket	2;3.1		
		wudi	(2;2.0)	wouldja	2;4
		try	2;2.0		
		shu	2;4.2		
		need	2;4	musta	2;6
		ku	2;4.2	couldja	2;6.0
				Da(dd)y-w(i)ll	2;6.3

Catenatives		Auxiliaries		Modals	
wanna	1;11	did	2;2	can	2;2.3
gonna	2;2.3	do	2;4	cannot	2;4.0
hafta	2;2.3	dont	2;4	cant	2;5.2
liketa	2;7	does	2;8	will	2;4.2
needta	2;11	didnt	2;9	would	2;4
tryta	2;11?	is, am	2;8	could	2;9
		are	2;4.2?	wont	2;10
		was, were	2;9		
		wasnt	3;2		

[a] I have deliberately avoided using apostrophes when there is not yet evidence that Seth has segmented the parts of an amalgam.

1.3 Overview

I will present evidence for the following developmental sequence: filler syllables emerge; they develop phonologically into protomodals and amalgams, which in turn evolve into a functionally defined class of request initiators; we can trace the slow emergence of three syntactically distinct classes: catenatives (with the most complex syntax), modals (which lack inflections), and auxiliaries (including inflections for both third singular present and past tense). Even though this sequence is not universal among English learners, it does have some general developmental implications.

2. The emergence of filler syllables

The data come from a longitudinal study of a severely visually-impaired child named Seth. The original materials on the development of Seth's language between 1;4 and 4;4 were collected by his father, Bob Wilson, who was a graduate student in linguistics at the University of Hawai'i during that period (Peters 1987; Peters 1993; Peters & Boggs 1986; Wilson & Peters 1988). I have been working with 33 half-hour transcriptions of audio tape spread over the time period; they almost exclusively contain father-son interactions at home or on outings.

As he first moved past the one-word stage, at about 1;7, Seth began preposing unglossable syllables ("fillers") to phonologically recognizable open-class

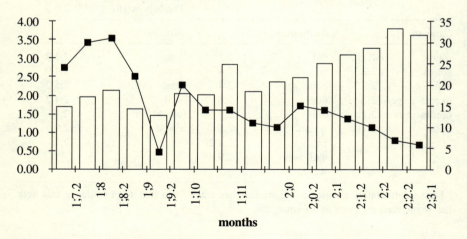

Figure 1. *Mean length of utterance in words (bars) and percent fillers (line)*

words; e.g. *cup* → *ng cup*. From as early as 1;8, he produced two relatively distinct kinds of fillers, one predominantly nasal, the other vocalic. His father's subjective impression at the time was that the nasal fillers were predominantly used in requests (perhaps an approximation of *want*), while the vocalic fillers were more attentional in function (Wilson, personal communication). Figure 1 shows Seth's early MLUs in words (bars) along with the percents of fillers he produced (line).[5]

At 1;11 Seth's ability to produce two open-class words in a single utterance increased: his open-class MLU jumped from about 1.25 to 1.7. Along with this increase in structure came the possibility of including more than one filler. The illustrative examples in (10) are from 1;10 and 1;11; nasal fillers are glossed as N and vocalic ones as ə.

(10) a. ɔ̃ gɛ' ə kəp?
        N get ə cup?
    b. n si ə bak?
        N see ə bark? (= of tree)
    c. m pɪk ə fawɪs?
        N pick ə flowers?
    d. ŋ gɛ ap?
        N get-up?

Not surprisingly, when Seth began producing fillers, an observer could not tell what they would develop into, if they survived at all. Later, however, once they had taken on more characteristics of adult targets, it has been possible to project both forwards and backwards, both to identify their eventual targets, and to uncover characteristics that distinguished subgroups of fillers almost from the beginning.

Peters & Menn (1993) examined five of Seth's filler positions in detail: subject of verb, object of transitive verb, copula, verbal particle, preposition. The distributional evidence suggests that each slot developed at a different time and rate. Of interest here is the position just in front of the verb. By 2;1 we find some utterances with **two** preverbal fillers, the second more nasal than the first, as in (11):

(11) **u wɔ̃** tak ɛdl 'talifon səmmor?   2;1
       ə wan' talk on-the telephone some-more?

Adopting a perspective as close to Seth's as the data allow, it appears that he simultaneously developed a pair of co-occurring preverbal slots, with the one farther from the verb evolving into the Subject, and the one closer to the verb

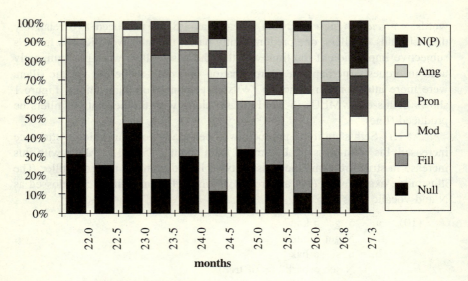

Figure 2. *Occupants of preverbal slots*

containing some sort of verbal modifier. I call this "inner" slot **protomodal** because its members seem to modify the verb's meaning in deontic ways, conveying possibility, desire, necessity, etc. Seth's fillers in Subject position primarily seem to be vocalic, while those in the Protomodal slot are predominantly nasal.

On the evidence that Seth does not at first differentiate his protomodals with respect to either co-occurrence or modality-marking function, I conclude that they are initially part of a single class. But from undifferentiated fillers, these forms evolve phonologically until adult targets can be recognized as members of three different classes: auxiliaries (*do, is*), modals (*can, would,* and *could*), and catenatives (*gonna, wanna, hafta,* and *liketa*).

Besides his protosubjects and protomodals, he produces a third set of preverbal forms which do not co-occur with either of the others; it consists of as yet unsegmented amalgams of pronouns with auxiliaries or modals (past-marking *didja,* interrogative *dyou, can-you,* and inchoative *lets* and *shou(ld)we*). Once Seth analyzes the members of this amalgamated group and discovers their adult morphosyntactic properties, he incorporates them into his other preverbal classes. Because of the simultaneity and inextricability of the analyses Seth is carrying out, the early development of the Subject and Protomodal slots is best understood in tandem. I will trace this process in as much detail as space permits.

A developmental overview can be seen in Figure 2. I computed developmental profiles for the Subject, Amalgam, and Protomodal slots by inspecting 150 of Seth's utterances at each data point between 1;10 and 2;3. For all sentences in which overt subjects were grammatically required, I calculated the relative proportions of preverbal constitutents: nulls, fillers, recognizable protomodals, pronoun-modal amalgams, pronouns, and full NPs. Figure 2 shows how the percents of nulls (black) and fillers (gray) steadily drop, and that amalgams are particularly important between 2;1 and 2;3.

3. Emergence of protomodals

3.1 *A single initial "functional category"*

Recall that Seth's nasal fillers primarily appear in the pre-verbal slot which is nearer the verb. Between 2;1 and 2;4, they evolve into recognizable lexical items (primarily *wanna, gonna, let, can*) that are as yet undifferentiated syntactically. The first nasal filler which Seth produces is homorganic, in that it assimilates to the initial consonant of the following word; it gradually acquires an initial /w/ and evolves into *wanna*, as illustrated by the developmental sequence in (12).

(12) a. ŋ gɪdlt?   1;9.2
         N get-it?
     b. wə kozɪt?
         wa(nt) close-it?
     c. əŋ gyæp?   1;10
         N get-up?
     d. wən gɛ əp?
         wan(t) get up?
     e. m pɪk ə fawis?   1;10.2
         N pick ə flowers?
     f. n si ə bak?
         N see ə bark? (= of tree)
     g. wə ʃekə maisælf.   1;11
         wa(nt) shake-ə myself.
     h. **wənnə** tek –
         wanna take –
     i. **wənnən** bæon?   2;0.2
         wanna bounce?

Within a single taped half-hour he could produce a number of phonetic variants of this preverbal protomorpheme, ranging from homorganic nasal, to *w*, to *wan* to **wanna**. It is the relative **proportions** of these forms that change with development, with the earlier forms on the list gradually giving way to the later ones (Figure 2).

Once *wanna* is established, a second nasal, a non-assimilating velar, appears, becomes recognizable as *gonna* at around 2;2.2.

(13) a. əŋə kɪt tə nɛdl wən? 2;1.2
 NG get da nother-one?
 b. əŋ go fwo də 'adr pɪtʃrs. 2;2.3
 NG go throw da other pictures.
 c. ŋ **gənə** 'it səm.
 NG gonna eat some.
 d. əm **gənə** 'klozɪt.
 Im? gonna close-it.
 e. **gɔ̃** fwo ɪ əp æt də 'pɪkʃr. 2;3.1
 gon throw i(t) up at da picture.
 f. əŋ **gɔ̃** fwoovr 'dɛr?
 NG gon throw-over dere?
 g. ŋ **gənə** 'gɛt ɪt?
 NG gonna get it?

One source of Seth's early protomodals may have been his father's heavy use of catenatives and modals, together with a parental concern that Seth's speech not seem rude.

3.2 *Differentiation of individual protomodals*

Seth's initial protomodals include fillers, the emerging catenatives *wan(na)*, *go(nna)*, *lets*, and *hafta*, a few auxiliaries (*is*, *do*, *are*), and the modal *can*. Evidence that they constitute a single pre-verbal class is found in their paradigmatic substitutability. All of the utterances in (14) were recorded at 2;3.3 while Seth was sitting in the car squeaking his seatbelt:

(14) can make it go squeak. 2;3.3
 want make go squeak.
 əm make go squeak.
 did make that squeak?

FROM PROSODY TO GRAMMAR IN ENGLISH

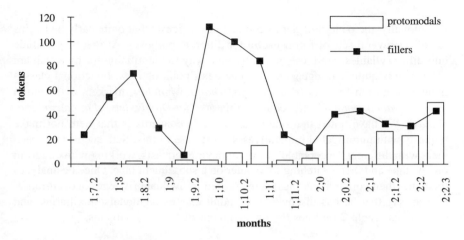

Figure 3. *Early fillers (line) and protomodals (bars)*

The development of protomodals to 2;3 is graphed in Figure 3: the initial dominance of fillers (line) is supplanted by a growing but as yet syntactically undifferentiated class of protomodals (bars).

Between 2;3 and 2;9, Seth begins to differentiate the members of this **positionally** defined class into at least three **syntactic** classes, each with its own co-occurrance privileges. These are the **auxiliaries**, the **modals**, and the **catenatives**.

4. Non-adult way-stations: Amalgams and request-initiators

If we consider which aspects of language must be salient to a toddler, two perspectives are helpful. A phonological perspective helps us identify those bits of the ambient language which might be easy to extract as units but hard to segment further. A functional approach suggests we look for sets of linguistic forms which a learner uses for identifiable functions.

Taking a phonological perspective, it is easy to identify a subset of Seth's pre-verbal forms that contains as-yet-unsegmented amalgams of pronouns with auxiliaries or modals. These include *didja, dya, a(re)ya, whatta, whatcha, lets, shu, canya, gonna,* and *əmmə*. Eventually, of course, after Seth has analyzed these forms and discovered their adult morphosyntactic properties, he redistributes their components into his other preverbal classes. We catch glimpses of this process as we follow their development.

4.1 Amalgams

Functionally, the pattern of Seth's productions suggests that quite early he begins to collect several sets of forms useful for different purposes. At first they include only filler syllables, but these gradually give way to identifiable forms which are nevertheless quite heterogeneous from an adult point of view. Functional classes include: question-formers (*dya, a(re)ya, whatta, whatcha*), markers of intention (*gonna, wanna, əmmə*), and request-initiators (*let-Daddy, lets, shu, canya, can-Daddy*). We have noted that one of his father's concerns is that Seth not make requests with unmitigated imperatives. In response to this, Seth seems to experiment with different "acceptable" ways of making requests, working with one form on one tape and then switching to another on a subsequent tape. Once he analyzes them into their components and discovers their individual privileges of occurrence, we can say that he has discovered the adult classes of modals, auxiliaries, and catenatives. Table 2 outlines the development of Seth's amalgams.

Table 2. *Emergence of amalgams*

amalgam	flourishes		sporadic remnants
IZ	1;11	2;4	(2;9)
didja	2;0	2;5	(3;0)
want-Daddy	2;3	2;9	
let-Daddy	2;3	2;3	
dyou	2;4	2;7	
əmmə	2;4	2;11	
əyə	2;4	2;4.2	
shu	2;4.2	2;5.2	
can-Daddy	2;6	3;2	
wouldja	2;4	2;11+	

4.1.1 IZ
A relatively infrequent but persistent proto-auxiliary is the form I gloss as **IZ**. It seems to be a blend or confusion of *lets* with *is, does*, and/or *didja*. These show up in ones and twos as early as 1;11; the largest group occurs at 2;4.

(15)   a.   /ezə/ wash ə put in the rack? [a request]   2;4
                let-Daddy(?) wash it and put it in the rack
       b.   ts   gonna cook ya   *two* eggs? [a request]
                lets? gonna cook you two eggs.

        c. Dayz find box.
            lets   find the box.
            [partial imitation of earlier utterance by Daddy]
        d. /wedz/ Da' finish wrapping?
            [Several lines earlier Daddy had said,
            "let Daddy finish wrapping this part."]

After 2;4, **IZ** appears only sporadically, up to 2;9.

4.1.2 *didja*

Seth's next earliest amalgam is *didja*, which appears at about 2;0. For a number of reasons, primarily interactive but too complex to go into here, he uses it when referring to his own past actions (Peters 1987, 1993; Wilson 1986). Here are examples with approximate glosses.

(16)	a.	didja hear car.	2;0
		I heard a car	
	b.	didja help you drive.	2;1.2
		I helped Daddy drive	
	c.	didja throw little blocks.	
		I threw little blocks	
	d.	didja break ya face.	2;2.3
		I bumped my face	
	e.	didja find it.	
		I found it	
	f.	didja dump it out.	2;4
		I dumped it out	
	g.	didja burp.	2;5
		I burped	
	h.	diya knock that tube down.	2;6.3
		I knocked that tube down. [immediate past]	
	i.	did you go to Mommy's new house.	
		I went to Mommy's new house. [longer ago]	

By 2;5 *didja* is beginning to break down phonologically into *did* + *you*, although its reference to himself persists sporadically through 3;0.

4.2 Request initiators

4.2.1 want/let-Daddy

Evidence for the emergence of a **class** of "requestives" by 2;3 is found in the intersubstitutability of *want* and *let* in (17) and (18).

(17) a. **want** Daddy si-down frow it. 2;3
 b. **let** Dad si-down frow it. asking Dad to throw the ball
(18) a. **wan(t)** Daddy da bat it? 2;3
 b. **let** Da(ddy) bat-it. asking Dad to bat the ball

Implicitly these are also Seth's first two-subject constructions, since the implied subject of *want* is *Seth* rather than *Daddy*. It is possible that *let-Daddy* is another requestive amalgam with which Seth experiments, preposing it to the label for any action he wants his father to perform: *le(t)-Daddy + VP*. An interesting construction at 2;3 is found in several instances of *let Da(dd)y come ta Dad*, which is a request for Daddy to pick Seth up.[6] The temporary-amalgam interpretation is supported by the subsequent virtual disappearance of *let AGENT VERB*.[7]

4.2.2 Dyou

At 2;4 Seth adopts *dyou* as a request-former. In each example in (19), culled from some twenty on this tape, Seth is asking for something for himself:

(19) **dyou** want a cookie? 2;4
 dy wan(t) sit up high chair?
 do y(ou) wanna hold it.

We note in passing that pronoun "reversals" are common in Seth's speech during this period (Peters 1987); in this case they arise because he co-opts the format of his father's suggestions to him into requests on his own behalf. This usage persists through 2;7.

4.2.3 əmmə

At 2;4 a new filler/amalgam, *əmmə*, appears. Phonologically it sounds like *I'm* and *I'm-gonna*; it functions both to state intention and to initiate requests.

(20) a. **əmmə** shishi[8] on the floor. [intention] 2;4
 I'm gonna shishi on the floor
 b. **m** make shishi some more. [intention]
 I'm gonna make shishi some more

c. **æw̃gettin'** ya blueberries.   [request]
   get me some blueberries
d. **aymə** erase it for ya —   [request]   2;4.2
   erase it for me
e. **əm** skyuwing you anonner one?
   show me a new letter

It has fully ceded to *am* by about 3;0.

4.2.4 *əyə, whatta, whichə*

Yet another auxiliary embedded in an amalgam which peeks in is *eyəgə(nə)*. It occurs three times at 2;4, and seven at 2;4.2 but does not become robust for a while longer. At the same time, this amalgam shows up in a *wh*-form, evidently modeled on the formulaic phrases (*what/which (one) are ya gonna do/take (next)?*)[9] which Daddy uses when inviting Seth to choose a card. The examples in (21) show Seth at 2;4.2 having difficulty segmenting *which-re* as well as *what-re*. Several of them occur more than once (with slight variations in parentheses).

(21)   now **whatcha** gonna do (next).   [n=5]   2;4.2
       which one ya gon' take.   [n=7]
       whichre (one) ya/we gon' take. [n=3]
       whatta ya gon' take.
       wisha we gon' take.
       whicha one a gon' take.
       whicha one ya gon' take.

The *whatcha* amalgam first appears at 2;6.3 (*whatchu drinking*), then reappears in some numbers at 2;8, consolidated into an idiosyncratic lexical item, the *wh*-word *whatta*, based not only on *what-are* but also on *what-did*, and possibly on *what-do* as well (Peters 1987, 1993; Wilson & Peters 1988).

(22)   **whattl** we're gonna buy (at the store).   2;8
       whatre ya gon' smell (first).
       whatta you're gonna smell.
       whatta we saw (at the zoo)

4.2.5 *Shu (< should/shall)*

Another requestive is *shu*,[10] which Seth produces nearly 50 times between 2;4.2 and 2;5.2. Examples (23) and (24) include a number of Daddy's interpretations.

(23)   they are drawing Hebrew and Roman letters with chalk   2;4.2
   a.   S: **shu** make a — **shu** make a kaf?[11]
        D: ⎰ oh, you want Daddy to make you some letters?
        S: ⎱ **shu** make a kaf. make a – kaf?
        D: ok.
   b.   S: **shu** make a /wuman/ letter? [= Roman letter]
             shu make He-brew letters?
             make He-brew letters?
             shu make He-brew letters?
        D: ok, Bird. what letters do you want.

(24)   they are in the bathroom, shining the flashlight on things   2;5.2
   a.   D: that light is white. oh, you shine it on the towels?
        S: **shu** shi(ne) on da *odder* tow(el)?
        D: yeah.
        S: ə — want — want Daddy to shine on the *ceiling*.
   b.   S: **shu** sit down on na rug?
        D: let's sit down on the rug and talk.
   c.   S: **should** turn the flashlight off?
        D: let's turn it off.
   d.   S: **shu**–should turnnn the lamp on.
        D: yeah – turn the lamp on,
             and let's turn on the *kitchen* light, too.

4.2.6 *Can-Daddy*

A somewhat later requestive is *can-Daddy* which appears at 2;6, e.g.

(25)   c'n Daddy get in your bed?   2;6
       can Daddy feel cars?
       can Daddy see cars Dad?

Between 2;8 and 3;2 Seth uses this formula very heavily — there are more than 100 tokens on these six tapes, with peaks on two tapes where his major activity seems to be to get his father to perform various actions. Interestingly there are no corresponding statements of the form *Daddy can VERB*, although there are a number with *I/you/we can*. Pairs of utterances using alternative constructions suggest that by 2;8 he has probably analyzed the *can-Daddy* sequence, but nevertheless finds it a handy construction unit.

(26)   can Da'y touch Da'y's hair?   2;8
       want Da'y ta touch Da'y's hair?

4.2.7 *Wouldja, couldja*

Two other modal-based requestive chunks are *wouldja* and *couldja*, both "polite" forms that Daddy encourages, but relatively infrequent. At 2;4 Seth imitates Daddy's production of *wouldja*:

(27) D: **wouldju** please throw this [wet diaper] in the rubbish? 2;4
S: **wouldja** throw this in ə rubbish for Daddy?

By 2;11 Daddy expects Seth to ask appropriately, and prompts for a polite form with an elliptical "say..."

(28) S: I want some water, Dad? 2;11
D: say ...
S: **wouldja** get some water?
D: yeah.

4.3 Further development

Almost immediately Seth begins the work of analyzing his amalgams into their adult components (2;3 to 2;9). Eventually he differentiates this **positionally** and **functionally** defined set into three **syntactic** classes (auxiliaries, modals, and catenatives), each with its own co-occurrence privileges. We consider first the small but syntactically complex set of **catenatives**; next the sparser and syntactically simpler **modals** (which require no inflection); finally the **auxiliaries**, including forms inflected for present and past tense.

5. Catenatives

5.1 *Wanna*

Seth needs to discover that several of his requestives, *wanna, liketa, hafta,* and *gonna*, possess the syntactic properties of raising verbs in the adult language. This process begins when Seth analyzes *wanna V* into *want+to V*, so that each verb can have a distinct subject ($SUBJ_i$ *want* $SUBJ_j$ *to VERB*). Evidence begins to appear at 2;4.2 in sentences such as those in (29) with *me* as subject of the infinitive.

(29) a. wã me **ta** cut-off Daddy? [ˈkədɔf] 2;4.2
gloss uncertain (4 times)
b. you wɔ̃me **ta** help?
requesting Daddy's help (5 times)

He quite consistently produces *want SUBJ to V* constructions, and they attain adult form relatively quickly.[12] The revealing exchanges in (30), which were recorded at 2;5, suggest that *want-Daddy* may still be only partially analyzed, or at least have been seized upon as a convenient production unit:

(30) a. D: you want Daddy ta help you?   2;5
             S: **wan' Daddy** ta help you, Dad.
             D: say, 'help me, Dad.'
             S: help me, Dad.
        b. S: I don' **wanna– wanna** build dat. *crying*
             D: d'you want Daddy ta help you build-tower.
             S: **wan' Daddy** ta help myou build-tower.
             D: ok. let's build one more.

At 2;5.2 Seth produces more than twenty *want-Daddy* sentences, all but one of the form *want Daddy to VP*. In no case does *want* have an expressed subject, although from context one can infer that in several cases an adult would include **I**:

(31) [I] **wan' Daddy** ta give [me] plenty.   2;5.2
       [I] **wan' Da'y** ta put sugar in it?
       [I] **want Daddy** [to] get in my [bath] water.

In other sentences what is omitted is more likely *do you*, but with the reversed-pronoun meaning *I*:

(32) [do you] **wan' Da'y** ta getchu some chocolate milk?   2;5.2
       [do you] **wa' Da'y** ta fix you raisins for Daddy.
       [do you] **wɛn Da'y** ta get in the bubble with you?

Of interest is a sequential pair in which Seth replaces the noun *Daddy* with the pronoun *me* as the agent of the proposed action (both sentences seem to mean 'I want you (= Daddy) to help me)'.

(33) **wan Da'y** ta help you?   2;5.2
       wan me ta help you?

By 3;6 this construction is truly productive, as seen in the flexibility for the subjects of both verbs.

(34) a. what**chu** want **us** to spell?   3;5.3
            now, Dad, **I** don't want**chu** ta play too hard, ok?
            I don't WANT **him** to play with it.
            I want **you and DJ** ta feed birds?

b. [d**you**] want **the sprinklers** ta go, or stop.   3;10
[d**you**] want **me** ta take you ta Bubby's or school.
[d**you**] want **the hair** to get on you
    or **you** don't want **it** ta get on you.
[do] you wanna make your lunch
    or **you** want **me** ta make your lunch.

While *wanna* is being analyzed as *want+to*, *go*, *gonna* and *hafta*, are emerging, with *go(nna)* later than *wanna* but earlier and more robustly than *hafta*.

5.2 *Go, gonna*

A functional difference between *gonna* and *wanna* is that *gonna* is used to express an intention rather than to request an action; a structural difference is that the subject of second verb must be a *pro* coreferential with the matrix subject (*SUBJ gonna VERB*). Before 2;4 Seth tends to use *go* or *gon'* rather than *gonna*, although the latter is beginning to appear as well.

(35) a. ng **go** frow Daddy's head.   2;3
ǝw **go** frow Daddy head —
ready to throw ball to/at Dad
b. ǝm **gonna** close it.
c. **go** see Myrna.
d. can make it **go** squeak.
squeaking his seatbelt

This sort of construction is one that Seth models on Daddy's usage, as can be seen in two interchanges in (36)

(36) a. D: lets **go** fix Mommy a present.   2;4
S: lets **go** fix.
b. D: let Daddy **go** find the wrapping paper.
S: 'ets **go** find ǝ wrap.

5.3 *Hafta*

Other catenatives that emerge more slowly during Seth's third year include *hafta*, *liketa*, *tryta*, and *needta*. Of these the most frequent is *hafta*, which first shows up at 2;1.2. Like *wanna* and *gonna* it seems initially to be an amalgam: *have-ǝ open it; have-ǝ open it an' clo(se)*. It continues to appear sporadically over the next year, at first without overt subjects:[13]

(37)	a.	**haddə** put'it back firs(t).	2;3
		now **hafta** go!	
	b.	**hafta** put it on the tray?	2;4
		hafta give it ta Dad.	
	c.	**hafta** help me ta make a nun.	2;4;2
		drawing Hebrew letters	
		hadda bui(ld) another blue, Dad.	
		building block towers	
	d.	**hafta** buy feathers at the store.	2;7

Subjects are added at 2;9, along with third-person singular:

(38)	a.	Daddy **hasta** tear dese up?	2;9
	b.	'cause we **hafta** refold the cord.	3;0

A single past-tense version is imitated at 3;2 as Dad describes his drive on snowy roads in Texas and Seth tries to join in to the narration:

(39)	D:	we hadta slide on the ice 'n' hadta go real slow.	3;2
	S:	an' I **hadta** go really fast.	
	D:	no, slow.	

5.4 Like(ta)

The tapes contain four productions of *liketa* during Seth's third year. Its first appearance, *I liketa do da(t)* at 2;7, is preceded by Dad's *I'd like ta do that*. The other three instances occur at 2;10 (*Miss Ellen likes ta clean the water up*), and 3;0 (*I would like ta do hair dryer, anyway*). During Seth's fourth year we find a few of the form *like N to V*.

(40)	a.	because I **like** you **to** have it slow.	3;10
	b.	I dont **like** you **ta** use this kinda paint.	

5.5 Need(ta)

Similarly, *need(to)* occurs twice during Seth's third year, at 2;4 (*I need down*), and again at 2;11 (*I don't need to*). Between 3;0 and 4;1 there are twelve more instances, including third-person constructions at 3;6 (*now, my bunny needs ta get in* [the car] *now*), 3;10 (*oh, I think– your hair needs ta get on you* [pretending to cut Daddy's hair]), and 4;1 (*she needs to do it like that*).

5.6 Try(ta)

At 2;0.2 we find a single construction with *try*: [14] *try pull it.* The transcriptions do not show another until 2;11, when, while discussing a picture book with Daddy he says: *he's tryin' ta put a orange on his stocking?* The next instances at 3;8 are in the past tense as Seth describes his swimming lesson:

(41)   and – we – uh – **tried** to – uh - put our chin in the water,   3;8
an' we **tried** to go under the water,
an' we **tried** to hold onto the side of the pool,
an' we hold on to the side of the pool, and that's what we did.

At 3;10 Seth produces *try* constructions in the progressive (*because I'm trying to squeeze — take the pancakes off, of here*) and imperative (*try ta get it out for me?*).

6. Modals

Reflexes of *can* appear quite early among the protomodals, but evidence for other modals does not show up until 2;4 or so.[15]

6.1 Can

Not only is *can* steadily produced, it immediately resembles the adult modal target, appearing inverted as well as uninverted, and occurring with several subjects (*Daddy, I, you, we*).

(42)   a.   now-I can throw it? /naɪ kɪn fwrowɪt?/   2;3
           b.   we can go ta coffee shop.
           c.   can Da'y frow [the ball] at da picture?

Between 2;3 and 2;4.2 some eighteen of the thirty-two tokens of *can* have no expressed subject, e.g. (from the same tape): [I] *can make it go squeak; now* [we] *can go ta da coff*[ee] *shop!* From 2;5, however, subjects of *can* are overtly expressed (with only one exception out of over 200 tokens).

6.2 Ket > cant ~ cannot

Negative forms of *can* develop in an interesting way. Between 2;3 and 2;10 Seth produces seven tokens of a form we gloss as *ket*; it seems to be a blend of *can* and *cant* although it is often impossible to tell which was Seth's actual target.

The attested instances are:

(43)　a.　S:　ū-ū **ke** ta(lk) ta Mommy.　　　2;2.3
　　　　　　D:　ya gonna get the phone and talk to Mommy?
　　　b.　S:　ɔ̃ **kɛ̃** get the ball? *going to get it*　2;3.1
　　　c.　S:　[wh]ere's ə ball. now **ket** get it?　2;3.1
　　　d.　S:　⎰ m wanna **ket** frow it at da picture.　2;3.1
　　　　　　D:　⎱ Daddy was holdin' it, not lettin' im - get it.
　　　　　　S:　**ket** frow [it at] ə picture.
　　　e.　S:　Da'y **ket** sit on the dresser.　　2;6.3
　　　f.　S:　I wan' go find da Braille.　　2;8
　　　　　　D:　ok.
　　　　　　S:　ohhh, **ket**.

Alongside *ket*, Seth produces twelve instances of *cant* and six of *cannot* (the more local (General Hawai'i English) form of the negative), as illustrated in (44).

(44)　a.　dɪsə kɔ̃nɔ̃ — tsə kɪn ræp ɪ əp.　　2;4
　　　　　'disə **cannot**-so **can** wrap it up.'
　　　b.　betcha **cant** get in the bubble [bath] with you.　2;5.2
　　　c.　we **cannot** see it Dad.　　2;6
　　　d.　oh, I **cant**.　　[with a clear /n/]　2;10
　　　　　I **cant** count 'em.
　　　　　I **cant** be quiet.
　　　e.　S:　Dad, you **cannot** use this (kinda) paint.　3;10
　　　　　D:　why not?
　　　　　S:　because you **cant**.

It is noteworthy that in this last exchange he chooses *cannot* for the full sentence and *cant* for his ellipted reply.

6.3 *Could*

Seth's first few productions of *could* are sporadic and probably formulaic, based on Daddy's *could-you* questions and *we-could* speculations. At 2;8 he begins to experiment with it as an alternative way to make requests or announce intentions:

(45)　a.　Daddy could lie down wiv you?　　2;8.0
　　　　　ca(n) Daddy lie down wiv you on the carpet?
　　　b.　sha' we brush our teeth?　　2;8.2
　　　　　we could brush our teeth.
　　　　　I'mma brush my teeth?

c. could I take more strawberry juice. 2;8.3
I want some more strawberry juice.
d. I could get down. 2;8.3
I can get down.

At 2;9, however, it emerges as a full-fledged modal: it occurs with several different subjects (*then I could draw; you could do spices; what Daddy could find*) in semantically appropriate ways, although inversion in *wh*-questions is not yet under control. At 4;1 *could* is used to express past possibility:

(46) D: tell me about her house. 4;1
S: oh, sh:e has a sofa there. she has a lanai there.
what can you do on the — lanai. [trying to initiate the asking]
D: tell me. [wants Seth to do the telling]
S: ohhh, you **could** talk about things — [what they had done]
D: what can you see from there.
S: oh, we **could** see:: — the place where we li:ve.
D: that's right. that's right, Bird, we sure could!
[D is surprised at Seth's memory; this happened at least a month earlier]
S: we **could** see my Mommy's hou:se.
where sh — where Mommy li:ves.
D: we could see the canal out there. [4 sec.]
S: or we **could** see cars going — out the tunnelllls,
going through — the tunnellls.

Not until 3;6 does *could* become one of Seth's request-initiators; at this time we find a few *could'I* as well as *could'you* requests; e.g.:

(47) **could you** stop doing that? [very politely] 3;6
couldju feed birds with me?
Dad, **could I** make pancakes?

6.4 *Will*

After a slow and tentative beginning, *will* also achieves a fairly adult-like status by 3;0. Seth's early approximations are rather mushy imitations of Daddy. For example, the following exchange occurs at 2;4 when they are preparing to wrap a present for Mommy:

(48) D: and when Mommy comes, we'll give her a present. 2;4
we'll wrap it up with paper.

> S: wə **wə** wrap i' paper.
> D: pretty wrapping paper.
> S: pre(tty) wrappi' paper. **we'll** wrap it.
> D: yeah.

By 2;10 he knows how to use *will* when the main verb is ellipted: *I wanna stand up* [on the table] *an' look at the pinwheels. I will. I will*. And at 3;0 he is able to make complex constructions:

> (49) Daddy **will** put the comb away, an' I **will** put the hair dryer away.   3;0
> Daddy **will** play the guitar an' I **will** play the banjo.
> Daddy **will** close the door and — turn the light off.

The final development we see for *will* is at 3;10 when it occurs with many different subjects, including full NPs:

> (50) **this'll** be black to paint your hair black, ok?   3;10
> and then **EVERYbody'll** say, "oh, you have a green hair."
> an' when you come home, **it'll** be ALL ready fer you, ok?
> when you come home, your table an' stool **w'll** be ALL ready.

6.5 Wont

The negative *wont* appears only twice. The earlier one is in an imitation requested by Daddy when Seth is 2;10.

> (51) S: I'm a-scared of it.   2;10
> D: no, don't be scared so much, ok?
> S: (wa)nna – scare – be a – ...
> D: say ok, Dad, I won't be scared.
> S: ok, Dad, I **won't** be a-scared.

The complexity of the second, at 4;1, suggests that by now Seth fully controls *wont*, despite the lack of evidence in the transcriptions: *'cause, if you don't roast them you won't be able to eat 'em* (talking about the seeds in his Halloween pumpkin).

6.6 Would

The last modal clearly to emerge is *would*.[16] In the amalgamated form *wouldja* it is another of the "polite-request-initiators" that Daddy encourages, but it is relatively infrequent, appearing only some seven times with this function. At 2;4 Seth imitates Daddy's production:

(52) D: wouldju please throw this [wet diaper] in the rubbish? 2;4
S: **wouldja** throw this in ə rubbish for Daddy?

By 2;11 Daddy expects Seth to ask politely, and prompts for a more acceptable form:

(53) S: I want some water, Dad? 2;11
D: say ...
S: **wouldja** get some water?
D: yeah.

Two similar prompts occur at 3;0. Other uses of *would*, however, suggest that it, too, is on its way to achieving modal status:

(54) a. **would** dis fit in dere? [putting saffron back in jar] 2;8
b. I **would** liketa do hair dryer, anyway. 3;0
c. you **would** pour da butter? [monolog about making popcorn] 3;0
d. what **would** I say if ya splash in da water. 3;4
what — **wouldju** say if I spl —
what will YOU say if I splash in the water.
e. oh, **I'd** like some breakfast. 3;10
f. we have three songs that we **would** like to sing with you. 3;10
[imitating the master of ceremonies he had seen earlier]

In summary, Seth seems to control *can, will, could,* and *would* by 4;0.

7. Auxiliaries

The largest class to differentiate out of the protomodals is the auxiliaries (*be, do,* and *have*), including inflected forms (present and past tense and negation). Since Seth produces almost no *have* auxiliaries in the transcripts[17] (and his father produces very few) the focus here is on forms of *do* (*do, does, dont, did*) and *be* (*is, are, am, was, were*). Rather than trace the full development of each auxiliary, we focus on their shift from syntactically undifferentiated protomodals or amalgams to auxiliaries. The primary evidence for a separate class of auxiliaries is their inflectability.

Incorporated into Seth's amalgams are the adult auxiliaries *did, do* and *are,* and from 2;4 more recognizable (proto)auxiliaries begin to appear: *do* and *is,* then *are,* then *am.* Seemingly distinct from *do, dont* also begins to combine with pronouns. The evidence suggests that at first each emerging auxiliary is locked in an amalgam.

7.1 Do *auxiliaries*

The *do* auxiliaries approach their adult targets fairly straightforwardly. The increases in variety of constructions produced suggest 3;2 as the best candidate for a "point of acquisition".

7.1.1 *Do*

In our discussion of amalgams we saw that, although *do* seems to burst in at 2;4 with some 20 instances, they are all *do+you*; we concluded that *dyou* was a request former. (See examples in (19).) This usage persists through 2;7. At 2;10 Seth seems to be becoming more aware of auxiliaries; he is showing some confusion about when to use *do* as opposed to *are*:

(55)   how **do** we gon' get down.[18]   2;10

The biggest breakthough comes at 3;3 when *do* attains a new versatility: the 15 occurrances include two *wh*-questions (*which color do you like, what do you call me*), seven *yn*-questions (one *do we*, six *do you know/ want/understand*), and six elliptical constructions (*yes you/they do!*).

7.1.2 *Does*

At 2;8, *does* makes its first appearance with four tokens:

(56)   **does** DA'Y'S like dill?   2;8
        d's it comes out of a plastic bag?
        does i' means 'down'? [n = 2]

From this small amount of evidence it looks as if Seth first uses *does* as a question-starter with third-person subjects, not yet aware that it incorporates the **third singular** inflection. There may be some confusion with *is*, since we find one occurrence of *is it taste good?*

After this first appearance, *does* seems to go underground until 3;3, when we find Seth actively struggling with it. He produces some 20 instances, formed on a small number of patterns:

(57)   what **does** your car do   [n = 1]   3;3
        where **does** lions/chickens/bees/cow live   [n = 5]
        what **does** squirrels/ cows/pigs/chickens eat   [n = 7]
        what sound **does** a pig/the lion make   [n = 4]

Evidence of the effort he is expending on the role and placement of *does* can be seen in the following set of variations:

(58)   what **does** the lion make   3;3
       what **d-** what sound **does** the lion make
       what **does** a sound **does** a pig make, Dad.

It seems likely that he still has not registered that *does* includes **third singular**: many of the subjects are plural *(lions, chickens, bees, pigs, squirrels)*, although we also find the singulars *car, cow, lion, sound*.
After 3;3 *does* subsides again. The only other constructions of interest are two *yn*-questions at 3;6 in which he is now able to invert *does*:

(59)   **does** this – have da one?   3;6
       does it have li'l yel- a little bit blue and orange?

7.1.3 Dont

At first *dont* seems to be unsegmented. At 2;4 Seth uses it primarily in self-prohibitions (negative imperatives), which he models on Daddy's directives to him. Examples are:

(60)   **dont** step on Daddy's feet!   2;4
       dont stand on Daddy's back.
       but **dont** drop it.

But by 2;5 there is evidence that *dont* is functioning like a negative auxiliary, even though it may not yet be fully analyzed into *do+not*:

(61)   I **dont** find da Y. [one of his letter cards]   2;5
       I **don'** wanna —
       ya **don'** like that hah?

At 2;9 Seth uses *dont* as an auxiliary in an elliptical response:

(62)   D: d'ya need ta go ta the potty?   2;9
       S: I **dont**.

I dunno is a formulaic phrase incorporating *dont* that appears at this time as well. The sixteen *dont* constructions at 2;11 and 3;0, all with *I* as subject, include:

(63)   I **don'** need to.   2;11
       I **don'** like you.   [n = 2]
       I **don'** want NP.   [n = 4]
       I **don'** wanna (VP).   [n = 7]
       I **don'** like da hairdryer.   3;0
       I **don'** remember dis.

At 3;3 we find the first negative imperatives with *dont*, all six of the form *dont say X*. An interesting construction, suggesting that *dunno* is not yet fully analyzed is:

(64)   I **dunno know** how ta burp.   3;3

Finally, at 3;4 Seth produces a *dont* construction with *you* as subject:

(65)   you **dont** have ta wash 'em.   3;4

He attempts a negated raised construction with *dont wannu* at 2;10, but does not yet seem to have sufficiently analyzed this chunk to be able to insert *you* in its proper position as subject of the raised verb:

(66)   I doN wannu — show me somep'm.[19]   2;10
   =   'I don't want you to show me anything.'

By 3;6 however, he controls raising with *dont*, as witness:

(67)   now, Dad, I **dont** wantchu ta play too hard, ok?   3;6
   I **dont** want him to play with it.

And by 3;8 *dont* appears in a variety of constructions, including elliptical *(no) I/we dont*, prohibitive *dont VP*, and statements with different subjects *I/we/you dont VP* and with a variety of verbs (*put, know, spank, say, like*). By 4;1 he is even producing counterfactuals:

(68)   'cause, if you **dont** roast them you wont be able to eat 'em.   4;1

7.1.4 *Did*

We have noted Seth's early amalgam *didja*. Except for two imitations (*I-did* at 2;4, *did-we* at 2;5), this is the only form in which *did* appears until 2;6 when we find a new amalgam with *did*, the *wh*-question-former *wha'did*:

(69)   **wha'dI** WE do.   2;6
   wha'dishu have ta eat.
   wha'didja get at that coffee shop?

At the same time, *did* is breaking free of the *you* in *didja*, so that we begin to find *yn*-questions with different subjects:

(70)   **did** Mommy sleep already?   2;6
   did Julia write'cher name?   [reporting an incident at school]
   did Myrna give you watermelon?
   did Daddy drink the water.
   did we throw da leave[s] in ə water fountain?

Although *didju/didja* retains the phonological character of an amalgam, other subjects continue to appear with *did*. It seems fair to claim full productivity for auxiliary *did* soon after 2;6.

7.1.5 *Didnt*

The past negative *didnt* first appears at 2;9, but only once. Although it is modeled by Dad on this occasion, Seth changes pronouns appropriately. On the other hand, he seems not to be sure whether *didnt* contains *not*:

(71) D: didju make doodoo? 2;9
 S: no —
 D: ya didnt? dya need to?
 S: **I didn nah.**
 D: dya need ta go ta the potty?
 S: I dont.

Since *didnt* occurs a total of only five times in the transcriptions we can not trace Seth's analysis of it with any certainty. At 2;10 he merely echoes Dad's *we didn't*, but the few subsequent examples suggest that *didnt* comes to function as a negative auxiliary with a variety of subjects, a variety of verbs, and in a variety of constructions:

(72) no you **didnt**. [response to an assertion by D] 3;3
 they [birds at the park] **didnt** eat out my hand. 3;6
 I **didnt** make pan(cakes) yet. 3;8
 they **di'nt** roast them [pumpkin seeds] yet. 4;1
 he made a noise, **didnt** he.

7.2 Be *auxiliaries*

We noted that the proto-auxiliary **IZ** may have blended *is*, *lets*, *does*, and *didja* (examples in (15), and that the first identifiable appearance of the *be* auxiliaries is in the amalgams *əmmə* (20), *areya*, *whichre*, and *whatre* (22). All 17 productions of auxiliary-like *is* at 2;4 are embedded in the amalgam *Daddys-gonna*, many echoing the ways Daddy tends to narrate ongoing actions. Seth's productions include:

(73) **Daddys-gonna** get you too'paste. 2;4
 Da's-ga gitchu some more water right now.
 Daddys-gon' put training pants on.
 Daddys-gonna cook you two eggs.

Auxiliary *is* emerges slowly, with some confusion as to its placement, possibly influenced by the prevalence of an amalgamated copula construction *whats*.

(74) what **Da'ys** gonna [do]. 2;6
 Daddys gettin' [i]n'a bubble[bath].
 Da'ys gonna drink a water. 2;7
 whats Daddys doing now? 2;8

From 2;9 Seth's *be*-auxiliaries become better segmented, increase in frequency, and are used in more adult-like ways.

7.2.1 *Is*

The variation at 2;9 suggests that Seth is still struggling with several aspects of auxiliary *is*: at least once he fails to add the progressive ending to the main verb (*whats Daddy take off*), and he is still working on inversion in questions, although he does get it right once:

(75) what **Daddys** giving you. 2;9
 (wh)ere **Daddys** going.
 Daddys making flash cards for you?
 an' **Dads** gon' put U? [referring to his letter cards]
 is Daddy gon' [do] [a]naddr —

Difficulties with inversion of *is* persist through 3;0 with the most obvious struggle taking place at that time.

(76) what **Seth's** doing. 2;10
 what **Daddy's** gonna have.
 what's Seth gonna do. 2;11
 wha' **Da'y is** doing 3;0
 is a ace **is** for play'in the band
 is a kitchen light **is** blinking?

I have found no further errors in placement of auxiliary *is* after 3;2. There is only a single transcribed instance of *isnt*, at 3;6:

(77) my bunny **isn't** gonna stay in here. 3;6

7.2.2 *Are*

Turning to *are*, at 2;9 Seth is working on the relation between *what-are*, *what-do*, *what-did*, and *what-does*. Examples include:

(78)	what it mean.	what does	2;9
	whatcha do at school.	what do/did?	
	what Daddy do/find.	what did	
	what Seth made?	what did	
	whatta I'm doing.	what am I	2;10
	whatta we do at Kailua beach.	what did	
	what d'Auntie put on [my sting].	what did	
	what Auntie put on.	what did	

Although the *whatta* seems to have gone underground on the tape at 2;9, it resurfaces at 2;10. Now, however, it seems to have lost its earlier and clearer connection with *what're*. We find further experimentation with *what'did*:

(79)	what d'Auntie put on [my sting].	2;9
	what Auntie put on.	

The only sentences with *are* at 2;11 are statements, and we see no problems with its inclusion or placement:

(80)	all da rabbits are goin' up da stairs.	2;11
	they're hanging [ornaments] on the Christmas tree?	

An elliptical *we're not* appears at 3;0, along with a single *yn*-question in which his recast suggests some lingering confusion about constituent order.

(81)	we're going to — we're going to — *we're not*.	3;0
	are gonna — *are* we gonna use ə hair dryer?	

Some small problems persist at 3;2 where we find variations in production of *wh*-questions in the progressive. Difficulty with placement of *are* in certain constructions is also evident in his elliptical *yes you're sure are!* (in response to his own question *are you talking?*), even though he generally has it correct in statements.

(82)	**what are** you putting your foot on?	[early in the tape]	3;2
	what're you put your head on?	[much later]	
	wha're you wearing?		
	what're you doing.	[several times]	
	are you talking?		
	yes **you're** sure **are**!		

From 3;4 no further problems with auxiliary *are* are found.

7.2.3 Am

The first person singular form *am* blossoms at 2;9, with eight instances. Since, however, seven of these are of the form *I'm gon(na) X*, *am* may be part of an amalgamated *I'm-gon'*. The eighth sentence, *I'm drinkin' my water*, supports at least an amalgamated *I'm*. Productivity increases sharply to some twenty-seven sentences at 2;10. Most of these are statements of intention: *I'm gonna X*. There are also two descriptions of activities in progress (*I'm doin' Braille; I'm rockin' in the rockin' chair*). Of greatest interest is a repeated question with both *whatta* and *I'm* (*whatta I'm doing?*), and a statement that suggests difficulty in segmenting *I'm gonna: I'mma do very good at Braille*. A similar utterance appears at 2;11: *mmə throw* ('I'm gonna(?) throw'), alongside some five *I'm gonna X*, and two *I'm* progressives.

Another surge of *I'm* constructions occurs at 3;3. These include three more *whatta I'm Xing* questions (*whatta I'm mm wearing; whatta I'm lying on*, twice), and three would-be progressives that lack the *-ing* inflection (all of the form *I'm put my foot on NP*). There are also eight well-formed progressives and twelve *I'm gonna X* constructions. There are no new developments with *am* at 3;4 except for the appearance of the first negative construction: *I'm not cleaning it up*. Two more negatives occur at 3;6, both variants of *I'm not gonna show him*, and seven at 3;10.2. The other progress can be seen in the series of quite well-formed questions that Seth produces at 3;10.2. His problem with segmentation of *whatta* that we saw at 2;10 and 3;2 is now resolved, although his pronunciation of *what am I* is sometimes a bit mushy. The *wh*-questions at 3;10.2 are:

(83) wha'**m I** doing. 3;10.2
  what'**m I** doing.
  what **am I** painting.
  where'**m I** goin' after bed.
  what color **am I** painting you.
  how **I'm** doin' da scissors.

There are also two correctly inverted *yn*-questions:

(84) 'm I goin to Bubby's? [Bubby is his baby sitter] 3;10.2
  am I painting?

Auxiliary *am* is quite adult-like by 4;0.

7.2.4 Was and were

The last *be* auxiliaries to appear are *was* and *were*, at 2;6. Both occur in the (memorized) context of story retelling: *da[t's] wha[t] I was thinking;* [*what*] *were'ya thinking*. The next instance is at 2;10, a single production of *was*, in response to a modelling question:

(85)   D: what were they doin'.   2;10
       S: they were playin' the banjo.

At 2;11 Seth seems a bit unsure of which form to use. Not only do we find the uninverted *I was — finished*, we also see him trying out *whatta* with these auxiliaries as well. The exchange in (85) shows both his use of *whatta* and his unsureness about whether to use *was* or *were*.

(86)   S: wha'a I **was** doing on my plastic bag. [what he sits]   2;11
       D: hunh?
       S: wha'a I **were** doing dere.

After this the few instances that occur are correct, with both ellipted and negative constructions occurring at 3;3 (*he wasn't; yes he was!*) At 4;1 he produces a pair correctly inflected for number: *he was making noise; they were making noise*.
In summary, by 4;0 Seth controls most forms of the auxiliaries *be* and *do*, including negative and past tense. There is as yet no evidence that he knows about *have*.

8. Conclusion

Although catenatives, which involve two verbs (the first finite, the second not) and a possibility of two subjects, seem complex in adult grammar, Seth's developmental sequence shows how they could originate in a **simple single-subject construction** in which the main verb is modified by one of a single class of protomodals: *SUBJ PM VP*. We have simply and naturally described the development of Seth's modals, auxiliaries, and catenatives as taking place through the phonological, functional, and syntactic differentiation of an initial fuzzy protomodal "slot". This approach to early syntactic development was driven by two assumptions:

– our understanding of language development must be grounded in what makes perceptual, functional, and cognitive sense for learners;
– learners can and do create **partial** and **increasingly specific** analyses of grammatical forms which **gradually** approach their adult targets.

At the outset I suggested that one mechanism through which such gradual analysis can take place is the "holding tank" afforded by an at first undifferentiated class of "fillers" — in this case the class of Protomodals. In association with such a position, enough information is accumulated about the members of the class to allow its analysis into more adult-like classes. If this developmental picture is at all general for English-learning children, the sequence goes something like this:

    Children in their second year can distinguish nouns from verbs from "other forms".[20]

    On the basis of **phonological presence** alone, they separate out an undifferentiated pre-verbal class of Protomodals, which includes all the regularly occurring catenatives, auxiliaries, and modals.

    They continue to collect information about the linguistic properties of these forms.

    They may or may not begin to reproduce their protomodals as filler syllables; if they do, they will not assume them to be forms to which inflections can be added.

    With experience with the language, they can use information from **phonology**, **semantics** (how the meaning of the following verb is modified), and **syntax** (cooccurrence privileges) to differentiate members of this class from each other.

    Eventually they subdivide the protomodals into three classes: catenatives, auxiliaries, and modals.

Notes

1. Even though not all of syntax can be accounted for in this way, it is nevertheless an instructive exercise.
2. Weissenborn (personal communication) notes that, because the complementizer **that** can be omitted in English, catenatives are useful as markers of upcoming embedded clauses. See also Höhle et al. (this volume).
3. George Grace proposed this to me. Levelt's suggestion that modals can be treated as main verbs that take verbal complements seems to me to be part of the same functional view of English verbs (1989, p. 197). See also Lebeaux, this volume.
4. This "holding tank" is somewhat similar to Slobin's "waiting room" (Johnston & Slobin 1979). However, in my understanding the waiting room is a place for a perceived form to "wait" until the learner knows enough to produce it, whereas the holding tank is a locus for the accumulation of further information concerning a class of forms.
5. Ages are given in years;months(.weeks).
6. Since Daddy regularly says **oh, come to Dad** as an offer to pick Seth up, Seth may have built this construction as **let-Dad + come-to-Dad**.
7. Except for one at 2;5.2, one at 3;6 and two at 4;1.
8. **shishi** is a local word for 'urinate'.
9. Elements in parenthesis are optionally included.

10. It is difficult to be sure of his intended target — candidates are **should we, shall we, should I, shall I**.
11. Name of a Hebrew letter.
12. Note, however, that the **to** often does not make it to the surface of an utterance.
13. Although Seth sometimes says **hadda** and sometimes **hafta**, there is no evidence until he is over 3 years old that he makes any systematic distinction between these forms. For this reason I interpret the ones in this set as phonological variants.
14. Seth's use of **try** may be based partly on the local variety of English, in which a common way to mitigate an imperative is to prepose **try**. Thus, **Try come** is considered more polite than **Come!** William O'Grady (personal communication) suggests that the absence of the infinitive marker **to** makes this similar to a serial verb construction at this stage.
15. Between 1;11 and 2;4 I only find three possible occurrences of **will**, two of which are parts of memorized phrases, and one of **would**.
16. I have already discussed **should** (and **shall**, since it is difficult to be sure of Seth's intended target) with the amalgams because its primary use is in the request-initiator **sh'we**. At 3;8 he does produce three clear instances of **shall we**, with a more modal meaning: **what else shall we talk about; shall we talk about Buzz's? shall we talk about, uh, Grandma and Grandpa's house?** No more recur in the transcripts, however.
17. The only two occurrences I find are one of contracted **have** at 2;1 (**I've got a red one**), and one of contracted **had** at 3;6 (**think I'd better do it a — try it again**).
18. One possibility is that he has substituted **do** for **are**; another is that he preposed an amalgamated **how-do-we** to a VP. I don't have frequency counts, but his father sometimes tried to elicit speech from Seth by asking him a **how do we X** question.
19. It looks likely that at some level this was formed by juxtaposing two partially analyzed amalgams: **I-dont-wannu + show-me-something**. The context was that they were looking at Seth's letter cards and Seth was resisting doing another one. BW often said **let me show you something**.
20. I do not think that they even need to be able to distinguish lexical from functional categories as Stromswold proposes; they only need be able to identify the most content-bearing words in an utterance and be predisposed to focus on them. The interaction patterns of several properties of the ambient language will aid in this task, including acoustical salience, frequency, and mappability to the surrounding context.

References

Bloom, L. 1991. *Language Development from Two to Three.* New York: Cambridge University Press.
Braine, M. D. S. 1994. "Is nativism sufficient?" *Journal of Child Language* 21: 9–31.
Brown, R. 1973. *A First Language: The Early Stages.* Cambridge, MA: Harvard University Press.
Johnston, J. R. & Slobin, D. I. 1979. "The development of locative expressions in English, Italian, Serbo-Croatian and Turkish." *Journal of Child Psychology* 6: 529–545.
Levelt, W. J. M. 1989. *Speaking: from intention to articulation.* Cambridge, MA: MIT Press.

Limber, J. 1973. "The genesis of complex sentences." In *Cognitive development and the acquisition of language*, T. E. Moore (ed.). New York: Academic Press.

Peters, A. M. 1987. "The role of imitation in the developing syntax of a blind child." *Text* 7: 289–311.

Peters, A. M. 1993. "The interdepencence of social, cognitive and linguistic development: Evidence from a visually-impaired child." In *Constraints on language acquisition: Studies of atypical children*, H. Tager-Flusberg (ed.). Hillsdale, NJ: Lawrence Erlbaum Associates.

Peters, A. M. 1997. "Language typology, prosody and the acquisition of grammatical morphemes." In *The Crosslinguistic Study of Language Acquisition*, Vol. 5, D. I. Slobin (ed.). Hillsdale, NJ: Lawrence Erlbaum Associates.

Peters, A. M. & Boggs, S. T. 1986. "Interaction routines as cultural influences upon language acquisition." In *Language socialization across cultures*, B. B. Schieffelin & E. Ochs (eds.). Cambridge, MA: Cambridge University Press.

Peters, A. M. & Menn, L. 1993. "False starts and filler syllables: Ways to learn grammatical morphemes." *Language* 69: 742–777.

Stromswold, K. 1995. "The cognitive and neural bases of language acquisition." In *The cognitive neurosciences*, M. S. Gazzaniga (ed.). Cambridge, MA: MIT Press.

Wilson, B. 1986. *The Emergence of the Semantics of Tense and Aspect in the Language of a Visually Impaired Child*. Unpublished Ph. D. dissertation; University of Hawai'i.

Wilson, B. & Peters, A. M. 1988. "What are you cooking on a hot?: A three-year-old blind child's 'violation' of universal constraints on constituent movement." *Language* 64: 249–273.

Input and Production in the Early Development of Function Words

Sven Strömqvist
University of Lund

Hrafnhildur Ragnarsdóttir
University College of Education, Reykjavík

Ulla Richthoff
University of Göteborg

Introduction

The present paper is concerned with aspects of the interaction between input and production in the early development of function words. For the present purpose function words are defined as a subset of closed class items distinguished by the syntactic property of being words or clitics and not affixes or process morphemes belonging to the internal morphological structure of word forms (cf., Bybee 1985).

Analyses are presented to shed light on dimensions and cues that play a role in the transition or "interface" between early phonetic development (perception and production) and early grammatical development. Exploring longitudinal case studies from the three closely related Scandinavian languages Danish, Icelandic and Swedish, the analyses focus on the dimensions of frequency, stress, and ambiguity. Our general research questions include: *What cues does the child make use of to arrive at a distinction between closed class and open class items? In particular, what cues are useful for discovering function words? Are particular configurations of cues (stress, frequency, ambiguity) conducive to particular developmental paths? What principles of continuity in development are instantiated in the data?*

In a first set of analyses the emergence of spatial particles or adverbs in Danish, Icelandic and Swedish children are analysed. Each of these three typologically minimally different languages has its own particular configuration of the verb + particle construction in terms of prosodic and syntactic properties. These different configurations, as evidenced in the input to the children, seem to push the children to learn the construction in different ways: either preferably by rote or preferably by analysis of the component parts. This first set of analyses explores the role of stress in the child's task of solving the "segmentation problem", that is, of ferreting out the units of the surrounding speech (cf., e.g., Clark & Clark 1977: 328).

A second set of analyses departs from the top 20 word forms (all function words) in the input and production data from 4 Swedish longitudinal case studies comprising in total around 350.000 tokens. The phonetic/phonological and semantic/functional properties of these forms are analysed and selective developmental analyses are presented. This second set of analyses thus also explore determinants to the child's task of solving the "mapping problem", that is, of mapping units of speech (forms) onto concepts (functions) (cf., again, Clark & Clark 1977).

Implications of these two sets of analyses for a theory of the interface between early phonetic development and early grammatical development are discussed.

The impact of stress: A within language group comparison

Several previous studies have demonstrated that child directed adult speech often differs from adult directed adult speech along many linguistic dimensions: lexical, syntactic, pragmatic and phonetic (see, e.g., Snow & Ferguson 1977). As to phonetic traits, in child directed speech adults often exaggerate the tonal and temporal profile of adult directed adult speech. For a crosslinguistic study demonstrating that effect, see Fernald et al. (1989). Moreover, it is likely that these prosodic modifications may help the child solve the segmentation problem in that they help the child direct his/her attention to certain elements of the input speech stream rather than others. The items in the input speech falling within the zones of this prosodic prominence tend to be major parts of speech, seldom function words, and almost never affixes.

A hypothesis concerned with the more exceptional situation when grammatical morphemes receive prosodic "spotlight" is formulated by Peters & Strömqvist (1996). Their "Spotlight Hypothesis" reads

Perceptually salient prosodic patterns, including pitch contours, rhythm, and increased duration, may serve as "spotlights" on any phonological forms that are regularly associated with these patterns; if such forms happen to be grammatical morphemes, learners will focus on them earlier than on morphemes not so spotlighted.

The Spotlight Hypothesis thus concerns children's *perception* of salient prosody that fortuitously coincides with grammatical morphemes, with evidence to be drawn from what children *produce* and from the parental input children receive. The Spotlight Hypothesis represents an attempt to bridge the gap between studies of infant perception (focusing on the first year of life) on the one hand and studies of early grammatical development (typically, from 18 months and onwards) on the other.

Peters & Strömqvist further argue in favour of a crosslinguistic approach using a within language group design comparing languages which are typologically minimally different. This would allow us to explore with greater accuracy the impact of linguistic details, such as variations in the prosodic configuration of an item or construction, on acquisition structure.

This kind of crosslinguistic design is implemented in an inter-Nordic project (Strömqvist et al. 1995b), where we explore the "natural linguistic laboratory" offered by the minimal variation between the Scandinavian languages. Our exploration of the typologically closely related Scandinavian languages Danish, Icelandic and Swedish, mainly on the basis of longitudinal case study materials from around 12 to 40 months of age, has yielded, among other things, some evidence in support of the spotlight hypothesis. More specifically, we will here review evidence of the impact of stress on acquisition structure in two linguistic domains: the development of particles and prepositions, and the development of the verb + particle construction. For reasons of the overall design in the inter-Nordic project, the analyses are restricted to items encoding spatial relations (see Strömqvist et al. 1995b).

Particles versus prepositions

Across the component longitudinal case studies from Danish, Icelandic and Swedish children, Ragnarsdóttir & Strömqvist (1997) found that

1. morphemes with both high input frequency and stress (as evidenced in the parental input) emerge earlier than items with high input frequency but no stress; thus, particles like *upp* 'up', *ner* 'down', *in* 'into', and *ut* 'out', emerge before prepositions.[1]

2. phonological forms which are ambiguous between particle and preposition make their debut as particle, that is, with stress. This last point will be discussed in greater detail below.

In Danish and Swedish, just as in English, prepositions are unstressed (except in adversative contexts) and verb particles are stressed. The phonological forms occurring as particles are thus prosodically spotlighted and can, in effect, be expected to be attended to and internalized earlier by the child than forms occurring as prepositions. Further, some phonological forms can occur both as prepositions and as particles, e.g., *i* 'in' and *på* 'on'. And we find across the two Danish and the two Swedish case studies we have analysed so far, that, indeed, the first prepositions to emerge in the children's production are forms that also occur as particles in the specific input to these children. Our "template" hypothesis (Strömqvist et al. 1995a) is that the child's representation of a form occurring in stressed position may serve as a template for the representation of the corresponding form occurring in non-stressed position. Assume that children first establish the phonological form of a particle/preposition on the basis of its occurrences in stressed (i.e., particle) position. They can then use this information to help them recognize these forms when they occur as unstressed phrase-internal prepositions. On this account we would expect that it is precisely these dual particle-prepositions that will be the first prepositions produced in early grammatical development. The template hypothesis is in harmony with the auditory priming learning mechanism postulated by Fisher & Church (this volume).

We observed above that the first handful of particles in Scandinavian child language development also includes the adverbs/particles *in* 'in$_{dir}$', *upp* 'up', *ner* 'down', and *ut* 'out'. If we turn to Icelandic, the corresponding items are ambiguous between adverb and preposition and their status is determined by context. When they occur in a verb phrase like *hljóp út*[2] 'ran out' they are classified as adverbs according to Icelandic grammatical descriptions (see, e.g., Þráinsson 1990). In this type of construction both the verb and the adverbial element receive stress, that is **V** + **PRT**, where boldface indicates the stressed item(s).[3] And when they occur in unstressed position before NP, they count as prepositions, for example *hljóp út ganginn* 'ran out$_{dir}$ the corridor', that is, **V** + PREP + NP. A consequence of this set of distributional properties is that the great majority of phonological forms that can serve as prepositions (unstressed) can also appear in stressed position, namely when they are used as adverbs. In Swedish (or Danish) the class of items of which the same distributional properties are true constitutes a smaller class. Again, on the assumption that children adopt the strategy of establishing the phonological forms in question on the basis of their occurrences in stressed (rather than unstressed) position, Icelandic children would be able to apply this strategy to a greater number of items than their Swedish or Danish peers.

To explore this hypothesis empirically, the set of prepositions which the Swedish longitudinal subject "Markus" produced by 24 months of age was compared with the corresponding data from the Icelandic subject "Ari". The difference found in the production data from Ari (Icelandic) and Markus (Swedish) at 24 months is striking: 13 different prepositions for Ari and only 3 for Markus. The respective sets of prepositions are specified in Table 1. There are no indications that this difference follows from an overall difference in grammatical level between the two children such that Ari would be more advanced than Markus. Across the data points from Ari at 24 months, Ari's MLU in terms of number of words per utterance is 2.33, that is, indicative of Brown's "stage 2" speech (Brown 1973). The corresponding figure for Markus is MLU 3.11.

Table 1. *Prepositions produced by Ari (Icelandic) and Markus (Swedish) at 24 months of age*

Ari (Icelandic)		Markus (Swedish)	
í	'in$_{loc/dir}$'	*i*	'in'
inní	'inside$_{loc/dir}$'		
oní	'down-into'		
á	'on'	*på*	'on'
uppá	'up-on$_{loc/dir}$'		
niðrá	'down-on$_{loc/dir}$'		
af	'off'		
til	'to'	*till*	'to'
frá	'from'		
hjá	'by/with'		
undir	'under$_{loc/dir}$'		
yfir	'over$_{loc/dir}$'		
upp	'up$_{dir}$'		

Also, there are no corresponding differences in the input data to the two children; in fact, the input data are identical in terms of type frequency: 23 different prepositions in the input to Ari and 23 to Markus. There is a striking difference between the Icelandic and the Swedish input, however, in terms of how the respective 23 items are distributed over positions with and without stress. Out of the 23 Icelandic items 13 were also used as adverbs. That means that the phonological forms of 13 of the 23 prepositions occurred with stress in the input to the child. The corresponding figures for Markus is just 3 of 23 (3 out of 23 prepositions were also used as particles). The three prepositions in question were the same three as Markus produced in his own speech by 24 months of age, i.e., *i* 'in', *på* 'on', and *till* 'to'.

The verb + particle construction

A linguistic sub-system where the otherwise minimally different Scandinavian languages reveal systematic differences is the verb + particle/adverb construction. (see Ragnarsdóttir & Strömqvist 1997; Strömqvist et al. 1995a; Strömqvist et al. 1995b). The different prosodic and syntactic configurations of the verb + particle construction in Danish, Icelandic and Swedish are illustrated by means of the phrase 'take it out' in examples (4)–(6).

(4) Danish   ta *det* **ud**
(5) Icelandic **taka** *það* **ut**
(6) Swedish   ta **ut** *det*
    where boldface indicates stressed words

The Danish pattern lays stress on the particle (**ud**) and places the pronominal object (*det*) between the verb and its particle. Icelandic stresses both the verb and the particle/adverb (cf., footnote 3) and places the pronominal object in the same way as in Danish. Swedish has phrasal stress on the particle and keeps verb and particle together, so that the pronominal object comes after the particle. Our hypothesis is that these differences should lead Danish, Icelandic and Swedish children to analyse their respective inputs in a somewhat different manner. The Swedish pattern with phrasal stress on the particle and syntactic contiguity between the verb and the particle would appear to make it easier, to begin with, to learn the construction as an unanalysed whole (rote-learning). The Icelandic pattern with separate stress on the verb and on the particle/adverb and syntactic material between them should on the other hand lead the child to analyse them as two separate units (instead of one). As for the Danish configuration with syntactic material between the verb and the particle and stress on the particle only, it helps make the particle very noticeable (stressed and in phrase final position, which often involves extra duration), with the verb more in the background.

In order to test the hypothesis as to whether the different patterns lead preferably to analysis or preferably to rote-learning, we consulted our longitudinal case study material of the inter-Nordic project. In order further to improve the precision of the crosslinguistic comparison, we selected case studies of children who had as similar a verb vocabulary as possible at the time of early language development (before the age of 24 months). This gave us three children with a very similar profile apart from the variables to be tested: "Anne" (Danish, 13;01–23;26), "Edda" (Icelandic, 8;00–25;01) and "Markus" (Swedish, 15;19–24;09). We then identified particle/adverb candidates in the children's utterances from the data points which were available for the three children up to the age of 24 months and classified these morphemes according to whether they constituted one-word utterances or were part of multi-word utterances. The results of this analysis are summarized in Table 2.

Table 2 shows that the Danish child (Anne) starts using particles earlier than the Icelandic or the Swedish child. Moreover she produces particles as one-word utterances at first (saying, e.g., *op* 'up'), which shows that she has analysed (extracted) these particles (forms) from the language to which she has been exposed. When Anne later begins to combine particles with other words into multi-word utterances, it is not verbs she chooses in the first place, but nouns, pronouns and certain adverbs (such as *ikke på* 'not on', *den op* 'that up', etc.). With the Icelandic child (Edda), particles/adverbs emerge later, alternating at first in one-word or multi-word utterances (and then preferably including a verb). Edda's pattern shows that she has analysed verbs and particles/adverbs as being different units, also that verbs and particles/adverbs are in close relationship with each other. When particles make their appearance with the Swedish child (Markus), it is exclusively in multi-word utterances and in the great majority of the cases with a verb — a pattern which indicates that, for a majority of verbs and particles, he has learnt verb + particle as one unit. The crosslinguistic analysis thus yields three distinct development patterns, — one for each characteristic combination of prosodic and syntactic properties in the child's specific language input.

For comparable studies of other languages within the Germanic language group, demonstrating a precocious development of verb particles, see Bennis et al. (1995) (Dutch and German) and Behrens (1998) (Dutch, English and German).

The most frequent word forms and their properties

Input versus production

Let us now redirect our attention from function words encoding spatial relations to the most frequent word forms in general. Which are the most frequent word

Table 2. *The distribution of particles/adverbs on one-word and multi-word utterances in the early language development of three Scandinavian children*

Danish, "Anne", 13–24 months

Period	one-word utterances with spat. adv/prt	multi-word utterances with spat. adv/prt
13;01–18;20	49	1
19;04–22;17	69	44
23;18–23;26	1	22

Icelandic, "Edda", 8–25 months

Period	one-word utterances with spat. adv/prt	multi-word utterances with spat. adv/prt
8;00–19;00	0	0
20;03–22;14	19	29
23;27–25;01	1	22

Swedish, "Markus", 15–24 months

Period	one-word utterances with spat. adv/prt	multi-word utterances with spat. adv/prt
15;19–20;05	0	0
21;07–22;25	0	18
23;00–24;09	1	92

forms a child gets to hear? And which are the most frequent ones in his own production? The Swedish child language corpus of our inter-Nordic project allows us to attempt a first reply to that question. The corpus, which is accessible in machine readable format, consists of longitudinal data (audio and video-recordings) from everyday activities (parent-child interaction) from four Swedish, monolingually raised children from around 18 to 40 months of age. At present, the corpus consists of around 350.000 words distributed over 120 data points. See further Strömqvist et al. (1993).[4]

In a first round, we carried out an analysis of the entire corpus (120 data points) as two sub-corpora: the one consisting of all adult utterances and the other of all child utterances. Frequency lists of all word forms were constructed for both sub-corpora. The frequencies were calculated on transcribed word forms and the transcriptions had been made in a speech-imitative variant of Swedish orthography, in contrast to a strictly orthographic written language representation of the word forms. For instance, the transcription reads *va e de* and not *vad är det* 'what is that'. In this example the transcribed form *va* is thus ambiguous between (at least) *vad*, 'what', *var* 'where', and *va* (as in the exclamation *va?!* 'what?!').[5]

Table 3 shows the 20 most frequent word forms in the two sub-corpora derived in the first round of analysis. The first column contains the top 20 forms derived from the adult input to the children (the transcripts of the child directed adult speech), and the second column contains the top 20 forms from the children's production data (the transcripts of the adult directed child speech). The column "Acc.%" further states their accumulated proportion to the total number of word tokens found in the sub-corpus in question. The figures in Table 3 were obtained by procedures developed and applied by Allwood (1996).

Now, what are the properties of the most frequent word forms resulting from the analysis procedure described above? First, a striking property is that already the 20 most frequent word forms make up such a large proportion of the total material: the 20 most frequent types of word forms in the input (on a total of 8545 types) represent 43.7% of all tokens ($n = 227764$); and in the children's production data the 20 most frequent types (on a total of 11856 types) represent 34.2% of all tokens ($n = 109156$).[6]

A second property is that there are almost exclusively closed class items to be found among the 20 most frequent word forms, in the adult input as well as in the children's production data.[7] And if we proceed to consider the top 50 word forms, the only forms that have an unequivocal interpretation as content words found in the children's sub-corpus are *mamma* 'mummy' (rank order 28), *pappa* 'daddy' (rank order 40), and *titta* 'look' (rank order 45). In effect, we are back to our focus on function words, although a broader range of types of function words than the ones we considered in our crosslinguistic comparisons. Among the top 20 word forms, we find pronouns, prepositions, particles, conjunctions, auxiliary verbs, and a number of feedback morphemes (see Allwood et al. 1992) such as *ja* 'yes', *nä* 'no', and *(h)mm*.

A third property of the top 20 items listed in Table 3 is that, from a phonological or phonetic point of view, they have a very simple structure. Almost all of them are monosyllabic and the syllables are constructed from a rather restricted set of segments or features, all of which are typically present in the late babbling stage (this is true of the children's production data and their adult input alike).

Fourth, in the top 20 list the better part of the forms are very ambiguous. Again, when such a form is considered in isolation, its interpretation can therefore often be very unsure, whereas if it appears in a linguistic context where

Table 3. *The top 20 word forms across all data points (around 18–40 months) from 4 Swedish children and their parents*

Adult input					Child production				
8545 types of word forms; 227764 tokens					11856 types of word forms; 109156 tokens				
Rank	Word	transl[a]	Freq	Acc.%	Rank	Word	transl	Freq	Acc.%
1	de	'that/it'	12547	0.0550877	1	dä	'there'	3750	0.0343545
2	du	'you'	10422	0.100846	2	de	'that/it'	3704	0.0682876
3	va	'what/was'	7851	0.135316	3	ja	'I/yes'	3431	0.0997197
4	e	'is/am/are'	7065	0.166334	4	e	'is/am/are'	3111	0.12822
5	ja	'I/yes'	6386	0.194372	5	ha	'have/yes'	2733	0.153258
6	den	'that (one)'	5038	0.216492	6	den	'that (one)'	2140	0.172863
7	å	'and'	4715	0.237193	7	å	'and'	1887	0.19015
8	då	'then'	4525	0.25706	8	ä	'is/there'	1842	0.207025
9	så	'so'	4382	0.276299	9	a	'yes'	1818	0.22368
10	ska	'shall'	4367	0.295473	10	hä	'here'	1705	0.2393
11	där	'there'	4277	0.314251	11	nä	'no'	1323	0.25142
12	vi	'we'	3926	0.331488	12	jaa	'yes'	1287	0.26321
13	en	'a/one'	3560	0.347118	13	aa	'yeah'	1284	0.274973
14	har	'has/have'	3344	0.3618	14	ia	'I (ideos.[b])'	1218	0.286132
15	han	'he'	3272	0.376166	15	i	'in'	1093	0.296145
16	här	'here'	2927	0.389017	16	nää	'no'	1078	0.306021
17	på	'on'	2860	0.401574	17	hmm	'aha'	1019	0.315356
18	inte	'not'	2682	0.413349	18	ka	'shall/can'	1014	0.324645
19	hmm	'aha'	2662	0.425036	19	haa	'aha'	975	0.333578
20	kan	'can'	2636	0.43661	20	nu	'now'	956	0.342336

[a] "transl" merely represents a "preferential" translation; the items translated are, as a rule, more ambiguous than the translation suggests, — cf. Table 4.
[b] "ideos" reads 'ideosyncratic', i.e., a particular child (non-target) form.

disambiguating cues are present, the form is more likely to get a satisfying interpretation. When, for instance *e* appears in the context *va _ de* 'what _ that', the interpretation *är* 'is' is the one one naturally turns to, and so on.

And fifth, it is true of all of the top 20 items that they are pronounced with various degrees of stress. For many of the items, this is due to the same dual stress property as we observed in relation to the spatial function words (e.g., *på* 'on' as either particle (stressed) or preposition (unstressed)). In this case the shift between stressed and unstressed is often associated with a change also in function (semantic and or grammatical value). E.g., the form *de* (rank order 1 in the adult input and 2 in the children's production data) is associated with deixis ('that one') when stressed, whereas it is always unstressed when it serves as expletive subject ('it'). ± stress thus interacts with the fourth property described above: functional ambiguity.

Before we proceed to a more detailed level of analysis, let us briefly consider the implications of these five properties for the child's acquisition task (including, importantly, the segmentation and mapping tasks). Let us, to begin with, think of the five properties in relation to the adult input only.

1. The implication of the first property is the force of input frequency. If input frequency does indeed play a role in acquisition, our top 20 items would surely be a case in point.
2. Second, a general characteristic of function words is that they are richly distributed across different communicative activities (discourse types) and across different linguistic contexts. Thus, the learner will get to hear them during free play, the preparation of food, bed time activities etc., and he will get to hear them in relation to a great variety of lexical items. The distribution of content words, in contrast, tend to be much more contingent upon communicative activity type, topic of conversation and the like.
3. An important implication of the third property is that the simple segmental structure provides for a continuity of forms in development: there are frequent old forms around for the learner to use/reuse in (partly) new functions.
4. Fourth, an implication of the functional (semantic/pragmatic) ambiguity of the most frequent items is that the child is left with a certain degree of freedom in organizing (and re-organizing) the relation between the forms in question and their functions.
5. From a strictly binary distinction between open class items and closed class items and the assumption that the former tend to be stressed and have concrete referential functions whereas the latter tend to be unstressed and have abstract, grammatical functions, one would expect the acquisition of closed class items to be relatively hard. Although function words constitute a proper subset of closed class items, our findings, however, suggest that function words constitute a more mixed class in terms of stress as well as function. The forms serving as function words are sometimes stressed and sometimes not. And some of them have more concrete meanings (e.g., the spatial particles) than others (e.g., the copula). By implication, the child could use the property of stress to proceed through the domain of function words in a more differentiated fashion. The "template hypothesis" applies here, that is, the child has the option to start out with the forms in stressed position and use them as templates for discovering and representing these forms as they appear in unstressed positions. The corollary tendency to a

distinction in terms of functional traits (concrete vs. abstract) reinforces this option: to start with stressed forms serving more concrete functions and move on to the corresponding unstressed forms and more abstract functions (cf., the example of *det* 'that one/it'). And to the extent that children follow this path, they will show a continuity of forms and a discontinuity of functions in their development, following the principle that old forms tend to be recruited for (partly) new functions (cf., Slobin 1971).

Now, if we return to the children's production data, we observe in Table 3 that all of the 5 properties characteristic of the adult input are present also in the data from the children. Some of the properties are even exaggerated as compared to the adult profile. For example, the child forms tend to be even more functionally ambiguous than the adult forms (for several examples, see Table 4). In what follows, we will analyse in greater detail data of relevance to the fourth and fifth developmental implications stated above. Among other things, the former data (fourth implication) provide a window on the child's mapping problem and way(s) of organizing and re-organizing the relation between form and function in the course of development. The latter type of data (fifth implication) lend themselves to further testing of our template hypothesis.

In a second round of analysis, all word forms produced by the children in the Swedish corpus were mapped onto target forms (adult glosses) and rendered in written language orthography. The specification of the child forms was made on the basis of their phonological form, their syntactic distribution, and the responses to the forms by the child's conversational partner in the activities transcribed. The analysis is exhaustive in the sense that all word forms produced by the children — whether conforming to the target or deviating from it — were mapped onto such adult glosses.

Table 4 shows the functional mappings (in terms of adult glosses) of the most ambiguous word forms produced by one of the four children in the Swedish corpus, "Anton", during the period 23;08–40;27. Table 4 shows the top fragment of Anton's ambiguity hierarchy (a list of the 14 most ambiguous forms ordered according to degree of ambiguity). His most ambiguous form is *e*, which has been matched with no less than 25 different adult glosses/interpretations (for a translation, see the footnote attached to the table).[8] As indicated in the table, 22 of these 25 interpretations are function words and 3 are content words.

Table 4. Anton's 14 most ambiguous word forms during the period 23;08–40;27

Degree of ambiguity	Child form	n tokens	Adult gloss by transcriber	Function words	Content words
25	e	1278	är, det, en, ett, när, vad, och, vi, ni, ner, blev, hos, till, där, som, för, med, var, på, vem, av, i/ge, vill, vet[a]	22	3
22	å	276	och, vad, var, å, om, då, får på, vart, av, vem, vad, när, varför, så, där, som, om/åka, ont, små, ål	18	4
16	ka	359	ska, han, kan/skal, glass, kalv, traktor, Karl, Kalle Anka, Skalman, kamera, kvar, ta, katt, tack, tass	3	13
15	ä	240	den, där, är, vad, på, var, i, när, det, en, att, här, ett, som/färg, vill	13	2
15	i	255	i, jag, vi, in, och, på, till, ni, hos, när/runt, jeep, vit, vill, ny	10	5
12	hå	138	dom, vad, på, får, så/fåren, hår, såg, trollen, hål, tåg, honung	5	7
13	a	296	ska, vara, ha, för, var, jag, vad, när, han, att, varför, vem, av	13	0
11	kacka	144	pannkaka, klappa, knacka, traktor, dansa, smörja, tacka, kaffe, Kalle Anka, tanka	0	10
10	de	1447	det, där, den, på, du, dit, dom, han, hon/vill	9	1
7	gå	100	dom, så, då/gå, grå, gång, golvet	3	4
7	ha	540	ha, han, när, kan, vad/svans, saft	5	2
7	kåcka	9	råtta, tanka, tomte, klocka, torka, kaka, trollen	0	7
6	ja	606	jag, var, vara, ska, vad/ta	5	1
4	hä	763	här/häst, sex, färg	1	3

[a] For reasons of space, we here restrict ourselves to translating the 25 adult glosses for the child form e: är 'am/are/is', det 'it/that', en 'a' (indef article, common gender), ett 'a' (indef article, neuter gender), när 'when', vad 'what', och 'and', vi 'we', ni 'you', ner 'down', blev 'became/got', hos 'at/with', till 'to', där 'there', som 'who/which/that', for 'cos' , med 'with', var 'was/where', på 'on', vem 'who', av 'of/off', i 'in', ge 'give', vill 'want', vet 'know'. The symbol "/" is used to demarcate the content words (to the right of /) from the function words (to the left) among the adult glosses.

An analysis of the whole fragment of Anton's ambiguity hierarchy shown in Table 4 reveals several constraints on the way Anton has organized the relation between the phonetic/phonological shape of the items and their functions. Thus, if a form is disyllabic, then it is a content word (open class item). If a form is monosyllabic, then it is either an open or closed class item. And if it consists of a vowel only, then either the great majority or all of the adult glosses/interpretations suggested are function words. In other words, Anton shows a tendency towards a phonological differentiation between function words and content words. More specifically, Anton honours a constraint that a function word should consist of one syllable, and he often reduces this syllable to its minimal component, namely, a vowel. In effect, Anton shows a preference for using a simplest segmental design to shape his function words.

Developmental patterns

The analyses of frequency distributions in the Swedish corpus reported above were based on a pooling of all longitudinal data in the corpus. Needless to say, an important task for further research is to carry out the same kind of analyses on each child, and longitudinally data point by data point. This is the only way to gain a detailed picture of the dynamics of the developmental process.

At this point, we will present two pilot analyses: one of "Anton"'s development of the form *e* (at the top of his ambiguity hierarchy in Table 4) from 23;08 to 40;27 (31 data points), and one of the development of the form *de* in the early development of "Markus" from 15;19 to 24;09 (12 data points), another component case study of the Swedish corpus.

Case study 1: "Anton"

Anton's development of *e* from 23;08 to 40;27 is summarized in Table 5. This period can be roughly divided into three phases. During a first phase, from 23;08 to 28;03, there is only a handful of instances of the phonological form *e* occurring as a wordlike entity in Anton's multiword utterances. The few tokens are either indeterminate as to their syntactic or functional status or they are distributed in a context where the copula (*e/är*) is expected from the point of view of the target norm.

In a second developmental phase, from 28;00 to 31;03, *e* becomes more frequent (around 10 to 30 tokens per data point) occurring in syntactic contexts where it seems to serve the function of the copula. In these contexts *e* is consistently unstressed. This usage, however, is at first extremely limited: it is constrained to the context *det _* 'it _', to form the expression *de e* 'it's'.

A third phase, from 31;19 and onwards, represents a dramatic leap, both in terms of functions and frequencies. There is a very substantial increase in Anton's usage of *e* as copula 'is/am/are'. Also, Anton sometimes uses *e* in syntactic contexts where different function words (not only the copula) would be expected from the point of view of the target language. We interpret this distribution of *e* as indicating that Anton has now entered an analysis phase proper with respect to the distributional constraints and function(s) of *e*. Possibly, Anton is trying out *e* as a generalized functor, a "multi-purpose" function word. In some respects, this usage of *e* resembles that of what has been termed "filler syllables" in children's early language development (Peters & Menn 1993). At the beginning of the third phase the great majority of Anton's tokens of *e* are distributed according to the target constraints associated with the copula. Later, this bias towards the target constraints is weakened and towards the end of the period observed the majority of the usages of *e* are not distributed according to the copula constraints. Only half a year later, around 46 months of age, Anton starts to narrow down the usage of *e* so that the great majority of his tokens of *e* are again distributed according to the target constraints associated with the copula (see Richthoff 2000).

Furthermore, in his development beyond 31;19, Anton is at first honouring the constraint that there should be a high degree of phonetic similarity between his *e* and the kernel vowel of the target item, both for target items that are typically stressed (e.g., verb particles) and for target items that are typically unstressed (e.g., prepositions) in the input. Later, Anton lifts this phonetic similarity constraint for those target forms which are typically unstressed. Among other things, Anton for a period uses *e* in place of most other prepositions, such as *hos* 'with/at', *till* 'to', *för* 'for', *med* 'with', *på* 'on', *av* 'of', and *i* 'in'.

Case study 2: "Markus"

Let us now turn to the other child, Markus, and the development of *de(t)* 'it/that'. Table 6 shows the distribution of stressed and unstressed *de(t)* in Markus from 15;19 to 24;09 (12 data points). The figures in the table are based on a study by Plunkett & Strömqvist (1992: 507–508).

Plunkett & Strömqvist analysed the early development of the word *det* 'that one/it' in two Danish and two Swedish children (one of whom was "Markus"). For all four children they found that the usage of *det* as a one-word utterance (stressed and deictic) preceded the usage of *det* in multi-word utterances in development. Further, for all four children the usage of *det* as one-word utterance decreased and ultimately vanished as the usage of *det* in multi-word utterances

Table 5. *Anton's development of* e *from 23;08 to 40;27*

Data point	n utterances	Child form	n tokens	Degree of ambiguity	Adult gloss by transcriber and (n tokens)	Percentage copula (e)
23;08 311	e	1			?[a](1)	
24;13 306	e	0				
24;26 196	e	1	1		är(1)	
25;21 383	e	0				
26;10 249	e	0				
27;00 427	e	2	1		är(2)	
27;21 370	e	2	1		är(2)	
28;03 470	e	0				
28;15 659	e	9	1		är(9)	
28;28 675	e	12	1		är(12)	
29;08 579	e	3	1		är(3)	
30;02 640	e	21	2		är(15) det(5) ?(1)	71.4%[b]
30;15 548	e	30	1		är(30) ?(1)	
31;03 591	e	23	1		är(21) ?(2)	
31;19 332	e	16	3		är(10) en(4) ner(1) ?(1)	62.5%
32;02 583	e	34	5		är(27) en(2) ett(2) i(2) av(1)	79.4%
32;11 472	e	27	2		är(26) på(1)	96.3%
32;29 590	e	82	5		är(68) ner(4) i(4) en(3) och(1) ?(2)	82.9%
33;18 564	e	32	5		är(25) ner(3) får(2) den(1) en(1)	78.1%
34;04 718	e	85	4		en/ett(38) är(32) i(3) för(3)	44.7%
34;25 431	e	72	8		är(51) en(5) det(2) och(3) vad(2) ett(3) vill(1) när(2) ?(3)	70.8%
35;17 558	e	94	4		är(74) en(8) och(8) vi(2) ?(2)	78.7%
36;08 642	e	86	11		är(53) en(14) ett(2) vi(3) ni(1) det(2) den(1) ner(1) och(2) dom(2) vad(1) ?(4)	61.6%
36;29 712	e	132	16		är(81) en(16) ett(3) vad(5) när(5) ge(2) vi(4) med(2) och(2) han(2) blev(1) hos(1) av(1) i(1) som(1) vill(1) ?(4)	61.4%
37;20 479	e	118	10		är(71) en(29) det(5) som(3) där(2) när(2) vad(1) till(1) ett(1) man(1) ?(2)	60.2%
38;03 326	e	37	10		är(17) en(6) hos(4) när(3) och(1) för(1) ge(1) med(1) ett(1) vill(1) ?(1)	45.9%
38;29 469	e	66	10		är(24) en(18) ett(5) och(7) när(4) där(2) det(2) vem(1) av(1) med(1) ?(2)	36.4%
39;20 522	e	114	12		är(92) en(2) ett(6) vi(2) i(1) vet(2) när(1) sig(1) och(1) det(1) man(1) ?(4)	80.7%
40;12 434	e	41	8		är(19) en(10) och/men(3) foer(2) ett(1) med(1) hos(1) vi(1) ?(3)	46.3%
40;27 275	e	40	6		är(12) en(13) det(5) när(2) i(3) vi(2) ?(3)	30%

[a] "?" signifies that the syntactic context was not rich enough for the transcriber to attempt an interpretation/adult gloss
[b] "71.4%" means that 71.4 percent of the tokens of *e* observed met the distributional constraints of the copula (*e/är*).

Table 6. *The distribution of stressed and unstressed* det *in Markus 15;19–24;09*

	15;19	16;27	18;10	19;25	20;05	21;03	22;14	22;25	23;00	23;12	23;25	24;09
One-word utterances	0	0	0	1	4	12	2	3	4	8	0	1
Multi-word utterances												
Gramm subj												
stressed "deictic"	0	0	0	2	0	5	1	4	0	9	9	14
unstressed "expletive"	0	0	0	0	0	0	0	2	0	0	2	11
Other	0	0	0	1		1	1	6	0	0	0	0

Based on Plunkett & Strömqvist (1992: 507–508)

emerged and gradually increased. In Table 6 Markus's distribution of *det* in multi-word utterances is further categorized in terms of whether he uses *det* as grammatical subject, and whether the subject *det* is stressed and deictic (as, e.g., *det är dillen* (pointing to the dill) 'that's the dill') or unstressed and expletive (as in, e.g., *så kommer det smulor där i* 'then it/there comes crumpets in there').

Table 6 shows that *det* as one-word utterance (stressed and deictic) reaches a peak at 21;03 and then decreases. Conversely, *det* (stressed and deictic) as grammatical subject increases towards the end of the period analysed (23;12–24;09), and *det* as unstressed expletive subject emerges for real only in the last data point (24;09) analysed by Plunkett & Strömqvist. The developmental structure summarized in Table 6 provides support for the developmental implications we formulated, especially the third ("continuity of forms") and fifth ("template hypothesis") ones. Markus starts out with stressed *det,* using that form with a deictic function, and later integrates *det* in syntactic patterns as grammatical subject. Finally he removes the stress from *det,* using the form as expletive subject in a purely syntactic function.

Conclusions

Our empirical investigations of input and production in the early language development of a handful of Scandinavian children offers a window on how aspects of the interface may be organized between phonetic development (perception and production) before 18 months of age and the development of function words in early grammatical development.

We interpret the precocious emergence of particles in the Danish child and the likewise precocious acquisition of prepositions in the Icelandic child as effects of a prosodic spotlight, more particularly, stress, — although not exclusively of prosodic spotlight. In a controlled experiment in which the task is to learn a fragment of an artificial language and the subjects of the experiment group would profit from the presence of, for example, stress, it would be possible more clearly to disentangle such a spotlight from other determining factors (such as input frequency, etc.). Real language development, however, takes place in multidimensional environments where a host of factors interact to determine the structure of acquisition. The purpose of our particular crosslinguistic approach, the within-group approach, is to study aspects of language development in naturalistic settings, keeping as many factors as possible under control, while varying the particular determining factor under scrutiny. On the basis of our intra-Scandinavian contrastive analyses, we conclude, then, that stress can interact with other determining factors (such as cognitive development, input frequency, etc.) in ways that facilitate the acquisition of particles and prepositions to a degree that is clearly observable. Our observations indicate that this facilitation process can already be evident at the beginning of the child's second year of life.

Now, more generally, could the distribution of stress and/or frequency in the input to the child be conducive to the child's construction of two sets of items, namely closed class and open class items? First, our analyses of the Swedish child language corpus suggest that a truly high token frequency implies a closed class item. However, there are closed class items which are infrequent, so a low token frequency does not imply a non-closed class item. Second, if a morpheme never occurs with stress, that implies that it is a closed class item. However, the particular subset of forms that serve as function words are distributed with stress in some usages and without stress in others. Thus, stress and frequency are neither necessary nor sufficient for the identification of the particular class of forms that serve as function words. But stress and frequency can still be supportive in the complex process of identifying such forms.

On the basis of our analyses of Scandinavian data, we would like to argue that function words present a special domain for the language learning child. The domain is a subdomain of closed class items, but it consists of items which vary in terms of both stress and function. A developmental scenario, then, in the transition from late infancy to early grammatical development supported by our data is that the child starts out with forms that are stressed, and which often have a more concrete function (e.g., stressed *det* 'that one' which has a deictic function), and then use these forms as templates for the perception and analysis of unstressed forms, — forms which often serve somewhat different functions than the stressed ones (e.g., unstressed, expletive *det* 'it'). The developmental principle that "new functions are first expressed by old forms" (Slobin 1971: 317) is thus instantiated in the developmental scenario for function words sketched here.

Further, we observe that the very simple phonetic/phonological structure of function words in the input to the Swedish children as well as in their own production data provides for a continuity from the children's early syllabic vocalizations to their early grammatical development proper. This further reinforces the developmental principle that new functions are first expressed by old forms. When the child directs his attention to function words in his early development, he is already in command of phonological forms that can be (re-)used for the production of these grammatical morphemes.

These tentative generalizations about the early interface, however, are limited to the particular configuration(s) of properties (frequency, stress, functional ambiguity) typical of function words in the Scandinavian languages. Languages which lack function words or where function words are configured in very different ways can be expected to be conducive to (partly) different approaches by the child in his transition from infancy to the early phases of grammatical development. Again, we want to underline that a given property, e.g. stress, may not be sufficient per se as an effective cue to the child for his segmentation task. Rather, the effectiveness of a particular cue may be a function of how it interacts with cues in other important dimensions in the particular language in question (cf., MacWhinney & Bates 1989). Our within-language group comparisons (Danish, Icelandic, Swedish) suggest that already subtle differences in the configuration of function words in terms of stress, word order, and ambiguity, do have an impact on the structure of acquisition.

Acknowledgments

This study was supported by Nordiska Samarbetsnämnden for Humanistisk Forskning (NOS H), project "Language Development a Scandinavian Perspective". We also want to thank Ann Peters for many fruitful discussions.

Notes

1. In our analyses, items such as *in, on, up* and *down* were coded as "particles/adverbs", "verb particles/adverbs", or "prepositions" depending on their syntactic and prosodic properties. Illustrations are given in examples (1)–(3). For further details see Ragnarsdóttir & Strömqvist (1997).

(1)	one-word utterance	*in*	"particle/adverb"
(2)	V prt/adv	go *in*	"verb particle/adverb"
(3)	prep NP	*in* the house	"preposition"

2. The diacritic signs in the Icelandic examples are there for orthographic reasons and are not related to stress.
3. In Icelandic, the construction V + **PRT** (i.e., with phrasal stress on the particle) is reserved for lexicalized (non-compositional) meanings, for example, *lita út* 'look'.
4. The corpus, the "Strömqvist and Richthoff corpus", is accessible on request from the Department of Linguistics, University of Lund, Sweden. Users of the Internet can download parts of the corpus from the CHILDES archive by anonymous ftp from poppy.psy.cmu.edu, where it is located in the file "swedish.tar" under the directory "childes/noneng/".
5. An important rationale for this way of transcribing spoken utterances rests on the assumption that individual morphemes and words are, as a rule, maximally ambiguous (or, "underspecified") taken out of context. It is therefore important to avoid overspecifying the morphological or lexical identity of the individual word forms encountered during the course of transcription. Especially on the assumption that the language learning child himself is ferreting out the semantic and grammatical properties of word forms he encounters on the basis of contextual cues (from the linguistic context as well as from the wider situational context).
6. The reason why there are more types of word forms in the children's production data than in the adult input, despite the fact that there are considerably fewer tokens in the children's data, is that the child speech recorded contains a large number of infrequent forms which do not occur in the adult input (e.g., *kåcka*). This is an effect of our transcription conventions, according to which we often keep close to the way a word form is actually pronounced by the child, in order to preserve lexical or grammatical ambiguities in the child's speech (e.g., *kåcka* can mean both clock (Sw *klocka*) and rat (Sw *råtta*) and so on. The typical effect, then, is that the amount of word types in the child sub-corpus increases, since we there encounter both *kåcka, klocka* and *råtta*, whereas in the adult sub-corpus we only encounter *klocka* and *råtta* etc.
7. The hedge "almost" is licensed by the fact that some of the word forms in the children's production data (e.g., *ka*) are ambiguous in the sense that they do not match target function words (e.g., *ka* matches *ska* 'shall') in all instances, but in some instances represent attempts at articulating content words (e.g., *ka* also matches *skal* 'shell'). See Table 4 for more examples.
8. As forms of spontaneous (child-directed adult) speech, these morphemes tend to be unstressed, which entails inter alia that they are "phonologically reduced"; for example vowels are often reduced to so-called central vowels, mostly to a schwa (roughly corresponding to unstressed e). Furthermore the 25 adult forms are all monosyllabic. The phonological distance between Anton's e and the 25 adult forms is therefore in reality (i.e., in spoken interaction) much less than their counterparts in written language would suggest.

References

Allwood, J. (ed.) 1996. *Talspråksfrekvenser.* Gothenburg Papers in Theoretical Linguistics S, Volume 20. University of Göteborg: Department of Linguistics.
Allwood, J., Nivre, J. & Ahlsén, E. 1992. "On the semantics and pragmatics of linguistic feedback." *Journal of Semantics* 9: 1–26.
Behrens, H. 1998. "How difficult are complex verbs?" *Linguistics* 36: 679–712.

Bennis, H., den Dikken, M., Jordens, P., Powers, S. & Weissenborn, J. 1995. "Picking up particles." In *Proceedings of the 19th Annual Boston University Conference on Language Development*, Vol. 1, D. MacLaughlin & S. McEwen (eds.). Boston: Cascadilla Press.
Brown, R. 1973. *A First Language: The Early Stages*. London: Allen and Unwin.
Bybee, J. 1985. *Morphology*. (Typological studies in language, Volume 9). Amsterdam: John Benjamins.
Clark, H. & Clark, E. 1977. *Psychology and Language*. New York: Harcourt Brace Jovanovich.
Fernald, A., Taeschner, T., Dunn, J., Papousek, M., de Boysson-Bardies, B. & Fukui, I. 1989. "A cross-language study of prosodic modifications in mothers' and fathers' speech to preverbal infants." *Journal of Child Language* 16: 477–501.
MacWhinney, B. & Bates, E. (eds.) 1989. *The crosslinguistic study of sentence processing*. Cambridge: Cambridge University Press.
Peters, A. & Menn, L. 1993. "False starts and filler syllables: ways to learn grammatical morphemes." *Language* 69: 742–777.
Peters, A. & Strömqvist, S. 1996. "The role of prosody in the acquisition of grammatical morphemes." In *Signal to Syntax: bootstrapping from speech to grammar in early acquisition*, J.L. Morgan & K. Demuth (eds.). Hillsdale, N.J.: Lawrence Erlbaum.
Plunkett, K. & Strömqvist, S. 1992. "The acquisition of Scandinavian languages." In *The Crosslinguistic Study of Language Acquisition, Volume 3*, D. Slobin (ed.). Hillsdale, New Jersey: Lawrence Erlbaum.
Ragnarsdóttir, H. & Strömqvist, S. 1997. "The linguistic encoding of spatial relations in Scandinavian child language development." In *The Proceedings of the Twenty-eighth Annual Child Language Research Forum*, E. Clark (ed.). Stanford: CSLI, Stanford.
Richthoff, U. 2000. *En svensk barnspråkskorpus — uppbyggnad och analyser*. Licentiate Dissertation, University of Göteborg: Department of Linguistics.
Slobin, D.I. 1971. "Developmental psycholinguistics." In *A Survey of Linguistic Science*, W. Dingwall (ed.). University of Maryland: University of Maryland Press.
Snow, C. & Ferguson, C. (eds.) 1977. *Talking to Children. Language Input and Acquisition*. Cambridge: Cambridge University Press.
Strömqvist, S., Peters, A. & Ragnarsdóttir, H. 1995a. "Particles and prepositions in Scandinavian child language development: effects of prosodic spotlight?" In *Proceedings of the XIIIth International Congress of Phonetic Sciences*, Vol. 4, K. Elenius & P. Branderud (eds.). Stockholm: Royal Institute of Technology.
Strömqvist, S., Ragnarsdóttir, H., Engstrand, O., Jonsdóttir, H., Lanza, E., Leiwo, M., Nordqvist, Å., Peters, A., Plunkett, K., Richthoff, U., Gram Simonsen, H., Toivainen, J. & Toivainen, K. 1995b. "The inter-Nordic study of language acquisition." *Nordic Journal of Linguistics* 18: 3–29.
Strömqvist, S., Richthoff, U. & Andersson, A.-B. 1993. "Strömqvist's and Richthoff's corpora — a guide to longitudinal data from four Swedish children." *Gothenburg Papers in Theoretical Linguistics* 66.
Þráinsson, H. 1990. *Setningafræði*. Reykjavík: Málvísindastofnun Háskóla Íslands.

Part IV

Neurophysiological Aspects of Language Acquisition

Part IV

Neurophysiological Aspects of Language Acquisition

Language Development during Infancy and Early Childhood
Electrophysiological correlates

Dennis L. Molfese, Dana B. Narter, Amy J. Van Matre,
Michelle R. Ellefson & Arlene Modglin
Southern Illinois University

The goal of the present chapter is to relate what is currently known regarding the brain's involvement in language processing during the early years of life. The primary focus will be on the event-related potential (ERP) as a means to study the neuroelectrical correlates of language in the brains of these infants and children. After reviewing general information concerning ERPs, this chapter reviews ERP studies investigating early language development in the areas of phonological, semantic, and syntactic development. Unfortunately, although the research reviewed here extends back over two decades, the literature in these areas remains sparse. The majority of ERP studies conducted with these populations have occurred in the area of speech perception and phonology, with only a handful of studies investigating early word acquisition and word discrimination. Only two studies have been identified dealing with syntactic issues. This paucity of electrophysiological studies of early language acquisition has occurred during a time when more traditional studies of language have blossomed. It is hoped that this review will serve in part to stimulate more research into this critically important yet largely uncharted area of early language acquisition and the brain.

The use of ERP techniques to study brain–behavior relationships

The ERP is a synchronized portion of the ongoing EEG pattern that is time-locked to the onset of some event in the infant's environment (Rockstroh, Elbert, Birbaumer & Lutzenberger 1982). The ERP is characterized by a complex waveform that varies in its amplitude and frequency over time and is thought to reflect ongoing brain processing. Fluctuations in the amplitude or latency of various positive or negative peaks within the ERP occur at different points throughout its time course (Callaway, Tueting & Koslow 1978). Research over the past 70 years has demonstrated that the ERP, because of this time-locked feature, can be used to effectively study both general and specific aspects of the organism's response to its external as well as its internal environment (Molfese 1978a, 1978b), in addition to an individual's perceptions and decisions (Molfese 1983; Nelson & Salapatek 1986; Ruchkin, Sutton, Munson, Silver & Macar 1981). Given that the ERP technique does not require a planned and overt response from individuals from which it is recorded, it is particularly well-suited for the neuropsychological study of the infant's and the child's early language development (Molfese, Freeman & Palermo 1975). One major advantage of the ERP is that it provides very fine temporal information (down to 1 ms or less) regarding the brain's response to language input. In addition, it does have some gross level spatial resolution capabilities that permit speculation concerning the distribution of brain mechanisms that subserve functions such as language.

In the following review, material will first be presented on ERP studies of phonological processing. This review will be followed by a review of studies on semantic development and the processing of syntactic information. Finally, material will be presented that suggests a link between these electrophysiological measures of infant and child language and later language development.

Phonetic discriminations and ERPs

A large number of studies conducted across the past two decades have investigated the neuroelectrical correlates of speech perception from the infancy period into adulthood. In general, these results suggest that some of the infant's perception of speech cues such as voice onset time (VOT) follow different developmental progressions than other cues such as place of articulation (POA). The two most notable differences are that (1) VOT discrimination along phonetic boundaries does not consistently appear in newborn infants, although it appears to be uniformly present by two to five months of age, and (2) VOT appears to elicit bilateral responses (i.e., equivalent responses from both hemispheres) earlier in the waveform than lateralized responses (Molfese & Molfese 1979a; Simos & Molfese 1997). POA, on the other hand, (1) does consistently appear in newborn infants and (2) evokes an initial lateralized response in the waveform that is then followed later in time by a bilateral response (Molfese, Burger-Judisch & Hans 1991; Molfese & Molfese 1979b, 1980, 1985).

Building on a base of behavioral research (Liberman, Cooper, Shankweiler & Studdert-Kennedy 1967), studies by Molfese and colleagues of VOT and POA have covered the developmental period extending from infancy (Molfese & Molfese 1979a, 1979b, 1980) into childhood and adulthood (Molfese 1978a, 1978b, 1980a, 1980b, 1984; Molfese & Hess 1978; Molfese & Schmidt 1983). For the purposes of this chapter, we have limited our review of the adult work to a few exemplars that provide a framework for interpreting the infant and child research that is more directly relevant to the theme of this chapter.

Voice onset time

Voice onset time (VOT) reflects the temporal relationship between laryngeal pulsing and the onset of consonant release and has long been recognized as an important cue for distinguishing voiced from voiceless stop consonants such as *b* and *p* (Liberman, Cooper, Shankweiler & Studdert-Kennedy 1967). Adult listeners readily discriminate between consonants from different phonetic categories, such as [ba] and [pa], while they perform at only chance levels when attempting to discriminate between different exemplars from the same phonetic category (Lisker & Abramson 1970). An adult's ability to discriminate between-category contrasts while failing to discriminate within-category contrasts is referred to as "categorical perception". Studies with infants (Eimas, Siqueland, Jusczyk & Vigorito 1971; Eilers, Wilson & Moore 1979), children (Streeter 1976), and adult listeners (Lisker & Abramson 1970) consistently demonstrate that adults and children from many different language environments exhibit categorical perception for a wide range of consonant contrasts.

Although Eimas et al. (1971) noted that young infants have categorical-like perception for stop consonants, nothing was known as to how the brain responded to these sounds and how such responses changed across development. Molfese (1978b), in a follow-up to work by Dorman (1974), provided the first evidence that speech cues such as VOT could elicit different ERP responses. To accomplish this, Molfese recorded ERPs from the left and right temporal regions of 16 adults during a phoneme identification task. Adults listened to randomly ordered sequences of synthesized bilabial stop consonants with VOT values of +0 ms,

+20 ms, +40 ms, and +60 ms. ERPs were recorded in response to each sound and then, after a brief delay, adults pressed different keys to identify the different consonant sounds they heard. Two regions of the ERP, one component centered around 135 ms and the second occurring between 300 and 500 ms following stimulus onset, changed systematically as a function of the consonant's phonetic category. The ERPs to stop consonant sounds with VOT values of +0 and +20 ms (identified as *ba*) were discriminated from those with VOT values of +40 and +60 ms (identified as *pa*). However, there were no waveform differences between the +0 and +20 ms tokens or between the +40 and +60 ms tokens, which were pairs of speech sounds from within the same category. This pattern of responding resembled what Lisker & Abramson earlier called categorical perception. That is, ERPs discriminated between sounds from different phonetic categories but not between sounds from the same phonetic category. Electrophysiological studies employing similar stimuli with a variety of different age groups replicated this finding (Molfese 1980a; Molfese & Hess 1978; Molfese & Molfese 1979a, 1979b, 1988). Surprisingly, however, in all these studies at least one region of the ERP in which this categorical discrimination effect was noted across the different age groups occurred over the right temporal region. This sense of surprise comes from the expectation that such speech sound discrimination effects are expected to originate from the left hemisphere (LH) since it, not the right hemisphere (RH), is associated with language functions (Lenneberg 1967).

Similar patterns of ERP effects were noted with 4-year-old children in a study involving the velar stop consonants, *k* and *g*. Molfese & Hess (1978) recorded ERPs from the left and right temporal scalp regions of 12 4-year-old children in response to randomly ordered series of synthesized consonant-vowel syllables in which the initial consonant varied in VOT from +0 ms, to +20 ms, to +40 ms, to +60 ms. In their analyses of the ERPs, they, like Molfese (1978b), also found a categorical discrimination effect whereby one late-occurring portion of the waveform (peak latency = 444 ms) changed systematically in response to consonants from different phonetic categories, but not differentially to consonants from within the same phonetic category. Also, as in the case of Molfese (1978b), this effect occurred over the RH. Unlike the adult study by Molfese, however, they found a second portion of the auditory ERP that occurred earlier in the waveform (peak latencies = 198 and 342 ms), before this RH effect, and which was detected by electrodes placed over *both* hemispheres. This earlier occurring bilaterally detected auditory ERP component also discriminated voiced from voiceless consonants in a categorical manner. Similar results were reported by both Molfese (1980b) and Segalowitz & Cohen (1989) with different populations of adults and by Molfese & Molfese (1988) with 3-year-old children.

This work has been extended to include newborn and older infants (Molfese & Molfese 1979a, 1979b). Molfese & Molfese (1979b) presented the four consonant-vowel syllables used by Molfese (1978b) to 16 infants between 2 and 5 months of age. ERPs were also recorded from the left and right temporal electrode sites. One auditory ERP component recorded from over the RH approximately 920 ms following stimulus onset discriminated between the different speech sounds categorically. As in the case of Molfese & Hess, they also noted a second portion of the auditory ERP detected at electrode sites over both hemispheres that also discriminated between the consonant sounds categorically. The major portion of this component occurred 528 ms following stimulus onset. Thus, these results paralleled the findings of Molfese & Hess in noting two portions of the auditory ERP that categorically discriminated between speech sounds. These included a bilateral component that occurred early in the waveform, followed by a RH lateralized component that occurred later in time, which also categorically discriminated between the speech sounds. The longer latencies found for the infants than for the four year-olds were most likely due to differences in maturation between these two populations.

Although another experiment described by Molfese & Molfese (1979a) failed to note any such bilateral or RH lateralized effects related to VOT discrimination with 16 newborn infants, a subsequent study by Simos & Molfese (1997) did find such effects with a different group of 16 newborn infants. They used two nonspeech auditory tones varying in tone onset time (TOT) which mimicked the temporal delays of the speech stop consonant voiced vs. voiceless distinction (see also Molfese 1980a). These TOT stimuli were obtained from Pisoni (1977) and had previously been used to study electrophysiological correlates of temporal differences in both adults (Molfese 1980a) and children (Molfese & Molfese 1988). The TOT stimuli consisted of two simultaneously occurring tones that differed from each other in the temporal onset of the lower frequency tone (500 Hz) relative to the higher frequency tone (1500 Hz). The lower tone began at the same time as the upper tone for the +0 ms TOT stimulus but lagged behind the upper tone by 20 ms for the +20 ms TOT stimulus. This delay increased to 40 ms and 60 ms, respectively, for the +40 ms and +60 ms TOT stimuli. Both tones ended simultaneously. Simos & Molfese found categorical-like discrimination effects at both the N200 and N530 negative peaks over parietal electrode sites and interpreted these results to indicate that the "temporal voicing cue used in speech perception may have an innate basis" (page 89). Notably, the latency for the bilateral effect reported for these non-speech stimuli was virtually the same as that reported by Molfese & Molfese (1979b) with a different population of older infants. This similarity in responses to speech and nonspeech temporal stimuli was also reported by Molfese (1980a) in adults and by Molfese & Molfese (1988) with preschool children. An overall summary of the infant speech perception research for VOT as well as for a second speech cue, POA, that is reviewed below, is outlined in Table 1.

Although the RH discrimination of the VOT cue appears paradoxical in light of traditional arguments that language processes are carried out primarily by the LH, the fact that identical responses are elicited by both speech and nonspeech sounds that contain the same temporal cues suggests that it may be the temporal quality of the sounds and not their speech-like quality that triggers the RH response. Furthermore, studies of clinical populations suggest that the VOT cue is discriminated, if not exclusively, then at least in part, by brain mechanisms restricted to the RH (for a review of this literature, see Molfese, Molfese & Parsons 1983, or Simos, Molfese & Brenden 1997).

Three general findings have emerged from this series of temporal discrimination studies involving the perception and discrimination of VOT and TOT. First, the discrimination of the temporal delay cue common to voiced and voiceless stop consonants can be detected by ERPs recorded from electrodes placed on the scalp over the two hemispheres. Second, from at least 2 months of age, if not before, the infant's brain appears capable of discriminating voiced from voiceless stop consonants in a categorical manner. That is, the ERPs appear to discriminate stimuli in one phonetic category from those with VOT values that characterize a second phonetic category. At the same time, these ERPs cannot discriminate between different VOT stimuli that come from the same phonetic category. Third, categorical discrimination across different ages appears to be carried out first by bilaterally represented mechanisms within both hemispheres and then, somewhat later in time, by RH lateralized mechanisms. The bilateral effects appear to be reflected with some consistency in the negative peak that occurs with a latency of approximately 530 ms in infants from birth onward. The lateralized effect, when noted in the infant ERPs, has a markedly longer latency. The presence of several different peaks with markedly different latencies that are responsive to the same temporal cues may signal that multiple regions of the brain respond to and perhaps process differently these temporal contrasts.

Place of articulation (POA)

In addition to studies of VOT, a second speech cue, place of articulation (POA) has been investigated in a number of studies with infants and adults (Molfese 1978a, 1980b, 1984; Molfese, Buhrke & Wang 1985; Molfese, Linnville, Wetzel & Leicht 1985; Molfese & Molfese 1979b, 1980, 1985; Molfese & Schmidt

Table 1. *Studies using event-related potentials to examine voice onset time (VOT) in infants*

Study	Participants	Electrodes	Task	Results
Molfese & Molfese (1979b)	2- to 5-month-old infants $n=16$	T3 & T4 referenced to linked ears	4 CV syllables comprised of an initial bilabial stop consonant with VOT values of +0, +20, +40 and +60 ms and the vowel /a/	For females, both hemispheres discriminated +0 and +20 ms VOT stimuli from +40 and +60 ms VOT stimuli (N528). For females, only the RH differentiated +0 and +20 ms VOT stimuli from +40 and +60 ms VOT stimuli (P920).
Molfese & Molfese (1979a)	Newborn infants $n=16$	T3 & T4 referenced to linked ears	4 CV syllables comprised of an initial bilabial stop consonant with VOT values of +0, +20, +40 and +60 ms and the vowel /a/	No categorical differentiation of the VOT stimuli
Simos & Molfese (1997)	Newborn infants $n=16$	FL, FR, T3, T4, PL, & PR referenced to linked ears	4 non-speech stimuli varying in TOT: +0, +20, +40 and +60 ms	Parietal sites differentiated +0 and +20 ms TOT stimuli from +40 and +60 ms TOT stimuli (N200 and N530)

1983). As in the case of the VOT temporal cue, these studies of the POA cue identified both lateralized and bilateral hemisphere responses that discriminated between different consonant sounds. However, unlike the discrimination abilities for VOT, the ability to discriminate the POA cue consistently appeared to be present from birth. There were some important differences, however, both in the development of ERP responses to the POA cue and in the character of the lateralized responses that distinguished the perception of this cue from that for VOT. A summary of these studies is presented in Table 2.

Molfese (1978a) first attempted to study POA in adults in order to obtain some reference for studying these abilities in infants. For the most part, this research focused on attempts to isolate the neuroelectrical correlates of changes in the second formant transition, the cue to which listeners attend in order to discriminate between different consonant sounds that are formed in different places within the vocal tract. In this study, Molfese presented a series of consonant-vowel syllables in which the stop consonants varied in POA, formant structure, and phonetic transition characteristics. Changes in POA signaled either the consonant *b* or *g*. The formant structure variable referred to two sets of sounds, nonspeech sounds consisting of formants composed of sinewaves 1 Hz in bandwidth, and speech sounds which contained speech-like formant bandwidths of 60, 90, and 120 Hz for formants 1 through 3, respectively. The phonetic transition cue referred to two stimulus properties in which one stimulus set contained formant transitions that normally characterize human speech patterns while the second set contained an unusual pattern not found in the initial consonant position in human speech patterns. Auditory ERP responses were recorded from the left and right temporal regions of 10 adults in response to randomly ordered series of consonant-vowel syllables that varied in consonant place of articulation, bandwidth, and phonetic transition quality. Two regions of the auditory ERP that peaked at 70 and 300 ms following stimulus onset discriminated the phonetic transition and POA cues only over the LH temporal electrode site. As in the case of Molfese (1978b), no bilateral place discrimination was noted. Similar LH POA discrimination effects later were reported by Gelfer (1987), Molfese (1980b, 1984), and Molfese & Schmidt (1983). Consistent discrimination of the place cues were also noted to occur over both hemispheres (bilateral effects) in these studies, even with the inclusion of additional electrode recording sites over each hemisphere.

Several general findings emerged from these adult POA studies. First, when multiple electrode sites are employed, bilateral stimulus discrimination effects are usually found in addition to LH lateralized ones. Second, these bilateral effects invariably occur early in the waveform and prior to the onset of the LH

Table 2. Studies using event-related potentials to examine place of articulation (POA) in infants

Study	Participants	Electrodes	Task	Results
Molfese & Molfese (1979b)	Full-term, newborn infants $n=16$	T3 & T4 referenced to linked ears	/bae/ and /gae/ speech syllables varying in formant structure and second formant consonant transition	LH differentiated between consonants with NF structure (N192) Both hemispheres discriminated between the 2 consonants with NF structure (N630)
Molfese & Molfese (1985)	Full-term, newborn infants $n=16$	T3 & T4 referenced to linked ears	6 speech CV syllables and 6 nonspeech control tones Presented in random order	LH response discriminated between /b/ and /g/ when they have NF structure (N168) Bilateral response (N664)
Molfese, Burger-Judisch, & Hans (1991)	Full-term, newborn infants $n=38$	FL, FR, T3, T4, PL, & PR referenced to linked ears	/bi/ and /gi/ speech syllables varying in formant structure and second formant consonant transition	AEPs recorded from LH frontal and parietal sites in females differed in response to /bi/ and /gi/ (N210)
Molfese & Molfese (1980)	Male preterm infants $n=11$	T3 & T4 referenced to linked ears	2 phonetic and 2 nonphonetic versions of /bae/ and /gae/, and 4 nonspeech controls (tones) matched to the center frequencies of each	LH discriminated between the consonant /b/ and /g/ for nonphonetic stimuli at region N848
Dehaene-Lambertz & Dehaene (1994)	2- to 3-month-old infants $n=16$	58 electrodes in a geodesic sensor net	Two conditions: Standard Trials — standard syllable repeated five times Deviant Trials — standard syllable repeated four times followed by a different syllable	/Ba/ response differed from /ga/ at 390 ms LH amplitude greater than RH amplitude over parietal regions

lateralized POA discrimination responses. This temporal relationship between bilateral and lateralized effects was noted earlier in our review of the VOT studies. Third, in addition to stimulus related hemisphere effects, portions of the ERPs also vary between hemispheres that are unrelated to stimulus, task, or subject features.

In an extension of these POA findings to younger populations, Molfese & Molfese (1979b) noted similar patterns of lateralized and bilateral responses with newborn and young infants. Unlike findings for VOT, however, POA discrimination was consistently found to be present at birth. In this study, ERPs were recorded from the left and right temporal regions of 16 full term newborn human infants. These data were recorded while the infants were presented series of consonant-vowel syllables that differed in the second formant transition (F2, which signaled POA information), and formant bandwidth. As with adults, one auditory ERP component that appeared only over the LH recording site discriminated between the two consonant sounds when they contained normal speech formant characteristics (peak latency = 192 ms). A second region of the auditory ERP varied systematically over both hemispheres and also discriminated between the two speech-like consonant sounds (peak latency = 630 ms). Notably, these latencies were markedly shorter than those found for VOT and TOT in young infants.

In a subsequent replication and extension of this work, Molfese & Molfese (1985) presented a series of consonant-vowel syllables that also varied in POA and formant structure. Two different consonant sounds, *b*, *g*, combined with three different vowel sounds were presented with speech or nonspeech formant structures. ERPs were again recorded from the left and right temporal regions. As in the case of Molfese & Molfese (1979b), analyses identified two regions of the auditory ERP that discriminated POA differences. One region, with a peak latency of 168 ms, was detected only over the LH site as discriminating between the two different consonant sounds; a second region with a peak latency of 664 ms, discriminated this POA difference and was detected by electrodes placed over both hemispheres. As can be readily seen when comparing Molfese & Molfese (1979b) with Molfese & Molfese (1985), these latencies and the pattern of bilateral and lateralized effects are remarkably stable across studies.

Also identical across POA infant studies was the finding that the lateralized effect noted in infants for the POA cue occurred prior to that for the bilateral effect, a finding opposite to that noted when adults were studied. However, the reversal of the temporal relationship between the bilateral and lateralized responses appears to be a legitimate one, given that virtually identical results were found by Molfese & Molfese (1985) and Molfese & Molfese (1979b) with different populations of infants and somewhat different stimulus sets that contained variations of the POA variable. A replication and extension of this work which involved recorded ERPs from 6 scalp locations of 38 newborn infants to a somewhat different stimulus set reported comparable effects at similar latencies (Molfese, Burger-Judisch & Hans 1991). This temporal pattern of initial lateralized responses followed by bilateral responses is also opposite to that noted previously for VOT cues for adults as well as that found for infants exposed to changes in the VOT temporal cue. Such differences in the patterns of ERP effects between VOT and POA lend support to the notion that different mechanisms subserve the perception and discrimination of the different speech related cues.

This relationship between lateralized and bilateral responses is not clear at this time. It does appear, however, that the bilateral response may develop after the lateralized ones for POA, both ontogenetically as well as phylogenetically. For example, Molfese & Molfese (1980) noted only the presence of LH lateralized responses in 11 preterm infants born on average 35.9 weeks postconception. Speech stimuli identical to those employed in Molfese (1978b) with adults were presented to these infants as well as a set of non-speech control stimuli. ERPs were recorded from the LH (T3) and RH (T4) temporal regions. As was found with full-term infants (Molfese & Molfese 1979b), a portion of the auditory ERP recorded from over the LH with a peak latency at 848 ms discriminated between speech stimuli containing different consonant transition cues. An additional LH component with a peak latency of 608 ms differentiated only between the nonphonetic consonants, a finding similar to that reported by Molfese (1978b) with adults, with the exception that adults were sensitive to both phonetic and nonphonetic contrasts.

While most studies of POA in infants involve newborns, one study by Dehaene-Lambertz & Dehaene (1994) noted a POA effect in older infants at 3 months of age. They recorded ERP activity to *ba* and *ga* syllables from 58 scalp electrodes placed on 16 infants. Two conditions were used: a repeated trials condition in which a standard sound was presented five times, and a deviant trial condition in which the standard was repeated four times, followed by one instance of a different syllable. Consonant discrimination changes were noted at one ERP peak (at 390 ms) which declined in amplitude as the standard stimulus was presented and then increased in amplitude with the presentation of the different syllable. They also noted a moderate LH asymmetry for this peak over posterior electrode sites. While this study is consistent with the neonatal research in reporting LH lateralized effects in young infants, the latency of the response occurs later than that reported by Molfese and colleagues. In addition, there is no report of the bilateral effect noted by Molfese and colleagues. However, it is difficult to determine whether such differences result from the different paradigms used, the differences in the ages of the infants sampled across the studies, differences in electrode sites sampled between studies, or other factors. It is clear that much more research is needed to fill in the missing gaps in our knowledge of the neuroelectrical correlates of POA from early infancy into the late adolescent years.

In summary, unlike the VOT studies, the POA cue evokes a relatively stable pattern of lateralized and bilateral responses from infancy into adulthood (Gelfer 1987; Molfese 1978b, 1980b; Molfese, Buhrke & Wang 1985; Molfese, Linnville, Wetzel & Leicht 1985; Molfese & Molfese 1979b, 1980, 1985; Molfese & Schmidt 1983). These effects appear to replicate well across laboratories (Gelfer 1987; Segalowitz & Cohen 1989), although a great deal more research is needed to characterize the changes in both the neuroelectrical correlates of VOT and POA through the infant and child years.

Vowel sounds

The ERP studies of vowel sounds have, for the most part, focused on steady state sounds such as *a* and *I* which do not vary in frequency. While consonant sound production is usually characterized by rapid movement of the articulators (tongue, jaw, lips, etc.) which translate into rapid frequency transitions, the mouth remains in a relatively steady state with no rapid change in the position of the articulators as the vowel sound is produced. There are four published studies investigating vowel discrimination abilities in young infants. Three of these studies used a mismatch negativity (MMN) paradigm (Cheour, Alho, Sainio, Reinikainen, Renlund, Aaltonen, Eerola & Naatanen 1997; Cheour-Luhtanen, Alho, Kujala, Sainio, Reinikainen, Renlund, Aaltonen, Eerola & Naatanen 1995; Cheour-Luhtanen, Alho, Sainio, Rinne, Reinikainen, Pohjavuori, Renlund, Aaltonen, Eerola & Naatanen 1996) while another used a paradigm comparable to that used by Molfese and colleagues to study VOT and POA information (Molfese & Searock 1986). These studies are summarized in Table 3.

The auditory MMN is produced in adults when an infrequent, physically deviant sound is presented in a sequence of standard repetitive sounds. The MMN component is appropriate for use with infants because its existence does not depend on the participant paying attention to the stimuli being presented. Cheour-Luhtanen et al. (1995) recorded ERPs from 12 healthy full-term newborns using electrodes placed at frontal, central, and parietal sites. The stimuli were synthesized (Klatt 1980) end points of the Finnish /i/-/y/ continuum, and a

Table 3. *Studies using event-related potentials to examine infants' responsivity to vowel sounds*

Study	Participants	Electrodes	Task	Results
Cheour-Luhtanen et al. (1996)	Preterm newborn infants $n=11$	F3, C3, T3, & P3 referenced to left mastoid, and F4, C4, T4, & P4 referenced to right mastoid	/y/ was the standard stimulus (probability of .8), /i/ and /yi/ were the deviant stimuli (probabilities of .1)	MMN between /y/ & /i/ was significant at 300–400 ms for F4 and P4, and at 400–500 ms for F3 and F4
Cheour-Luhtanen et al. (1995)	Full-term newborn infants $n=12$	F3, C3, & P3 referenced to left mastoid, and F4, C4, & P4 referenced to right mastoid	/y/ was the standard stimulus (probability of .8), /i/ and /yi/ were the deviant stimuli (probabilities of .1)	MMN between /y/ and /i/ was significant at 100–150°ms, 200–250°ms, and 250–300°ms at F3 and F4
Cheour et al. (1997)	3-month-old infants $n=6$	F3, C3, T3, & P3 referenced to left mastoid, and F4, C4, T4, & P4 referenced to right mastoid	/y/ was the standard stimulus (probability of .8), /i/ and /yi/ were the deviant stimuli (probabilities of .1)	MMN between /y/ and /i/ was significant at 200–300°ms at C4 and P3
Molfese & Searock (1986)	12-month-old infants $n=16$ Divided into High and Low Groups based on Median Split of McCarthy Verbal Scores at 3 years of age	T3 & T4 referenced to linked ears	3 vowel sounds (I, ae, au) and their nonspeech controls matched to the center frequencies of each vowel	RH discriminated I from au (P60) High Group discriminated nonspeech control I from ae and ae from au. (N200) In High Group, RH discriminated speech vowels I from ae, and nonspeech vowels I from ae and I from au. LH discriminated ae from au (P300) In Low Group, RH discriminated ae from au (P300)

boundary /y/i/ stimulus. The boundary stimulus was a vowel sound that was identified as /i/ approximately half of the time and /y/ half of the time. It should be noted that native speakers of Finnish perceive vowels categorically, whereas native speakers of English do not. The standard /y/ stimulus (probability = .8), the deviant /i/ stimulus (probablility = .1), and the deviant boundary stimulus /y/i/ (probability = .1) were presented in a random order. ERPs were averaged separately for standards and each deviant across the stimulus blocks presented during quiet sleep.

Repeated measures ANOVAs (Stimulus × Hemisphere) compared ERP amplitudes at frontal sites for the /y/ and /i/ stimuli. Significant differences in the ERPs elicited by the /y/ and /i/ stimuli were found at 100–150 ms, 200–250 ms, and 250–300 ms. No hemisphere differences were observed. Cheour-Luhtanen and her associates concluded that the MMN observed in newborns is similar to the MMN observed in adults. However, the MMN to deviant vowel /i/ was smaller than MMNs in previous studies. The frontally dominant scalp distribution found in this study resembled the scalp distribution for MMN found in adults.

In a closely related study of MMN in infants, Cheour-Luhtanen et al. (1996) extended their findings to include preterm infants using an identical set of vowel sounds. The participants were 11 preterm infants. Electrodes were placed at frontal, central, temporal, and parietal sites. T-tests indicated that the MMN was significant at 300–400 ms for right hemisphere frontal and right hemisphere parietal sites, and bilaterally at 400–500 ms for frontal sites. The response to the boundary stimulus did not differ significantly from that to the standard /y/ stimulus. The MMN found in the present study resembles, both in morphology and scalp distribution, the MMN response previously recorded from full-term newborns.

In order to study the development of the MMN in older infants, Cheour et al. (1997) conducted a research project using 6 healthy 3-month-old full-term infants as participants. Electrodes were placed bilaterally at frontal (F3, F4), central (C3, C4), temporal (T3, T4), and parietal sites (P3, P4). This study employed the same stimuli used by Cheour-Luhtanen et al. (1996). Difference waves were submitted to two-tailed t-tests. For the deviant /i/ stimulus, the MMN amplitude differed significantly from 0 microvolts at 200–300 ms at right hemisphere central (C4) and left hemisphere parietal (P3) sites. However, no hemispheric differences were found. Although both newborns and 3-month-olds demonstrated an MMN-like response, the MMN in the older group was larger in amplitude. This latter finding might be explained by differences in arousal states (asleep versus awake) or due to nervous system maturation.

In sum, studies of MMN to speech stimuli have revealed several consistent findings in newborn infants born prematurely, full-term newborns, and 3-month-old full-term infants. Across all three studies, a consistent MMN difference was found between the standard /y/ stimulus and the deviant /i/ stimulus. In adults, the MMN has a frontally dominant scalp distribution that was also found for the preterm and full-term newborn infants. Strangely, the 3-month-old infants were not found to have such a scalp distribution. The negativity to the deviant boundary stimulus /y/i/ was not significant in any of the studies. Finally, no significant hemispheric differences were noted across the three studies.

A study with older, one-year-old infants used a very different strategy to test auditory discrimination of vowel sounds (Molfese & Searock 1986). They recorded auditory ERPs from 16 one-year-olds. The infants heard three vowel sounds with normal speech formant characteristics (/i/, /ae/, /au/) and three nonspeech controls which contained one-hertz sinewave formant bandwidths instead of the normal speech formant bandwidths of 60, 90, and 120 Hz for formants 1, 2, and 3, respectively. The auditory stimuli were presented randomly while ERPs were collected from scalp electrodes placed at the left and right temporal regions. Upon test completion, the infants were divided using a median split into two groups based on their McCarthy verbal scores at three years of age. The High Group had a mean McCarthy verbal score of 77.25 (SD = 15.5) and the Low Group had a mean McCarthy score of 20.5 (SD = 12.6). Three regions of the ERP changed for both groups following the presentation of the vowel sounds. An initial positive component (P60) changed systematically over the RH of both groups to the vowel sounds, /i/ and /au/. A second region of the waveform, the N190, which characterized a negative peak at 190 ms post-vowel sound onset, only changed systematically for the High Group at the RH temporal site and discriminated the nonspeech control sounds, /i/ from /ae/ and /ae/ from /au/. Finally, a positive peak at 340 ms discriminated the vowel speech sounds, /i/ from /ae/, for the high group and the nonspeech sounds, /i/ from /ae/ and /i/ from /au/ at the RH site. The only LH discrimination of sounds for the High Group occurred in response to the nonspeech sounds for /ae/ versus /au/. Only one discrimination over the RH was noted for the Low Group who discriminated /ae/ from /au/.

On the basis of these electrophysiological data, it appears that brain responses to speech materials from infancy into adulthood are multidimensional and that they develop in a dynamic fashion. First, it is clear that discrimination of different speech cues emerge at different times in early development. This is true from both the standpoint of behavioral research (Eimas et al. 1971) as well as ERP research (Molfese & Molfese 1979a, 1979b, 1985, 1997). Relatively stable and reliable ERP correlates of consonant POA discrimination have been noted in newborns. At the same time, however, VOT does not appear to develop until sometime after birth, at least in the majority of the population (Molfese & Molfese 1979a; Simos & Molfese 1997). Second, different regions of the auditory ERP elicited by the different auditory stimuli appear to lateralize differently, depending on the evoking stimuli. The temporal cue, VOT, elicits a differential RH response, while the POA cue elicits a differential LH response. Third, the scalp distributions for ERP effects in relation to speech sound discrimination change with development. Thus, for example, Molfese & Molfese (1979a) noted temporal lobe lateralized effects in newborn infants, while more pronounced temporal-parietal effects are noted in children (Molfese & Molfese 1988) and adults (Molfese 1978a). The fourth point is that different portions of the ERP waveform appear sensitive to phonetic speech sound contrasts at different developmental stages. Thus, shortly after birth, speech sound discriminations are noted to occur at relatively long latencies (520–920 ms, see Molfese & Molfese 1979b; Simos & Molfese 1997), while these effects shift forward in the ERP wave to 180–400 ms for one-year-olds (Molfese & Searock 1986) and for preschoolers (Molfese & Hess 1978; Molfese & Molfese 1988), and from 50 to 350 ms for elementary school children and adults (Molfese 1978a, 1978b, 1980). Fifth, and finally, at some point during the auditory ERP to virtually all stimuli tested to date using this procedure, the two hemispheres, in both infants and adults, respond differently to all stimuli. This general hemisphere difference seems most pronounced in the preterm infants, with many different regions of the ERP varying between the two hemispheres (Molfese & Molfese 1980). However, this difference is also present in newborns (Molfese & Molfese 1979b, 1985), one-year-old infants (Molfese & Searock 1986), preschool age children (Molfese & Hess 1978; Molfese & Molfese 1988), and adults (Molfese 1978a, 1978b, 1980a, 1980b, 1984; Molfese & Schmidt 1983).

Infant speech perception responses generally appear to occur at approximately 200, 530, and 900 ms post stimulus onset for VOT, at approximately 200, 400, 630, and 850 ms for POA, and at approximately 60, 200, 300, and 400–500 ms for vowel sound discrimination. The major discrepancy between studies for these three cues appears to be centered on variations in the ERP's middle latencies between 400 and 630 ms, as well as the scalp distributions for these effects. This suggests that different mechanisms must subserve the perception of these three different speech cues. With age, responses to all three speech cues appear to occur earlier in time as indicated by shorter latency responses in the ERP waveforms. In addition, ERPs to speech materials appear to generate multiple responses in the infant waveform with an earlier ERP peak varying bilaterally while a second, later peak occurs in a lateralized fashion. Across both speech cues bilateral responses appear to occur with similar latencies. The lateralized responses for two of these cues, VOT and POA, however, show much more variability. POA and VOT thus elicit different lateral patterns with different latencies. This is a further indication that different mechanisms must underlay the perception of these three different types of speech information.

Electrophysiological correlates of infant word acquisition

While our knowledge of infants' speech perception has expanded rapidly over the past two decades (Eimas et al. 1971; Kuhl 1985; Molfese & Molfese 1979b, 1980, 1985; Morse 1974), little remains known about the infant's beginning comprehension of "names" for objects/events (Bates 1979). While some investigations have documented and catalogued the words first comprehended by infants, beginning around 8 months of age (Benedict 1975; Kamhi 1986; Macnamara 1982; Miller & Chapman 1981), investigations only recently have probed the nature of the older infant's early word meanings (Bloom, Lahey, Hood, Lifter & Fiess 1980; Clark 1983; Retherford, Schwartz & Chapman 1981; Snyder, Bates & Bretherton 1981) and to study the very beginning stages of the infant's ability to perceive and remember the names for objects and events (Bates, Benigni, Bretherton, Camaioni & Voltera 1979; Bates, Bretherton, Snyder, Shore & Voltaire 1980; Golinkoff, Hirsh-Pasek, Cauley & Gordon 1987; Hirsh-Pasek & Golinkoff 1996; Kamhi 1986). Moreover, virtually nothing is known about the role that the brain plays in the early acquisition of such word meanings (Molfese 1989a, 1990; Molfese, Morse & Peters 1990). Furthermore, while scientists have speculated that the LH plays a major role in early language acquisition (Best 1988; Lenneberg 1967), little actual work has been conducted to address this issue. Indeed, six recent papers indicate that ERPs can be successfully used to study the developmental neuropsychology of early word comprehension in infants from 12- to 20-months of age (Mills, Coffey-Corina & Neville 1993, 1994; Molfese 1989a, 1990; Molfese, Morse & Peters 1990; Molfese, Wetzel & Gill 1993). These early word acquisition studies are summarized in Table 4.

The youngest group to be studied during word acquisition using ERPs was a population of 12-month-old infants (Molfese, Wetzel & Gill 1993). This investigation represented a direct attempt to determine whether ERPs recorded from 12-month-old infants could discriminate between words confidently believed by the infants' parents to be known to these young infants from those

Table 4. *Studies using event-related potential (ERP) procedures to study infant and toddler word acquisition*

Study	Subjects	Electrode	Task	Results
Molfese, Wetzel & Gill (1993)	12-month old infants $n=12$	F_L, F_R, T3, T4, P_L, & P_R referenced to linked ears	Randomly ordered words rated as known to the infants and words rated as unknown	Known vs Unknown word effects: LH frontal, temporal, parietal; RH frontal, temporal 210–300 ms All electrode sites; 210–300 ms
Molfese (1989a)	14-month old infants $n=14$	F_L, F_R, T3, T4, P_L, & P_R referenced to linked ears	Experiment 1: Randomly ordered words rated as known to the infants and words rated as unknown	Known vs Unknown word effects: LH frontal, temporal, parietal; RH frontal, temporal 30–220ms All electrode sites 270–380 ms LH and RH parietal 380–500 ms
Molfese (1990)	16-month old infants $n=16$	F_L, F_R, T3, T4, P_L, & P_R referenced to linked ears	Experiment 1: Randomly ordered words rated as known to the infants and words rated as unknown	Known vs Unknown word effects: Females: T3; Males: F_L,T3, F_R 180–340 ms Females: LH frontal, temporal, parietal; Males: All electrode sites 580–700 ms
Molfese, Morse & Peters (1990)	14-month old infants $n=14$	F_L, F_R, T3, T4, P_L, & P_R referenced to linked ears	Pretraining test: ERPs to meaningless CVCVs 5 days training, 2 blocks of 15 minutes per day training one CVCV to one novel object and another CVCV to another novel object Post training test: Parents rate training effectiveness; ERPs to same CVCVs used in pre-training test	Pretraining test: No ERP differences for Match vs. Mismatch Post training test: Match vs. Mismatch word effects: LH and RH frontal 30–120 ms; LH frontal, temporal, parietal 530–600 ms

Study	Subjects	Electrode	Task	Results
Mills, Coffey-Corina & Neville (1994) Experiment 1	13–17-month-old infants ($n=22$) & 20-month-old infants ($n=24$)	"Bilateral frontal, temporal, parietal, and occipital sites", Cz and Pz all referenced to linked mastoids	Words consisted of comprehended (known) & unknown words	*13–17 Months*: N200 & N350; known > unknown words over both hemispheres and at all sites anterior to occipital sites *20 Months*: N200 & N350; known > unknown words over LH temporal and parietal sites *Across Age*: N200; latency was earlier for 20- than for 13–17-month-olds; "Responsiveness to known & unknown words differed for 2 age groups"
Mills, Coffey-Corina & Neville (1994) Experiment 2	13–17- month-old infants ($n=22$) 2 groups: talking, & not talking *20-month-old infants ($n=24$) 2 groups: high producers and low producers	Presumably the same as Experiment 1	Presumably the same as Experiment 1	*13–17 Months*: 2 groups "differed in responsiveness" to comprehended and unknown words over occipital regions Non-talkers: ERPs differed to known and unknown words at all sites Talkers: ERPs differed to known and unknown words at sites anterior to occipital regions *20 Months*: High producers: N200 to known words larger over temporal and parietal than over frontal or occipital regions Low producers: N200 of equal amplitude over frontal, temporal, and parietal regions
Mills, Coffey-Corina & Neville (1993)	20-month old infants $n=24$	F7, F8, 33% distance from T3/4 to C3/4, 50% of distance from T3/4 to P3/4, O1, O2 referenced to linked mastoids	Ten known words, unknown words, and backward presented words	*N200*: 90% showed N200 for known > unknown words at T3, P3 sites 80% showed known > unknown words at F7 and T4, P4 sites Known: Temporal, parietal > frontal, occipital Unknown: RH amplitude > LH Larger to known than backward at frontal, temporal & parietal sites; Larger to unknown than backward at RH sites; Backward ERPs more positive over LH anterior than LH posterior sites *N350*: Latency: Known < backward (by 20 ms) Amplitude: Known > unknown at LH temporal & parietal sites; Known > backward at LH sites; Unknown > backward at RH sites; Unknown larger for RH than LH sites *N600-900*: For all stimuli, anterior RH > LH No sex related effects

*The 20-month-old infants in Mills et al (1994) Experiment 2 are assumed to be the same participants described in Mills et al. (1993).

words that parents strongly believed were not known to the infants. It was hoped that multiple electrode sites over various areas of each hemisphere would provide more information concerning the involvement of different brain regions in early word discrimination. Because the details of this study are relevant to subsequent studies that will be reviewed here, this review of Molfese et al. (1993) will be more extensive.

A group of nine 12-month-old infants were tested. Unique stimulus tapes were constructed for each infant, based upon the parental ratings obtained during a telephone interview during that parents were asked to identify all of the words from an original list of ten (i.e., "bottle", "book", "cookie", "key", "kitty", "ball", "dog", "baby", "duck", and "cat"), that they believed that their infant understood. Next, they were asked to rate their confidence in their identification using a five-point scale. Parents were told that a rating of "5" indicated that they were "very confident" that the infant did or did not know the word, while a rating of "1" signified that the parents were "not confident at all" about their decision. Following the interview, parent ratings were converted to a range from "1" to "10", with "1" signifying high confidence that the infant did not know the word, and "10" signifying high confidence that the infant knew the word. The stimuli which were used as the "known" words in the present study had a mean rating of 9.7 out of 10.0 (SD = .4). For the "unknown" words, there was a mean rating of 1.9 (SD = .5).

Each audio tape contained stimulus repetitions of two spoken words produced by an adult male speaker using flat intonation. Each word began with a voiced, stop consonant to minimize ERP variations due to acoustic factors such as voicing or rise time. One of these two words was identified by that infant's parent as known to the infant while the second word was believed by that parent to be unknown to the infant. The known and unknown words were arranged on the tape in a block random order, with 54 occurrences of each and a randomly varied interstimulus interval.

The six electrode placements included two electrodes placed respectively over the left (T3) and right (T4) temporal areas (Jasper 1958), a third electrode placed at FL, a point midway between the external meatus of the left ear and Fz; a fourth electrode placed at FR, a position midway between the right external meatus and Fz; a fifth electrode placed at PL, a point midway between the left external meatus and Pz; and a sixth electrode placed at PR, a point on the right side of the head midway between the right ear's external meatus and Pz. Such placements, it was hoped, would provide information concerning not only LH versus RH responses to the known and unknown words, but in addition, information within each hemisphere concerning general language perception areas commonly thought to be localized to the left temporal and parietal language receptive regions of the brain as well as the language production areas of the frontal lobe. The electrical activity recorded from these scalp electrodes was obtained in response to a randomly arranged series of words matched in duration and peak intensity levels. The words were presented auditorily through a speaker positioned approximately one meter over the midline of the infant's head while the infant was in a quiet awake state.

Twelve averages were obtained for each infant, including averages for the known and unknown words for each of the six scalp electrode sites. As in the case of the speech perception studies, the average ERPs were submitted to a two step analysis procedure (Brown, Marsh & Smith 1979; Chapman, McCrary, Bragdon & Chapman 1979; Donchin, Teuting, Ritter, Kutas & Heffley 1975; Gelfer 1987; Molfese 1978a, 1978b; Molfese & Molfese 1979b, 1980, 1985; Ruchkin, Sutton, Munson, Silver & Macar 1981; Segalowitz & Cohen 1989). This procedure first involved the use of a Principal Components Analysis (PCA) and then an Analysis of Variance. Six rotated factors accounted for 77.84% of the total variance (Cattell 1966). The ANOVAs were based on the design of Subjects (9) × Word Understanding (2) × Electrode Sites within Hemispheres (3) × Hemispheres (2). These were conducted to determine if any of the regions of the ERPs identified by the six factors varied systematically as a function of the specific levels of the independent variables in this study.

Two ERP regions were noted to vary as a function of whether parents believed that the infant could recognize the meaning of a word or not. The first region, which reflected variations in the initial portion of the waveform until approximately 140 ms following stimulus onset, indicated that ERP activity recorded from over all LH sites discriminated the known from the unknown words. However, only electrical activity from the frontal and temporal regions of the RH made similar discriminations. The ERPs elicited by the known words were characterized by a larger negative (or downward) peak prior to 140 ms while a markedly smaller negative peak characterized the ERPs evoked by the unknown words. Thus, the vertical amplitude appears larger for the known words than the unknown words. A second region of the averaged ERPs between 210 and 300 ms post stimulus onset also varied systematically as a function of whether the word was thought to be understood by the infant. This effect was reflected by amplitude differences in the second major negative component of the ERP where the overall negative peak-to-peak amplitude in the region between 210 and 300 ms was generally larger for ERPs elicited by the known than by the unknown words.

Molfese and colleagues interpreted these results to indicate that auditory evoked ERPs successfully discriminated between words that parents believed their 12-month-old infants knew from those that the infants were thought not to understand. Moreover, Molfese et al. noted that even at this young age the process of word comprehension appeared to be dynamic in that different regions of the brain responded differently over time following the onset of the word that was known to the infant. Initially, differential electrical activity was generated early in the waveform for approximately 200 ms over the entire LH and most of the RH except the right parietal area. Such early responses suggest that the infant begins to process known words as meaningful virtually from the time they begin to hear the auditory signal. This initial response period then was followed for a 100 ms period by a spreading of the discrimination to all ERP scalp regions. Thus, the differential response of the ERPs to words appears to continue through much of the time that the infant hears the word, although it appears to be carried out by different brain regions.

A related study with older infants showed a similar pattern of discrimination. In Experiment 1, Molfese (1989a) recorded auditory evoked responses from frontal, temporal, and parietal scalp locations over the LH and RH of 10 infants, 14 months in age, who also listened to a series of words, half of which were determined to be known to the infants (based on behavioral testing and parental report) and half of which were believed not to be known to the infant. As in the case of the 12-month infant study (Molfese et al. 1993), parents rated words from a list as either words the infant knew or words they did not know. In addition, however, each infant received four behavioral trials, with two independent observers rating whether or not the infant knew the word presented. In order to assess the infant's comprehension, a specially constructed multi-shelved cabinet was used. The object representing the known or the unknown word (as appropriate) was placed in one of the four compartments of a test cabinet. Two compartments of the test box each contained distracter items randomly selected for each trial from a sack of toys while the fourth compartment remained empty. The parent then instructed the infant to look at or retrieve various toys using instructions to the infant such as, "Go get the book" or "Look at the duck". The compartments that contained the test object, the empty space, and the distracters were randomized for each trial for each infant. On each trial the raters independently determined whether they believed that the infant responded to the instructions correctly and recorded their confidence in these judgments on a 5-point scale identical to that previously used by the parents. For the children in this study, both the parents (across the two interviews) and the raters reliably rated the words they believed were known to the infant as different from those that they believed the infant did not understand.

Analyses of the ERP data isolated three regions of the evoked potential waveform that discriminated known from unknown words in this population. Initially, ERP activity across both hemispheres (with the exception of the right parietal region) between 30 and 220 ms following stimulus onset discriminated known from unknown words. This effect appeared as a positive peak for the known words and a negative peak in this same region for the unknown words. This activity was followed shortly by a large positive to negative shift in the waveform between 270 and 380 ms across all electrode sites for both the LH and RH that was larger for the known than for the unknown words. Finally, a late negative peak between 380 and 500 ms, detected only by electrodes placed over the left and right parietal regions, was larger for the known than for the unknown words.

Molfese speculated that such known vs. unknown word effects could result from familiarity differences. That is, words known to the infant would be expected to be more familiar while unknown words would be unfamiliar and novel. To determine whether the results from Experiment 1 reflected meaning differences or differences in item familiarity, Molfese (1989a) conducted a second experiment to determine whether familiarity with speech stimuli produced brain responses similar to those found for the known vs. unknown word materials. A different set of ten 14-month-old infants first listened to a nonsense bi-syllable (CVCV) over a two-day period. Parents encouraged their infant to play with a box on which a large orange Frisbee was mounted and connected to a series of hidden switches. Infants played with the device for three times on each of the 2 days designated for training, with 15 minutes allowed for each of the six play sessions. Five infants heard "toto" during the familiarization process while five children heard "gigi" to decrease the likelihood that any experimental effects were due to acoustic differences between the stimuli instead of due to differences in amount of previous exposure to the different stimuli. On the third day, ERPs were recorded to this now familiar CVCV and to the novel CVCV. Electrode placements were identical to those used in Experiment 1. If the latencies and scalp distributions of the brain responses found in this study were identical to those found in the known–unknown word study, the familiarity hypothesis could not be rejected. In fact, no conclusion could be reached concerning whether the effects were due to familiarity or meaning related effects, since the infants could also be using the familiarized bi-syllable to label the device. However, results did differ between the two tasks. ERPs recorded over both the LH and RH frontal areas discriminated between the familiar and unfamiliar CVCVs. In addition, the major peak in the ERP that discriminated these differences occurred at 360 ms, not between 30 and 220 ms or at the 630 ms previously found to discriminate known from unknown words. Consequently, Molfese concluded that the earlier ERP findings discussed in the first experiment did indeed reflect meaning differences and not differences in familiarity (see also Molfese & Wetzel 1992).

A study with 16-month-old infants (Molfese 1990) which utilized procedures similar to those employed by Molfese, Wetzel & Gill (1993) and Experiment 1 of Molfese (1989a), found comparable differences in an older group of infants in response to known and unknown words. Molfese tested 18 infants with a mean age of 16.57 months. As in his previous studies, parent handedness was measured and found to indicate strong right hand preferences across parents. In addition, parents were asked to rate a set of 10 words during a telephone interview and a subsequent lab visit in order to identify at least one word that parents confidently believed their infant knew and another word they believed the infant did not know. As in the case of Experiment 1 of Molfese (1989a), two independent raters evaluated infants' word knowledge using the four-shelf cabinet. Only infants were tested whose parents and raters agreed on the same set of known and unknown words, and who displayed high confidence that the infant did or did not know specific words. ERP testing then commenced with 54 repetitions of each of the two words presented auditorily in random order, separated from each other by a varied ISI random.

Two ERP regions varied as a function of the known vs. unknown distinction. The first region, between 180 and 340 ms with a peak latency of 270 ms contained a larger N180–P340 complex for unknown words at only the T3 site for females while the left and right frontal regions as well as T3 showed a similar effect for males. A second region, between 580 and 700, with a peak latency of 650 ms, also discriminated known vs. unknown words for females but this time at all LH sites while for males, both the LH and RH sites discriminated known vs. unknown words. In all cases, this discrimination was reflected by larger negative shifts for unknown words.

A fourth study by Molfese, Morse & Peters (1990) also investigated aspects of the infant's early word comprehension, but this time in a training situation. Fourteen infants at 14 months of age participated in a training study in which specific CVCV nonsense syllables were systematically paired with specific objects of specific shapes and colors over a five-day training period. On the day before the training period, infants first were tested in a Match–Mismatch task in which on half of the trials each object was paired with its CVCV label (i.e., the label that the infant would later learn during the training period was the "name" of that object) while on the other half of the trials the objects were mispaired with the CVCV "names" of other objects. The parents and infants then returned home for 5 days of training. On the sixth day and immediately prior to the post-training session, parents indicated whether or not their infants knew the name of the object in question and then to rate their own confidence in that judgment using the 5 point scale and rating system used earlier by Molfese (1989). All parents rated the terms as "known" by the infant with a mean confidence rating for "bidu" at 8.71 (SD = .88) and for "gibu" at 8.79 (SD = .94), indicating that the parents were confident that their infants understood which terms labeled which objects. Next, during the post-training test, infants again were tested in a Match–Mismatch task in which on half of the trials each object was paired with its CVCV label (Match condition) while on the other half of the trials the objects were mispaired with the CVCV "names" of other objects (Mismatch condition). The electrophysiological techniques used during this phase were identical to those employed during the pretest phase of this study.

Two regions of the ERP waveform reliably reflected Match related effects during this task — an early component of the ERP which changed bilaterally over the frontal regions of both hemispheres and a late occurring lateralized response which was restricted to only the LH electrode sites. The first, which occurred between 30 and 120 ms post stimulus onset, was characterized by a marked negativity for the Mismatch condition. A second region, which began 520 ms after stimulus onset, reached its peak at 580 ms, and then diminished by 600 ms, produced a positive going wave for the Mismatch condition over all of the LH electrode sites. Interestingly, since both auditory stimuli were equally familiar to the infant, no bilateral negative deflection occurred at 360 ms.

Since no such Match or Mismatch effects were noted in the pre-training ERP session, it is clear that the ERPs detected changes that occurred as a function of training. When a correct match occurred between the auditorily presented word and the object that the infant held, both the left and right frontal regions of the brain emitted brain responses that contained an initial positive deflection or peak between 20 and 100 ms following the auditory onset of the object name. If a mismatch occurred, however, this early positive deflection inverted 180 degrees and became a negative deflection. Later in time, between 520 and 600 ms, just before the conclusion of the ERP, a large positive going wave occurred over only the three LH electrode sites when the infant listened to a stimulus that did not name the object that the infant held. Given the short latency of the initial changes in the ERP waveshapes across the frontal regions, it appears that the young infant must recognize almost immediately if there is agreement between something that it hears and something that it sees and touches.

Mills, Coffey-Corina & Neville (1994) reported two experiments investigating ERPs to speech materials from somewhat older infants. In Experiment 1, 22 13- to 17-month-olds and 24 20-month-olds were tested. First, the Early Child Language Inventory (ELI) was administered to the children's parents to assess whether infants knew certain words. In the first experiment, ERPs were collected from bilateral frontal, temporal, parietal and occipital electrode sites, as well as Cz and Pz while infants listened to (1) comprehended words (words whose meanings were known by the child), and (2) unknown words (words whose meanings were not known). ERPs were then averaged separately for known and unknown words and baseline amplitudes were calculated relative to a prestimulus baseline. Specified time windows were then assessed for peak amplitudes and latencies: P100 (50–75 ms), N200 (125–250 ms), and N350 (275–450 ms), and N600–900 (calculated as the mean negative amplitude between 600 and 900 ms).

The 13- to 17-month-olds generated larger N200 and N350 amplitudes to known than unknown words over both hemispheres and at all electrode sites anterior to occipital sites. For 14 of the children (64%), this effect was larger from RH than LH. ERPs recorded from the 20-month-olds also elicited larger N200 and N350 responses for known than unknown words; although these differences were only noted at LH temporal and parietal electrode sites. While latency differences were noted between the two age groups for the N200, it occurred only slightly earlier (11 ms) for the 20-month-olds than for the 13- to 17-month-olds.

In Experiment 2, the same 22 13- to 17-month-old infants from the first experiment were divided into 2 subgroups. One subgroup ($n=11$) contained children who had started to talk and produced on average approximately 70 words (range = 17–97 words). The other subgroup ($n=11$) contained children who were matched on chronological age (CA), showed similar performance on language comprehension tests, and produced fewer than 10 words (range = 0–9 words). The 24 20-month-olds from Experiment 1 were also divided into two subgroups based on their performance on the ELI: High Producers (above 50th percentile) and Low Producers (below 50th percentile). Mean productive vocabularies were 310 and 77 words respectively. In this case, when the infants were divided on the basis of their productive vocabularies, some variations in ERP patterns were noted. The two groups of 13- to 17- month-olds differed in responsiveness to comprehended and unknown words over occipital regions. For children who had not begun to talk, ERP differences between known and unknown words were significant at all electrode sites; whereas for children who had begun to talk, these differences were restricted to areas anterior to the occipital regions. At 20 months of age the two groups showed marked differences in the distribution of the N200 to known words. The High group produced a larger N200 to known words over temporal and parietal than over frontal or occipital regions. The Low group, in contrast, produced a uniform amplitude N200 over frontal, temporal and parietal regions.

In a related study with older toddlers, Mills, Coffey-Corina & Neville (1993) recorded auditory ERPs from 24 20-month-old children to a series of comprehended (known), unknown, and backward presented words. The Early Language Inventory (ELI), was administered one week before ERP testing. Parents rated each word on 1–4 scale of confidence that the child did or did not comprehend the word. Also a Comprehension Book with 50 object names, 9 verbs and modifiers was presented to the child who then pointed to each picture verbalized by experimenter. The child's language production was tested separately.

ERPs were collected from each child to auditorily presented known, unknown, and backward words. An electrode cap was used with electrodes placed at F7, F8, 33% distance from T3 to C3 and from T4 to C4, 50% of distance from T3 to P3, and from T4 to P4, O1, O2. Prior to analyses the children were divided into two groups based on whether their ELI was above or below the 50th percentile. Subsequent tests confirmed that these groups differed on productive vocabulary and comprehension. In general, Mills et al. reported larger temporal and parietal responses than for frontal or occipital sites for known words, while there were larger RH responses overall to unknown words. A number of known vs. unknown word effects were noted.

For the N200 region, 90% of the children produced a larger N200 to known versus unknown words at LH temporal and parietal sites while 80% showed a larger N200 to known versus unknown words at LH frontal and RH temporal & parietal sites. When comparisons included backward speech, larger responses were noted to known and unknown words than to backward speech, with generally more positive responses over LH anterior than LH posterior sites.

At the next major peak measured (N350 — the most negative point between 275 and 450 ms), the known words elicited a faster N350 than backward speech (by 20 ms). Amplitude measures of this peak found larger responses to known than unknown words at LH temporal and parietal sites. Unknown words overall elicited larger responses over RH than LH sites. Finally, responses to known words were larger than to backward stimuli at LH sites while unknown words elicited larger responses than backward stimuli at RH sites. Measures of the negative wave in the region between 600 and 900 ms noted that all stimuli elicited larger anterior RH than LH responses.

When ERP sensitivity to language abilities was compared between the two language groups, a number of additional effects were noted. Overall, the N200 amplitude was greater for Low language producers for both known and unknown words. N350 latency was fastest to known words for the High production group. Additionally, High production group had larger N350 amplitudes at LH temporal and parietal sites.

Other later effects were also noted within the 600–900 ms region. The negative amplitude was largest for known words for the High production group at RH frontal site, and the Low production group at bilateral anterior sites. Known words also produced larger responses for the Low than High producers at LH temporal and parietal sites while the unknown words produced larger responses for the Low than for the High producers at RH parietal site. Unlike Molfese (1990), who tested a more restricted range of 16-month-olds, Mills et al. did not note any sex-related effects.

While there are a growing number of recent studies investigating word vs. non-word discriminations in infants and very young toddlers, we could find no such work with preschool children. Only a few studies have been reported with older children such as Licht, Kok, Bakker & Bouma (1986) with 5 to 6 year olds, Berman and Friedman (1993) who included a group of 7 to 10 year olds along with an adolescent and adult groups, Shelburne (1973) who tested 8 to 12 year olds, and Taylor & Keenan (1990) who tested three groups of children between 7 and 12 years of age.

Summary of early word acquisition studies

There are remarkable similarities in terms of scalp electrode effects and known–unknown word discrimination effects across studies. For example, Molfese (1989a, Experiment 1) noted that three regions of the ERP waveform discriminated known from unknown words. Initially, ERP activity across both hemispheres (with the exception of the right parietal region) between 30 and 220 ms following stimulus onset discriminated between known and unknown words. Thus, in two different ages of infants, 12-month-olds and 14-month-olds, similar regions of the ERP waveform distributed over the same electrode recording areas discriminated known from unknown words. A similar effect was also reported by Molfese, Morse & Peters (1990). Furthermore, in all three studies, this activity was followed shortly by a large positive to negative change in amplitude across all electrode sites for both the LH and RH that was larger for the known than for the unknown words or match versus mismatched labels. Molfese (1989a) reported that this effect occurred between 270 and 380 ms while Molfese et al. (1990) identified this area between 210 and 300 ms. These studies differ, however, in that Molfese (1989a) reported a third, late negative peak between 380 and 500 ms, that was detected only by electrodes placed over the left and right parietal regions, an effect that was larger for the known than for the unknown words. No such effect was noted by Molfese et al. The absence of such a late effect in the ERP responses of 12-month-old infants could reflect differences in the developmental stages between the younger infants tested by Molfese, Wetzel & Gill (1993) and the older infants tested by Molfese (1989a, 1990).

Molfese et al. (1993), as in the case of both Molfese (1989a) and Molfese et al. (1990), observed an effect in the initial portion of the ERP that discriminated known from unknown words. Given other behavioral and electrophysiological investigations of co-articulated speech cues as noted above (Ali, Gallagher, Goldstein & Daniloff 1971; Daniloff & Moll 1968; MacNeilage & DeClerk 1969; Molfese 1979), it is possible that the infants can use acoustic correlates of articulatory information in the initial portion of words to identify words. If so, this suggests that such perceptual strategies are mastered by the infant at a very early stage of the language learning process.

It is interesting to note that, although a general belief exists that language perception is carried out by mechanisms within the LH (Lenneberg 1967), none of the known versus unknown word related effects were exclusively restricted to only the LH electrode sites in infants younger than 16 months of age. Even the Mills et al. (1994) study with 20-month-old infants indicate that a large percentage of children (80%) showed larger N200 responses to known than unknown words at both LH frontal and RH temporal and parietal sites. The N350 latency difference between known and unknown words also occurred across both hemispheres, rather than for only LH sites. These data can be used to argue that, at least in the early stages of language acquisition, both hemispheres of the brain are dynamically involved in the process of learning to relate word speech sound sequences to word meanings. If this is indeed the case, then perhaps the reason that young infants experiencing LH brain damage during the initial stages of language acquisition are able to recover language skills more quickly than those injured later may be due to the duplicated mechanisms subserving language abilities of the RH at that stage. Consequently, after the loss of the LH, the infant's language functions may continue to be served by these RH mechanisms. If, on the other hand, the child experiences LH damage later in development, the outcome could be quite different. Either due to changes in brain plasticity or further specialization of the brain with development, the ability of the non-language specialized hemisphere in the normally developing child becomes more restricted with age. Consequently, following injury to the LH at this later stage of development, there may not be a right hemisphere that is capable of performing these functions and therefore language performance would be impaired because the RH is unable to continue this process in the absence of a fully functioning LH. Instead, the RH would only have residual abilities that reflected its involvement at a much earlier stage of development.

Syntax

There have been virtually no attempts to study syntax development in infants or children. One exception to this is a study by Tan (1996) in which auditory ERPs were collected to words used as nouns or verbs in a task modeled after Molfese, Burger-Judisch & Gill (1996). ERPs were recorded to auditory presentations of nouns and verbs while 22 preschool-age children (range = 3.17–5.5 years) viewed videotaped segments in which an actor manipulated objects using different actions. Based on comparisons with adult data from previous work (Molfese et al. 1996), her findings suggested that the pattern of brain involvement underlying syntactic class discriminations undergo developmental changes between the preschool years and adulthood. While bilateral frontal areas of the brain are primarily involved in subserving the syntactic discriminations in preschool-age children, the functions become more lateralized in adulthood. Moreover, the pattern of brain involvement progresses in an anterior to posterior direction with age.

Visual and auditory stimuli were previously created for presentation in a similar study involving adults by Molfese et al. (1996). These stimuli consisted of a videotaped presentation depicting separate scenes of actions with objects. Each visual scene was accompanied by an auditorily presented word, either a noun or a verb, that was presented twice during that scene. In addition, each visual scene was paired to a word that was either congruous or incongruous with the action or the object in the scene. The visual portion of the stimuli consisted of eight individual scenes. Each scene involved a female actor manipulating an object while seated at a table. The actions shown were that of the actor eating a cookie, bouncing a ball, patting a toy stuffed dog, pouring milk into a glass, pushing a toy car, rocking a baby doll cradled in her arms, drinking from a cup, and dropping a toy baby bottle on the table. Auditory stimuli consisted of a recorded female adult voice saying four nouns (i.e., "cookie, baby, bottle, doggie"), and four verbs (i.e., "bouncing, drinking, pouring, pushing"). Each child was instructed to watch the television screen where the video scenes were presented and told that these scenes would be accompanied by auditorily presented words that would either match ("go with") or not match ("not go with") the video scenes.

ERPs were recorded from electrode placements that were identical to those used by Molfese (1989). Two different analysis approaches, one involving a traditional baseline-to-peak (BTP) analysis and the other using a Principal Components Analysis (PCA) approach were used for the data analyses and good agreement was noted between the two approaches. The first window comprised the P1-N1 peaks (latency range = 1–250 ms), P2-N2 were encompassed in the second (latency range = 250–450 ms), while the third subsumed the P3 wave (latency range = 450–700 ms). The fourth window contained the final portion of the wave (latency range = 600–900 ms) for which an area measure was computed. Baseline-to-peak (BTP), peak-to-peak (PTP) and area measures were performed on the individual ERPs collected for each subject. A baseline average was calculated based on the first 80 ms sampled during the 100 ms prestimulus period of the wave.

As Tan had predicted, the ERP waveforms clearly discriminated nouns from verbs. Four different ERP regions carried out this discrimination. Furthermore, hemispheric differences in responding to the different syntactic classes were evident in two adjacent ERP regions. For the first region, the RH discriminated nouns from verbs as evidenced by the PCA-ANOVA procedure while the BTP measure indicated that this discrimination occurred over the LH. In the second region, the RH discriminated between nouns and verbs only in the match condition, while the LH discriminated between mismatched nouns and verbs. These findings are partially in keeping with those of Molfese et al. (1996).

The hemisphere effects related to syntactic differences occurred later in children than in the adults. Lateralized noun–verb differences occurred at the peak latency of 355 ms in the adults, while the preschool children showed a much later effect, between 590 ms and 790 ms. Despite the difference in latency, the findings from both age groups converged to reveal somewhat consistent hemispheric differences in subserving language functions.

Tan's second hypothesis was also supported. ERPs recorded to match and mismatches differed for both noun and verb classes, a conclusion similar to the one reached in the earlier study conducted with adults (Molfese et al. 1996). However, while those authors found that several components in the adults' ERPs beginning at 150 ms and continuing to the end of the wave reliably discriminated match from mismatch conditions, Tan found these discrimination effects within two widely separated regions of the waveform. The ERPs differentiated between match and mismatched nouns in the initial (between 1 ms to 250 ms) and final (600 ms to 900 ms) regions of the ERPs. Both these effects occurred at the bilateral frontal recording sites, once again emphasizing the role of the anterior regions within the two hemispheres that underlie the processing of syntactic classes early in life.

In summary, Tan noted that ERPs recorded from preschool children clearly discriminated nouns from verbs at different times and within various matching situations. In addition, the bilateral frontal regions of the brain appeared to be the most involved areas in the overall processing of syntactic class information. This finding is in part similar to those obtained from adults in which anterior-posterior scalp differences were observed as a function of varying syntactic meanings (Brown, Marsh & Smith 1976, 1979). When viewed in conjunction with the adult findings, the data from Tan's study provide evidence for a developmental change in syntactic class processing.

Summary syntactic development studies

Several consistent trends in the ERP data reviewed thus far can be noted. First, it is clear that discrimination of different speech cues emerge at different times in early development. This is true from both the standpoint of behavioral research (Eimas et al. 1971) as well as ERP research (Molfese & Molfese 1979a, 1979b, 1985, 1997). For example, relatively stable and reliable ERP correlates of consonant place of articulation (POA) discrimination occur in newborn infants. At the same time, however, discrimination of a different speech cue, voice onset time (VOT), does not appear to develop until sometime after birth, at least in the majority of the population (Molfese & Molfese 1979b; Simos & Molfese 1997). Second, the scalp distributions for ERP effects in relation to speech sound discrimination and word discrimination change with development. Thus, for example, Molfese & Molfese (1979a) note temporal lateral effects in newborn infants, while more pronounced frontal effects are noted in 12–16 month old infants (Molfese 1989b, 1990), and temporal-parietal effects in children (Molfese & Molfese 1988) and adults (Molfese 1978a). The third point is that different temporal regions of the ERP waveform appear sensitive to phonetic, semantic, and syntactic contrasts at different developmental stages. Thus, shortly after birth, speech sound discriminations are noted to occur at relatively long latencies (520–920 ms, see Molfese & Molfese 1979a; Simos & Molfese 1997), while these effects shift forward in the ERP wave to 180–400 ms for preschoolers (Molfese & Hess 1978; Molfese & Molfese 1988), and from 50 to 350 ms for elementary school children and adults. Finally, the scalp distributions for ERPs change as a function of age, stimuli, and task. While early patterns of lateralized responses are noted across different domains, from speech perception to syntactic processing, bilaterally distributed responses often co-occur, although at different latencies during the processing of these materials.

Such lateralized and bilateral patterns may have important implications for later language development (Molfese & Betz 1988). Of particular concern are questions such as: Are these patterns of lateralized responses to phonetic contrasts related to later language development or do they reflect only some basic pattern of auditory processing in the brain that have little relation to language development? Given Lenneberg's (1967) notion that lateralization is a biological sign of language, could such early patterns of lateralized discrimination for speech sounds predict later language outcomes? Theoreticians have speculated that the absence of hemispheric differences in a child indicates that the child is at risk for cognitive or language disabilities (Travis 1931). Although the data generally have not supported such a position with regard to the absence of hemispheric differences and disabilities, predictions concerning later performance could be enhanced when hemispheric differences are considered in light of specific language or speech processing capacities.

Multivariate approaches to language prediction using ERPs to predict later development

One recent development trend in the study of ERP correlates of language acquisition is the use of ERPs to predict later language development. Such studies have recorded ERPs to speech sounds in very young infants and then used these brain responses to predict factors such as later vocabulary size. These results have been used to argue that neonatal auditory discrimination abilities as measured by ERPs are an important factor for later language development. The children who performed better on language tasks at age 3 years, as newborn infants could discriminate between consonant sounds alone and consonant sounds in combination with different vowel sounds. Such a pattern of responding suggests that more linguistically advanced children are already at an advantage at birth because their nervous systems can make finer discriminations along a variety of different dimensions. As D. Molfese (1989b) suggests, "Perhaps the earlier an infant can discriminate between speech sounds in its environment, the more likely that infant will be able to use such information to discriminate word sound differences" (p. 55). Such early discrimination abilities may later play a major role in the infant and young child's vocabulary and syntax development.

In this regard, Molfese & Molfese (1985, 1986) attempted to establish the predictive validity of a variety of factors in predicting long-term outcomes in language development from measures taken shortly after birth and during the first years of life. In the first study, 16 infants were studied longitudinally from birth through 3 years. Information was collected on gender, birthweight, length at birth, gestational age, scores on the Obstetric Complications Scale (Littman & Parmelee 1978), the Brazelton Neonatal Assessment Scale (Als, Tronick, Lester & Brazelton 1977; Brazelton 1973), the Bayley Scales of Infant Development (Bayley 1969), the Peabody Picture Vocabulary Test (Dunn 1965), and the

McCarthy Scales of Children's Abilities (McCarthy 1972). Information on parental ages, incomes, educational levels, and occupations was also obtained. In addition, ERPs were recorded from the left and right temporal areas (T3 and T4) at birth and again at six-month intervals until the child's third birthday. These ERPs were elicited in response to speech stimuli chosen because they produced reliable general hemispheric difference effects as well as bilateral and lateralized discrimination effects. Eight other stimuli were added to facilitate tests of generalizability across different consonant and vowel contrasts. Such stimuli appeared ideally suited for determining whether general hemispheric differences or specific lateralized discrimination abilities were the best predictors of later language skills.

Analyses of the ERP data indicated that electrophysiological measures recorded at birth could identify children who performed better or worse on language tasks 3 years later. Two particularly important components in the brain waves were identified. One component of the auditory ERP that occurred between 88 and 240 ms reliably discriminated between children whose McCarthy Verbal Index scores were above 50 (the high group) and those with lower scores (i.e., the low group). Only ERPs recorded over the LH of the HIGH group systematically discriminated between the different consonant speech sounds. The RH responses of this group, on the other hand, discriminated between the different nonspeech stimuli. The low group displayed no such lateralized discrimination for either the speech or the nonspeech sounds. A second component of the ERP with a late peak latency of 664 ms also discriminated between the high and low groups. Unlike the earlier component, however, the second component occurred over both hemispheres and, consequently, reflected bilateral activity. This second component differed in other ways from the first component. While the second component discriminated between speech and nonspeech sounds, this discrimination depended on which vowel followed the consonant. A third ERP component (peak latency = 450 ms), that only characterized a gross electrical difference between hemispheres, failed to discriminate between the two different language performance groups. Thus, hemispheric differences at birth by themselves did not discriminate between infants who would develop better or poorer language skills 3 years later. Instead, if one hemisphere specifically shows better speech perception discrimination abilities, it is the one more likely to relate to better later language outcomes. Furthermore, given that the ERP components discriminating between the two groups were sensitive to certain speech and nonspeech contrasts but not to others, it appears that the ERPs reflected the infant's sensitivity to specific language related cues rather than the overall readiness of the brain to respond to any general stimulus in its environment.

In subsequent analyses of these data, a stepwise multiple regression model was developed in which the Peabody scores and McCarthy Verbal Index scores were used as the dependent variables and the ERP components obtained at birth that best discriminated the different consonant sounds were used as the independent variables. This model accounted for 78% of the total variance in predicting McCarthy scores from the brain responses, whereas 69% of the variance was accounted for in predicting Peabody scores (Molfese 1989b). Clearly, there appears to be a strong relationship between early ERP discrimination of speech-related stimuli and later language skills. Efforts to improve the amount of variance accounted for were undertaken in which perinatal measures and Brazelton scores were also entered into the equations. While these regression models were significant, the improvement in the amount of variance accounted for less than 3%.

Molfese & Searock (1986) later noted that the relationship between neonatal ERP activity and later language also exists using ERPs recorded at one year of age. In this study ERPs were recorded from 16 infants at birth and again within two weeks of their first birthday. A series of three vowel sounds with normal speech formant structure bandwidths and 3 nonspeech tokens containing 1-Hz-wide formants that matched the mean frequencies of the speech sounds were presented to these infants, and their ERPs were recorded in response to each sound. Two regions of the ERPs, one centered between 300 and 400 ms, and another centered around 200 ms following stimulus onset, discriminated between the one year old infants who two years later would perform better or worse on the McCarthy language tasks. Infants who were able to discriminate between more vowel sounds at one year of age performed better on the language tasks at 3 years of age. Thus, it appears that ERPs at birth and at one year can both be successfully used as the basis for making predictions concerning language performance at three years.

Subsequently, Molfese (1989b) utilized a different type of statistical procedures with a different longitudinal sample of infants. ERPs were recorded at birth from frontal, temporal, and parietal scalp areas over the LH and RH in response to speech and nonspeech sounds. The sample consisted of 30 infants who had McCarthy verbal scores at 3 years of age that ranged from 32 to 69 (mean = 53, SD = 9.41). The mean for the infants who scored 50 or below on the McCarthy test was 45. The mean for the infants who scored above 50 was 61. Overall, both groups of children possessed largely average language scores. A Discriminant Function Procedure used the time points of the averaged ERPs to discriminate the language scores. The stepwise analysis, with an F-to-enter of 3.0, selected 17 points in order of their effectiveness in classifying each of the

720 original averaged ERPs into one of the two groups. These points clustered in four regions of the ERP — the first between 20 and 140 ms, the second between 230 and 270 ms, the third between 410 and 490 ms, and the fourth between 600 and 700 ms. The likelihood of correctly classifying a brain response as belonging to a low or high language performance child was 50%, but the actual classification accuracy was significantly higher than chance. For the high group, the classification accuracy was 68.6%, whereas it was 69.7% for the low group. A Z-test of proportions indicated that the actual classification was significantly better than chance for each group. Applying a rule that at least 51% of an individual's ERPs must be classified into the low group before that infant would be classified as a lower than average language performing child, Molfese noted that only one infant from the low group would be misclassified along with one infant from the high group.

More recently, Molfese (1992) collected data from a second and larger longitudinal sample of infants. Analyses involving one subset of data included a sample of 1,296 ERPs recorded from 54 neonates. The language performance of these children again was measured with the McCarthy Verbal Index at 3 years of age. The children were divided into two groups such that half of the children scored above 54 (High Group, mean = 61) on the McCarthy test and half scored 50 or below (Low Group, mean = 45). The early region of the ERP was again found to vary as a function of 3-year language performance scores (Low vs. High). As in the case of Molfese & Molfese (1985), the region between 70 and 210 ms with a peak latency of 140 ms discriminated between groups. The LH auditory evoked responses from the high language group discriminated between the two consonant sounds, /b/ and /g/. This was not the case for the low language group. These findings are especially exciting because they are similar in both latency and lateralized effect to the results reported from the earlier Molfese & Molfese (1985) study even though Molfese (1992) used a different population of infants and the stimuli comprised a smaller subset of that employed earlier by Molfese & Molfese (1985).

A follow-up to this study, using 79 infants (Molfese 1995), showed that this effect continued to hold even when finer distinctions were made between groups (see Table 5). For the discriminant function procedure, three groups were established based upon the Stanford-Binet Verbal Reasoning subtest scores obtained for these children at three years of age. Of 79 children, 16 children scored at least one standard deviation below the mean with scores that ranged between 85 and 94, 47 children scored within one standard deviation of the average score of 105.4, and 16 children scored at least one standard deviation above the mean with scores between 116 and 130.

Two discriminant functions discriminated between these three language groups at 3-years-of-age. Function 1 accounted for 89.02% of the total variance while function 2 accounted for 10.98%. Thus, these two functions together accounted for 100% of the total variance for this data set and indicate that auditory evoked ERPs can successfully discriminate between infants at birth for different levels of language skills.

A striking aspect of these replications concerns the range of language abilities assessed at three years between the Molfese & Molfese (1985) study and the Molfese (1992) and Molfese (1995) studies. While the language skills of the first study covered a considerable range from relatively poor receptive and productive skills to well above average skills, the language skills in the later Molfese (1992, 1995) studies are from samples of children whose language skills cover a much narrower range. In spite of the dissimilarity of these samples, the brain responses continued to be robust in their ability to distinguish groups of children who perform differently on language tasks.

More recently, Molfese & Molfese (1997) noted that this relationship between early neonatal ERPs and later language performance measures continues into the kindergarten years. In fact, Molfese & Molfese present data indicating that this relationship remains a strong one over this longer time period. They tested a sample of 71 term infants within 36 hours of birth using auditory ERPs. The ERPs were recorded to 9 consonant-vowel (CV) syllables that combined the initial consonants, b, d, or g with a following vowel, a, i, or u. Twenty repetitions of each CV were presented in blocked random order with the other sounds. Electrodes were placed at FL, FR, T3, T4, PL, and PR. In this manner, 3834 ERPs were obtained from the 71 infants and then submitted to a PCA that generated 7 factors that accounted for 89.02% of the total variance. These children were subsequently tested again at 5 years of age using the Stanford-Binet verbal score. These 71 children were then divided into two groups based upon their verbal scores: 62 children with verbal IQ above 100 (High group) and 9 with verbal IQ less than 100. Comparisons of these groups indicated no differences in birth weight, Apgar scores, or gestational ages.

The investigators selected two factors in their analysis that had the same temporal characteristics of that previously identified by Molfese & Molfese (1985) as discriminating children at three years of age in terms of their verbal skills. Using discriminant function analyses to discriminate between these two groups based on their newborn ERPs, Molfese & Molfese correctly classified 78.87% of the children in terms of their verbal skills at five years of age based on three variables (LTBG2, RTBG2, RPBD2) that reflected variations in the ERP waveform between 170 and 320 ms as elicited by different CV sounds. LTBG2 was derived by subtracting the left temporal hemisphere factor score for /g/ initial syllables from those obtained for the left temporal hemisphere response to /b/ initial syllables, while RTBG2 reflected the same difference score obtained for the right temporal hemisphere, and RPBD2 was derived by subtracting RH parietal factor scores obtained for /d/ initial syllables from those obtained at this electrode site from /b/ initial syllables.

The inclusion of three additional variables (RTDG6, RTA6, HAU6) for the region between 70 and 210 ms allowed Molfese & Molfese to correctly classify 91.55% of the children (65 of 71 children). In this case, seven of nine children again were correctly identified as scoring below 100 while 58 of 62 children now were correctly classified as scoring above 100. RTDG2 reflected the difference score obtained by subtracting the right temporal hemisphere factor score for /g/ initial syllables from those obtained for the right temporal hemisphere response to /d/ initial syllables, RTA6 reflected the RH temporal response to the vowel /a/; and HAU6 summarized the difference in the way the two hemispheres responded to the /a/ vs. /u/ vowels.

A final discriminant analysis was conducted using one additional variable, LTA6, that summarized the LH temporal response to all CV syllables ending in /a/. In this analysis, 68 of 71 children were correctly classified at 5 years of age based upon their newborn brain responses. Virtually all of the children belonging to the Low group (8 of 9 for 88.9%) were correctly classified along with 60 of 62 children (96.8%) belonging to the High group.

These results indicate that auditory ERPs recorded at birth can successfully discriminate the verbal performance of children even up to five years later with high accuracy. These results extend the predictive accuracy of neonatal ERPs two years beyond that first demonstrated by Molfese & Molfese (1985). Confirmation in this study of the findings from Molfese & Molfese (1985) regarding the use of neonatal ERPs to predict later language performance outcomes are especially intriguing when it is remembered that different verbal performance measures were used across these two studies. The McCarthy Verbal scores were used by Molfese & Molfese (1985) while the verbal scores derived from the Stanford Binet were used by Molfese & Molfese (1997). Thus, given this ability to classify children across different performance measures, it is clear that ERP factor scores obtained from similar brain regions can provide an effective and powerful means to discriminate performance on different standardized tests and at different ages. In addition, Molfese & Molfese (1997) accurately classified children's language performance on verbal tests based upon their birth measures despite a narrower range of verbal skills. Indeed, the children in the Molfese & Molfese (1997) study showed a narrower range of scores than that shown by the children originally tested by Molfese & Molfese (1985). Nevertheless, despite this relatively narrow range of scores, their measures continued to show high classification accuracy.

The Molfese & Molfese (1997) study varied in other ways from their earlier study with 3-year-old children. In contrast to Molfese & Molfese (1985) who used ERPs recorded from only the left and right temporal regions, T3 and T4, Molfese & Molfese (1997) employed a total of six scalp recording sites, two of which were identical to those used in the original study. As in their previous study, factor scores derived from the temporal sites were important in discriminating between children with different levels of verbal skills. In fact, for the most part, the discriminative models in the Molfese & Molfese (1997) study included ERPs recorded primarily from the temporal sites and comprised two of three components in the three variable model, four of six in the second model, and five of seven in the third model. However, it is clear that the additional factor scores derived from frontal and parietal leads improved the classification accuracy beyond that produced by the temporal sites alone. The ability of the right parietal region to discriminate between consonant sounds also contributed to the discrimination between variations in language skills. Another variable that collapsed electrode sites within each hemisphere and then subtracted the contribution of the RH from that of the left also contributed to this discrimination. A final variable that characterized a more general level of hemisphere difference related to vowel discrimination further served to improve the discrimination. Thus, overall, while ERPs recorded from over the temporal regions of the two hemispheres continued to play a prominent role in predicting later developmental outcomes, additional contributions were noted at other electrode sites. These studies are presented in Table 5.

The obvious question that arises from such highly predictive results as these is why any type of measure, behavioral or brain, should discriminate developmental outcomes over a large age range with such high accuracy. Are human accomplishments predetermined from birth? Are genetic factors so potent that they all but force certain developmental outcomes despite the influence of any environmental factors? Rather, Molfese & Molfese have hypothesized that these data reflect the state of an underlying perceptual mechanism upon which some aspects of later developing and emerging verbal and cognitive processes are based. As a result of genetic and intrauterine factors, the developing organism develops a set of perceptual abilities responsive to variations in its environment. For most of us, these perceptual abilities are similar and readily enable us to discriminate elements within our environment in quite similar ways. For others, however, aspects of these perceptual skills may not respond to environmental

Table 5. *Studies using neonatal ERPs to predict later cognitive development*

Study	Subjects	Electrodes	Task	Results
Molfese & Molfese (1985)	Infants studied longitudinally from birth through 3 years $n = 16$	T3, T4 referenced to linked ears	ERPs recorded to speech and nonspeech consonant-vowel sounds at birth McCarthy Scales of Children's Abilities administered at 3 years	Newborn ERPs identified children performing better or worse on language tasks 3 years later ERPs: 88–240 ms discriminated High vs. Low Groups on McCarthy Verbal Index at 3 years ERP component at 664 ms discriminated High vs. Low Groups at 3 years
Molfese & Searock (1986)	One-year-old infants retested at 3 years $n = 16$	T3, T4 referenced to linked ears	At 1 year, ERPs recorded to speech and nonspeech vowel sounds McCarthy test administered at 3 years	Children with above-average language skills at 3 years exhibited ERPs at 1 year that discriminated different vowel sounds
Molfese (1989b)	Newborns retested at 3 years $n = 30$ 15 with McCarthy scores below 50 and 15 with scores above 50	T3, T4 referenced to linked ears	At birth, ERPs to speech and nonspeech consonant-vowel sounds were recorded McCarthy test administered at 3 years	Discriminant function correctly classified 68.6% of the ERPs recorded from High Group and 69.7% of the ERPs recorded from Low Group
Molfese (1992)	Newborns tested again at 3 years of age Total $n = 54$ High Group = 27 who scored above 54 (mean = 61, SD = 4.95, range = 54–72); Low Group = 27 scored 50 or below (mean = 45, SD = 4.97, range = 32–50)	T3, T4, FL, FR, PL, PR referenced to linked ears	At birth, ERPs collected to 9 consonant-vowel syllables Stanford-Binet administered at 3 years of age	PCA-discriminant function analysis performed ANOVA found LH of the High Group (70–210ms, peak = 140 ms) discriminated /b/ from /g/. No such discrimination was noted for the Low group Second region (480–620 ms) at both LH and RH parietal sites discriminated /b/ from /g/ for only the High Group
Molfese (1995)	Newborns tested again at 3 years of age $n = 79$	T3, T4, FL, FR, PL, PR referenced to linked ears	At birth, ERPs collected to 9 consonant-vowel syllables Stanford-Binet administered at 3 years of age	PCA-discriminant function analysis performed Three groups established based on Stanford-Binet Verbal Reasoning subtest scores at 3 years 2 discriminant functions classified children with 100% accuracy
Molfese & Molfese (1997)	Newborns tested again at 5 years of age $n = 71$	T3, T4, FL, FR, PL, PR referenced to linked ears	At birth, ERPs collected to 9 consonant-vowel syllables Stanford-Binet administered at 5 years of age	2 groups based on Stanford-Binet Verbal Reasoning subtest scores at 5 years: 62>100 VIQ; 9 < 100 VIQ 3 discriminant functions classified children with 78.9%, 91.6%, and 95.8% accuracy using 3, 6, and 7 variables

elements in the same way. It is these fundamental differences in perceptual skills that set the stage for early detection of responses that influence later language development.

Such findings as outlined above raise exciting possibilities regarding the early identification of children with potential language problems and enhance the possibility that successful intervention for such language problems could be carried out before they become fully manifested in the child's behavior. At present, the identification of children with language and other cognitive problems occurs relatively late, often occurring in the elementary school years after it is established that the child is performing below grade level. One consequence of this delayed identification strategy is that it occurs so late in the child's overall cognitive and linguistic development. Thus, it may already be pushing the edge of the child's cognitive flexibility and its ability to master new skills. Witelson & Swallow (1987) noted that 10 years of age could mark an important transition or major "breaking point" in development since there are marked changes in abilities such as spatial pattern recognition, Braille and map reading after this time. Others (e.g., Curtis 1977) have shown that the onset of puberty appears to set limits on the acquisition of certain language and cognitive skills. Thus, interventions begun at approximately 10 years of age could face ceiling limits placed upon their success by the child's developmental level and age. If, however, potential problems in language or cognitive development could be identified much earlier in time, the planned interventions could be introduced earlier to the child and, consequently, be more successful in remediating the child's emerging language or cognitive problems.

Summary and implications of prediction studies

These data obtained using ERP measures from neonates are supportive of the position that these early physiological indices are highly predictive of later emerging language skills over a three year time period. The utilization of several brain wave components rather than one component or one latency measure seems to impact importantly on the effectiveness of brainwaves as predictors of later functioning. The identification of brainwave components related to specific stimulus conditions permits them to be used in analyses in a theory driven manner to predict specific types of later language functioning. These analysis procedures, which have been described by Molfese (1978a), have also been effective in attempts to use brainwave components to assess other aspects of cognitive functioning and performance abilities (Molfese 1978a, 1978b, 1980a, 1980b, 1983, 1984).

Further work is underway to identify when in development the best predictions of later functioning can be made. The use of a longitudinal sample makes this work feasible because measures appropriate for use across the birth to 13-year age range are being used. Unlike some measures, ERP methods can be used with infants and children to provide measures of brain processing. Furthermore, the ERP methods have shown promise as providing a basis by which accurate predictions of language and cognitive status can be made even when the scales used for assessments of cognitive and language functioning must change as the children mature. We are very hopeful that ERP measures, in combination with other measures (V. Molfese 1989), will provide a highly accurate assessment methodology for use with infants.

Conclusions

There are, of course, some marked differences in the ages of the infants tested for each cognitive domain and such differences could contribute to the overlapping latency results. Younger infants might simply produce longer latency responses regardless of the cognitive area of test because of their more immature nervous system and the additional time needed for information to travel along incompletely myelinated pathways to dendritic trees which are still relatively early in their developmental life. The bulk of the infant speech perception studies focus on infants from birth through 5 months of age. The earliest work with word discrimination appears to be have the least overlap in subject ages tested with these other cognitive areas since testing did not commence until 12 months of age (Molfese, Wetzel & Gill 1993) and then extended upwards to 20 months of age (Mills et al. 1993, 1994). Nevertheless, from the existing data with vowel perception and word discrimination studies (Molfese 1989a, 1990; Molfese, Morse & Peters 1990; Molfese, Wetzel & Gill 1993) we can still discern that by one-year of age some speech discrimination effects occur slightly earlier in time than some word related effects, which all occur earlier than the memory effects reported for older infants. Are speech perception and word discrimination more automated at this stage and consequently require less time for processing or are there some innately specified mechanisms which subserve at least some aspects of speech perception which contribute to those faster response times? Does the infant's early knowledge of perception for coarticulated speech information tap such mechanisms and consequently results in such faster processing time for word discrimination?

It is obvious from this review that there are a large number of gaps in our knowledge about each of these three domains. In fact, we still know very little about the neurophysiological development of mechanisms underlying not only speech perception, but early language development as well. Clearly, there is a great deal of work that still needs to be done before questions concerning the integration of infant cognition can be adequately addressed.

Acknowledgments

Support for this work was provided by the National Science Foundation (BNS8004429, BNS 8210846), and the National Institutes of Health (R01-HD17860).

References

Ali, L., Gallagher, T., Goldstein, J. & Daniloff, R. 1971. "Perception of Coarticulated Nasality." *Journal of the Acoustical Society of America* 49: 538–540.
Als, H., Tronick, E., Lester, B. & Brazelton, T. 1977. "The Brazelton Neonatal Behavioral Assessment Scale." *Journal of Abnormal Child Psychology* 5: 215–231.
Bates, E. 1979. *Emergence of Symbols.* New York: Academic Press.
Bates, E., Benigni, L., Bretherton, I., Camaioni, L. & Volterra, V. 1979. *The Emergence of Symbols: Cognition and Communication in Infancy.* New York: Academic Press.
Bates, E., Bretherton, I., Snyder, L., Shore, C. & Volterra, V. 1980. "Vocal and Gestural Symbols at 13 Months." *Merrill-Palmer Quarterly* 26: 407–423.
Bayley, N. 1969. *Bayley Scales of Infant Development: Birth to Two Years.* New York: Psychological Corporation.
Benedict, H. 1975, April. "The Role of Repetition in Early Language Comprehension." Paper presented at the meeting of the Society for Research in Child Development, Denver, CO.
Berman, S. & Friedman, D. 1993. "A Developmental Study of ERPs during Recognition Memory: Effects of Picture Familiarity, Word Frequency, and Readability." *Journal of Psychophysiology* 7: 97–114.
Best, C. T. 1988. "The Emergence of Cerebral Asymmetries in Early Human Development: A Literature Review and a Neuroembryological Model." In *Brain Lateralization in Children: Developmental Implications*, D. L. Molfese & S. J. Segalowitz (eds.). New York: Guilford Press.
Bloom, L., Lahey, M., Hood, L., Lifter, K. & Fiess, K. 1980. "Complex Sentences: Acquisition of Syntactic Connectives and the Semantic Relations They Encode." *Journal of Child Language* 7: 235–261.
Brazelton, T. 1973. "Neonatal Behavior Assessment Scale." *Clinics in Developmental Medicine 50.* Philadelphia: Lippincott.

Brown, W. S., Marsh, J. T. & Smith, J. C. 1976. "Evoked Potential Waveform Differences Produced by the Perception of Different Meanings of an Ambiguous Phrase." *Electroencephalography and Clinical Neurophysiology* 41: 113–123.

Brown, W. S., Marsh, J. T. & Smith, J. C. 1979. "Principal Component Analysis of ERP Differences Related to the Meaning of an Ambiguous Word." *Electroencephalography and Clinical Neurophysiology* 46: 706–714.

Callaway, C., Tueting, P. & Koslow, S. 1978. *Event-Related Brain Potentials and Behavior.* New York: Academic Press.

Cattell, R. B. 1966. "The Scree Test for the Number of Factors." *Multivariate Behavior Research* 1: 245.

Chapman, R. M., McCrary, J. W., Bragdon, H. R. & Chapman, J. A. 1979. "Latent Components of Event-Related Potentials Functionally Related to Information Processing." In *Progress in Clinical Neuropsychology: Vol. 6. Cognitive Components in Cerebral Event-Related Potentials and Selective Attention,* J. E. Desmedt (ed.). Basel: Karger.

Cheour, M., Alho, K., Sainio, K., Reinikainen, K., Renlund, M., Aaltonen, O., Eerola, O. & Naatanen, R. 1997. "The Mismatch Negativity to Changes in Speech Sounds at the Age of Three Months." *Developmental Neuropsychology* 13: 167–174.

Cheour-Luhtanen, M., Alho, K., Kujala, T., Sainio, K., Reinikainen, K., Renlund, M., Aaltonen, O., Eerola, O. & Naatanen, R. 1995. "Mismatch Negativity Indicates Vowel Discrimination in Newborns." *Hearing Research* 82: 53–58.

Cheour-Luhtanen, M., Alho, K., Sainio, K., Rinne, T., Reinikainen, K., Pohjavuori, M., Renlund, M., Aaltonen, O., Eerola, O. & Naatanen, R. 1996. "The Ontogenetically Earliest Discrimination Response of the Human Brain." *Psychophysiology* 33: 478–481.

Clark, E. V. 1983. "Meanings and Concepts." In *Handbook of Child Psychology: Vol. 3*, Paul H. Mussen (ed.). New York: Wiley.

Curtis, S. 1977. *Genie: A Psycholinguistic Study of a Modern Day "Wild Child".* New York: Academic Press.

Daniloff, R. & Moll, K. 1968. "Coarticulation of Lip Rounding." *Journal of Speech and Hearing Research* 11: 707–721.

Dehaene-Lambertz, G. & Dehaene, S. 1994. "Speed and Cerebral Correlates of Syllable Discrimination in Infants." *Nature* 370: 292–295.

Donchin, E., Tueting, P., Ritter, W., Kutas, M. & Heffley, E. 1975. "On the Independence of the CNV and the P300 Components of the Human Averaged Evoked Potential." *Journal of Electroencephalography and Clinical Neurophysiology* 38: 449–461.

Dorman, M. 1974. "Auditory Evoked Potential Correlates of Speech Sound Discrimination." *Perception & Psychophysics* 15: 215–220.

Dunn, D. 1965. *Peabody Picture Vocabulary Test.* Circle Pines: American Guidance Series.

Eilers, R., Wilson, W. & Moore, J. 1979. "Speech Discrimination in the Language-innocent and Language-wise: A Study in the Perception of Voice Onset Time." *Journal of Child Language* 6: 1–18.

Eimas, P. D., Siqueland, E., Jusczyk, P. & Vigorito, J. 1971. "Speech Perception in Infants." *Science* 171: 303–306.

Gelfer, M. 1987. "An AER Study of Stop-consonant Discrimination." *Perception & Psychophysics* 42: 318–327.

Golinkoff, R. M., Hirsh-Pasek, K., Cauley, K. M. & Gordon, L. 1987. "The Eyes Have It: Lexical and Syntactic Comprehension in a New Paradigm." *Journal of Child Language* 14: 23–45.

Hirsh-Pasek, K. & Golinkoff, R. M. 1996. *The Origins of Grammar: Evidence from Early Language Comprehension.* Cambridge, MA: The MIT Press.

Jasper, H. 1958. "The Ten-twenty Electrode System of the International Federation of Societies for Electroencephalography: Appendix to Report of the Committee on Methods and Clinical Examination of Electroencephalography." *Journal of Electroencephalography and Clinical Neurophysiology* 10: 371–375.

Kamhi, A. G. 1986. "The Elusive First Word: The Importance of the Naming Insight for the Development of Referential Speech." *Journal of Child Language* 13: 155–161.

Klatt, D. 1980. "Software for a Cascade/parallel Formant Synthesizer." *Journal of the Acoustical Society of America* 67: 971–995.

Kraus, N., McGee, T. J., Carrell, T. D., Zecker, S. G., Nicol, T. G. & Koch, D. B. 1996. "Auditory Neurophysiologic Responses and Discrimination Deficits in Children with Learning Problems." *Science* 273: 971–973.

Kuhl, P. K. 1985. "Constancy, Categorization, and Perceptual Organization for Speech and Sound in Early Infancy." In *Neonate Cognition: Beyond the Blooming, Buzzing Confusion*, J. Mehler & R. Rox (eds.). Hillsdale, NJ: Erlbaum.

Kurtzberg, D., Hilpert, P. L., Kreuzer, J. A. & Vaughan, H. G., Jr. 1984. "Differential Maturation of Cortical Auditory Evoked Potentials to Speech Sounds in Normal Fullterm and Very Low-birthweight Infants." *Developmental Medicine and Child Neurology* 26: 466–475.

Lenneberg, E. 1967. *Biological Foundations of Language.* New York: Wiley & Sons.

Liberman, A. M., Cooper, F. S., Shankweiler, D. & Studdert-Kennedy, M. 1967. "Perception of the Speech Code." *Psychological Review* 74: 431–461.

Lisker, L. & Abramson, A. S. 1970. "The Voicing Dimension: Some Experiments in Comparative Phonetics." In *Proceedings of the Sixth International Congress of Phonetic Sciences.* Prague: Academia.

Licht, R., Kok, A., Bakker, D. & Bouma, A. 1986. "Hemispheric Distribution of ERP Components and Word Naming in Preschool Children." *Brain and Language* 27: 101–116.

Littman, B. & Parmelee, A. 1978. "Medical Correlation of Infant Development." *Pediatrics* 61: 470–474.

Macnamara, J. 1982. *Names for Things.* Cambridge, MA: The MIT Press.

MacNeilage, P. F. & DeClerk, J. L. 1969. "On the Motor Control of Coarticulation in CVC Monosyllables." *Journal of the Acoustical Society of America* 45: 1217–1233.
McCarthy, D. 1972. *Manual for the McCarthy Scales of Children's Abilities*. New York: Psychological Corporation.
Miller, J. F. & Chapman, R. S. 1981. "The Relation between Age and Mean Length of Utterance in Morphemes." *Journal of Speech and Hearing Research* 24: 154–161.
Mills, D. L., Coffey-Corina, S. A. & Neville, H. J. 1993. "Language Acquisition and Cerebral Specialization in 20-month-old Infants." *Journal of Cognitive Neuroscience* 5: 317–334.
Mills, D. L., Coffey-Corina, S. A. & Neville, H. J. 1994. "Variability in Cerebral Organization during Primary Language Acquisition." In *Human Behavior and the Developing Brain*, G. Dawson & K. Fischer (eds.). New York: The Guilford Press.
Molfese, D. L. 1972. "Cerebral Asymmetry in Infants, Children and Adults: Auditory Evoked Responses to Speech and Music Stimuli." Unpublished doctoral dissertation, The Pennsylvania State University.
Molfese, D. L. 1978a. "Left and Right Hemisphere Involvement in Speech Perception: Electrophysiological Correlates." *Perception and Psychophysics* 23: 237–243.
Molfese, D. L. 1978b. "Neuroelectrical Correlates of Categorical Speech Perception in Adults." *Brain and Language* 5: 25–35.
Molfese, D. L. 1979. "Cortical and Subcortical Involvement in the Processing of Coarticulated Cues." *Brain and Language* 7: 86–100.
Molfese, D. L. 1980a. "Hemispheric Specialization for Temporal Information: Implications for the Processing of Voicing Cues during Speech Perception." *Brain and Language* 11: 285–300.
Molfese, D. L. 1980b. "The Phoneme and the Engram: Electrophysiological Evidence for the Acoustic Invariant in Stop Consonants." *Brain and Language* 9: 372–376.
Molfese, D. L. 1983. "Event Related Potentials and Language Processes." In *Tutorials in ERP Research: Endogenous Components*, A. W. K. Gaillard & W. Ritter (eds.). The Netherlands: North Holland Publishing Co.
Molfese, D. L. 1984. "Left Hemisphere Sensitivity to Consonant Sounds Not Displayed by the Right Hemisphere: Electrophysiological Correlates." *Brain and Language* 22: 109–127.
Molfese, D. L. 1989a. "Electrophysiological Correlates of Word Meanings in 14-month-old Human Infants." *Developmental Neuropsychology* 5: 79–103.
Molfese, D. L. 1989b. "The Use of Auditory Evoked Responses Recorded from Newborns to Predict Later Language Skills." In *Research in Infant Assessment 25 (6)*, N. Paul (ed.). White Plains: March of Dimes.
Molfese, D. L. 1990. "Auditory Evoked Responses Recorded from 16-month-old Human Infants to Words They Did and Did Not Know." *Brain and Language* 38: 345–363.
Molfese, D. L. 1992. "The Use of Auditory Evoked Responses Recorded from Newborn Infants to Predict Language Skills." In *Advances in Child Neuropsychology 1*, M. G. Tramontana & S. R. Hooper (eds.). New York: Springer-Verlag.

Molfese, D. L. 1995. "Electrophysiological Responses Obtained during Infancy and Their Relation to Later Language Development: Further Findings." In *Advances in Child Neuropsychology 3*, M. G. Tramontana & S. R. Hooper (eds.). New York: Springer-Verlag.

Molfese, D. L. & Betz, J. C. 1988. "Electrophysiological Indices of the Early Development of Lateralization for Language and Cognition and Their Implications for Predicting Later Development." In *Developmental Implications of Brain Lateralization*, D. L. Molfese & S. J. Segalowitz (eds.). New York: Guilford Press.

Molfese, D. L., Buhrke, R. A. & Wang, S. L. 1985. "The Right Hemisphere and Temporal Processing of Consonant Transition Durations: Electrophysiological Correlates." *Brain and Language* 26: 289–299.

Molfese, D. L., Burger-Judisch, L. M. & Gill, L. A. 1996. "Electrophysiological Correlates of Noun-verb Processing in Adults." *Brain and Language* 54: 388–413.

Molfese, D. L., Burger-Judisch, L. M. & Hans, L. L. 1991. "Consonant Discrimination by Newborn Infants: Electrophysiological Differences." *Developmental Neuropsychology* 7: 177–195.

Molfese, D. L., Freeman, R. & Palermo, D. 1975. "The Ontogeny of Lateralization for Speech and Nonspeech Stimuli." *Brain and Language* 2: 356–368.

Molfese, D. L., Gill, L. A., Simos, P. G. & Tan, A. 1995. "Implications Resulting from the Use of Biological Techniques to Assess Development." In *Assessment and Intervention across the Lifespan*, L. F. DiLalla & S. M. Clancy-Dollinger (eds.). New Jersey: Lawrence Erlbaum Associates.

Molfese, D. L. & Hess, R. M. 1978. "Speech Perception in Nursery School Age Children: Sex and Hemispheric Differences." *Journal of Experimental Child Psychology* 26: 71–84.

Molfese, D. L., Linnville, S. E., Wetzel, W. F. & Leicht, D. 1985. "Electrophysiological Correlates of Handedness and Speech Perception Contrasts." *Neuropsychologia* 23: 77–86.

Molfese, D. L. & Molfese, V. J. 1979a. "Hemisphere and Stimulus Differences as Reflected in the Cortical Responses of Newborn Infants to Speech Stimuli." *Developmental Psychology* 15: 505–511.

Molfese, D. L. & Molfese, V. J. 1979b. "VOT Distinctions in Infants: Learned or Innate?" In *Studies in Neurolinguistics: Vol. 4*, H. Whitaker & H. Whitaker (eds.). New York: Academic Press.

Molfese, D. L. & Molfese, V. J. 1980. "Cortical Responses of Preterm Infants to Phonetic and Nonphonetic Speech Stimuli." *Developmental Psychology* 16: 574–581.

Molfese, D. L. & Molfese, V. J. 1985. "Electrophysiological Indices of Auditory Discrimination in Newborn Infants: The Basis for Predicting Later Language Development." *Infant Behavior and Development* 8: 197–211.

Molfese, D. L. & Molfese, V. J. 1986. "Psychophysical Indices of Early Cognitive Processes and Their Relationship to Language." In *Child Neuropsychology: Vol 1. Theory and Research*, J. E. Obrzut & G. W. Hynd (eds.). New York: Academic Press.

Molfese, D. L. & Molfese, V. J. 1988. "Right Hemisphere Responses from Preschool Children to Temporal Cues Contained in Speech and Nonspeech Materials: Electrophysiological Correlates." *Brain and Language* 33: 245–259.

Molfese, D. L. & Molfese, V. J. 1994. "Short-term and Long-term Developmental Outcomes." In *Human Behavior and the Developing Brain*, G. Dawson & K. Fischer (eds.). New York: Guilford Press.

Molfese, D. L. & Molfese, V. J. 1997. "Discrimination of Language Skills at Five Years of Age Using Event Related Potentials Recorded at Birth." *Developmental Neuropsychology* 13: 135–156.

Molfese, D. L., Morse, P. A. & Peters, C. J. 1990. "Auditory Evoked Responses from Infants to Names for Different Objects: Cross Modal Processing as a Basis for Early Language Acquisition." *Developmental Psychology* 26: 780–795.

Molfese, D. L. & Schmidt, A. L. 1983. "An Auditory Evoked Potential Study of Consonant Perception." *Brain and Language* 18: 57–70.

Molfese, D. L. & Searock, K. 1986. "The Use of Auditory Evoked Responses at One Year of Age to Predict Language Skills at 3 Years." *Australian Journal of Communication Disorders* 14: 35–46.

Molfese, D. L. & Wetzel, W. F. 1992. "Short and Long Term Memory in 14-month-old Infants: Electrophysiological Correlates." *Developmental Neuropsychology* 8: 135–160.

Molfese, D. L., Wetzel, W. F. & Gill, L. A. 1993. "Known versus Unknown Word Discrimination in 12-month-old Human Infants: Electrophysiological Correlates." *Developmental Neuropsychology* 3–4: 241–258.

Molfese, V. J. 1989. *Perinatal Risk and Infant Development: Assessment and Prediction.* New York: Guilford Press.

Molfese, V. J., Molfese, D. L. & Parsons, C. 1983. "Hemispheric Involvement in Phonological Perception." In *Language Functions and Brain Organization*, S. Segalowitz (ed.). New York: Academic Press.

Morse, P. A. 1974. "Infant Speech Perception: A Preliminary Model and Review of the Literature." In *Language Perspectives: Acquisition, Retardation, and Intervention*, R. Schiefelbusch & L. Lloyd (eds.). Baltimore: University Park Press.

Nelson, C. A. & Salapatek, P. 1986. "Electrophysiological Correlates of Infant Recognition Memory." *Child Development* 57: 1483–1497.

Pisoni, D. B. 1977. "Identification and Discrimination of the Relative Onset Time of Two Component Tones: Implications for Voicing Perception in Stops." *Journal of the Acoustical Society of America* 61: 1352–1361.

Retherford, K. S., Schwartz, B. C. & Chapman, R. S. 1981. "Semantic Roles and Residual Grammatical Categories in Mother and Child Speech." *Journal of Child Language* 8: 583–608.

Rockstroh, B., Elbert, T., Birbaumer, N. & Lutzenberger, W. 1982. *Slow Brain Potentials and Behavior.* Baltimore: Urban-Schwarzenberg.

Ruchkin, D., Sutton, S., Munson, R., Silver, K. & Macar, F. 1981. "P300 and Feedback Provided by Absence of the Stimulus." *Psychophysiology* 18: 271–282.

Segalowitz, S. & Cohen, H. 1989. "Right Hemisphere EEG Sensitivity to Speech." *Brain and Language* 37: 220–231.
Shelburne Jr., S. A. 1972. "Visual Evoked Responses to Word and Nonsense Syllable Stimuli." *Electroencephalography and Clinical Neurophysiology* 32: 17–25.
Shelburne Jr., S. A. 1973. "Visual Evoked Responses to Language Stimuli in Normal Children." *Electroencephalography and Clinical Neurophysiology* 34: 135–143.
Simos, P. G. & Molfese, D. L. 1997. "Electrophysiological Responses from a Temporal Order Continuum in the Newborn Infant." *Neuropsychologia* 35: 89–98.
Simos, P. G., Molfese, D. L. & Brenden, R. A. 1997. "Behavioral and Electrophysiological Indices of Voicing Cue Discrimination: Laterality Patterns and Development." *Brain and Language* 57: 122–150.
Snyder, L., Bates, E. & Bretherton, I. 1981. "Content and Context in Early Lexical Development." *Journal of Child Language* 8: 565–582.
Streeter, L. A. 1976. "Language Perception of Two-month-old Infants Shows Effects of Both Innate Mechanisms and Experience." *Nature* 259: 39–41.
Tan, A. A. 1996. "The Processing of Nouns and Verbs in Preschool Children: Electrophysiological Correlates." Unpublished Masters thesis, Southern Illinois University at Carbondale.
Taylor, M. J. & Keenan, N. K. 1990. "Event-related Potentials to Visual and Language Stimuli in Normal and Dyslexic Children." *Psychophysiology* 27: 318–327.
Travis, L. 1931. *Speech Pathology.* New York: Appleton-Century.
Witelson, S. & Swallow, J. A. 1987. "Neuropsychological Study of the Development of Spatial Cognition." In *Spatial Cognition: Brain Bases and Development*, J. Stiles-Davis, M. Kritchevsky & U. Bellugi (eds.). Hillsdale, N.J.: Erlbaum.

Development Patterns of Brain Activity Reflecting Semantic and Syntactic Processes

Angela D. Friederici & Anja Hahne
Max Planck Institute of Cognitive Neuroscience

Introduction

Our knowledge concerning whether and how language acquisition and development covaries with changes of the underlying neuronal correlate is sparse and at most quite indirect.

Traditionally lesion studies were used to describe the relationship between language function and brain structure in children (Lenneberg 1967; for an overview see Basso, Bracchi, Capitani, Laiacona & Zanobio 1987; Basso & Scarpa 1990, and Friederici 1994). In these studies researchers correlated particular brain lesions with a particular clinical classification of the child's language behavior and/or investigated the child's recovery from a given language impairment as a function of lesion type and age. It is not clear in how far these types of investigations can enlarge our knowledge about language acquisition and development in the intact brain as the brain's plasticity is remarkable at early age (Bates, Thal & Janowsky 1992; Neville 1990, 1991). Although plasticity is an interesting issue in itself, it interferes with an adequate description of the normal relationship of brain structure and language functions in early language acquisition. Moreover, concerns must also be raised with respect to the majority of the studies correlating brain lesions with clinical classifications of different aphasia types as they often lack a detailed linguistic description of the child's language behavior as well as a precise description of the lesion. Therefore, these studies can only provide a non-precise picture of the language-brain relationship.

Given the data at hand, it is interesting to note that brain lesions in children up to the age of 8 years produce language impairments different from those seen in adults with comparable lesions (Friederici 1994). For example, adults with a unique brain lesion in the posterior (post rolandic) parts of the left hemisphere often show a Wernicke's aphasia which is characterized by a fluent, paragrammatic output and a severe comprehension deficit. Adult brain lesions involving the anterior (pre rolandic) parts of the left hemisphere often cause a Broca's aphasia characterized as a language deficit with a non-fluent, agrammatic output and, dependent upon the additional involvement of post rolandic tissue, either good or deficient comprehension.[1] In contrast to these two types of language disorders no such pattern of brain lesion and language behavior observed for adults can be found in childhood. Instead, an overview of the cases available in the literature reveals that children up to the age of 8 years do not display a fluent, paragrammatic Wernicke's type of aphasia, neither with lesions in the posterior part of the left hemisphere nor with lesions at other sites (Friederici 1994). Aphasia in children up to that age manifests itself as non-fluent Broca's type of aphasia independent of whether the lesion is localized in the anterior or the posterior part of the left hemisphere. Fluent paragrammatic Wernicke's types of aphasia are only reported in children beyond the age of 9 years (Van Hout & Lyon 1986; Van Dongen, Loonen & Van Dongen 1985).[2] Unfortunately, these studies on childhood aphasia only provide sparse information about the children's comprehension abilities. Nonetheless, the available data suggest the following difference between the language behavior-brain relationship. Adults with lesions in the Wernicke's area produce a fluent output characterized by a lack of content words, but mostly correct local phrase structure and prosody with an inability for correct attachment between phrases and clauses. Thus it appears that these patients are left with some automatic, procedural knowledge concerning the local phrase structure. This knowledge may be subserved by the intact Broca's area. It is assumed that this knowledge not only supports language production but also language comprehension, in the sense that highly automatic procedures check the incoming information with respect to its local phrase structure (Friederici 1994). The observation that children up to the age of 8 years do not show a fluent aphasia with lesions in the Wernicke's area may suggest that the intact Broca's area does not yet provide the highly automatic procedures to synthesize and analyze local phrase structures. The hypothesis is that the underlying processes are not yet established as automatic procedures.

In the following we will test this hypothesis in the domain of language comprehension, assuming that the left inferior frontal cortex supports automatic syntactic processes during production and comprehension.[3]

We will test this hypothesis in the domain of language comprehension by first describing the adult language-brain relationship and then consider the childhood aphasia data with respect to the adult target model, taking developmental aspects into account. Since the model is based on neuropsychological as well as electrophysiological evidence (Friederici 1995) we will have to introduce the reader to the research on event-related brain potentials.

Language related event-related brain potentials in adults

Event-related brain potentials (ERPs) reflect the summation of synchronous postsynaptic discharges of a large population of neurons engaged in information processing. ERPs allow researchers to distinguish particular stimulus related brain activity from the background electrical activity of the brain by averaging the ERP signal time-locked to the onset of a given stimulus. When averaging over a number of similar stimuli, the average to a particular stimulus event usually displays a number of positive and negative voltage peaks at different latencies and particular distributions across the scalp. Several ERP components have been correlated with specific language processes in the normal adult. We will briefly discuss them below.

One particular component, the so-called N400 component, has been shown to correlate with lexical-semantic aspects of processing (for review see Kutas & Van Petten 1994; Osterhout & Holcomb 1995). The N400 is a negative deflection in the ERP waveform which is maximal over centroparietal electrode sites, and present between 250 and 600 ms (peaking at 400 ms) after stimulus onset. Kutas & Hillyard (1980) first observed this component in correlation with sentence endings that were semantically anomalous (*He spread the warm bread with socks*). Later it was shown that the amplitude of the N400 systematically varies inversely with the word's expectedness (Kutas, Lindamood & Hillyard 1984). This N400 component is taken to reflect the ease or difficulty with which a word can be integrated into preceding context, at least with respect to its lexical-semantic attributes (Brown & Hagoort 1993).

Two different ERP components have been shown to correlate with the processing of syntactic information: (1) an early left anterior negativity, labeled LAN or ELAN, and (2) a late centroparietal positivity, labeled P600. In several studies an early negativity with a left anterior maximum was found to covary with the processing of word category information in different phrasal contexts. An early left anterior negativity around 120 ms (followed by a left anterior negativity around 400 ms) was reported by Neville, Nicol, Barss, Forster & Garrett (1991) coincident with reading word-category errors (e.g. *Max's of proof the theorem*). Friederici, Pfeifer & Hahne (1993) examined word-category errors such as *"Der Freund wurde im **besucht**"* (literal translation: *The friend was in visited*) in an auditory task. They found an early negativity peaking around 180 ms with a left anterior maximum. Studies investigating other types of syntactic violations also report left anterior negativities, however, mostly only around 400 ms. The processing of a verb's subcategorization information (i.e. transitivity information; e.g., *"Der Lehrer wurde **gefallen**"*, literal translation: *The teacher was fallen*; Rösler, Friederici, Pütz & Hahne 1993) as well as verb agreement information (e.g. *Every morning he **mow** the lawn*; Coulson, King & Kutas 1998; Gunter, Stowe & Mulder 1997; Münte, Heinze & Mangun 1993) have been shown to correlate with a left anterior negativity occurring between 300 and 500 ms following the critical element's onset.[4]

Late centroparietally distributed positivities were observed with the processing of a number of different syntactic anomalies, including violations of syntactic structures and violations of syntactic preferences requiring syntactic reanalyzes. Osterhout & Holcomb (1992, 1993) investigated sentences that at a given point required a complete structural reanalysis of the preceding sentence (i.e. deriving a reduced relative clause analysis from an initial analysis as a simple declarative sentence) and found a positivity around 600 ms after the disambiguating lexical element. When examining noun phrase versus complement ambiguities Osterhout, Holcomb & Swinney (1994) found a late positivity around 600 ms when the critical word (e.g., *was*) violated syntactic constraints (e.g., (a) *The doctor forced the patient **was** lying*) or syntactic preferences (e.g., (b) *The doctor charged the patient **was** lying*). The positivity (labeled P600) was larger for the violation of syntactic constraints (a) than for the violation of the syntactic preferences (b). Only in condition (a) was the P600 preceded by a negativity. Similar positivities have been observed with a number of different syntactic anomalies (Hagoort, Brown & Groothusen 1993; Mecklinger, Schriefers, Steinhauer & Friederici 1995; McKinnon & Osterhout 1996). A biphasic ERP pattern, i.e. an early left anterior negativity followed by a late centroparietal positivity was observed by Friederici, Hahne & Mecklinger (1996) in correlation with word category errors (e.g., *Das Metall wurde zur **veredelt** ...*, literal translation: *The metal was for **refined** ...*). When trying to generalize over the different studies it appears that an early left anterior negativity is only seen in response to a phrase structure violation and not in response to either violations of long distance dependencies or to so-called garden path sentences, i.e. temporarily ambiguous sentences. The early left anterior negativity and the late positivity may thus reflect functionally different aspects of syntactic processes.

Moreover, these two ERP components are differentially influenced by attentional factors. They behave differently as a function of the probability of incorrect sentences in an experimental set. While the late positivity is only present when the experimental set contains more correct than incorrect sentences (80% : 20%), but not when the experimental set contains more incorrect than correct sentences (20% : 80%), the early left anterior negativity remains unaffected by this variation (Hahne & Friederici 1999). The two components not only reflect functionally different processes, but moreover, it appears that those processes which are reflected by the early left anterior negativity are highly automatic whereas those reflected by the late positivity are more controlled. But what type of processes are reflected by these two components?

The adult model for language comprehension

The model we will use as a reference for the children's data was formulated on the basis of electrophysiological as well as neurophysiological data obtained from adults (Friederici 1995; Friederici et al. 1996). It describes language comprehension as consisting of three functionally distinct processing phases reflected in brain activity patterns, which are neurotopologically and temporally distinct. Two of these distinct phases of language are primarily syntactic in nature, whereas one is viewed to represent semantic aspects of processing. During the first phase, the parser assigns the initial syntactic structure on the basis of word category information. These first-pass parsing processes are assumed to be subserved by the anterior parts of the left hemisphere. Event-related brain potentials show an early left anterior negativity, ELAN, when phrase structure violations are processed (Friederici et al. 1993; Neville et al. 1991). Furthermore, circumscribed lesions in this area lead to an absence of the early left anterior negativity (Friederici, Hahne & von Cramon 1998). During the second phase, lexical-semantic information is processed. This phase is neurophysiologically manifest in a negative component in the event-related brain potential observed around 400 ms after the onset of a semantic anomaly. This component is distributed over the left and right temporo-parietal areas (Kutas & Hillyard 1984). During the third phase, the parser tries to map the initial syntactic structure onto the available lexical-semantic information. In the case of an unsuccessful match between the two types of information, reanalysis may become necessary. These processes of structural reanalysis are correlated with a centro-parietally distributed late positive component, P600, in the event-related brain potential (Osterhout & Holcomb 1992; Mecklinger et al. 1995). The centro-parietally distributed late positivities observed with different types of syntactic anomalies appear to reflect secondary processes of reanalysis and repair (Friederici et al. 1996; Münte et al.

1997), whereas the early anterior negativity may be considered to reflect automatic first-pass parsing processes (Friederici et al. 1993; Friederici et al. 1996; Hahne & Friederici 1999).

In addition to the data from the event-related brain potential studies, some aspects of aphasics' comprehension behavior support the view that the assumed different processing phases are distinct and that the left anterior cortex, in particular, is responsible for the fast and automatic on-line assignment of syntactic structure. Focusing on aphasic behavior we have formulated the idea that the left anterior areas may be necessary to guarantee first-pass parsing in a highly automatic fashion since adult patients with lesions in these areas are particularly deficient when it comes to processing syntactic information on-line (Kilborn & Friederici 1994). Patients, with lesions in the anterior part of the left hemisphere, however, do show sensitivity to syntax when tested in a sentence grammatically judgment task (Linebarger, Schwarz & Saffran 1983). These findings suggest a functional distinction between the anterior language area and the temporal language area with the former subserving syntactic procedures and the latter representing grammatical knowledge. This view seems to be supported by the behavior of patients with lesions in the posterior part of the left hemisphere, since these patients are not able to judge a sentence's grammaticality. They do, however, show some proficiency in syntactic priming for local structures during perception (Friederici 1985; Blumstein, Milberg & Shrier 1982). Moreover, these patients show a fluent paragrammatic output during production. Thus it could be hypothesized that the intact anterior part of the left hemisphere is responsible for the observable automatic, paragrammatic behavior in patients with temporal lesions. How can we relate these observations from adult aphasia to the pattern of aphasia seen in children?

The language-brain relationship in children

Children with a left temporal lesion do not show a fluent, paragrammatic output. Unfortunately none of the case reports of childhood aphasia provides information about these children's ability to process syntactic information on-line during language comprehension such as measured by reaction time tasks.

There are two possible explanations for the behavioral pattern seen in childhood aphasia: (1) either the automatic parsing procedures necessary for a fast first-pass parse are not yet established and language comprehension must be based on other syntactic processes, possibly those that allow the adult Broca's aphasic to perform grammaticality judgments, or (2) language comprehension is based on adult-like parsing routines which are, however, not yet able to automatically produce the fluent syntactic processes during production and perception seen in adults.[5] These two hypotheses make different predictions with respect to the expected pattern of event-related brain potentials. Under the first hypothesis we would predict an absence of the early left anterior negativity and a presence of the late positivity in early childhood, whereas under the second hypothesis we expect the left anterior negativity to be present in addition to the late positivity, although the former would be expected to be somewhat delayed in time.

The obvious possibility to test these hypotheses is to conduct an experiment registrating event-related brain potentials (ERPs) in children. Before we turn to our study in which we pursued this possibility we will briefly review the studies conducted in order to identify specific language-related ERP patterns in children.

The relation between brain and language function in a prelinguistic phase has been studied extensively by Molfese and coworkers (see this volume). Molfese (1980) recorded ERPs from 14-month-old and 16-month-old infants as they listened to words whose meaning the child comprehended and to words that the child did not appear to know. The data suggested different ERP patterns to these two types of words. More recently Mills, Coffey-Corina & Neville (1993; see also St. George & Mills, this volume) investigated the ERP patterns of 20-month-old children in response to words they understood, words which they did not understand and words played backwards. Again, the data indicate different ERP components discriminating comprehended words from unknown words and backward words. Holcomb, Coffey & Neville (1992) studied subjects between 5 and 26 years in a sentence listening experiment, presenting sentences with a highly expected completion word or a semantically inappropriate completion word. Children, like adults, showed a N400 component for the semantically inappropriate completion. The ERP latency and amplitude was increased in young children and then decreased linearly with age. Neville (1995) reports a study in which the processing of function words and content words in correct sentences was investigated using ERPs. Averages were calculated over all content words and function words in the sentences. A specific difference was observed for the ERP pattern for the function words. For adults a N280 component localized over the anterior temporal region of the left hemisphere was found as a function of processing function words. This component was not present in children before the age of 11 years.

The study

The present study was designed to test whether the early left anterior negativity observed in adult listeners in response to a phrase structure violation is present in childhood or not. In addition, as a control we tested the children's ERP pattern with respect to a lexical-semantic violation known to elicit the N400 component in adult listeners as a control.

The experiment presented a total of 192 German sentences. As indicated below half of the sentences were correct (1) and (3) and half were either (2) semantically incorrect because they contained a selectional restriction violation or (4) syntactically incorrect because they contained a phrase structure violation. The phrase structure violation was realized as a word category error, as the case marked preposition *im* necessarily requires the completion by a noun (as in (3)) or an adjective-noun combination. Instead the listener is confronted with a past participle verb form terminating the clause.[6]

Semantically and syntactically correct:

(1)   *Der Fisch wurde geangelt.*
      the fish was caught

Semantically incorrect:

(2)   **Die Schule wurde geangelt.*
      the school was   caught

Semantically and syntactically correct:

(3)   *Der Fisch wurde im   See geangelt.*
      the fish was   in.the lake caught

Syntactically incorrect:

(4)   **Der Fisch wurde im   geangelt.*
      the fish was   in.the caught.

Prior tests confirmed that the sentence material was adequate for children beginning at the age of 6 years. The sentences were presented auditorily in a quasi-random mixed order in blocks of 48 sentences. Three thousand milliseconds after each sentence, participants were required to judge the sentence's grammaticality by pressing one of two buttons. The side of the "yes" button (e.g., right button) corresponded to a smiling face displayed on a computer screen in front of the child (e.g., right half of the screen) and the "no" button's side (e.g., left button) corresponded to a frowning face at the left half of the screen.

To keep the children's attention during sentence listening, this task was embedded in a brief scenario which proceeds as follows: at the beginning of the session a magic man appears on the screen. The child is told that the magic man performed magic on the sentences, turning some of the sentences into incorrect sentences. The child's task is to carefully listen to each sentence and to indicate which of the sentences are magical (i.e. ungrammatical) and which are correct. Between each block the magic man appears on the screen, but before each block the magic man becomes smaller and smaller, and stays as a small fixation "point" on the middle of the screen throughout the block. Children are required to fixate on this small magic man when listening to the sentences.[7]

Since findings from the aphasia research suggested that 8 years of age could be of special interest to the question asked here, we included children from two age groups, 7.3 year of age (ranging from 6.1 to 7.8 years) and 8.7 year of age (ranging from 8.2 to 9.2 years) in addition to an adult control group (mean 26 years, ranging from 22 to 34 years). Each group consisted of 16 individuals. Children were all from a middle class housing area of Berlin, they were all native speakers of German and had no known hearing or neurological deficits. Adult participants were students of the Free University of Berlin. All participants were right handed according to the Edinburgh handedness test (Oldfield 1971). ERPs were recorded from 19 scalp electrodes distributed over the participant's scalp. In order to control for artifacts due to eye movements EOG (electro-occulogram) was registered by four additional electrodes placed lateral to the eyes and above and below the right eye.

Analyses were conducted separately for the behavioral and the ERP data (for further details see Hahne & Friederici, in preparation). Only those trials were included in the ERP analysis that were judged correctly by the participants. As can be gathered from Table 1 all groups performed above 90% correct in each condition. Performance increased with age, but particularly between childhood and adulthood.

The ERP pattern observed for the adult group replicates earlier results with similar sentence material (Friederici et al. 1993; Hahne & Friederici 1999). For the semantic violation condition, we found a N400 component, i.e. a negative

Table 1. *Correct answers (in %) by condition and age group*

	correct	semantically incorrect	syntactically incorrect
7.3 years	90.1	90.6	92.0
8.7 years	91.5	91.3	95.8
26 years	98.5	96.9	97.7

going wave distributed over centro-parietal areas with a maximum between 350 and 650 ms after the onset of the critical word. Figure 1 displays this N400 component at the central electrode Cz. For the phrase structure violation condition, we observed an early left anterior negativity (ELAN) illustrated at the left frontal electrode F7 in Figure 2. This negativity starts as early as 150 ms and extends up to 350 ms. In addition to this negativity, we observed a late centro-parietal positivity (P600) illustrated at the centro-parietal electrode Pz. This positivity starts around 350 ms and extends up to 1300 ms (Figure 2).

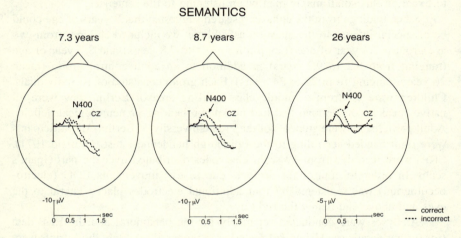

Figure 1. *Grand average event-related brain potentials at one critical electrode site (CZ) elicited by the critical word in the correct (solid line) and semantically incorrect (broken line) condition for three different age groups. The N400 component is marked by an arrow. Note that due to a general difference in amplitude size between children and adults different scales are used.*

Children at the age of 8.7 years showed the same three components, although these were slightly different in their temporal structure and scalp topography. The N400 component for the semantic violation condition similar to adults started at 350 ms, peaked around 400 ms but extended beyond 1000 ms (Figure 1). For the phrase structure violation condition, we found an early left anterior negativity (ELAN) between 150 and 350 ms just like in adults. However, the late centro-parietal positivity (P600) contrary to adults, only started around 750 ms and extended beyond 1500 ms (Figure 2). In contrast to adults, however, it was lateralized to the right hemisphere. These findings suggest that children at the age of 8.7 years perform the first-pass parsing routines reflected by the ELAN similar to adults, but need more time for secondary processes including a possible repair of the sentences indicated by the latency differences in the P600.

SYNTAX

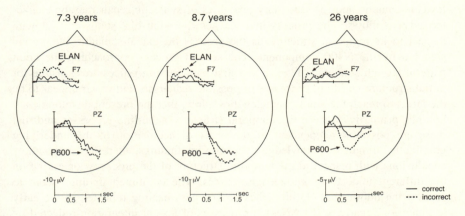

Figure 2. *Grand average event-related brain potentials at two critical electrode sites (F7 and PZ) elicited by the critical word in the correct (solid line) and syntactically incorrect (broken line) condition for three different age groups. The early left anterior negativity (ELAN) and the late positivity (P600) are marked by the arrows. Note, that due to a general difference in the amplitude size between children and adults, different scales are used.*

Children at the age of 7.3 years differed in their ERP pattern both from 8.7 year olds and from adults, in particular with respect to the component reflecting early syntactic processing. Their ERP pattern for the semantic violation condition looks similar to that of the 8.7 years old, with the N400 starting around 400 ms extending up to 1000 ms (Figure 1), though the N400 in this age group is again more widely distributed than that observed for the adults. It included central, parietal and frontal electrodes. For the phrase structure violation condition we do observe a left anterior negativity which, however, is delayed as compared to the 8.7 year olds and to the adults. The left anterior negativity for the 7.3 year olds only started around 200 ms, peaked around 400 ms and extended beyond 1000 ms. Differences to the adult data pattern could also be observed with regard to the positivity (P600). Similar to the 8-year-olds this component started only around 750 ms and extended beyond 1500 ms. The observed pattern of the left anterior negativity for the 7 year olds suggests that children at this age based their first-pass parsing processes on brain systems similar to those of adults, but it appears that the routines operating on those systems are still much slower than those of healthy adults.

Discussion

The age related differences in the temporal structure of (1) first-pass parsing, (2) lexical-semantic and (3) secondary processes of syntactic repair may be characterized as follows. The process that reaches the adult-like status earliest with respect to its temporal structure, is the process of lexical-semantic integration signaled by the N400 component. The second process approaching the adult pattern, though somewhat later, is the first-pass parsing process responsible for initial structure building. Processes of possible reanalysis and repair appear to be the latest to reach the adult characteristics. Note, that the present developmental findings primarily concern the temporal structure of on-line processes and that these are possibly independent of the order of acquisition of the underlying grammatical/linguistic knowledge. The present findings, therefore, only allow conclusions with respect to the temporal structure of the processes operating on the different underlying knowledge sources. The combined findings seem to support the notion that (1) processes of first-pass parsing reflected in the early left anterior negativity (ELAN), (2) processes of lexical integration reflected by the N400 component as well as (3) secondary processes of reanalyzes and repair reflected in the P600 change their temporal parameters as the brain matures. However, the different processes appear to change temporal parameters at different times. In the present study we have only investigated two age groups during childhood. Although the age difference between these two groups is only 1.4 years (i.e. 7.3 years versus 8.7 years) and although the general age level is quite high with respect to language acquisition, we were able to demonstrate subtle differences in the way these two age groups process syntactic information during the first-pass parse. In particular, the reported findings suggest that during the age of 7 years children's parsing routines are similar to those of adult listeners, but these routines only reach a highly automatic status around the age of 8 years. Research including younger age groups will have to show whether our hypothesis that the same brain systems which support adult parsing are also used during language acquisition, although with slower routines also holds for earlier stages of acquisition.

Notes

1. Note, that there are exceptions to this description of lesion-behavior relationship (see for example Wilmes & Poeck 1993; De Bleser 1988).
2. There is, however, one case report of fluent aphasia around the age of 5 years which manifests as a phonological jargon type of fluent aphasia though not as a paragrammatic type of aphasia

(Wood & Teuber 1978). This phonological jargon is described as fluent speech in which words seem to be substituted by pseudowords following the phonotactic rules of the target language, in this case English.
3. Recent results from functional magnet resonance imaging indicates that the critical brain structure involved is the left frontal operculum, adjacent to the Broca's area (Friederici, Meyer & von Cramon, in press).
4. Note that a left anterior negativity around 400 ms was also reported to correlate with processes of verbal memory (Kluender & Kutas 1993). Given that neuroanatomically adjacent areas in the left frontal cortex subserve the different function of verbal memory (Brodman area 46/45) and syntactic processes (Brodman area 44 that is Broca's area) it is not unlikely that the observed left anterior negativities reflect different functions. There is most recent evidence that two LAN effects can be dissociated: a local LAN effect reflecting the processing of morphosyntactic information and a global LAN (spanning between a filler and its gap) reflecting memory processes (Kluender & Münte 1998).
5. It may not be trivial to note that there is a case of a fluent jargon aphasia at the age of 5 years. This may give rise to the speculation that parts of these left anterior areas developmentally first establish the automatization of *phonotactic* routines and then the automatization of *syntactic* routines. Interestingly, brain imaging studies suggest that both syntactic and phonotactic phonological procedures are supported by Brodman area 44. While the latter procedures seem to be supported by the superior-dorsal portion of BA44, the former appear to be supported by inferior part of BA44 (see Friederici 1998).
6. Note, that German is a verb-finite language, thus requiring the past participle to occur in the sentence final position.
7. Loudness of sentence presentation was adjusted for each child in a pretest ensuring good comprehension.

References

Basso, A., Bracchi, M., Capitani, E., Laiacona, M. & Zanobio, M. E. 1987. "Age and evolution of language area functions: A study on adult stroke patients." *Cortex* 23: 475–483.
Basso, A. & Scarpa, M. T. 1990. "Traumatic aphasia in children and adults: A comparison of clinical features and evolution." *Cortex* 26: 501–514.
Bates, E., Thal, D. & Janowsky, J. 1992. "Early language development and its neural correlates." In *Handbook of Neuropsychology*, I. Rapin & S. Segalowitz, S. (eds.). Amsterdam: Elsevier.
Blumstein, S. E., Milberg, W. & Shrier, R. 1982. "Semantic processing in aphasia: Evidence from an auditory lexical decision task." *Brain and Language* 17: 301–315.
Brown, C. M. & Hagoort, P. 1993. "The processing nature of the N400: Evidence from masked priming." *Journal of Cognitive Neuroscience* 5: 34–44.
Coulson, S., King, J. & Kutas, M. 1998. "Expect the unexpect: Event-related brain responses to morphosyntactic violation." *Language and Cognitive Processes* 13: 21–58.

De Bleser, R. 1988. "Localization of aphasia: Science or fiction." In *Perspectives on Cognitive Neuropsychology*, G. Denes, C. Semenza & P. Bisiacchi (eds.). London: Lawrence Erlbaum.
Friederici, A. D. 1985. "Levels of processing and vocabulary types: Evidence from on-line comprehension in normals and agrammatics." *Cognition* 19: 133–166.
Friederici, A. D. 1994. "Funktionale Organisation und Reorganisation der Sprache während der Sprachentwicklung: Eine Hypothese." *Neurolinguistik* 8: 41–55.
Friederici, A. D. 1995. "The time course of syntactic activation during language processing: A model based on neuropsychological and neurophysiological data." *Brain and Language* 50: 259–281.
Friederici, A. D. 1998. "The neurobiology of language comprehension." In *Language Comprehension: A biological Perspective*, A. D. Friederici, (ed.). Berlin/Heidelberg/ New York: Springer.
Friederici, A. D., Hahne, A. & Mecklinger, A. 1996. "The temporal structure of syntactic parsing: Early and late ERP effects elicited by syntactic anomalies." *Journal of Experimental Psychology: Learning, Memory and Cognition* 22: 1219–1248.
Friederici, A. D., Meyer, M. & von Cramon, D.Y. (in press). "Auditory language processing: Brain images evoked by syntactic and lexical information." *Brain and Language*.
Friederici, A. D., Pfeifer, E. & Hahne, A. 1993. "Event-related brain potentials during natural speech processing: Effects of semantic, morphological and syntactic violations." *Cognitive Brain Research* 1: 183–192.
Gunter, T. C., Stowe, L. A. & Mulder, G. 1995. "When syntax meets semantics." *Psychophysiology* 34: 660–676.
Hagoort, P., Brown, C. & Groothusen, J. 1993. "The syntactic positive shift as an ERP-measure of syntactic processing." *Language and Cognitive Processes* 8: 439–483.
Hahne, A. & Friederici, A. D. 1999. "Functional neurotopography of syntactic parsing: Early automatic and late controlled processes." *Journal of Cognitive Neuroscience* 11: 193–204.
Hahne, A. & Friederici, A. D. (in preparation). "Syntactic and semantic processing in children as revealed by event-related brain potentials."
Holcomb, P. J., Coffey, S. A. & Neville, H. J. 1992. "Visual and auditory sentence processing: A developmental analysis using event-related brain potentials." *Developmental Neuropsychology* 8: 203–241.
Kilborn, K. W. & Friederici, A. D. 1994. "Cognitive penetrability of syntactic priming in Broca's aphasia." *Neuropsychology* 8: 83–90.
Kluender, R. & Kutas, M. 1993. "Bridging the gap: Evidence from ERP's on the processing of unbounded dependencies." *Journal of Cognitive Neuroscience* 2: 196–214.
Kluender, R. & Kutas, M. 1993. "Subjacency as a processing phenomenon." *Language and Cognitive Processes* 8: 573–633.

Kluender, R. & Münte, T. F. 1998. "ERPs to grammatical and ungrammatical subject/object asymmetries in German wh-questions." Paper presented at the 11th Annual CUNY Conference of Human Sentence Processing. New Brunswick, NJ, USA.

Kutas, M. & Hillyard, S. A. 1980. "Reading senseless sentences: Brain potentials reflect semantic incongruity." *Science* 207: 203–205.

Kutas, M. & Hillyard, S. A. 1984. "Brain potentials during reading reflect word expectancy and semantic association." *Nature* 307: 161–163.

Kutas, M., Lindamood, T. & Hillyard, S. A. 1984. "Word expectancy and event-related brain potentials during sentence processing." In *Preparatory States and Processing*, S. Kornblum, J. Requin (eds.). New Jersey: Erlbaum Press.

Kutas, M. & Van Petten, C. K. 1994. "Psycholinguistics electrified: Event-related brain potential investigations." In *Handbook of Psycholinguistics*, M. A. Gernsbacher (ed.), 83–143. San Diego: Academic Press.

Lenneberg, E. 1967. *Biological foundations of language*. New York: Wiley.

Linebarger, M. C., Schwartz, M. & Saffran, E. M. 1983. "Sensitivity to grammatical structure in so-called agrammatic aphasia." *Cognition* 13: 361–392.

McKinnon, R. & Osterhout, L. 1996. "Constraints on movement phenomena in sentence processing: Evidence from event-related brain potentials." *Language and Cognitive Processes* 11: 495–523.

Mecklinger, A., Schriefers, H., Steinhauer, K. & Friederici, A. D. 1995. "Processing relative clauses varying on syntactic and semantic dimensions: An analysis with event-related potentials." *Memory and Cognition* 23: 477–494.

Mills, D. M., Coffey-Corina, S. A. & Neville, H. 1993. "Language acquisition and cerebral specialization in 20-month-old infants." *Journal of Cognitive Neuroscience* 5: 326–342.

Molfese, D. L., Narter, D. B., Van Matre, A. J., Ellefson, M. R. & Modglin, A. (this volume) "Language development during infancy and early childhood: Electrophysiological correlates."

Molfese, D. L. 1980. "Neuroelectric correlates of language processes: Evidence from scalp recorded evoked potential research." *Brain and Language* 11: 222–397.

Münte, T. F., Heinze, H.-J. & Mangun, G. R. 1993. "Dissociation of brain activity related to syntactic and semantic aspects of language." *Journal of Cognitive Neuroscience* 5: 335–344.

Münte, T. F., Matzke, M. & Johannes, S. 1997. "Brain activity associated with syntactic incongruencies in words and pseudo-words." *Journal of Cognitive Neuroscience* 9: 318–329.

Neville, H. J. 1990. "Intermodal competition and compensation in development: Evidence from studies of the visual system in congenitally deaf adults." In *The Development and Neural Bases of Higher Cognitive Function*, A. Diamond (ed.). New York: New York Academy of Sciences.

Neville, H. J. 1991. "Whence the specialization of the language hemisphere?" In *Modularity and the motor theory of speech perception*, I. G. Mattingly & M. Studdert-Kennedy (eds.). Hillsdale, NJ: Lawrence Erlbaum Associates.

Neville, H. J. 1991. "Neurobiology of cognitive and language processing: Effects of early experience." In *Brain Muturation and Cognitive Development: Comparative and Crocc-cultural Perspectives*, K. R. Gibson & A. C. Petersen (eds.). Hawthorne, NY: Aladine de Gruyter Press.

Neville, H. J. 1995. "Developmental specificity in neurocognitive development in humans." In *The Cognitive Neuroscience*, M. S. Gazzaniga (ed.). Cambridge, MA: MIT Press.

Neville, H. J., Nicol, J., Barss, A., Forster, K. & Garrett, M. 1991. "Syntactically based sentence processing classes: Evidence from event-related brain potentials." *Journal of Cognitive Neuroscience* 3: 155–170.

Oldfield, R. C. 1971. "The assessment and analysis of handedness: The Edinburgh Inventory." *Neuropsychologia* 9: 97–113.

Osterhout, L. & Holcomb, P. J. 1995. "Event-related potentials and language comprehension." In *Electrophysiology of mind*, M. D. Rugg & M. G. H. Coles (eds.). Oxford, NY: Oxford University Press.

Osterhout, L. & Holcomb, P. J. 1992. "Event-related brain potentials elicited by syntactic anomaly." *Journal of Memory and Language* 31: 785–804.

Osterhout, L. & Holcomb, P. J. 1993. "Event-related potentials and syntactic anomaly: Evidence of anomaly detection during the perception of continuous speech." *Language and Cognitive Processes* 8: 413–437.

Osterhout, L., Holcomb, P. J. & Swinney, D. A. 1994. "Brain potentials elicited by garden-path sentences: Evidence of the application of verb information during parsing." *Journal of Experimental Psychology: Learning, Memory and Cognition* 20: 786–803.

Rösler, F., Friederici, A. D., Pütz, P. & Hahne, A. 1993. "Event-related brain potentials while encountering semantic and syntactic constraint violations." *Journal of Cognitive Neuroscience* 5: 345–362.

St. George, M. & Mills, D. L. (this volume) "Electrophysiological studies of language development."

Van Dongen, H. R., Loonen, M. C. B. & Van Dongen, K. J. 1985. "Anatomical basis for acquired fluent aphasia in children." *Annals of Neurology* 17: 306–309.

Van Hout, A. & Lyon, G. 1986. "Wernicke's aphasia in a 10-year-old boy." *Brain and Language* 29: 268–285.

Willmes, K. & Poeck, K. 1993. "To what extent can aphasic syndromes be localized?" *Brain* 116: 1527–1540.

Wood, B. T. & Teuber, H. L. 1978. "Changing pattern of childhood aphasia." *Annals of Neurology* 3: 273–280.

Electrophysiological Studies of Language Development

Marie St. George & Debra L. Mills
University of California at San Diego

A central question which has motivated much of the research in the field of developmental cognitive neuroscience is to what extent cerebral organization depends on, and is modified by, experience. With regard specifically to *language* development one wonders the extent to which individual language experience impacts the organization of language in the brain and the developmental timecourse for this dynamic process.

One way to study how the developing brain processes language is to look at the organization of language in the brain early in development and measure the patterns of brain activity in response to language stimuli at many different time points across infants and children with a wide range of language abilities. An obvious problem with measuring language comprehension in a child age 13 months is that they cannot tell you what they understand. The use of ERPs (event-related brain potentials) provides a unique opportunity to study ongoing brain development and specialization by recording the electroencephalogram (EEG) while children listen to words without the necessity for a behavioral response. By using ERPs, complex but reliable patterns of brain activity can be recorded from infants in response to known or unknown words (such as ball, cat, bath) and compared to the patterns of activity obtained from children and adults at different levels of development. To use the technique, one records the EEG from a number of electrodes placed over the scalp. Stimuli are presented and the data are subsequently averaged across the brain response to different types of stimuli of interest (for a detailed description of the ERP technique, see Rugg & Coles 1995). Using this measure one can tell at what point in development children make a distinction between a familiar word and an unfamiliar word, and between different word classes. More importantly, we can track the changing patterns of brain activity associated with language milestones. More complex questions can be asked, such as whether developmental patterns observed in brain activity in response to words reflect the developmental age of the child or something specifically linked to language ability, such as vocabulary size.

In the present paper, we will focus on ERP studies of language development in children ages 13 to 42 months, with data from both normally developing children as well as those showing signs of language impairment. We examine developmental changes in neural systems linked to specific language milestones during the first 4 years of life. Changes in the organization of language-relevant brain systems in children of different ages are contrasted with changes linked to vocabulary size when the age of the child is held constant. Brain activity during language comprehension will also be examined from a group of 28 to 30 month-old late talkers, whose ERP patterns were predictive of their language performance at a later age.

Known vs. unknown words

Between 13 and 17 months of age, children are learning to produce their first words. By 20 months, they typically show a marked increase in the number of words they produce, called the "vocabulary spurt" (Goldfield & Reznick 1990). The increase is roughly from about 10 words to 150 words (Barrett 1995). Mills et al. (1993, 1997) sought to track the brain activity associated with this rapid change in language ability by studying children at ages 13 months and 20 months, i.e., before and after the vocabulary spurt. For 13 to 17 month-olds, ERPs were different for known and unknown words. Word knowledge was assessed by parental report using two different measures: the MacArthur Communicative Development Inventory (CDI) as well as a vocabulary checklist and rating scale in which parents were asked to give confidence ratings for both comprehension and production for 120 words typically known by children in this age range. As can be seen in Figure 1, both the N200 and the N350 were larger to known than unknown words. The differences were observed across the head, including frontal, temporal, parietal and occipital locations over both hemispheres. By 20 months, after the vocabulary spurt, these ERP differences were limited to the left hemisphere over temporal and parietal regions. Thus, there seems to be a dramatic difference in the processing of words before and after the vocabulary spurt, from 13 to 20 months of age.

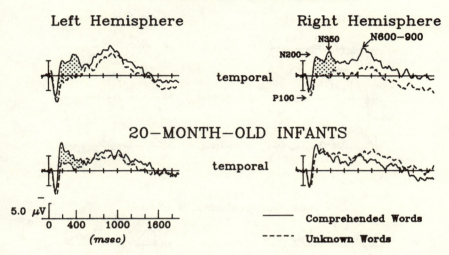

Figure 1. *ERPs elicited by comprehended (known) and unknown words for 13 to 17 month old (top) and 20 month old (bottom) children, over the temporal region of both hemispheres. At 13 to 17 months ERPs are greater to comprehended than unknown words over both hemispheres. By 20 months of age, the differences between comprehended and unknown words are limited to the left hemisphere. Dotted areas indicate differences between the waveforms which reached significance.*

In order to determine if these changes were associated with language comprehension, the 13 to 17 month old children were split into two groups according to the size of their receptive vocabularies. Vocabulary size was determined by asking parents to complete the MacArthur Communicative Development Inventory (Fenson et al. 1989). The low comprehenders (lower 50 percent on the CDI) showed broadly distributed ERP differences, just as their age group overall. In contrast, the high comprehenders (upper 50 percent on the CDI) showed a more focal distribution of differences between known and unknown words, much like the 20 month-olds after the vocabulary spurt. The 13–17 month-old high comprehenders did however show bilateral differences over frontal and temporal regions, which is unlike the pattern observed in 20 month olds. Thus, the observed changes in brain activity from 13 to 20 months are at least in part associated with increasing vocabulary size.

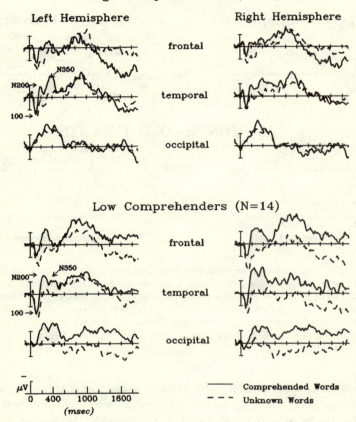

Figure 2. *ERPs to comprehend (known) and unknown words for 13 o 17 months old children, divided by high and low comprehension. The ERPs for the high comprehenders (upper 50% on CDI) are shown in the top half of the figure, and the ERPs for the low comprehenders (lower 50% on CDI) are shown in the bottom half of the figure. The low comprehenders showed the broad distribution of known/unknown differences typical of their age group (notice the large differences over occipital regions, and the right hemisphere), whereas the high comprehenders showed a more focal distribution, with differences between known and unknown words only over more frontal areas (notice there is no difference over occipital region).*

Open class words vs. closed class words

Open class and closed class words were chosen for study during development because they have different timecourses for acquisition, and have different roles in sentences. Open class words, also known as "content" words, are named such because we can, and often do, add members to this class of words. As a language grows, new nouns, verbs, adjectives and adverbs become members. In contrast, closed class words, or "function" words, which include prepositions, conjunctions, and articles, do not typically acquire new members, and are referred to as "closed". Their labels of "content" and "function" refer to their roles in sentence processing. Content words are thought of as the "meat" of the sentence, carrying the bulk of the meaning in the form of nouns, verbs, adjectives and adverbs. Function words carry the grammatical information of the sentence which link and clarify the content words in the form of prepositions, conjunctions, articles and auxiliaries. With regard to development, these two word classes are interesting because of their different developmental trajectories. Open class words tend to be acquired first, and are less vulnerable to abnormal development than closed class words, although several investigations have shown that children may perceive closed class words well before they produce them (e.g., Gerken & McIntosh 1993). Because of their different developmental trajectories, their different roles in sentences, and the different pattern of electrical activity they elicit (see Holcomb, Coffey & Neville 1992; Neville, Mills & Lawson 1992; King & Kutas 1998), we chose to study how children process open and closed class words as they are beginning to speak in single (predominantly open class) words and through their production of closed class words and sentence formation. For all age groups studied (20 to 42 months) production was measured by both the CDI as well as the parental report (vocabulary checklist and confidence rating scale, mentioned above). Comprehension scores were also provided by parents on the vocabulary checklist and confidence rating scale. Additionally, comprehension was measured by using a comprehension book task in which children pointed to one of two pictures which matched the word spoken by the experimenter. Comprehension of both open and closed class words was assessed (e.g., for the closed class word "more" children were shown pictures of a few ducks and many ducks and asked "show me *more* ducks"). The standard open class words were "nose, milk, dog, cat, ball" and the standard closed class words were "out, up, down, off, more". Other words were used if these were not known by an individual subject based on parental report.

20 months

At 20 months of age, when children are producing single words and just beginning to put words together, there are no reliable ERP differences to open and closed class words (see Figure 3a). This result obtained despite the fact that all of these children understood and produced all of the words, both open and closed class. Although their ERPs did not reflect open versus closed class differences, both open and closed class words elicited waveforms which look like the ERP response to *known* words, specifically in the region of the N200 component. That is, the N200 component elicited by open and closed class words was of similar amplitude to that elicited by known words, and of greater amplitude than that elicited by unknown words.

28–30 months

By 28 to 30 months of age, as children are beginning to speak in phrases, differences in ERPs elicited by open and closed class words are observed. Over the left hemisphere, a component at approximately 200 ms, called the N200, is larger in response to the open class words than to the closed class words (see Figure 3b). A few hundred milliseconds later, at approximately 500 ms following the word, closed class words are more negative than open class words over the right hemisphere. While ERPs to open class words are symmetrical, ERPs to closed class words are greater over the right than the left. Thus, as children are beginning to understand the role of grammar, different patterns of brain activity are elicited by the processing of open and closed class words.

36–42 months

By 3 years of age, ERPs to open and closed class words differ by 150 ms after the onset of the word. The N200 is larger to open class words than to closed class words at frontal, temporal, parietal, and occipital sites over both hemispheres. A second negative component, the N450, is also larger to open class words than closed class words, but this difference is confined to the right hemisphere (see Figure 3c). More specifically, the N450 to open class words is symmetrical, whereas the N450 to closed class words is larger over the left than the right. Note that at *both* 200 ms and at 450 ms closed class words are larger over the left hemisphere than the right. Thus, at 3 years of age, the differences between open and closed class words can be summarized as follows: the N200 and N450 are symmetrical to open class words, whereas for closed class words

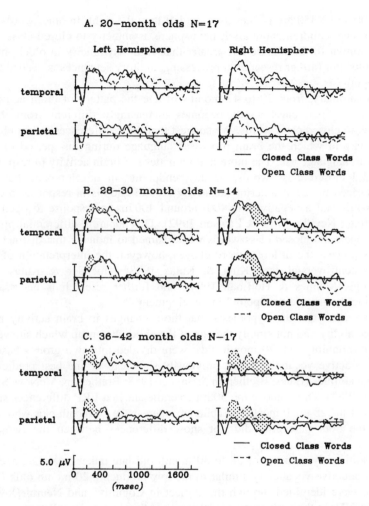

Figure 3. *ERPs to open and closed class words at (a) 20 months old, (b) 28 to 30 months old, and (c) 36 to 42 months old. Dotted areas indicate differences between the waveforms which reached significance. Note that there are no differences between the word classes at 20 months. At 28 to 30 months, the waveforms differ by 200 msec following word onset; closed class words elicit activity greater over the right than the left hemisphere, and open class words elicit symmetrical activity. By 36 to 42 months, ERPs to closed class words elicit a left greater than right asymmetry, whereas ERPs to open class words are symmetrical.*

the N200 and N450 are greater over the left than the right. In other words, by 3 years of age, children show a left hemisphere asymmetry to closed class words that is similar to the mature left-greater-than-right asymmetry in older children and adults, but further research in processing auditory sentences is needed to test this hypothesis.

In summary, from 20 to 42 months of age the pattern of brain activity in response to open class words becomes increasingly different from that in response to closed class words. We suggest that these differences reflect changes in the way in which the brain processes language during this period of rapid growth in language use. The more mature pattern of brain activity in response to open and closed class words, or the "endpoint" in development, has been characterized by a left anterior negativity around 280 ms in response to closed class words and a negativity (N400) around 400 ms in response to open class words (e.g., Neville, Mills & Lawson 1992). This apparent differential processing for open and closed class words was assumed to indicate that distinct brain systems process the different word classes, however, the interpretation of these data is controversial (see King & Kutas 1998; Kluender & Kutas 1993; St. George, Mannes & Hoffman 1994), and further research is necessary to determine the mature "endpoint" in development.

To further test the hypothesis that these changes in brain activity reflect language ability and not simply the age of the child, the group which showed the greatest variability, the 20 month olds, were divided into two groups based on their productive vocabulary size, previously shown to be the best predictor of language abilities (Bates, Bretherton & Snyder 1988; Bretherton, McNew, Snyder & Bates 1983). Those above the 50th percentile showed ERP differences similar to those of the 28 to 30 month old children, whereas the 20 month olds who scored below the 50th percentile did not show differences between the two word classes.

Additionally, a group of 28 to 30 month old late talkers were studied who had a productive vocabulary similar to the low producing 20 month olds. These children were identified through the Project in Cognitive and Neural Development (PCND) at the University of California at San Diego, in collaboration with Dr. Donna Thal. Just as the 20 month olds, the 28 to 30 month old late talkers did not show any differences between open and closed class words (see Thal et al. 1997). Thus, their pattern of brain activity is similar to language-matched rather than chronological age-matched children.

Furthermore, ERP data from children with focal brain lesions reflect a similar pattern (Mills et al. 1995, see also Bates et al. 1997). Just as we found with high producing 20 month olds and late talking 28 to 30 month olds, their patterns of brain activity in response to open and closed class words do not follow chronological age, but rather, are predictable by level of language ability. In a study of three year olds with focal brain lesions (n=5), three children with productive vocabularies equivalent to 30 month olds showed all of the ERP differences associated with open and closed class words at that level of language development in normal children. The remaining two children with focal lesions who scored below the 50th percentile on productive vocabulary for normal 20 month olds displayed no differences between open and closed class words, just as normal 20 month olds with low productive vocabularies. Taken together, these data, (1) studies of high producing 20 month olds, (2) late talking 28 to 30 month olds, and (3) both low and high producing children with focal brain lesions, strongly suggest that the pattern of brain activity elicited by open and closed class words is linked to language abilities rather than to chronological age.

ERP predictors of later language abilities

In addition to tracking the brain's electrical activity which is correlated with language ability, it seems we may also be able to use ERPs to predict later language performance. Children at three age groups (13 to 17 months, 20 months, and 28 to 30 months) were split into two categories based on the size of their productive vocabularies, as was done in the above experiments (Mills et al. 1995). In this study, children scoring below the 30th percentile made up the low producer groups, and those scoring above the 50th percentile made up the high producer group. In the 28 to 30 month group, most of the low producers were by this point considered "late talkers". The study focused on an ERP component which is earlier than the others mentioned in this chapter. The P100 component is thought to be an index of early sensory processing (Hillyard & Picton 1987; Wood & Wolpaw 1982). Since older children with language deficits show abnormal auditory sensory processing (Neville, Coffey, Holcomb & Tallal 1993; Tallal 1978), it is possible that these differences may be detectable much earlier in development. As can be seen in Figure 3, the P100 amplitude in response to familiar, open class words is quite different for the high and low producers at every age group. Specifically, at 13 to 17 months, 20 months, and 28 to 30 months the P100 component in the high producer group was much larger over the left hemisphere than the right. For the low producer groups at every age, however, P100 peak amplitude was symmetrical over the two hemispheres.

Thus, unlike the N200 and N350 described above, the P100 seems to be linked to the performance of children relative to children their age. Whereas the

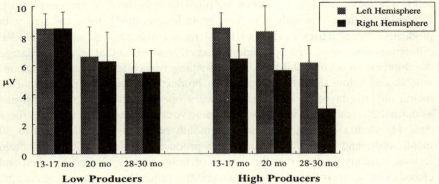

Figure 4. *P100 peak amplitude to familiar words at three age groups (13–17 months, 20 months, and 28–30 months), each divided by productive vocabulary size. It is the high producers who show a P100 asymmetry (left greater than right), but not the low producers.*

N200 and N350 reflect differences in language abilities regardless of age, that is, different language milestones, the P100 reflects differences in language performance within an age group. Namely, the 13 month old high producers and the 20 month old low producers had the same productive vocabulary size — but only the 13 month old high producers demonstrated the asymmetry.

An exciting, though preliminary, finding from this study is the follow up data from the 28 to 30 month old children who were late talkers (below the 10th percentile in productive vocabulary for their age). When tested in the original experiment, three of the nine late talkers showed a P100 asymmetry more typical of high producers, that is, amplitude greater over the left hemisphere than the right. By 42 months, these three children had all caught up considerably and scored within the normal range on the Reynell test of language comprehension. In contrast, five of the six late talkers who demonstrated the low producer pattern at 28 to 30 months old (symmetrical P100s to words) continued to show evidence of delayed language, scoring significantly below their age on the Reynell for comprehension, production, or both. Further research is clearly needed to investigate the predictive power of ERP component differences when both age and language performance is identical. It is an intriguing finding that children of the same age and same language ability — thus indistinguishable by behavioral measures — can be distinguished based on the asymmetry in the P100 component, and furthermore, the *outcome* of their early language delay can be predicted based on the presence or absence of this asymmetry at 28 to 30 months.

Conclusion

The ERP is clearly a powerful methodology to use in the study of both normal and delayed or abnormal language development. This window on the rapidly developing mind can provide much more information about how and when each stage of language development occurs than can be gleaned from more traditional behavioral measures. This is especially true in the study of the late talkers, in which their later language performance was predicted by an ERP asymmetry, not by age or language performance at testing. This is much like looking into a crystal ball for scientists seeking a way to determine how to help, how to understand, how to characterize and chart the developmental path of language not only in the mean but in the individual.

Acknowledgments

We are grateful to the NIH for support (grant DC0289 from the National Institute on Deafness and Other Communication Disorders), and to the parents and children who helped make these studies possible.

References

Barrett, M. 1995. "Early lexical development." In *Handbook of Child Language*, P. Fletcher & B. McWhinney (eds.). Oxford: Basil Blackwell.

Bates, E., Bretherton, I. & Snyder, L. 1988. *From first words to grammar: Individual differences and dissociable mechanisms*. Cambridge, MA: Cambridge University Press.

Bates, E., Thal, D., Trauner, D., Fenson, J., Aram, D., Eisele, J. & Nass, R. 1997. "From first words to grammar in children with focal brain injury." *Developmental Neuropsychology* 13(3): 275–343.

Bretherton, I., McNew, S., Snyder, L. & Bates, E. 1983. "Individual differences at 20 months: Analytic and holistic strategies in language acquisition." *Journal of Child Language* 10: 293–320.

Fenson, L., Flynn, D., Vella, D., Omens, J., Burgess, S. & Hartung, J. 1989. San Diego State University, *Tools for the assessment of language in infants and toddlers by parental reports.* Paper presented at the Society for Research in Child Development, Kansas City.

Gerken, LA. & McIntosh, B. J. 1993. "Interplay of function morphemes and prosody in early language." *Developmental Psychology* 29(3): 448–457.

Goldfield, B. A. & Reznick, J. S. 1990. "Early lexical acquisition: rate, content, and the vocabulary spurt." *Journal of Child Language* 17: 171–183.

Hillyard, S. A. & Picton, T. W. 1987. "Electrophysiology of the brain." In *Handbook of Psychology: The Nervous System*, F. Plumb (ed.). Bethesda, MD.

Holcomb, P. J., Coffey, S. A. & Neville, H. J. 1992. "Visual and auditory sentence processing: A developmental analysis using event-related brain potentials." *Developmental Neuropsychology* 8: 203–241.

King, J. W. & Kutas, M. 1998. "Neural plasticity in the dynamics of human visual word recognition." *Neuroscience Letters* 244: 61–64.

Kluender, R. & Kutas, M. 1993. "Subjacency as a processing phenomenon." *Language and Cognitive Processes* 8(4): 573–633.

Mills, D. L., Coffey-Corina, S. A. & Neville, H. J. 1993." Language acquisition and cerebral specialization in 20-month-old infants." *Journal of Cognitive Neuroscience* 5: 317–334.

Mills, D. L., Coffey-Corina, S. A. & Neville, H. J. 1997. "Language comprehension and cerebral specialization from 13 to 20 months." *In Special Issue: Origins of Language Disorders*, D. Thal & J. Reilly (eds.). *Developmental Neuropsychology* 13(3): 397–445.

Mills, D. L., Coffey-Corina, S. A. & DiIulio, L. 1995. "The development of cerebral specialization for different lexical items in normal infants and infants with focal brain lesions." *Center for Research in Language Technical Report CND-9507.*

Mills, D. L., Thal, D., DiIulio, L. et al. 1995. "Auditory sensory processing and language abilities in late talkers: An ERP study." *Center for Research in Language Technical Report #CND-9508.*, Project in Cognitive and Neural Development. La Jolla, CA: University of California, San Diego.

Neville, H. J., Coffey, S. A., Holcomb, P. J. & Tallal, P. 1993. "The neurobiology of sensory and language processing in language-impaired children." *Journal of Cognitive Neuroscience* 5: 235–253.

Neville, H. J., Mills, D. L. & Lawson, D. S. 1992. "Fractionating language: Different neural subsystems with different sensitive periods." *Cerebral Cortex* 2: 244–258.

Rugg, M. D. & Coles, M. G. H. 1995. *Electrophysiology of Mind: Event-related Brain Potentials and Cognition.* Oxford: Oxford University Press.

St. George, M., Mannes, S. & Hoffman, J. E. 1994. "Global semantic expectancy and language comprehension." *Journal of Cognitive Neuroscience* 6(1): 70–83.

Tallal, P. 1978. "An experimental investigation of the role of auditory temporal processing in normal and disordered language development." In *Language Acquisition and*

Language Breakdown: Parallels and Divergences, A. Caramazza & D. Zurif (eds.). Baltimore, MD: The John Hopkins University Press.

Thal, D., Bates, E., Goodman, J. & Jahn-Samillo, J. 1997. "Continuity of language abilities: An exploratory study of late- and early-talking toddlers." *Developmental Neuropsychology* 13(3): 239–273.

Wood, C.C. & Wolpaw, J.R. 1982. "Scalp distribution of human auditory evoked potentials. II. Evidence for overlapping sources and involvement of auditory cortex." *Electroencephalography and Clinical Neurophysiology* 54: 25–38.

Part V

Additional Perspectives on Language Acquisition

Interactionist Approaches to Early Language Acquisition

Kim Plunkett
Oxford University

Abstract

What features of brain processing and neural development support linguistic development in young children? To what extent is the profile and timing of linguistic development in young children determined by a pre-ordained genetic programme? Does the environment play a crucial role in determining the patterns of change observed in children growing up? Recent experimental, neuro-imaging and computational studies of developmental change in children promise to contribute to a deeper understanding of how the brain gets wired up for language. The multi-disciplinary perspectives of cognitive neuroscience, experimental psycholinguistics and neural network modelling are brought to bear on four distinct areas in the study of language acquisition: early speech perception, word recognition, word learning and the acquisition of grammatical inflections. Each area demonstrates how linguistic development can be driven by the interaction of general learning mechanisms, highly sensitive to particular statistical regularities in the input, with a richly structured environment. This interaction provides the necessary ingredients for the emergence of linguistic representations that support mature language processing. Similar epigenetic principles, guiding the emergence of linguistic structure, apply to all these domains, offering insights into the precocity of young infants' sensitivity to speech contrasts as well as to the complexities of the problem facing the young child learning the Arabic plural.

1. Introduction

Very few of the major landmarks in language development have been tagged to specific aspects of brain development. Although many critical events in neural development occur during the language learning years and their potential role in language development has been discussed (Bates, Tahl & Janowsky 1992; Elman et al. 1996; Quartz & Sejnowski 1997) in most cases the causal link between language development and behaviour remains unclear. Language development may depend on changes in the neuroanatomical and neurophysiological changes in the brain. Conversely, language development may reflect a fine-tuning of pre-fashioned, genetically-determined structures and a consolidation of cortical representations. Recent neuro-imaging and neuropsychological research on infants and children shows that the developing language system undergoes striking changes in neural organisation, displaying extensive plasticity (see Appendix, Box 1), and that its final layout depends critically on experience. At the same time, experimentalists have uncovered an increasingly detailed picture of the sophisticated linguistic propensities of the young infant. These findings indicate the need for learning mechanisms which are finely tuned to extracting statistical properties of the speech input. Computational implementations of these learning mechanisms provide the language acquisition researcher with important clues as to how the brain gets wired up for language.

2. Early speech perception

Newly born infants can discriminate the speech contrasts of all human languages (Eimas et al. 1971; Jusczyk 1992). Furthermore, their way of categorising speech sounds is universal, so that a child born to Japanese-speaking parents has the same phonemic category boundaries as a child born to Spanish-speaking parents. For some non-native speech contrasts, the ability to discriminate remains intact until fairly late in the first year. For example, 6–8 month old infants from an English-speaking background have been shown to be able to distinguish the glottalised velar/uvular stop contrast [k'i]–[q'i] in Nthlakapmx[1] and the Hindi voiceless aspirated versus breathy voiced contrast [th]–[dh] — neither of which are exploited in English. For English-learning infants, this ability declines after the age of 10–12 months as their phonological processing develops (Werker & Tees 1984). For other contrasts, discrimination sensitivity can decline even earlier. For example, Polka & Werker (1994) have shown that English infants have already lost the ability to discriminate the German vowel contrasts [Y]–[U] by 6–8 months of age. Sensitivity to non-native contrasts appears to decline earlier for vowels than for consonants (Jusczyk 1996). Interestingly, however, not all sensitivities to non-native contrasts decline in this fashion. Best et al. (1988) have shown that even English-learning 12–14 month olds are able to discriminate Zulu click contrasts — as are English-speaking adults.

The mechanisms by which the newly born infant can discriminate all human speech sounds, and the process by which the child becomes attuned to the parental language are not well understood. Dehaene-Lambertz & Dehaene (1994) have shown that auditory Evoked Related Potentials (ERPs) can be used to unravel the temporal and spatial organisation of the neuronal processes underlying phoneme discrimination. They played two-month old infants synthesized speech stimuli as groups of five syllables (e.g., /ba/, /ba/, /ba/, /ba/, /ga/) where the first four syllables were identical (the standard) and the fifth was either identical or phonetically different (deviant). A significant difference in auditory ERPs between standard and deviant stimuli showed that the infant could discriminate the deviant stimuli. Christophe & Morton (1994) suggest that this technique might be used to study the developmental profile of responses to native and non-native contrasts thereby shedding light on whether the brain is still sensitive to non-native speech contrasts but ignores the information, or whether the ability to discriminate non-native speech contrasts is truly lost.

Auditory ERPs offer an important new tool for studying which aspects of the acoustic stimulus young infants are sensitive to, when they are sensitive to it and even, in some cases, the parts of the brain that are most revealing of these discriminatory capacities. However, ERP measures are unlikely to tell us how the brain gets the job done. Nakisa & Plunkett (1998) have developed a neural network model of early phonological development. The model is based roughly on Jusczyk & Bertoncini's (1988) proposal that the development of speech perception should be viewed as an innately guided learning process: learning the speech contrasts of the native language takes place rapidly because the system is innately structured to be sensitive to correlations of certain distributional properties of the speech stimulus and not others.

The model is based on vertebrate neuronal development. Neurons are allowed to migrate, grow axons and synapses under the control of genes for various trophic factors. Other genes then control the means by which synapses are modified by experience. A population of these neural networks is generated and allowed to breed, with a selective pressure for networks that respond in the desired way to speech sounds. Network fitness is calculated using the stored output unit activities after the network has been exposed to a test set of spoken English sentences. The fitness function favours networks that represent occurrences of the same phoneme as similarly as possible and different phonemes as differently as possible. When, after many generations of this evolutionary process, one of these neural networks is exposed to speech spectra from any of 14 human languages (including English, Cantonese, Swahili, Farsi, Czech, Hindi, Korean, Hungarian Polish, Russian, Slovak, Spanish, Ukrainian and Urdu), it rapidly modifies its connections and creates a representation of speech sounds that is the same regardless of the language to which it has been exposed. Furthermore, the internal representations of speech in the network show the same categorical boundaries that are observed in adult and infant perception (see Appendix, Box 2). Once a network architecture has been selected by the evolutionary process, only two minutes of speech are required to train the network.

The innately guided learning exhibited by this network enables it to learn very fast and make it less dependent on the 'correct' environmental statistics. The model offers an account of how infants from different linguistic environments can learn the same featural representation so soon after birth. In this sense, innately guided learning as implemented in this model is half-way between nativism and constructivism. It shows how genes and the environment can interact to ensure rapid development of a featural representation of speech on which further linguistic development depends.

3. Word recognition

During the first year of life, infants become attuned to more than the phonemic contrasts of their native language. They pick up knowledge that enables them to identify words and other linguistic units in speech. Jusczyk & Aslin (1995) have used the familiarization-preference procedure (see Appendix, Box 3) to demonstrate that even 7½-month-olds have some ability to detect words in fluent speech. Jusczyk et al. (1993a) showed that 9-month-old American and Dutch infants prefer to listen to word lists that conform to the phonetic and phonotactic structure of their own language. In contrast, 6-month-old American infants showed no preference for lists from either language. There is also evidence that infants are sensitive to the prosodic organization of their native language. Jusczyk, Cutler & Redanz (1993) report that prelinguistic infants have identified a regularity of English wherein disyllabic words tend to adhere to a trochaic (strong-weak) stress pattern (Cutler & Carter 1987). Newsome & Jusczyk (1995) have shown that 7½-month-old infants can use this knowledge to segment disyllabic words from the main speech stream. Young children are also more likely to imitate syllables that are stressed or word-final than syllables that are both unstressed and nonfinal (Echols & Newport 1992). Fernald, McRoberts & Herrera (1996), using a preferential looking task, have shown that infants are more likely to recognise familiar words in utterance-initial or final position than when the word occurs in the middle of the utterance.

Saffran, Aslin & Newport (1996) have focused on the ability of young children to acquire linguistic structure via statistical cues. They point out that the one potentially useful type of information for infant word segmentation is the statistical properties of multisyllabic words. Over a corpus of speech sounds, there are measurable regularities that distinguish those recurring sound sequences which comprise words from the more accidental sound sequences which occur across word boundaries. Using the familiarization-preferential looking procedure (see Appendix, Box 3), Saffran et al. (1996) showed that 8 month old infants are able to perform the necessary statistical computations. Following a two minute exposure to a synthetic speech stream containing only statistical cues to word boundaries, the infants' listening preferences demonstrated that they had extracted and remembered serial order information about the familiarization items, distinguishing 'words' (recurrent syllable sequences) from syllable strings spanning word boundaries. This preferential behaviour indicates that the infants computed the co-occurrence frequencies for pairs of sounds across the familiarization corpus. Jusczyk, Luce & Charles-Luce (1994) report that 9-month-old infants (but not 6-month-olds) are attentive to the frequency with which phonotactic sequences occur within English. These results, together with Saffran et al.'s (1996) findings, suggest that infants have access to a powerful mechanism for the computation of statistical properties of the language input even from very brief exposures and that this develops sometime between the age of 6–9 months. They indicate that infants may be far better at deriving structure from statistical information than has often been assumed in the acquisition literature. In particular, certain aspects of language which are argued to be unlearnable and thus innately specified may be discoverable by appropriately constrained statistical learning mechanisms.

More recent research suggests that infants can do more than detect co-occurence frequencies in the linguistic input. Bailey & Plunkett (1998) have shown that 6 month olds can extract novel stress patterns (not attested in English) from sequences of tones during a familiarisation session and generalise these to test sequences which obey the stress assignment rule, while ignoring those sequences which conform to stress patterns not attested in the familiarisation sequences. Similarly, Marcus et al. (1999) demonstrate that 7½ month olds can abstract a rule underlying the structure of simple multisyllabic words and generalise the rule to words consisting of different syllables but obeying the same rule.

Recent connectionist and statistical analyses (Brent & Cartwright 1996; Cristiansen, Allen & Seidenberg 1998; Reddington & Chater 1998) of the properties of real language corpora have contributed to the view that the distributional information in the input may be of considerable utility to the language learning child. For example, Christiansen et al. (1998) trained a simple recurrent network on a phoneme prediction task. The model was explicitly provided with information about phonemes, relative lexical stress and boundaries between utterances. Individually, these sources of information provide relatively unreliable cues to word boundaries and no direct evidence about actual word boundaries. After training on a large corpus of child directed speech, the model was able to use these cues to reliably identify word boundaries. The model demonstrates how aspects of linguistic structure that are not overtly marked in the input can be derived by efficiently combining multiple probabilistic cues. Further work needs to be done to demonstrate that simple recurrent networks can generalise distributional information to novel stimuli in the manner that infants do in the Bailey & Plunkett (1998) and Marcus et al. (1999) studies.

4. Word learning

One of the most dramatic manifestations of language development during the first two years of the life is the rapid increase in rate of vocabulary development observed around 18 months of age. This spurt in development usually occurs in both comprehension and production (Goldfield & Reznick 1992). There are three main families of theories about the mechanism underlying the vocabulary spurt. These are linguistic development (Dore 1978; Lock 1980; Plunkett 1993), conceptual development (Corrigan 1978; Gopnik & Meltzoff 1987), and the development of constraints on word learning (Markman 1991; Golinkoff et al. 1992; Clark 1993). All of these theories postulate the triggering of a new principle of organisation in the child's understanding of the object/label relationship. Woodward, Markman & Fitzsimmons (1994) argue that these explanations imply that learning a new word prior to the vocabulary spurt is likely to be a time-consuming process, requiring considerable exposure to a new word. There is growing evidence, however, that the young (pre-vocabulary spurt) child may not be as hampered in learning new words as was previously thought. Woodward et al. report that 13-month-olds can, under favourable circumstances, learn novel words from as few as nine presentations of a novel word token. Baldwin (1996) argues that joint attention between the infant and its instructor is necessary for word learning. However, Schafer & Plunkett (1996) have succeeded in replicating

Woodward et al.'s results under conditions which do not require the presence of an instructor, suggesting that the pre-vocabulary spurt child is already equipped with a powerful learning mechanism for forming object-label associations.

4.1 *Imaging early language development*

Event-related potentials have been used to examine developmental changes in neural processing in normal children. Mills, Coffey-Corina & Neville (1997) examined the changes in the organization of brain activity linked to comprehension of single words in 13 to 20-month-old infants. ERPs were recorded as children listened to a series of words whose meanings they did or did not understand, as well as to backwards words. The ERPs differed as a function of word comprehension within 200ms after word onset. At 13–17 months comprehension-related differences were bilateral and broadly distributed over anterior and posterior cortex. In contrast, at 20 months these effects were limited to temporal and parietal regions of the left scalp.

These results indicate that the neural organisation for word comprehension shifts, precisely during the period of development when language acquisition is most pronounced. The implication is that plasticity and reorganisation may be a natural property of the developing system, and is not restricted to compensatory changes in damaged brains. Mills et al. suggest that aspects of their ERP findings are linked to changes in early lexical development that typically occurs between 13 and 20 months. Still unclear, however, is whether the ERP changes reflect qualitative changes in the underlying language processing of lexical items or a consolidation of existing lexical representations. Combining novel-word teaching techniques such as that used by Schafer & Plunkett (1998) with ERP measures offers an opportunity to evaluate whether the observed hemispheric specialisation for lexical processing arises from prolonged experience with words or from the development of new cognitive processing strategies.

4.2 *Connectionist modelling of non-linear word learning*

Recent work in connectionist modelling has demonstrated that small and gradual changes in a network, not involving the maturation of new systems, can lead to dramatic non-linearities in its behaviour. For example, Plunkett et al. (1992) have developed a connectionist model of children's vocabulary development that involves an auto-associative process of relating labels to images. Although the training of the model involved small continuous changes in the connection strengths within and across the different processing modalities in the network (see Appendix, Box 4), the linguistic behaviour of the network exhibited dramatic non-linearities in vocabulary development, mimicking the well known vocabulary spurt that occurs in young children toward the end of their second year. Furthermore, the model showed clear cut dissociations in receptive and expressive vocabulary development, suggesting that the asymmetries between comprehension and production, which are often observed in young children, may be a natural outcome of the child's attempt to integrate multiple representations. This modeling work suggests that the results observed in children with focal lesions (see Appendix, Box 1) and in ERP studies of word comprehension need not necessarily imply pre-wired, dedicated modules. The results are entirely consistent with the view that the non-linear onset of overt behaviours is linked to gradual experience-driven learning processes and coordination of multiple representations in the underlying neural system.

5. Inflectional morphology

Symbolic accounts of the acquisition of inflectional morphology (Marcus et al. 1992; Pinker & Prince 1988) assume a dual-route mechanism for the processing of regular and exceptional words: A rule-governed process attempts to inflect all words while an associative memory attempts to identify the exceptions to the rule and block its application. For example, on this view, plural formation of 'sheeps' is blocked by the identification of the exceptional plural form 'sheep' in associative memory whereas plural formation of 'boys' is achieved by application of the rule (add /s/) to the word 'boy'. The rule-governed process acts as a default that applies to any word, offering the language user economy in representation (no need to store information about inflected forms that conform to the default) and creativity (the capacity to inflect forms previously not encountered).

In contrast, connectionist accounts of the acquisition of inflectional morphology (Rumelhart & McClelland 1986; MacWhinney & Leinbach 1991; Plunkett & Marchman 1991, 1993, 1996) assume a single-route mechanism for the processing of both regular and exceptional forms. There is no distinction in the manner in which regular and exceptional forms are handled on this account. They are processed by the same network of connections which maps an uninflected form of the word to its inflected form. The network's capacity to inflect novel forms is shaped by its experience with the forms on which it has already been trained.

In English, the inflectional systems of the past tense and the plural are highly regular. Irregular past tense forms and irregular noun plurals constitute only 14% and 2% of their respective systems (Marcus 1995). The dual-route account of inflectional morphology is very efficient at representing these systems since only a minority of forms need to be stored in associative memory. The default rule can deal with the rest. A connectionist network stores information about all the words. Nevertheless, the dominance of the regular words in the system results in the network producing regular responses to novel words. Consequently, dual-route and connectionist approaches can both explain the preponderance of regular responses to novel words by English speakers but for different reasons: the dual-route account exploits a default rule which attempts to regularise any word available to the language user. The connectionist account exploits the skewed distribution in favour of regular words in the language.

5.1 *Minority defaults*

There is evidence from speakers of other languages that their ability to produce a default response to novel words or overgeneralise the default to exceptional words does not rely upon a numerical superiority of the words that epitomise the default in the language. For example, Clahsen et al. (1992) and Marcus et al. (1995) claim that the 's' plural in German is the default process even though it constitutes a minority of the plural forms in the language. A similar claim is made for the default status of the 'sound' plural in Arabic. These authors claim that languages whose speakers conform to a minority default pattern, appear to present a major challenge to connectionist accounts of inflectional morphology since networks operating on the principle of 'similar inputs produce similar outputs' are unlikely to produce a default response to novel forms.

Hare, Elman & Daugherty (1995) have demonstrated that connectionist models of inflectional morphology can learn a default response even in the absence of superior numbers for the default class. Two factors contribute a network's capacity to respond in a default-like fashion: First, words which look similar at the input need not have similar internal representations. Second, the distribution of the words in the language influences the ability of the network to act in a default-like fashion (see Appendix, Box 5). Under appropriate conditions, it is possible for a network to learn a *distributional* default.

Plunkett & Nakisa (1997) trained a neural network on the Arabic plural and evaluated its performance on words not encountered in the training set. They showed that the network was superior to the dual-route model at predicting the plural class of Arabic words on which it had never been trained. In particular, prediction of membership in the sound plural class was more accurate in the neural network model. In a similar fashion, Nakisa, Plunkett & Hahn (in press) have shown that a connectionist network trained on a subset of German plurals accurately predicts the class membership of German plurals that it has never seen before. The network is in much the same position as the Arabic or German child who may have to guess how to form the plural of a word. These results indicate that the distribution of nouns in Arabic and German may provide subtle clues to plural class membership which are not obvious to even sophisticated professional linguists.

6. Conclusions

None of the domains of language acquisition described above are yet properly understood. However, the picture of the language learning child is becoming increasingly refined as we uncover the details of *what* is developing and *when* it develops, *where* the neural systems in the brain are for controlling these linguistic behaviours, and *how* these systems actually function. Behavioural, neuropsychological and computational studies reveal the young infant as richly endowed with neural systems well-adapted to the business of linguistic information processing. At the same time, a multi-disciplinary approach to the study of language acquisition points to the utility of viewing linguistic development as driven by the interaction of powerful general learning mechanisms with a richly structured environment that provides the necessary ingredients for the emergence of mature linguistic representations.

Notes

1. A language spoken by people in a tribe indigenous to the Pacific Northwest.

Appendix

Box 1. *Language development in children with focal lesions*

> Children with early unilateral brain injury to either brain hemisphere typically go on to achieve levels of language performance that are within the normal range. Earlier reports on recovery of language in children with focal brain injury led some investigators to conclude that the two hemispheres are initially equipotential for language (Lenneberg 1967). This remarkable plasticity of the developing language system was investigated at different stages of language acquisition in a recent neuropsychological study with a large sample of subjects. Bates et al. (1996) report on the effects of focal brain injury during the early language development in 53 children. All children had suffered a single, unilateral brain injury to the left or right hemisphere, incurred before 6 months of age.
>
> The results indicated a striking difference between the critical functional anatomy of the developing and the mature language system. All of the most consistent hypotheses regarding language organisation in the adult were violated: left-hemisphere dominance, left temporal involvement in language comprehension, and left frontal involvement in expressive language functions and grammar. The results from 10–17 month olds showed that children with right-hemisphere injuries are at greater risk for comprehension impairments. Left temporal lesions during 10–44 months correlated with significantly greater delays in expressive vocabulary and grammar. Frontal lesions to either hemisphere disrupted the typical dramatic increase in vocabulary growth observed around 21 months, independently of motor impairments. The implication of this study is that the localisation of language and other cognitive functions in the adult may reflect the developmental or experience-dependent status of a behaviour.

Box 2. *Categorical perception in the Nakisa & Plunkett (1998) model*

Categorical perception of phonemes is a robust phenomenon observed in both infants and adults. The network was tested on a series of eleven spectra which formed a linear continuum from the pure /sh/ to a pure /s/. Each of the eleven spectra in the continuum were individually fed into a network that had been trained on 30 sentences of continuous speech in English. The output feature responses were stored for each spectrum in the continuum. The distances of these feature vectors from the pure /sh/ and pure /s/ indicated the categorical nature of the network's internal representations of the speech spectra as shown in the figure below.

All of the human languages tested seemed to be equally effective for training the network to represent English speech sounds. To see whether any sounds could be used for training, the network was trained on white noise. This resulted in slower learning and a lower final fitness. The fitness for a network trained on white noise never reached that of the same network trained on human speech. An even worse impediment to learning was to train on low-pass filtered human speech.

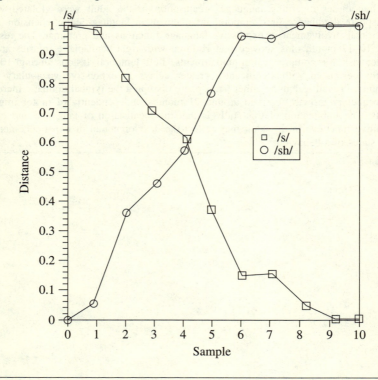

Box 3. *Familiarization-preference procedure used in the Saffran et al. Study*

The familiarization-preference procedure was developed by Jusczyk & Aslin (1995). In this procedure, infants are exposed to auditory material that serves as a potential learning experience. They are subsequently presented with two types of test stimuli: (a) items that were contained within the familiarization material, and (b) items that are highly similar but were not contained within the familiarization material. During a series of test trials that immediately follows familiarization, infants control the duration of each test-trial by their sustained visual fixation of a blinking light. If infants have extracted the crucial information about the familiarization items, they may show differential durations of fixation (listening) during the two types of test trials.

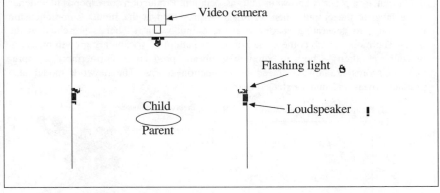

Box 4. *Multi-modal model of vocabulary acquisition*

(a) Profile of vocabulary scores typical for many children during their second year — taken from Plunkett (1993). Each data point indicates the number of different words used by the child during a recording session. The vocabulary spurt that occurs around 22 months is observed in many children. It usually consists of an increased rate of acquisition of nominals — specifically names for objects (McShane 1979). (b) Simplified version of the network architecture used in Plunkett, Sinha, Møller and Strandsby (1992). The image is filtered through a retinal pre-processor prior to presentation to the network. Labels and images are fed into the network through distinct "sensory" channels. The network is trained to reproduce the input patterns at the output — a process known as auto-association. Production corresponds to generating a label at the output when an image is presented at the input. Comprehension corresponds to generating an image at the output when a label is presented at the input. The model exhibits the same non-linear pattern of vocabulary growth observed in young children — both in comprehension and production. Furthermore, comprehension scores are always ahead of production scores. The network model also produces over- and under-extension errors.

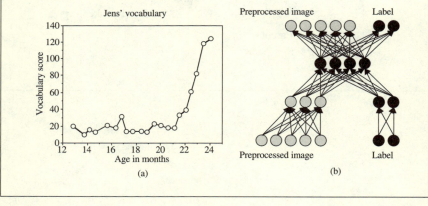

Box 5. *How to obtain a minority default from a neural network*

Forrester & Plunkett (1994) trained a neural network to categorise input patterns as belonging to one of three classes. Each input pattern identified a point on a two-dimensional plane. The distribution of the points is shown below. The majority of the points are clustered in two squares. All the points within a square are deemed to belong to the same class. These can be thought of as the exceptional patterns. The minority of the points are distributed outside these square regions. All the points outside the square regions belong to the same class. These can be thought of as the patterns representing the default (or elsewhere) class. The question of interest is how a neural network trained on this distribution of points responds to novel patterns, i.e., the points in the two-dimensional plane on which it has never been trained? The classifier network used by Forrester & Plunkett (1994) contained two input units to specify the x, y coordinates in the two dimensional plane, 20 hidden units that formed internal representations of the input patterns permitting a non-linear classification of the input space, and three output units to classify the input patterns. The network was trained with the points shown below and then tested on every point in the plane. The surface plots show the activation of the three classifier units at different stages in training. Darker regions indicate higher activation. The final column (late training) shows that all the classifier units do a good job at partitioning the space by the end of training. In particular, most of the points in the two-dimensional plane are treated as though they belong to the third class, the so-called default, even though the training set contained a minority of forms in this class. This example demonstrates how a neural network can be trained to produce a default-like response provided it has the resources to construct internal representations that permit a non-linear partitioning of the input space and provided the forms in the 'language' are appropriately distributed.

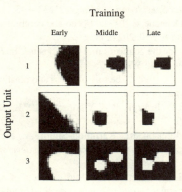

References

Bailey, T. M. & Plunkett, K. 1998. *Learning prosody: Infants' learning of two word stress rhythms*. Paper presented at the International Conference on Infant Studies, Atlanta.

Baldwin, D. A. 1996. "Understanding the link between joint attention and language." In *Joint Attention: its origin and role in development*, C. Moore & P. Dunham (eds.). Hillsdale, NJ: Lawrence Erlbaum Associates.

Bates, E., et al. (in press). "From first words to grammar in children with focal brain injury." *Developmental Neuropsychology*.

Bates, E., Thal, D. & Janowsky, J. 1992. "Early language development and its neural correlates." In *Handbook of Neuropsychology, Vol. 7: Child Neuropsychology*, I. Rapin & S. Segalowitz (eds.) Amsterdam: Elsevier.

Best, C. T., McRoberts, G. W. & Sithole, N. M. 1988. "Examination of the perceptual reorganization for speech contrasts: Zulu click discrimination by English-speaking adults and infants." *Journal of Experimental Psychology: Human Perception and Performance* 14: 345–360.

Brent, M. R. & Cartwright, T. A. 1996. "Distributional regularity and phonotactic constraints are useful for segmentation." *Cognition* 61: 93–125.

Christiansen, M. H., Allen, J. & Seidenberg, M. S. 1998. "Learning to segment speech using multiple cues: A connectionist model." *Language and Cognitive Processes* 13: 221–268.

Christophe, A. & Morton, J. 1994. "Comprehending Baby-Think." *Nature* 370: 250–251.

Clahsen, H., et al. 1992. "Regular and irregular inflection in the acquisition of German noun plurals." *Cognition* 45: 225–255.

Clark, E. V. 1993. *The Lexicon in Acquisition*. Cambridge: Cambridge University Press.

Corrigan, R. 1978. "Language development as related to stage 6 object permanence development." *Journal of Child Language* 5: 173–189.

Cutler, A. & Carter, D. M. 1987. "The predominance of strong initial syllables in the English vocabulary." *Computer Speech and Language* 2: 133–142.

Dehaene-Lambertz, G. & Dehaene, S. 1994. "Speed and cerebral correlates of syllable discrimination in infants." *Nature* 370: 292–295.

Dore, J. 1978. "Conditions for the acquisition of speech acts." In *The social context of language*, I. Markova (ed.). New York: Wiley.

Echols, C. H. & Newport, E. L. 1992. "The role of stress and position in determining first words." *Language Acquisition* 2: 189–220.

Eimas, P. D., Siqueland, E. P., Jusczyk, P. & Vigorito, J. 1971. "Speech perception in infants." *Science* 171: 303–306.

Elman J. L., Bates, E. A., Johnson, M., Karmiloff-Smith, A., Parisi, D. & Plunkett, K. 1996. *Rethinking Innateness: A connectionist perspective on development*. Cambridge, MA: MIT Press.

Fernald, A., McRoberts, G. W. & Herrera, C. 1996. "Effects of prosody and word position on infants' ability to recognize words in fluent speech." Unpublished manuscript.

Forrester, N. & Plunkett, K. 1994. "Learning the Arabic plural: The case for minority default mappings in connectionist networks." In *Proceedings of the Sixteenth Cognitive Science*

Society Annual Conference, Atlanta, GA, A. Ram & K. Eiselt (eds.). Hillsdale, NJ: Lawrence Erlbaum Associates.

Goldfield, B. & Reznick, J.S. 1992. "Rapid change in lexical development in comprehension and production." *Developmental Psychology* 28: 406–413.

Golinkoff, R.M., et al. 1992. "Young children and adults use lexical principles to learn new nouns." *Developmental Psychology* 28: 99–108.

Gopnik, A. & Meltzoff, A. 1987. "The development of categorization in the second year and its relation to the other cognitive and linguistic developments." *Child Development* 58: 1523–1531.

Hare, M., Elman, J.L. & Daugherty, K.G. 1995. "Default generalization in connectionist networks." *Language and Cognitive Processes* 10: 601–630.

Jusczyk, P.W. 1992. "Developing phonological categories from the speech signal." In *Phonological Development: Models, Research, Implications*, C.A. Ferguson, L. Menn, & C. Stoel-Gammon (eds.). Timonium, MD: York Press.

Jusczyk, P.W. 1996. *The discovery of spoken language*. Cambridge, MA: MIT Press.

Jusczyk, P.W. & Aslin, R.N. 1995. "Infants' detection of sound patterns of words in fluent speech." *Cognitive Psychology* 29: 1–23.

Jusczyk, P.W. & Bertoncini, J. 1988. "Viewing the development of speech perception as an innately guided process." *Language and Speech* 31: 217–238.

Jusczyk, P.W., Cutler, A. & Redanz, N. 1993. "Preference for the predominant stress patterns of English words." *Child Development* 64: 675–687.

Jusczyk, P.W., Friederici, A.D., Wessels, J.M.I., Svenkerud, V.Y. & Jusczyk, A.M. 1993. "Infants' sensitivity to the sound patterns of native language words." *Journal of Memory and Language* 32: 402–420.

Jusczyk, P.W., Luce, P.A. & Luce, J.C. 1994. "Infants' sensitivity to phonotactic patterns in the native language." *Journal of Memory and Language* 33: 630–645.

Lenneberg, E.H. 1967. *Biological foundations of language*. New York: Wiley.

Lock, A. 1980. *The guided reinvention of language*. London: Academic Press.

MacWhinney, B. & Leinbach, J. 1991. "Implementations are not conceptualizations: Revising the verb learning model." *Cognition* 40: 121–157.

Marcus, G. 1995. "Children's overregularization of English plurals: a quantitative analysis." *Journal of Child Language* 22: 447–459.

Marcus, G.F., et al. 1992. "Overregularization in language acquisition." *Monographs of the Society for Research in Child Development* 57.

Marcus, G.F., Vijayan, S., et al. 1999. "Rule learning by seven-month-old infants." *Science* 283: 77–80.

Marcus, G., et al. 1995. "German inflection: The exception that proves the rule." *Cognitive Psychology* 29: 189–256.

Markman, E.M. 1991. "The whole object, taxonomic and mutual exclusivity assumptions as initial constraints on word meanings." In *Perspectives on language and thought: Interrelations and development*, J.P. Byrnes & S.A. Gelman (eds.). Cambridge: Cambridge University Press.

McShane, J. 1979. The development of naming. *Linguistics* 17: 879–905.

Mills, D. L., Coffey-Corina, S. A. & Neville, H. J. (in press). "Language comprehension and cerebral specialization from 13 months to 20 months." *Developmental Neuropsychology.*

Nakisa, R. C. & Plunkett, K. 1998. "Evolution of a rapidly learned representation for speech." *Language and Cognitive Processes* 13: 105–127.

Nakisa, R. C., Plunkett, K. & Hahn, U. (in press). "A cross-linguistic comparison of single and dual-route models of inflectional morphology." In *Models of Language Acquisition: Inductive and Deductive Approaches*, P. Broeder & J. Murre (eds.). Cambridge, MA: MIT Press.

Newsome, M. & Jusczyk, P. W. 1995. "Do infants use stress as a cue for segmenting fluent speech?" In *Proceedings of the 19th Boston University Conference on Language Development*, D. MacLaughlin & S. McEwen (eds.). Somerville, MA: Cascadilla Press.

Pinker, S. & Prince, A. 1988. "On language and connectionism: Analysis of a parallel distributed processing model of language acquisition." *Cognition* 28: 73–193.

Plunkett, K. 1993. "Lexical segmentation and vocabulary growth in early language acquisition." *Journal of Child Language* 20: 43–60.

Plunkett, K. & Marchman, V. 1991. "U-Shaped learning and frequency effects in a multi-layered perceptron: Implications for child language acquisition." *Cognition* 38: 43–102.

Plunkett, K. & Marchman, V. 1993. "From rote learning to system building: acquiring verb morphology in children and connectionist nets." *Cognition* 48: 21–69.

Plunkett, K. & Marchman, V. 1996. "Learning from a connectionist model of the acquisition of the English past tense." *Cognition* 61: 299–308.

Plunkett, K. & Nakisa, R. C. 1997. "A connectionist model of the Arabic plural system." *Language and Cognitive Processes* 12: 807–836.

Plunkett, K., et al. 1992. "Symbol grounding or the emergence of symbols? Vocabulary growth in children and a connectionist net." *Connection Science* 4: 293–312.

Polka, L. & Werker, J. F. 1994. "Developmental changes in perception of non-native vowel contrasts." *Journal of Experimental Psychology: Human Perception and Performance* 20: 421–435.

Quartz, S. R. & Sejnowski, T. J. 1997. "The neural basis of cognitive development: a constructivist manifesto." *Behavioral and Brain Sciences* 20: 537–596.

Reddington, M. & Chater, N. 1998. "Connectionist and statistical approaches to language acquisition: A distributional perspective." *Language and Cognitive Processes* 13: 129–191.

Rumelhart, D. E. & McClelland, J. L. 1986. "On learning the past tense of English verbs." In *Parallel distributed processing: explorations in the microstructure of cognition*, J. L. McClelland & D. E. Rumelhart (eds.). Cambridge: MIT Press.

Saffran, J. R., Aslin, R. N. & Newport, E. L. 1996. "Statistical learning by 8-month-old infants." *Science* 274: 1926–1928.

Schafer, G. & Plunkett, K. 1996. "Rapid word learning by 15-month-olds under tightly controlled conditions." *Center for Research in Language Newsletter* 10(1).

Werker, J. F. & Tees, R. C. 1984. "Cross language speech perception: Evidence for perceptual reorganisation during the first year of life." *Infant Behaviour and Development* 7: 49–63.

Woodward, A. L., Markman, E. M. & Fitzsimmons, C. M. 1994. "Rapid word learning in 13- and 18-month-olds." *Developmental Psychology* 30: 553–566.

Repertoires of Primitive Elements
Prerequisite or result of acquisition?

Manfred Bierwisch
Humboldt-University, Berlin

1. Conceptual and empirical questions

The study of language acquisition is inevitably based on sufficiently specific assumptions about the structure of linguistic knowledge and its underlying, species specific conditions, by means of which the acquisition and use is possible. For the same reason, the elucidation of language acquisition is one of the important sources of insight into the structure of language, its internal representation, and the biological basis of this capacity. With this interdependence in mind, I will explore the nature and content of basic elements of linguistic knowledge. This problem plays a crucial role not only as an indispensable aspect of the structure of knowledge, but also with respect to the question of their origin in ontogenetic development. Are the basic elements of structural representations invented or learned during the process of language acquisition, or are they rather part of the preconditions that make the acquisition possible in the first place? Are primitive elements the product or rather the presupposition of language acquisition? By primitive elements I have in mind the basic units of structural representation that are not reducible to more basic terms of linguistic structure — although they may be complex in terms of extralinguistic structure, such as motoric patterns, perceptual properties, or acoustic and other physical correlates. The concern with these problems has a remarkable tradition, with highlights like Hjelmslev (1935) and Jakobson (1936) for morphological categories, Jakobson (1941) for phonetic features, or Berlin & Kay (1969) and Clark (1973) for semantic components, to mention just a few different approaches. As a matter of fact, theoretically oriented empirical analyses of linguistic knowledge abound with more or less explicit contributions to the discussion of primitive terms of structural organization, although certain basic assumptions are usually left implicit and are still in need of clarification. This is the rationale of the present discussion.

A first point to be noted is the non-trivial observation that there are indeed basic elements of linguistic structure. This does not refer to the trivial fact that any characterization of a given domain must rely on elements that are basic in the sense that they simply are not (but possibly could be) reduced to more elementary terms. What I am interested in is the quest for elements that are primitive in the more genuine sense that they cannot be analysed further within the given domain, which means that they must be assumed to have a real status in the organization and acquisition of knowledge in general and language in particular. The assumption of primitive terms is uncontroversial for representational conceptions of knowledge, and it is the problems arising in this connection that I will be concerned with. It is worth noting, though, that genuine primitive terms seem to be indispensable also in subsymbolic conceptions of knowledge, based on distributed activation, rather than symbolic representations. Without going into details, it can be observed that any network intended to characterize aspects of linguistic — or other cognitive — capacities requires so-called input-nodes, specifying the character of information that can be processed, and output nodes determining the potential result of processing.[1]

According to standard assumptions, knowledge of language, viz. lexical items, complex expressions, and the rules and principles on which they are based, is organized in terms of three types of primes:

(1)   a.   Phonetic features, on which the sound structure is based
        b.   Semantic components, organizing the conceptual interpretation
        c.   Formal features, specifying morphological and syntactic categories.

The nature of these elements, their status, origin, and properties raise conceptual as well as factual questions, among which I want to sort out the following:

(2)   a.   To what extent are basic elements fixed in or determined by Universal Grammar?
        b.   How do basic elements emerge ontogenetically: are they triggered or constructed?
        c.   To what extent are the elements determined by external conditions?

Questions like these can reasonably be discussed only with respect to some general assumptions about the character of the domain which they are supposed to support. I will therefore first sketch the relevant background assumptions, and then consider the problems arising with respect to the types of primes indicated in (1).

2. Language design and its primes

What we need to be interested in is the organization of linguistic knowledge, i.e. the internal or I-language in terms of Chomsky (1986), rather than its external instantiation. It is easy to see that relevant primes can be identified in external realizations of language only to the extent to which they are projected by the underlying knowledge on the basis of which signals are produced and interpreted: Acoustic events instantiating linguistic expressions are not *per se* structured in terms of phonetic features, let alone grammatical categories.

Knowledge of a natural language L in this sense is a mental structure that constitutes a systematic correspondence between two mental systems, namely:

(3) a. the system A–P, which accomplishes the articulation and perception of signals, and
 b. the system C–I, in terms of which conceptual and intentional experience is organized.

The assumption of these two mental systems is anything but trivial, it raises in fact a number of intricate questions some of which will be taken up below. For the time being, I will assume that A–P and C–I are (fairly complex) aspects or components of mental organization, which are, moreover, phylogenetically independent of the capacity of language, although the emergence of I-language might reveal and enrich invisible properties of the systems in question, just as playing piano recruits and systematically elaborates hidden possibilities of the motor coordination of the hand.

The observation that language establishes a connection between signals and thoughts has, of course, a long tradition, including Saussure's (1916) influential notion that a linguistic sign combines a *signifiant* and a *signifié*. The conception pursued here is essentially the version adopted in Chomsky (1995), with I-language being interpreted at the interface with A–P and C–I, respectively. The next point to be noted is the fact, that the mapping between articulation/perception A–P and intentional conceptualization C–I provided by a language L ranges over an open (potentially infinite) domain of coordinated structures in A–P and C–I determined by the expressions of L. As articulatory and conceptual patterns do not in principle exhibit strict analogous structure, such that one domain would directly reflect the organization of the other,[2] the correspondence in question is possible only if the expressions of L defining the relevant mapping can be computed by recursive, combinatorial operations. Assuming the systems of (3), elements of the potentially infinite set of expressions of L can thus be characterized as ordered pairs (α, σ), where α and σ belong to the interface of

L with A–P and C–I, respectively. Let us call these interfaces the Articulatory Form AF of L for α, and the Semantic Form SF of L for σ. Two things might be noted with respect to these interfaces: First, they must draw on the systems they interface with. This means that they must be based on (or even participate in) articulatory/perceptual and intentional/conceptual configurations, respectively. I will have to say more about this relation below. Second, whatever properties might characterize the patterns in A–P and C–I, the structure of configurations in AF and SF must be discrete, in order to allow for the recursive computation of the correspondence between A–P and C–I. The relevant components of mental organization and their mutual dependencies can be indicated as follows:

(4)   Signal ⟷ A–P ⟺ AF ⟷ SF ⟺ C–I ⟷ Environment

$$\underbrace{}_{\text{Language}}$$

$$\underbrace{}_{\text{Mental Systems}}$$

The relation abbreviated by the arrow '⟷' comprises complex mechanisms by means of which the organism interacts with specific aspects or domains of its internal and external environment. I have nothing to say here about the processes involved in this interaction and will simply take it for granted that A–P and C–I make available the patterns for production and perception of signals on the one hand and the representation of relevant aspects of experience on the other. The double-arrow '⟺' indicates the conditions by which interface structures of language are extracted from and embedded in representations of what Chomsky (1995) calls performance systems.[3] We will return to this relation in more detail below, noting at this point, however, that the interface structures AF and SF are the actual representations of I-language, in terms of which the correspondence between form and meaning of arbitrary complex linguistic expressions is computed. This correspondence is indicated by the relation '⟷' in (4), connecting the two domains, whose systematic coordination constitutes the core of linguistic behavior.[4]

As already mentioned, the relation between AF and SF must be computable by recursive operations. These operations require representations of AF and SF to be based on the rules or principles of the grammatical system G determining the language in question. I will follow the standard assumption that the organization of G develops ontogenetically within the framework of general conditions usually referred to as Universal Grammar UG. In other words, the structure of G is due to individual experience, constrained by the fact that the biological endowment abbreviated by UG provides the preconditions of this experience. These preconditions must obviously be the result of phylogenetic processes leading to the human language capacity.[5] We furthermore note, that grammatical rules and principles are crucially dependent on the formal or grammatical properties γ specifying the syntactic and morphological categorization of a given linguistic expression (α, σ). Thus a lexical item like *play* is not simply an articulatory pattern paired with a semantic interpretation, but it has different combinatorial properties if it is marked as a noun with case, number and gender information, or as a verb with tense and agreement information. Similarly, the phrase *his plays* combines form and meaning of this expression with the grammatical properties of a definite plural noun phrase, as opposed to the phrase *he plays*, which has the properties of a finite clause. More generally, linguistic expressions defining the relation between A–P and C–I are to be characterized as follows:

(4) An expression E of a given I-language L is a configuration (γ, (α, σ)), where:
α belongs to the Articulatory Form AF, and
σ belongs to the Semantic Form SF,
with AF and SF constituting the interface of L with A–P and C–I, respectively; and
γ specifies the morpho-syntactic properties of E.

For reasons mentioned before, α, σ and γ must be discrete entities. To the extent to which they exhibit internal structure, they must ultimately be made up from component parts belonging to sets of discrete primitive elements. These sets seem to differ remarkably with respect to size, i.e. the number of primes, their formal character, and their interpretation, with corresponding differences for their status in acquisition. It is thus a highly intriguing question, whether these primitive elements are fixed by UG, that is whether and to what extent they belong to the biological prerequisites for linguistic experience, and which of their aspects result from ontogenetic experience. In what follows, we will have to consider the tension between the two views indicated in (5a) and (b), which might be called the nativist and the empiricist position with respect to basic elements:

(5) Linguistic primes must be construed
a. as fixed by UG providing the basis for ontogenetic development, or
b. as the inductive result of individual experience, shaped by external conditions.

For obvious reasons, (a) and (b) cannot be reconciled by an unprincipled compromise which would end up in the middle of no man's land. We will discuss the relevant problems of the three types of primitive elements in turn.

3. Articulation

Let me begin with the discussion of AF-primes relying on the system A–P of articulation and perception. It appears that they are reasonably well understood with respect to their number as well as their interpretation.

A–P is normally construed as the system of production and perception of spoken language, i.e. the coordination of vocal articulation and auditory perception. Under this assumption, AF is more specifically to be taken as representing the Phonetic Form PF, such that expressions of L are constituted by $(\gamma, (\pi, \sigma))$, where π is based on phonetic features as primitive elements of PF. This has, of course, direct — and non-trivial — consequences for the status of PF and its primes.

Before turning to these consequences, we notice that PF and its primes must be assumed to be abstract in the sense that A–P contains various sorts of systematically determined information that has nothing to do with linguistic knowledge underlying the structure and interpretation of signals. We do, for instance, identify age and sex, or the personal identity, of the speaker, we distinguish different moods or rates of speech. In other words, the language capacity must provide a rather robust filter that extracts linguistic properties of the signal from information processed by other mental systems.

We notice next that, for obvious reasons, PF must be assumed to rely on conditions applying to articulation as well as perception. In this sense, the first systematic account of phonetic features proposed in Jakobson & Halle (1956) gave in fact a characterization of each element in both perceptual/acoustic and articulatory terms. Subsequent developments shifted the characterization of PF to strictly articulatory terms, indicating the relevant articulator (Root, Dorsum, Corona of the tongue, ...), as well as place and manner of articulation (Voiced, Nasal, Continuant, ...). These conditions are linked to the slots of the time skeleton, along which PF organizes segmental and prosodic properties, leading to abstract, three-dimensional articulatory patterns. See e. g. Halle (1983, 1995), Clements (1985) for exposition. Conditions emerging from the articulatory apparatus are furthermore the source of substantive constraints on the combination of basic elements, restricting the range of possible PF-configurations.

On this account, the coordination of perception and articulation is presupposed, rather than created by the structure of PF and its primes. To put it differently, I-language does not interface with articulation and perception separately, PF instead recruits patterns of the articulatory system — presumably the more specific domain — while double interpretation for each primitive element is obviated by independently established perceptual control and monitoring of motoric articulation.[6] In any case, the particular load to be carried by the language capacity would be reduced if the interpretation of PF could be restricted to articulatory gestures, presupposing mechanisms, however general, to integrate perceptual categorization and patterns of motor control. This is of particular interest if one asks for the role of UG in providing primes of PF.

Notice next, that however the correspondence between A–P and C–I is determined, the repertoire provided by UG must leave sufficient space to accommodate the remarkable variation exhibited by the phonetic form of different I-languages. This condition can be accomplished in at least two alternative ways:

(6)   UG defines the set of possible phonetic features Π, with each grammar G selecting a subset of Π, where the structure of Π might exhibit conditions determining the choice of possible selections.[7]

(7)   UG does not define the set Π directly, but only the character of PF (discrete features, organized in segments, syllables, ...) while the content of Π and the properties of its elements emerge from the interaction of UG with A–P under actual conditions.

The difference does not seem very impressive at first glance, especially with respect to language acquisition: Under both assumptions the actual repertoire emerges from the interaction of UG with individual experience. In both cases the result of this interaction is a grammar G whose phonetic features are made up from exposure to pertinent experience, but clearly predetermined by UG, accounting for well-known generalizations like 'affricates presuppose stops', 'mid vowels presuppose high vowels', etc. The character of UG and the role it plays is nevertheless clearly different under both assumptions. According to (6), the articulatory patterns must be triggered by appropriate stimuli, selecting within certain constraints from options that are genetically fixed. According to (7), UG provides only boundary conditions, within which actual stimuli lead to the construction of motoric patterns that provide abstract, discrete items to be recruited by the component of linguistic computation. At least implicitly, most of the literature on distinctive features seems to rely on the assumption (6).

The conditions UG imposes on articulation and perception seem to favor a more abstract perspective, along the lines of (7), however. It is the remarkable research on sign language that specifically points in this direction. Beginning with interesting results in Klima & Bellugi (1979), it became clear that sign language is not only a fully equivalent variety of natural language, but is organized with respect to its articulatory form AF along essentially the same principles as spoken language. Without going into the interesting details of sign language,[8] one might say that under the pressure of lacking auditory perception, the construction of PF is replaced by AP, related to visual perception and signing articulation, where basic elements are not based on gestures of tongue, velum, lips etc., but on position, shape and movement of the hand.

It is worthwhile to notice some general points based on observations about sign language. First, the coordination of perception and production, i.e. the visual control and monitoring of motoric patterns of the hand, must obviously be assumed to be established in much the same way as the coordination of auditory perception and articulation for spoken language, even though on the basis of characteristically different conditions. The observations about sign language clearly support, however, the strictly articulatory, rather than perceptual foundation of primitive elements discussed with respect to spoken language.[9] In general, then, UG presupposes, rather than creates the coordination of articulation and perception, recruiting specific motoric gestures to build up the structure of AF.

Second, if UG is responsible for possible repertoires of spoken and signed language alike, it cannot fix the substance — i.e. the specific interpretation — of the primitive terms, but may only provide the conditions in terms of which an interpretation can be constructed. This implies first of all the requirement just noted: only motoric patterns for which a perceptual categorization is available (possibly stabilized by proprioceptive loops) can be recruited as primes of AF. It also implies formal constraints as to the character of primitive elements, i.e. the type of combination they require or allow for. We will have to return to this aspect with respect to primes of SF and GF in more detail below; for AF it implies that primes represent conditions on the production of signals that are linked to positions in a linear, time dependent skeleton. Even though this simply requires primes to represent properties that make up simultaneous clusters of structured conditions assigned to linearly ordered positions, a fair amount of organizational consequences will follow from or be imposed on intrinsic properties,[10] the discussion of which would go beyond the present topic, though.

One corrolary of this formal aspect should be noted, however: Expressions of natural language seem to be based on one-dimensional, linear ordering on very principled grounds, no matter what type of realization applies. While the linearity of phonetic articulation is an obvious consequence of the conditions of speech production, no such external condition applies to sign language, which could rely on the use of two hands to obviate the strict linearity of spoken language,[11] but it is linear in essentially the same sense in which phonetic articulation is linear.

We finally observe that the set of primitive elements recruited in sign language — i.e. the articulator's position, shape, movement etc. — is of the same order of magnitude (about a dozen or so) as the set of phonetic features, in spite of the rather different resources available to the two modalities. This supports the assumption that it is the inner, formal conditions of UG that set the stage for the organization of primes of Articulatory Form, whatever the domain of interpretation might be.

One should add, that there is, of course, a natural preference for auditory as opposed to visual manifestation of linguistic expressions. The reasons for this preference, which we need not speculate about here, may — but need not — be due to adaptive selection in the phylogenesis of the language capacity. They are, in any case, a clear condition on normal language acquisition.

To sum up, there are strong reasons to assume that UG provides the basis for a finite repertoire of candidates for primitive elements of AF, but presumably not in terms of a fixed set Π of phonetic features, but rather by formal constraints, imposed on candidates of a set of discrete articulatory properties the actual content of which is determined by the child's motoric activity controlled by the exposure to perceptual input. The conditions inherent in the articulatory apparatus together with the control patterns of motoric action could then substantially contribute to the organization of the actual subset of Π (or X, if X represents the set of possible primes for AF of sign language).

4. Concepualization

Although the interfaces of I-language with A–P and C–I are similar in certain respects, the problems they raise in specific respects differ enormously. This applies especially to the nature and status of the primitive elements from which the structures σ of the semantic form SF are made up. The difference is clearly reflected in the relevant literature: While there is general agreement with respect to the inventory of PF, at least in principle, positions with respect to primitive elements of SF differ remarkably. It is not even clear to what extent different positions would ultimately be compatible.

In any case, SF must be build up from elements that are interpreted in or taken from C–I. Technically, the primes of SF are conceptual categories of different types, illustrated by examples like MALE, HUMAN, VERTICAL, PROXIMAL, AT, CAUSE, BECOME, etc.[12] and (presumably) variables x, y, z, etc. to be filled in by linguistic or conceptual context. Let us consider, for the sake of discussion, the status of a potential inventory Σ of primes of SF determined by UG, from which every language L can draw, just as L would draw on Π with respect to PF. There are some fundamental differences between Π and Σ to be observed.

First, there does not seem to be any reason to assume that SF could manifest itself in alternative conceptual systems, corresponding to the alternation between auditory and visual perception for AF. This difference has a more principled character as one might be aware of at first glance. The important point is that AF, even if its articulatory realization is privileged, does not exhaust the range of patterns that might control the production and perception of signals; SF on the other hand must be assumed to cover the complete domain of intentional conceptualizations, i.e. the range of possible thoughts — to put it in non-technical terms. To push the issue one step further, one might assume that effability in the sense of Katz (1972) or expressibility in the sense of Searle (1970) is a constitutive property of natural language and hence a condition supported by UG. Expressibility is defined as follows:

(8)   For a speaker S of language L, who has a thought T, it is possible to find an expression $E = (\gamma, (\alpha, \sigma))$ of L, where T is the exact interpretation of σ in C–I.

Thus, according to (8), UG must grant the possibility that what can be thought can be said.[13] This has far-reaching consequences for the repertoire Σ of semantic primes, which obviously must be complete in the sense, that every conceptual distinction is, at least in principle, accessible in SF. The possibility of alternative interpretations of semantic primes would therefore be at variance with the notion that SF must be complete with regard to its domain of interpretation: A conceptual domain reserved for an interpretation of SF that differs from the actual one would only be possible if SF were not already complete in the sense of (8).

On the other hand, the contrast between actual and constructed primes indicated in (6) vs. (7) for the set Π carries over to Σ, as we will see in a moment. Once again, the preferred option, albeit for quite different reasons, is assumption (7), according to which UG has to determine the 'skeleton' of Σ (to which I will return immediately), rather than its actual elements, which emerge only through interaction of UG and C–I.[14]

The next point to be made concerns the fact that what I have called the skeleton of Π differs essentially from its counterpart in SF, although it is equally crucial for the intrinsic conditions on the nature of SF and its primes. Two interdependent conditions seem to be conceptually necessary in this respect. On the one hand, while AS is based on linear organization, related to the temporal structure of articulation and perception, SF does not exhibit sequential structure. It is based, however, on hierarchical organization, corresponding to connections in intentional conceptualization.[15] On the other hand, the hierarchy in question must essentially be determined by the nature of the components to be combined. The most general characterization of this requirement leads to the principle which assigns conceptual conditions to appropriate entities, thereby representing the structure of situations or events and the objects they involve. Formally, this principle leads to functor-argument-combination, a well known structure, formalized for instance in the operator-operand-combination of categorial systems.[16] To illustrate the point, elements like HUMAN, BECOME and CAUSE would be of category $\langle 1, 0\rangle$, $\langle 0, 0\rangle$, and $\langle 0, \langle 0, 0\rangle\rangle$, indicating properties, one-place- and two-place propositional functions, respectively, if one assumes the following definition of categories:

(9)   a.   0 and 1 are basic categories, categorizing propositions and individuals, respectively

        b.   If α and β are (basic or complex) categories, then $\langle \alpha, \beta\rangle$ is a complex category, categorizing a functor that combines with an argument of category β to form a complex unit of category α.[17]

In other words, while the primes of PF represent articulatory properties linked to segmental positions in temporal order, primes of SF must be construed as elements assigned to characteristic categories of a representational system that provides nested structures by which language interfaces with C–I.

Finally, while the set of features (determined by the skeleton of) Π is closed and of highly restricted magnitude, this can hardly be assumed for the potential inventory Σ of SF. Although the actual repertoire of any given I-language L is finite, it is always extendible, provided the skeleton of Σ can accommodate additional primes. There seem to be at least two reasons for this conjecture. One is the fact that there is no a priori limit for the possibility to represent distinctions along various dimensions in C–I by means of expressions in L. Different taxonomies — of e.g. artefacts, materials, attitudes, natural kinds — are one domain, nameable individuals — persons, places, pets, etc. — are another illustration of the issue. The other reason is the diversity of subdomains and modalities of C–I that primes of SF can rely on. For the sake of illustration, consider the notorious problems of natural kinds. Standard assumptions for terms like *cat* and *dog*, or *elm* and *oak* is that besides conditions classifying them as e.g. PHYSICAL-OBJECT and ANIMAL or TREE, they need primes like DOG, CAT, ELM, and OAK, respectively. Notice that e.g. DOG, according to (9) a prime of category $\langle 1, 0\rangle$, would recruit not only information about typical shape and its variation, but also about barking and other aspects of characteristic behavior. Similar observations would apply to the distinction between e.g. *shuffle, sneak,* and *creep*, and a large number of other terms for types of motoric behavior, and, in fact, to items representing coneptually organized distinctions in general.[18]

These problems can be met by one of two assumptions, corresponding, *mutatis mutandis*, to the alternatives (6) and (7) regarding the inventory of phonetic primes. Assuming, first, that semantic primes cannot be learned by inductive generalization, one might conclude that they must be provided by UG, such that different conditions in individual and cultural experience would merely trigger more or less different selections from a fixed, innate set of possibilities. Call this the actual innateness- or (A)-position. This would be the counterpart of (6) with respect to SF. One of the problems with position (A) is that by definition the set of primes could not be unbounded.[19] Alternatively, one would have to assume that UG, instead of providing a fixed set of primes, merely determines conditions along which basic elements of SF can be constructed, relying on options made available by or extracted from C–I, presumably as an extension of some initial core to start with. Call this the construction or (C)-position. Under this construal, the inventory Σ of L would have the status assumed for Π in (7), even though for rather different reasons, as should be clear by now. More specifically, according to position (C), UG defines (a) the character of SF, viz. non-linear, nested representations based on a system like (9) categorizing constants and variables, and (b) certain basic domains in C–I to recruit interpretations for initial elements of Σ.[20] Basic domains in this sense are e.g. conditions on spatial and temporal orientation, perception of color and shape, as studied e.g. in Berlin & Kay (1969), Clark (1973), Bierwisch (1996), or Jackendoff (1996).

The problems just sketched have been treated in different ways, not always easily associated with position (A) or (C). Some observations might be of interest, nevertheless. Thus, a rather definite version of position (A) seems to be defended by Fodor (1981, 1988), who argues that (the vast majority of) lexicalized concepts are undefinable, i.e. primitive and hence innate, such that together with the set of primes even the majority of possible lexical meanings must be taken as fixed by UG.[21] In spite of Fodor's vigorous argumentation, it is not clear, however, whether he is prepared for an infinite set of innate primes, or how the set is to be restricted in principled ways. As an example of position (C) on the other hand, one might refer to Pustejovsky's (1995) notion of *qualia structure*, which relates to units most naturally construed as basic with respect to semantic representation, but possibly complex in terms of extralinguistic specifications, allowing for an indefinite range of possible primitive elements. From a somewhat different perspective, Katz (1972) set up *semantic markers* as elements of semantic representation, allowing them, however, to be composed in systematic ways from more basic markers, leaving open the question where this reduction ends. A similar sort of telescoping is recognized in Jackendoff (1983) and subsequent work. This apparent ambivalence with respect to the irreducible semantic primes does not come as a mere incident: It rather reflects an implicit recognition of what I have called position (C).

To sum up, the set Σ of semantic primes is even less likely to be actually fixed by UG without recourse to individual experience than the set Π of articulatory features, although for systematically different reasons: While there is no problem to consider Π to be finite, and in fact limited in magnitude to less than 10 to the power of 2, there is no reasonable bound limiting the magnitude of Σ to say 10 to the power of 3 or even 4, although one must not allow for actual infinity. Thus, while Π must presumably be considered to be constructed according to abstract conditions of AF because of the possible choice of modality with respect to the system A–P of production and perception, the reason for Σ to be constructed according to more abstract principles of SF is the range of distinctions to be captured within the domain C–I. In other words, both interface levels of language are presumably based on primes to be recruited by experience, but on the basis of conditions of UG by means of which the construction of repertoires of primitive terms becomes possible. The relevant principles include the format of interface representations and the choice of primary dimensions of interpretation in A–P and C–I, respectively. The reason for this assumption is on the one hand the actual experience needed to fix the modality of signals, and on the other hand the range of conceptual distinctions, which must be open to actual experience of the individual speaker/hearer.

5. Grammaticalization

Considerations about the status of formal features, i.e. basic elements underlying the internal computation by means of which the interface representations are related, should start with a brief survey of the properties represented by the grammatical information γ associated with the pair (α, σ) of an expression E as indicated in (4) above. Roughly speaking, γ must provide the categorization and subcategorization of E by means of which E combines — as head, complement, or adjunct — with other expressions to form complex units of L. More specifically, γ comprises the following types of information:

(10) a. The categorization Cat of E by means of a structured set of syntactic and morphological features;

b. the subcategorization or Argument Structure AS of E specifying the complements E combines with and the morpho-syntactic conditions imposed on them.

(10a) is straightforward. Syntactic and morphological features categorize e.g. *found* as a finite Verb marked for past tense, or *Hundes* (dog's) as the Genitive Singular of a Masculine Count Noun.[22] As to (10b), two points seem to be uncontroversial. First, Argument Structure or subcategorization is made up from hierarchically organized Argument Positions, each position specifying a Thematic Role θ. Second, each argument position may be associated with conditions specifying morpho-syntactic properties to be met by the co-constituents in question. These conditions can be systematic, i.e. structurally predictable, or idiosyncratic and hence lexically specified.[23] More formally:

(11) The Argument Structure AS of an expression E is an ordered set $P_1 \ldots P_n$ of Argument Positions, where each P_i is an ordered pair $\langle \theta_i, F_i \rangle$, such that θ_i is an operator binding a variable in the SF of E, and F_i is a set of morpho-syntactic features associated with θ_i.

With respect to the nature of the Thematic Roles θ_i, two conceptions are under discussion. Drawing on Fillmore's (1968) notion of abstract Case and the θ-Theory assumed in Chomsky (1981), a universal set of roles, including Agent, Experiencer, Theme, Goal and a few others, has been discussed e.g. by Jackendoff (1990), Grimshaw (1990), or, in slightly different guise, by Dowty (1991). Under this view, Thematic Roles constitute a particular set of primitive elements alongside with those of Semantic Form, and hence interpreted in C–I. An alternative assumption, adopted e.g. in Haider (1993), Bierwisch (1997), Wunderlich (1997), and related work, considers Thematic Roles as operators making variables of SF available for saturation by (the SF of) appropriate complements. Given the nature of SF discussed in Section 4, a Thematic Role θ can formally be construed as an abstractor or lambda operator binding a variable x in SF. Under this view, the purport of θ derives from the position x occupies in SF. In both versions, however, θ_i must relate a syntactic position to semantic slots or variables.[24]

As to the features appearing in F_i associated with θ_i, it can easily be seen that they must necessarily be a (proper or improper) subset of the features that can appear in Cat: Only features that can be matched or checked by those of the arguments in question could be justified by their selective effect. Hence, considerations about the repertoire Γ of possible morpho-syntactic primes can be restricted to Cat. Two questions are to be raised in this respect:

(12) a. What sort of interpretation — if any — is available for formal features?
b. To what extent can there be a universal set of formal features?

These questions might require different answers in view of the following distinction:

(13) The properties represented by γ include:
a. syntactic categories, such as V, N, A, P, D, C, and a few others;
b. morphological categories, i.e. specification for Case, Number, Gender, Tense, etc.

Turning first to question (12a), I will assume here, that the categories in (13) are specified in terms of (presumably binary) features, which are formal in the sense that they have no direct interpretation in any extralinguistic domain. This seems to be at variance with the observation, that features like [±Plural], [±Feminine], or [±Past] do in fact usually correspond to elements of SF with a straightforward interpretation in C–I. This is obvious for the contrast between e.g. *dog* vs. *dogs*, *country* vs. *countries*, etc, or *der Angestellte* (the employee, male), vs. *die Angestellte* (the employee, female), and even for Case, there is a long tradition of attempts to rely on conceptual interpretation. See Hjelmslev (1935) for a comprehensive survey. Notice, however, that the correspondences of formal and semantic properties are often completely discarded, as shown by cases like *Weib* (woman), *Mädchen* (girl), both of which are [−Feminine], or *scissors*, which is [+Plural] even for single objects. Thus, morphological features may correspond to semantic conditions, but they are still elements of their own. They are not interpreted by elements of SF in the sense in which elements of Π and Σ are interpreted by configurations in A–P and C–I, respectively. They may, but need not, be related to configurations in SF by default rules.[25]

A somewhat different problem concerns syntactic categories like Noun, Adjective, Verb, which are often considered to correspond to ontological categories like object, property, event or state, respectively. Again, even though there is a preference for properties to be denoted by Adjectives, and processes and events by Verbs (which can hardly represent objects), there are still all sorts of systematic and idiosyncratic mismatches. Obvious cases are words like *sleep, walk, jump*, which can show up either as Verb or as Noun with identical Semantic Form and conceptual interpretation. The same point can be made for cases like *Eva ist ihrer Schwester ähnlich, Eva ähnelt ihrer Schwester* (Eva resembles her sister), characterizing Eva as similar to her sister once by the Adjective *ähnlich* in combination with the copula, once by the Verb *ähneln*. In other words, there is no strict, general correspondence between ontological types and syntactic categories.

If conceptual distinctions and categories do not provide the content of morphological and syntactic categories, two questions arise: First, what else is the actual content of morpho-syntactic primes? Second, what is the relationship between morpho-syntactic features and semantic components? We will discuss these questions in turn.

In order to answer the first question, one has to make explicit the notion of morphological and syntactic properties of an expression E. The essential point concerns the combinatorial possibilities and requirements of lexical items and of complex expressions made up from them. The major conditions can be indicated as follows:

(14) a. Morphological features represent conditions on relations between constituents of a complex expression E, in particular
   i. Linking between head and complement by features expressed at the head (Agreement) or the complement (Case-marking etc.)[26]
   ii. Concord between grammatically related elements, such as head and adjunct, or anaphor and antecedent, where features are realized by both constituents.
b. Syntactic features determine essentially conditions on permissible Argument Structures, regulating in particular
   i. obligatory vs. optional, internal vs. external (or designated), and referential vs. complement positions;
   ii. the range of predictable as well as idiosyncratic features associated with the different Argument Positions.[27]

Although these specifications are oversimplified, it should be clear what is meant by combinatorial properties and their effect. Syntactic categories constrain the sort of complements a head admits or requires, and they define the category of the resulting combination. Thus in the construction *he fears to speak* the concept expressed by *fear* is complemented by a nominative and an infinitive and projects verbal properties to the construction as a whole, while *fear* takes a possessive instead of the nominative in *his fear to speak*, which comes out as a Noun Phrase. Morphological categories on the other hand regulate in a sense the traffic within complex expressions. Thus the distinction between Dative and Accusative in *Er fährt in der Stadt* (He drives in the city) vs. *Er fährt in die Stadt* (He drives into the city) discriminates locative vs. directional prepositional phrases, while in *Er traut ihnen* (he trusts them) vs. *Er traut sie* (he marries them) it indicates selectional conditions of different (homonymous) verbs. Different antecedens possibilities are indicated by the Singular of *him* in *Max expected her to ask him*, which may be coreferential with *Max*, while this is excluded by the Plural of *them* in *Max expected her to ask them*.

These considerations indicate the main part of an answer to question (12a): Formal features regulate the traffic between form and meaning, i.e. between AF and SF.

This does not seem to be the full answer to (12a) yet, for the following reason: Although the combinatorial effects of formal features do not depend on semantic distinctions related to them, it is still obvious, that syntactic and morphological features preferably correspond to certain characteristic conceptual conditions. This has already been mentioned for morphological features like Gender, Number, and Case. And it holds also for syntactic categories, which apparently correspond to common sense ontology in the following way: Verbs refer to events or states, prepositions denote relations, and adjectives denote properties. Nouns, on the other hand, refer preferably to objects (*dog, hammer, tree*, etc.), but allow practically every ontological type, as shown by e.g. *water, traffic, anger, jump, color, height*. On closer inspection, however, this interpretation becomes circular in crucial respects. Compare e.g. *he equals her in size* and *he is equal to her in size*, where the claim that *equal* expresses a situation in the first case, but a relation in the second, would have no other justification than the syntactic categorization, which it is meant to explain. Similar observations hold for pairs like *this is above the norm* vs. *this exceeds the norm* and many others. What is left are constraints, according to which verbs and prepositions do not refer to objects or substances, with consequences for a category shift that verbalizes a noun as in *he shelved the books*, or nominalizes an adjective as in *the blue of the sky*.[28]

In general, then, the domain interpreting morphological and syntactic features is the computational system, by means of which AF is related to SF. This does not exclude preferred correspondences between certain formal features and configurations of these interface levels.[29] The raison d'être of these features, however, is the combinatorial systematicity of the language capacity. The features controlling this systematicity may be contaminated with or supported by configurations in SF — as in systems of Tense and Aspect in many languages — and they can be made 'visible' in AF in various ways in different languages. This is in fact the content of what is usually called morphology. Halle & Marantz (1993) and Wunderlich (1997a) provide two recent versions to account for these components of the grammatical system.

This leads us directly to question (12b), concerning the possibility of a universal set Γ of grammatical features or distinctions γ. Different considerations seem to be indicated for syntactic and morphological features. Let us turn first to syntactic categorization. Although I have argued that syntactic categories cannot be reduced to ontological or semantic types, it seems still uncontroversial that there is only a very restricted range of distinctions to be made in this domain. Languages differ with respect to morphological distinctions that are realized by elements of particular syntactic categories; the basic distinctions, however, reduce to a limited range of categories, like Noun, Verb, Adjective, Preposition, and a number of functional categories, based on a very small set of universal features, providing guidelines for the combinatorial possibilities, including options for morphological distinctions to be expressed. In other words, syntactic categories pave the way for universal syntax, diversified in different languages by different indicators for morphological categories. A moments reflection shows, that under these assumptions the distinction between a fixed set of features and a skeleton of possibilities to construct features does not yield a real distinction: The alternative between possible features that may be realized, and principles according to which they can be constructed, based on strong, albeit different arguments for AF and SF, appears to be vacuous in case of the syntactic categories, as the range of distinctions is restricted to the core combinatorial properties of basic and derived expressions. What is at issue is neither a choice of the domain from which features could be recruited, as in AF, nor an unlimited range of possible distinctions to be captured, as in SF. It is here that the tenet of Chomsky (1995) applies, according to which natural languages exhibit essentially the same structure.

Turning to morphological features, we seem to have a different situation. According to well motivated assumptions, natural languages differ remarkably with respect to the morphological distinctions they realize. As a matter of fact, morphology (besides lexical arbitrariness) is taken to be the characteristic domain for idiosyncratic aspects in linguistic structure. This seems to be correct, even if we observe that e.g. abstract Case (see Kiparsky 1992), or Tense (see Hornstein 1981) are based on highly restricted, universal distinctions. Languages may differ with respect to inflectional systems, let alone derivational possibilities, in unpredictable ways. On closer inspection, however, the arbitrariness is to a large extent a matter of the overt realization and the specific combination of the categories in question. Two things are to be noted on principled grounds, however.

First, morphological features define classes of expression with respect to their grammatical, i.e. language internal behavior. In this respect, they differ from elements of Σ and Π, which are interpreted in C–I and A–P, respectively.

Second, they go beyond the basic combinatorial conditions fixed by syntactic features, which define possible Argument Structures and referential capacity of linguistic expressions. Hence morphological classification must draw on either properties of SF or AF — or particular correspondences between them. This is the source of the preferred correspondence between morphological features and semantic components mentioned above.[30] Hence morphological features realize options that rely on two conditions: (a) Linguistic expressions can be classified according to distinctions in their grammatical (i.e. language internal) behavior. (b) These distinctions are anchored in configurations of either SF, or AF, or both, where a feature γ is anchored in some configuration if the correspondence to it is above chance.

We thus arrive at the following answer to question (12a) and (b): For Γ, as opposed to Π, the domain of interpretation is unique, viz. the language internal combinatorial categories, and the range of options, as opposed to Σ, is fairly limited (to the order of some dozen). Hence there are no principled reasons preventing the assumption that Γ consists of a fixed universal repertoire, from which individual languages make their choice.[31] Grammars of different languages result from alternative selections out of this universal set, plus language particular options of combination in lexical entries and patterns of inflection and derivation. On the other hand, it seems to be sufficient, and hence preferable, to rely on assumptions that seem to be necessary for Π and Σ anyway, according to which UG provides the framework to construct the necessary primes. Under this assumption, the actual repertoire of formal features would emerge from patterns realizing the basic combinatorial options on which the mapping between AF and SF is based.

6. Perspectives

Summarizing the considerations about the three types of basic elements UG is responsible for, we seem to be lead to a paradox: On the one hand, there is no representational system — whether symbolic or subsymbolic — without primitive elements of representation. Hence these primes must be available in order to make the acquisition of representations possible. On the other hand, primitive elements of linguistic structure are unlikely to be fixed before the domain of interpretation and the range of relevant distinctions are identified. This is only an apparent paradox, however, if units of representation are allowed to emerge from the accommodation of actual data according to general principles of the representational system.[32] One might argue that this view merely shifts the burden of basic elements from elements of representation to underlying principles, determining the format of representations, including their primitive terms. Instead of features or components, we get principles of representation as proper primitive elements, i.e. the conditions I have called the skeleton or framework on which primes are based.

It should be noted that this step is by no means just a terminological shift, replacing elements by principles. If it is a step in the right direction — as I think it is — then we have to distinguish the organizing principles of representation, which belong to UG, from the primitive elements of representation, which are not as such part of UG, although they depend on UG for principled reasons, and are still basic and irreducible in a well motivated sense, as they cannot be reduced to smaller units within the realm of linguistic structure.

With respect to language acquisition, these considerations lead to the following view: Universal Grammar must provide the general functional architecture of linguistic knowledge, i.e. the system providing the correspondence between A–P and C–I over an unlimited range, and the principles of representation and combination supporting this architecture. These principles include the conditions to establish representational primes on the basis of actual data. In other words, primes are indispensable constituents of representation, they are created during the process of acquisition, but they crucially depend at least as much on genetically fixed dispositions as on actual experience and are thus not arbitrary products of external stimulation. The answer to our initial question would thus be as follows: Primitive elements are the result of language acquisition, emerging, however, on the basis of biologically fixed prerequisites.

Notes

1. The program of subsymbolic representational systems was developed in Rumelhart & McClelland (1986). For a survey of related approaches see Schnelle (1994), and Elman et al. (1998) for recent programmatic elaboration. It might be noted that the various sorts and layers of nodes in spreading activation models like e.g. Dell (1986) or the TRACE-model of McClelland & Elman (1986) are proper primitive terms with respect to the internal architecture of the model; they cease to be primitive, however, as soon as one tries to account for processes from which the input information emerges. Similarly, output-nodes might be abbreviations of assemblies of nodes, if they are looked at from outside the network under consideration. In general, the problems arising with respect to nodes of subsymbolic networks are complex and in many respects different from those related to primes of the sort I will be concerned with. I will not pursue these differences any further, noting merely that there are various unsolved problems with respect to neuronal network models of linguistic capacities that need not concern us here.
2. Direct correspondence by analogy between articulation and the particular type of (essentially intentional) interpretation is characteristic for music and dance or — with different domains of

articulation and interpretation — for visual art. For some discussion of this type of correspondence in case of music see Bierwisch (1979).
3. The term is meant to comprise the mental systems recruited by the computational system of I-language to implement the correspondence established by linguistic expressions. The term is slightly misleading, as performance systems, notably the subsystems of A–P as well as C–I, are based on their own types of knowledge requiring appropriate performance mechanisms. Not much depends on the terminology, though, once the status of the mental systems in question is understood.
4. One might in fact consider I-language as the interface system in terms of which signals, structured by A–P, and meanings, organized by C–I, can be mutually accessed, such that the origin of language consists essentially in the creation of a highly complex interface system integrating two independently given, heteromorphic domains.
5. The details of this aspect are anything but trivial, but they are not the topic of the present discussion. For a critical discussion see e.g. Pinker et al. (1990).
6. Early proposals to implement this sort of coordination include the motor theory of speech perception of Liberman et al. (1962) and the model of analysis by synthesis of Stevens & Halle (1967). For a more general, i.e. language independent, account of the perceptual control loop of motor behavior see Powers (1973).
7. Conditions of this sort can be stated in various ways; an important tradition dealing with these facts is the theory of markedness as formulated e.g. in Chomsky & Halle (1968). It assumes that primes of PF are binary features, one value being marked, the other unmarked or neutral, with the consequence that G cannot include a marked value of a feature F unless it also manifests the corresponding unmarked value. A somewhat different proposal is made within the framework of Optimality Theory initiated by Prince & Smolensky (1993), where UG is assumed to provide general constraints, that can be ranked differently with respect to their strength in the grammar of different languages. I cannot go here into the details of these alternative theories.
8. Although there is general agreement that sign language has clearly components that correspond strictly to phonology, morphology, and syntax of spoken language, details of the organization are still under discussion. Issues to be clarified include e.g. the assumption that the Articulatory Form of sign language, like that of natural language in general, is based on features, segments, and syllables as layers of organization, as argued, e.g., in Perlmutter (1992).
9. While perceptual characterization in terms of acoustic properties like frequency patterns as given e.g. in Jakobson & Halle (1956) is possible and reasonable for primes of PF, no comparable visual characterization, i.e. a visual description not referring to the articulator and its properties, is possible or has ever been attempted for primes of AF in sign language.
10. The most important aspect is presumably the scale of sonority and its counterpart of primary movement in sign language which give rise to syllable structure as an inherent layer of AF, as argued by Perlmutter (1992).
11. It might be noted, that even writing systems of different sorts preserve the linear ordering of letters or characters, although two-dimensional structures could easily be used, as in notational systems like Frege's (1879) 'Begriffsschrift' and various other artificial languages. This is remarkable in view of the fact that writing — in contrast to sign language — is a derivative system that does not only presuppose spoken language, but is an 'invented' product of cultural evolution and does in fact exploit different principles of organization.
12. Whether and to what extent these elements should be associated with model-theoretic interpretations along the lines of intensional logic proposed in Montague (1974) and related work, in

order to capture the referential properties of natural language expressions, is still a matter of debate. While e.g. Dowty (1979) proposed an explicit account of terms like CAUSE, BECOME in this framework, Jackendoff (1983) and subsequent work does not take this to be an appropriate program. In a similar vein, Chomsky (1993) construes conceptual structures as providing a 'perspective' on, rather than reference to the environment, with reference taken in the technical sense. Although I strongly tend to agree with the position of Jackendoff and Chomsky, the issue can be left open, if we admit that the system C–I necessarily mediates the relation between linguistic expressions and whatever they are about.

13. Katz (1972) distinguishes general effability, according to which any thought T that can be expressed in L_i can also be expressed in every other natural language L_k, from what he calls 'local effability', according to which the principle (8) holds for the thoughts of the speaker of a given language L, but does not imply that any T expressible in L_i is equally expressible in L_k.

14. It should be noted that even under local effability, where languages would differ as to what they can express, it would be logically possible to have the inventory Σ completely predetermined by UG, as language acquisition could lead to different systems of SF by triggering different subsystems of Σ, just as — logically — the ontogenesis of PF could activate different selections from Π, accounting for the differences in the PF of different languages.

15. The structural organization of SF must not be confused with the fact, that there is a temporal aspect in the creation and understanding of thoughts interpreting linguistic expressions. The temporal aspect of these processes can be remarkably different from the organization of the conceptual structure, as simple examples like (i) or (ii) clearly demonstrate:

    (i)   He backed his claims up with strong evidence
    (ii) Eve switched the light on/off.

    The speaker of (i) must activate the meaning of *back up* before he gets to the production of *up*, as the concept expressed by *back up* is not properly composed from that of its parts, while the hearer can activate the concept only after the particle *up* has been processed. Hence the temporal structure of the process constructing SF cannot be the same for production and perception — differing from AS, where the processes of articulation and perception run along identical temporal organization.

16. For the use of those systems, originally introduced by Ajdukiewicz (1935), in the analysis of natural language semantics see e.g. Dowty (1979) and much related work.

17. The choice of two basic categories in (9a) is an empirical assumption, albeit close to the conceptual minimum; the recursive definition in (9b) however is conceptually necessary in one or the other notational variant, in order to capture the hierarchical nature of SF. Notice, that the combination determined by functor categories based on (9b) is, of course, without linear order. — It might be useful to point out, incidentally, that basic categories may categorize complex structures, while complex categories might comprise basic elements, as shown by the structure (i), indicating standard assumptions about the SF of the verb *die*, where the primes BECOME, ALIVE, and NOT are functors, while the whole structure (as well as its nested parts) are of the basic category 0:

    (i) $[\text{BECOME}_{\langle 0,0 \rangle} \, [\text{NOT}_{\langle 0,0 \rangle} \, [\text{ALIVE}_{\langle 1,0 \rangle} \, x_1]_0]_0]_0$

18. A special case of the capacity to identify complex perceptual and conceptual patterns in some kind of holistic manner is the domain of human faces. Even though the identity of faces cannot be verbalized in compositional way, the identification is invariant under a wide variety of changing conditions. Now, there are, on the one hand, strong reasons to assume that faces are special in several respects, they are, on the other hand, indicative for the capacity to identify

19. In order to be unbounded, i.e. potentially infinite, the system of primes would have to be based on some sort of constructive operation, like e.g. the construction of natural numbers by the successor operation. But then, of course, the elements of this set would be composite, and not primes.

20. It must be noted that construction of primes under this perspective cannot properly be an operation within the system of SF — or Language, for that matter — since otherwise constructed primes would cease to be primitive elements for the reason already mentioned in note 18 and 19. Construction of primes must be construed as associating simple elements — having roughly the status of variables — with configurations created in C–I. This is possible only, if UG formally provides an infinite set of uninterpreted elements, which don't have other properties than those determined by the formal skeleton of SF.

21. Fodor's argument against decomposition of lexical meanings rests on the assumption that concepts that cannot be defined by necessary and sufficient conditions cannot be complex either. For the sake of argument, he claims that e.g. the meaning of the verb *paint* cannot be complex, containing in particular the concept PAINT assigned to the noun *paint*, as it does not seem to be appropriately defined as CAUSE[BECOME[COVERED-WITH PAINT]]. Without going through the full range of pertinent issues, I merely want to point out that the SF of a verb like *paint* may well contain the semantic constituent represented by the homonymous noun, even if it could not be reduced to the definition in question. — It should be added, moreover, that the issue of lexical decomposition is not identical to that of the actual innateness of the set of primitive concepts.

22. There is a not incidental ambiguity here with regard to categorization in the sense of (10a) and the categorization assumed in (9) for the organization of SF. On the one hand, categorial grammars, based on initial ideas of Ajdukiewicz (1935), are not only motivated by conceptual types, but are clearly bound to conditions of conceptual combination; on the other hand, syntactic and morphological categories like Verb, Adjective, or Case, Number and Gender, categorize linguistic, rather than conceptual entities. We will return to this point shortly.

23. For the sake of illustration, German verbs with indirect and direct object, such as *geben* (give), *sagen* (say), *zeigen* (show), require these objects by default to be nominal constituents in the Dative and Accusative, respectively. The verb *fragen* (ask), however, requires the indirect object idiosyncratically to be realized by an Accusative. For details see Bierwisch (1996a).

24. As a matter of fact, the two conceptions can in part be reconciled, if Roles like Agent etc. are considered as Relations in SF, providing an argument that is accessed by the corresponding position in AS. This is essentially the view adopted in Davidson (1967) and subsequent work, where Agent is construed as a relation between an event and an individual. In any case, to the extent to which argument positions are subject to interpretation, this is a matter of SF and its interpretation in C–I.

25. The introduction of morphological features obeying those correspondences seems to be a crucial aspect of what is usually called grammaticalization in linguistic change. — It might be noted that the correspondence between e.g. [+Feminine] and the SF-component FEMALE differs in crucial respects from the interpretation of elements of SF by conceptual (or elements of PF by articulatory) conditions. Even though the interpretation of SF-elements must allow for conceptual variation and 'plasticity' in the sense mentioned above, such that e.g. FEMALE may or may not involve social aspects of prototypical behavior alongside with biological conditions, but it never allows for strictly opposite interpretation, a standard possibility for [+Feminine], as

shown in *eine männliche Person* (a male person), which is male, in contrast to its lexically fixed Gender marking, or [+Feminine] as the Gender of ships in English. Similar observations hold for cases of *plurale tantum* and other idiosyncracies.

26. The proposal to look at grammatical marking of the head-complement relation in these ways comes from Kiparsky (1989), who draws, among others, on the Case Theory of Chomsky (1981). — What it means to express morphological features, i.e. to realize the distinctions made by them in terms of articulatory features is the content of morphological rules and principles. For concrete proposals see e.g. Halle & Marantz (1993) or Wunderlich (1997a).

27. The conditions in (b-i) include the fact that complements of Nouns and Adjectives are usually optional, that Verbs and Nouns have a referential position; conditions in (b-ii) include facts dealt with in terms of structural as opposed to inherent or lexical Case. See Bierwisch (1997) for further discussion.

28. The system of categorial grammar based on Ajdukiewicz (1935) suggests a different notion of syntactic category, according to which intransitive, transitive, and ditransitive verbs belong to completely different categories such as S\NP (e.g. *sleep, walk*), (S\NP)/NP (e.g. *lose, kill*), and ((S\NP)/NP)/NP (e.g. *give, show*). Similarly for simple or relational nouns or adjectives. See Montague (1974), Steedman (1989), and related work for systematic exposition. As mentioned in fn. 21, this is the notion of categorization adopted in (9b) above to account for semantic categories (or types, for that matter), distinguishing one-place, two-place, n-place predicates etc. It does not express, however, the common properties according to which *sleep, meet, give* do not only share properties of Argument Structure (Nominative subject), but also the need for morphological categories like Tense, Mood, Person, and Number, by which they differ from nominal one- and two-place predicates like *sleep, loss,* etc. In other words, the conceptually crucial notion of n-place functor does not provide an interpretation for morpho-syntactic features. It rather distinguishes semantic categories (or types) from properties captured by syntactic category features like [±Verb] or [±Noun].

29. This does not only apply to the semantic background considered so far, but with equal strength to the articulatory aspect. To take just one example for the syntactic categories, for English items like *adult, conduct, content, decrease, object, produce*, which are categorized as Nouns and simultaneously as Verbs and/or Adjectives, the categorization [−Noun] corresponds to word final stress, although, of course, the feature [+Noun] cannot to be interpreted as initial stress, just as it must not be interpreted as 'thing' or 'object'.

30. From this perspective, it is natural that there are morphological features like [±Strong], [±Umlaut] etc., which are anchored in configurations of AF, besides features like [±Plural] or [±Past], which correspond to conceptually interpreted configurations in SF.

31. This appears to be paradox at first glance, as universal phonetics and universal semantics are notions to which traditionally at least some plausibility is ascribed, which would hardly be the case for the notion of universal morphology. Notice, however, that Γ does *not* represent the morphological combinatorial systems of natural language, but merely the repertoire of primes, from which actual systems of morphology can be constructed. For reasons discussed earlier, this repertoire is in fact the domain, for which an autonomous module defining the species specific language capacity might be indicated.

32. This is by no means an exotic assumption. Units of currency, for instance, must have emerged on the basis of exchange and comparison of goods, units of time measurement emerged according to demands of systematisation, etc. What is necessary besides raw data are, of course, principles of representation or organization, for that matter.

References

Ajdukiewicz, K. 1935. "Über die syntaktische Konnexität." *Studia Philosophica* 1: 1–27.
Berlin, B. & Kay, P. 1969. *Basic Color Terms*. Berkeley and Los Angeles: University of California Press.
Bierwisch, M. 1979. "Musik und Sprache." In *Jahrbuch Peters 1978*. Leipzig: Edition Peters.
Bierwisch, M. 1996. "How Much Space gets into Language?" In *Language and Space*, P. Bloom, M. Peterson, L. Nadel & M. Garrett (eds.). Cambridge, Mass.: MIT Press.
Bierwisch, M. 1996a. "'Fragen' zum Beispiel." In *Wenn die Semantik arbeitet*, G. Harras & M. Bierwisch (eds.). Tübingen: Niemeyer.
Bierwisch, M. 1997. "Lexical Information from a Minimalist Point of View." In *The Role of Economy Principles in Linguistic Theory*, C. Wilder, H.-M. Gärtner & M. Bierwisch (eds.). Berlin: Akademie-Verlag.
Chomsky, N. 1981. *Lectures on Government and Binding*. Dordrecht: Foris.
Chomsky, N. 1986. *Knowledge of Language: Its Nature, Origin, and Use*. New York: Praeger.
Chomsky, N. 1993. *Language and Thought*. Wakefield, Rhode Island: Moyer Bell.
Chomsky, N. 1995. *The Minimalist Program*. Cambridge, Mass.: MIT Press.
Chomsky, N. & Halle, M. 1968. *The Sound Pattern of English*. New York: Harper and Row.
Clark, E. V. 1973. "What's in a Word?" In *Cognitive Development and the Acquisition of Language*, T. E. Moore (ed.). New York: Academic Press.
Clements, G. N. 1985. "The Geometry of Phonological Features." *Phonology Yearbook* 2: 245–252.
Davidson, D. 1967. "The Logical Form of Action Sentences." In *The Logic of Decision and Action*, N. Rescher (ed.). Pittsburgh: University of Pittsburgh Press.
Dell, G. S. 1986. "A spreading activation theory of retrieval in sentence production." *Psychological Review* 93: 283–321.
Dowty, D. R. 1979. *Word Meaning and Montague Grammar*. Dordrecht, Holland: D. Reidel.
Dowty, D. 1991. "Thematic proto roles and argument selection." *Language* 67: 547–619.
Elman, J. L, Bates, E., Johnson, M. H., Karmiloff-Smith, A., Parisi, D. & Plunkett, K. 1998. *Rethinking Innateness — A connectionist Perspective on Development*. Cambridge, Mass.: MIT Press.
Fillmore, C. J. 1968. "The Case for Case." In *Universals in Linguistic Theory*, E. Bach & R. T. Harms (eds.). New York: Holt, Rinehart and Winston.
Fodor, J. A. 1981. *Representations*. Cambridge, Mass.: MIT Press.
Fodor, J. A. 1987. *Psychosemantics*. Cambridge, Mass: MIT Press.
Frege, G. 1879. *Begriffsschrift, eine der arithmetischen nachgebildete Formelsprache des reinen Denkens*. Halle a. S.: L. Nebert.
Grimshaw, J. 1990. *Argument Structure*. Cambridge, Mass.: MIT Press.
Haider, H. 1993. *Deutsche Syntax generativ*. Tübingen: Narr.

Halle, M. 1995. "Feature Geometry and Feature Spreading." *Linguistic Inquiry* 26: 1–46.
Halle, M. 1983. "On Distinctive Features and their Arrticulatory Implementation." *Natural Language and Linguistic Theory* 1: 91–105.
Halle, M. & Marantz, A. 1993. "Distributed Morphology and the Pieces of Inflection." In *The View from Building Twenty*, K. Hale & S. Jay Keyser (eds.). Cambridge, Mass.: MIT Press.
Hjelmslev, L. 1935. *La Categorie des Cas, I. Partie.* Aarhus: Universitetsforlaget.
Hornstein, N. 1981. "The Study of Meaning in Natural Language: Three Approaches to Tense." In *Explanation in Linguistics,* N. Hornstein & D. Lightfoot (eds.). London: Longman.
Jackendoff, R. 1983. *Semantics and Cognition.* Cambridge, Mass.: MIT Press.
Jackendoff, R. S. 1990. *Semantic Structures.* Cambridge, Mass.: MIT Press.
Jackendoff, R. S. 1996. "The Architecture of the Linguistic-Spatial Interface." In *Language and Space*, P. Bloom, M. Peterson, L. Nadel & M. Garrett (eds.). Cambridge, Mass.: MIT Press.
Jackendoff, R. 1997. *The Architecture of the Language Faculty.* Cambridge, Mass: MIT Press.
Jakobson, R. 1936. "Beitrag zur allgemeinen Kasuslehre." *Travaux du Cercle Linguistique de Prague* 6: 240–288.
Jakobson, R. & Halle, M. 1956. *Fundamentals of Language.* The Hague: Mouton.
Katz, J. J. 1972. *Semantic Theory.* New York: Harper and Row.
Kiparsky, P. 1989. *Agreement and Linking Theory.* Ms. Stanford University.
Kiparsky, P. 1992. *Structural Case.* Ms. Stanford University.
Klima, E. & Bellugi, U. 1979. *The Signs of Language.* Cambridge, Mass: Harvard University Press.
Liberman, A. M., Cooper, F. S., Harris, K. S. & Mc Neilage, P. F. 1962. "A Motor Theory of Speech Perception." In *Proceedings of the Speech Communication Seminar, Vol 2.* Stockholm: Royal Institute of Technology.
McClelland, J. L. & Elman, J. L. 1986. "The TRACE model of speech perception." *Cognitive Psychology* 18: 1–86.
Montague, R. 1974. *Formal Philosophy, Selected Papers,* edited by Richmond H. Thomason. New Haven: Yale University Press.
Pinker, S. & Bloom, P. and Commentators 1990. "Natural Language and Natural Selection." *Brain and Behavioral Sciences* 13: 707–784.
Perlmutter, D. 1992. "Sonority and Syllable Structure in American Sign Language." *Linguistic Inquiry* 23: 407–442.
Powers, W. T. 1973. *Behavior: The Control of Perception.* Chicago: Aldine.
Prince, A. & Smolensky, P. 1993. *Optimality Theory: Constraint Interaction in Generative Grammar.* Rutgers University & University of Colorado at Boulder, to appear in Cambridge, Mass.: MIT Press.
Pustejovsky, J. 1995. *The Generative Lexicon.* Cambridge, Mass.: MIT Press.
Rumelhart, D. E., McClelland, J. L. & the PDP Research Group 1986. P*arallel Distributed Processing.* Cambridge, Mass.: MIT Press.

Saussure, F. de 1916. *Cours de Linguistique Générale*. Paris: Payot.
Searle, J. R. 1969. *Speech Acts*. Cambridge: Cambridge University Press.
Steedman, M. 1989. "Constituency and Coordination in a Combinatory Grammar." In *Alternative Conceptions of Phrase Structure*, M. Baltin & A. Kroch (eds.). Chicago: The University of Chicago Press.
Stevens, K. N. & Halle, M. 1967. "Remarks on Analysis by Synthesis." In *Models for the Perception of Speech and Visual Form*, W. Wathen-Dunn (ed.). Cambridge, Mass.: MIT Press.
Wunderlich, D. 1997. "Cause and the Structure of Verbs." *Linguistic Inquiry* 28: 27–68.
Wunderlich, D. 1997a. "A Minimalist Model of Inflectional Morphology." In *The Role of Economy Principles in Linguistic Theory*, C. Wilder, H.-M. Gärtner & M. Bierwisch (eds.). Berlin: Akademie-Verlag.

Developmental Trajectories of Complex Signal Systems in Animals
The model of bird song

Henrike Hultsch & Dietmar Todt
Free University, Berlin

1. Introduction

Animal signal systems have a long phylogenetic history during which they were adapted to surviving in particular biological niches. Here, animal signals are tools for problem solving through communication. This view has two implications. By referring to the large number of biological niches to which species have adapted, it explains why the diversity of signal systems found across animals is so huge. On the other hand, the number of biological problems that a given species normally solves through communication is limited, and this explains why the sizes of species-typic signal repertoires are rather small: even in many vertebrates such repertoires do not exceed 25 different display behaviors. There is an exception from this rule, however, which is given by the signal patterns of songbirds (oscines). Songbirds often orchestrate more than hundred different vocalizations and their singing may be so dynamical that it clearly ranks among the most complex signal systems of animals.

Inquiries into the mechanisms of human communication have raised questions about their biological roots and whether there are homologous or at least analogous mechanisms in animals too. Although there is no doubt that a large number of human-typic traits, such as the ability and use of language, are unique to men, at least some of these characteristics may result from neural mechanisms which have evolved during our biological history. To be challenged by this idea entails to be inquisitive about accomplishments of other creatures, that seem comparable the human-typic achievements. In this article, we embark to such endeavor and invite readers to contrast features of language development (given in other chapters of this volume) to features documented for the ontogenetic development of complex signal systems in animals. To be fair, we will deal only with vocal signals that are acquired by individual learning. Currently, the singing behavior of birds is the only signal system of animals, that is both vocal and learnt and at the same time studied in a profound manner. Thus, it seems expedient to selecting this behavior as a paradigmatic model here, and to concentrate on recent findings of bird song studies. As an introduction to results showing how bird song is specifically acquired, developed and eventually retrieved, we first give a brief description of its organization and use.

2. How birdsong is organized and used

The singing of birds can be described as a stream of behavior where acoustically filled segments alternate with silent segments (pauses). The most conspicuous segment that is well known to the human listener is the so-called 'song' ('strophe'). In the typical case, songs have a length of about 3 seconds and are separated by pauses of about the same duration. Birds sing and hear, and such time patterns are obviously an adaptation to modes of vocal interaction. From the perspective of information processing, song duration seems to be selected for providing optimal 'chunks' of information (cf. Pöppel 1978 for human dialoguing). A song is long enough to convey a distinct message and, at the same time, not so long to constrain a sensory check for signals of a neighbor or delay a potential reply (Todt & Hultsch 1996).

In addition, also the acoustical organization of songs makes them optimal units of vocal communication. Songs form an intermediate level of a structural hierarchy in which the highest level is given by an episode of singing or a sequence of songs (term: inter-song level). On hierarchically lower levels one can distinguish several structural compounds that compose the songs (term: intra-song levels). In a top-down order these are, for example, song sections, trills, motifs, syllables and elements or notes. Although the number of distinguished intra-song levels, as well as their acoustical constituents vary a lot across species, the basic level is always given by the so-called song elements. Usually, this level serves for an analysis in which basic units are compared and told apart according to parametric cues, e.g. values assessed by frequency spectrography. The pool of classified song elements is then taken to categorize the songs and thus assess the repertoire of song-types (Todt 1968; Lemon & Chatfield 1971; Bondesen 1979; Kroodsma 1982; Thompson et al. 1994; Todt & Hultsch 1996).

Bird species differ in the sizes of their song-type repertoires, and this fact is due to genetic factors that obviously constrain the number of song-types. A Zebra Finch, for instance, develops one single type of song only, whereas a Chaffinch or a Great Tit usually produces three to eight different songs. Eurasian Blackbirds are able to acquire and sing approximately 50 song-types and Common Nightingales master even more than 150 types of song. In spite of such species-typic diversity, in most songbirds the composition of vocal repertoires follows a basic rule: The element-type repertoire of a given individual is clearly larger in size than his song-type repertoire. Thus, if we compare this relation to the relations documented for units and higher level compounds in human language, a crucial difference appears. In the latter case a small number of basic units (e.g. phonemes) serves as a pool to compose an almost unlimited amount of verbal patterns, such as words or sentences. Nevertheless, for reasons that will be treated later in this chapter, songs appear somehow comparable to sentences: both can be regarded as units of interaction where they obviously play a role as chunks of exchanged information ('units of sense').

Lessons from the structural hierarchy of bird song have stimulated studies on the rules encoded in the sequencing of songs or song elements, respectively, and these rules have been described by a procedural hierarchy. The concept of a procedural hierarchy allows to investigate the significance of sequential positions, namely by assuming that a given pattern can be taken as a hierarch for the next unit in the sequence. Such studies showed that the sequencing of songs reflects a remarkably high degree of freedom. That is, in principle, no song-type succession is excluded, and this facilitates pattern specific responses during vocal interaction. Nevertheless, one can find preferred sequential combinations of particular types of songs, which according to recent studies can be explained as a result of individual learning (cf. p. 316).

Studies investigating the procedural hierarchy on the intra-song level showed that the sequencing of elements is much less flexible than that of songs. With the Eurasien Blackbird (*Turdus merula*) and the Common Nightingale (*Luscinia megarhynchos*) as model species the intra-song hierarchy can be described by the following rules: First, particular types of elements occur at a particular song position only. Second, some element-type combinations are produced in a predictable manner, whereas others reflect certain degrees of permutational freedom. Third, element-types occurring at the beginning of songs are more frequent than others at later positions (Figure 1).

Viewed from another perspective this rule means that many songs share initial element compounds, but differ in the subsequent ones. Thus the intra-song branching usually reflects a 'diffluent flow' schema (one-to-many principle). In terms of decisional aspects this means that a bird has a number of alternative

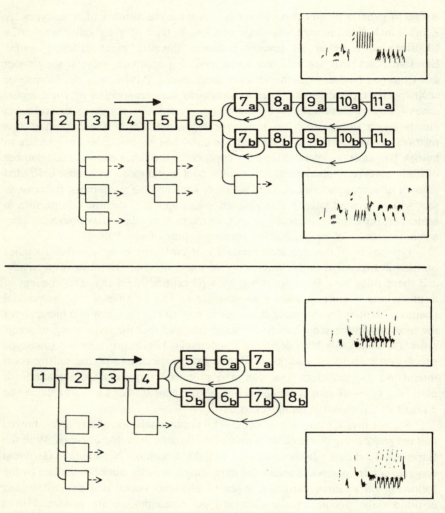

The upper two song-types share six element-types, the lower two four ones. Please note: The flowchart illustrates a diffluent procedural hierarchy (one to many). This is typical for the song patterns of many birds and entails that many songs start with the same type of element (e.g. 1), but end differently (e.g. by (11a) or (11b)). Vacant cells stand for element-types that do not constitute the song-types given here. In the repertoire of this individual, they occur as units of further song-types (after Hultsch 1980).

Figure 1. *Spectrograms of four song-types and schematic flowcharts of their element-types (cells with ID numbers) produced by a nightingale*

options to continue a song after the first element has been produced (Todt 1970; Todt & Hultsch 1980; Hultsch 1980; Naguib et al. 1991; Naguib & Kolb 1992).

Song birds modify their singing according to the time of season or day, ecological features and, above all, the social context. The influence of social context on singing has been described for a number of species suggesting that differences in repertoire delivery vary according to whether the subject is advertising its territory, counter singing, or addressing a mate. In situations of courtship or close range male-male interactions, for instance, the singing typically is more complex and versatile than singing used in territorial advertisement (Todt 1970; Kroodsma 1977; Catchpole 1983; Catchpole & Slater 1995; Hultsch 1980, 1993a; Falls & d'Agincourt 1982; Horn & Falls 1988; Todt & Hultsch 1996).

With a few exceptions, song production is the domain of territorial males; their singing is addressed to conspecific females or to territorial neighbors. Around their breeding season neighbors often engage in vocal interactions during which they mutually respond to a perceived song pattern. Various analyses have shown that such interactions can follow sophisticated rules, including both pattern specific and time specific relationships between the exchanged songtypes. Especially the so-called alternating singing provides evidence that birds actually may both listen and respond to a neighbor's songs. In addition, birds use to insert their songs into the silent intervals of another songster's vocalizations, then, and often this is so precise that the mutual alternation of songs can be described as a sort of turn-taking. In line with this, interactions by song have been compared to the schema of 'dialogues' (Figure 2; Todt & Hultsch 1994).

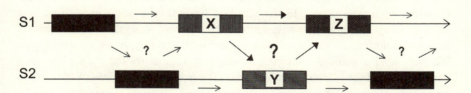

The bars symbolize their songs, and the question marks indicate temporal and pattern relationships that we study. The interaction is "dialogue-like" if the timing of songs is adjusted, indicating a type of turn-taking, and if "Z" is a function of both "X" and "Y," but is not determined exclusively by either of them.

Figure 2. *Schematic section of a dialogue-like interaction between two songsters*

3. Rules of song acquisition

Studies on the rules of song acquisition have been conducted in a number of bird species such as the Song Sparrow (*Melospiza melodia*; Marler & Peters 1982a), Marsh Wrens (*Cistothorus palustris*; Kroodsma 1979), the Canary (*Canarius serinus*; Nottebohm et al. 1986), the Starling (*Sturnus vulgaris*, Chaiken et al. 1993), and the Common Nightingale (*Luscinia megarhynchos*). However, most of these approaches have concentrated on the intra-song level and systematic investigations on the learning of information encoded on the inter-song level are currently available only for the Common Nightingale. This species is renowned for an outstanding vocal virtuosity, and the repertoire of an adult individual comprises about 200 different types of songs which are performed in a versatile singing style.

Several characteristics make nightingales good candidates for studying song learning also in the laboratory. First, the early period of auditory song acquisition begins around day 15 post hatching and continues for, at least the first three months of life, thus providing an extended time span in which to conduct learning experiments. Second, young nightingales readily accept a human caretaker as their social tutor (Todt et al. 1979; Todt & Boehner 1994), thus allowing us to standardize variables (e.g. by presenting our master songs through a loudspeaker) and also enabling us to check for factors which affect the acquisition process (e.g. by audiovisual control). Third, nightingales easily develop excellent copies of conspecific songs presented in a laboratory learning program, which often is a problem in other oscine species (Figure 3).

To compose a learning program, particular songs are selected at random from our catalogue of master song-types and recorded on tape to form a particular string of master songs. In the standard design, each song in a string is a different song-type and, likewise, each of the different strings to which a subject is exposed during the period of tutoring consists of a unique set of song-types. We thus label a particular tutoring situation or regime by the particular string which is played then (Hultsch et al. 1984). The acquisition success of the tutored males then allows inferences on whether and how a particular exposure variable influenced their singing. Additional checks for an impact of variables is done by an analysis of audiovisual recordings which permit access to e.g. an individual bird's motility during a given tutoring experiment (Müller-Bröse & Todt 1994).

Song acquisition depends on exposure variables. In some respect, however, it can be remarkably resilient to changes in such variables. For example, while the acquisition success of nightingales is low (appr. 30%) for songs experienced only 5 times, these birds imitate around 75% of those song-types which they

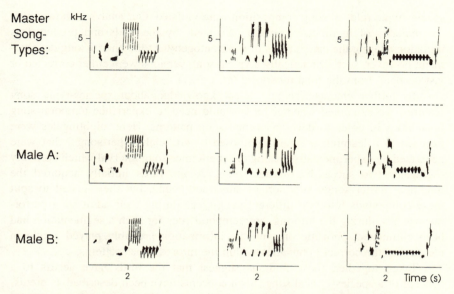

Top: Three song-types recorded from a free-ranging Nightingale. These songs served as master song-types. Bottom: Copies of the master songs by two laboratory-raised males (A, B).

Figure 3. *Sound spectrograms of Nightingale songs illustrating the birds' normal copy quality*

heard 15 times. On the other hand, a more frequent exposure does not significantly improve acquisition success. Also, the number of songs in a string can be considerably increased (e.g. from 20 to 60 song-types) without raising exposure frequencies accordingly. As the birds cope well with such an increase in the number of stimuli to be acquired (Hultsch & Todt 1989a), the results contrast with paradigms from Learning Theory, which state that exposure frequency must grow proportionally with the number of stimuli to be acquired (review in Crowder 1976). Implications of our findings are relevant to the issue of song acquisition as a special process or template learning (Marler 1976) and any inquiry into the memory mechanisms has to take into account that specific adaptations are involved in the process.

As with many other species, the accuracy of song imitations is remarkably high in nightingales. To examine whether this accomplishment is based on an innately specified concept of the species song, we exposed young birds to song patterns in which we modified particular syntactical rules in a way that the species-typic rules of song composition were violated. Our analyses showed that the majority of modifications were 'accepted' by the birds and produced as imitations during the early stages of song ontogeny. At the end of song development, however, such syntactically atypical song versions were either corrected or just dropped from the final repertoire (cf. p. 321).

To further characterize any latent knowledge about species-typic song features, we examined whether birds would need to experience temporal song boundaries in order to develop normal song patterns. Here, nightingales were exposed to a learning program composed of artificial 'super-songs' that were generated by experimentally erasing the silent inter-song interval which normally segregates two successive master songs. Again, birds initially acquired the modified master songs as a sort of super-compound, but they tended to split these compounds into two different song-types during their adult song performances. As, during the tutoring, any temporal cues for such a segmentation had been eliminated, phonetic or syntactic information probably played a role in identifying the correct boundaries within the tutored super patterns.

Taken together, these findings suggest that the birds have access to a concept of a species-typical song. Such concepts have been described as predispositions allowing the young birds to selectively acquire appropriate, i.e. species typical songs from a 'noisy' acoustic environment. As the birds in our studies were also exposed to natural, i.e. unmodified song patterns, we cannot exclude that such predispositions were shaped through experience as well. Anyway, in most of the tested syntactic inconsistencies, prescriptions from preordained or acquired information did not restrict the acquisition during auditory exposure. That is, the majority of modifications were initially accepted by the birds and produced as imitations during the early stages of vocal development. And only after a certain amount of vocal practice had been accomplished, 'analysis' based on structure dependent knowledge came into play to set performance parameters according to species-typic rules. Thus, the findings presented here may be accounted for by a rule-bound selection process.

These findings invite to address features of singing above the level of 'song' and ask whether and how its organization is shaped through experience. Recent studies on this matter provided a number of interesting results. To recall, the degree of permutational freedom of unit successions is higher at the inter-song level than within songs (cf. p. 311). This principle suggests that genetically prescribed constraints on generative rules mainly act on the level of song patterns, but less so on the sequential combinations of songs. A test of these assumptions should be done in species which develop large song-type repertoires, because their singing very clearly exemplifies the problem. As a rule, conspecific birds, e.g. neighboring nightingales, share song-types, whereas a sharing of their song-type sequencing is quite rare.

Our studies on nightingales have shown that birds do indeed acquire information encoded in the serial succession of master song-types presented during their training. Mainly, the evidence has been collected from three effects: the formation of song-type packages and context groups, and the imitation of the serial order of song-types in a master string (Hultsch & Todt 1989a, b, c, 1992, 1996; Hultsch 1991a).

(1) Package effect: The effect documents that a large body of serial data, here information from a string of master songs, is segmented into subsets of sequentially associated items. Such subsets have a number of characteristics. Two striking features are: First, strong sequential associations exist among members of a given package, here the learned song-types. As a rule, these relationships are not uni-directional (i.e. A → B → C), but bi- or multi-directional (A ↔ B; A ↔ C; B ↔ C). Second, subsets have a limited size: the frequency distribution of package sizes shows a prominent peak between three and four song-types. In other words, a limited number of learned song-types use to occur sequentially associated, and these association groups are termed packages.

(2) Context effect: The effect documents that birds learn a given master string as a sort of super-unit that they sequentially separate from another super-unit, that is, from songs learned from another master string. These super-units are termed context groups. In contrast to the package groups, context groups are not limited in size and are determined by the length of a tutored song string.

(3) Serial order effect: The effect documents that birds are able to learn and memorize serial information encoded in a string of master song-types. The strength of this effect is, in contrast to the packaging of song-types, related to the presentation frequency of a master string, and the birds have to hear it sufficiently often in order to make such learning evident. Only if high presentation frequencies are used serial order learning can modify consequences of the package effect, for instance, by changing multidirectional relationships among package members to unidirectional ones or by blurring the boundaries between different packages.

A comparison of these effects reveals two hierarchy levels appearing above the level of songs. The first involves the packages, composed of songs; the next involves the context groups, composed of packages. Both song order and context groups clearly reflect the serial organization of input during auditory learning. Consequently they are exposure-induced compounds, and thus are to be distinguished from the package groups, which have been characterized as self-induced associations (Hultsch 1993b). A crucial question on the formation of exposure induced song-type associations is whether they simply reflect the memorization of stimulus chains or whether they are based on cognitive accomplishments, such as 'categorization'. For the context groups, for instance, such categorical cues would be 'song-types heard from a particular individual', 'at a particular location or time' or 'song-types specified by a particular quality'. Preliminary evidence suggests that birds are indeed using such cues and experiments which systematically examine this matter are underway.

4. Rules of song development

The ontogenetic development of singing shows a number of characteristic traits that are wide-spread across oscine birds (Marler 1991). For example, in the typical case, the early phase of auditory learning is segregated from the phase of vocal production by an interval of several weeks. Vocal activity of the young bird then, covers another longer time span that is often lasting for several months until they reach the adult vocal competence (Figure 4). Early in life, all birds perform temporally coherent arrays of vocalizations that first are phonologically amorphous and only gradually improve in terms of form and structure. Due to the high variation of vocal patterns, these behaviors have been compared to the playful activities found in young mammals. Referring to the profile of the developmental progress, Marler & Peters (1982a) have suggested a tripartite model which distinguishes among (a) subsong, (b) several stages of plastic song and (c) crystallized fullsong. The study of these stages allowed to identify a set of ontogenetic trajectories that will be described in the following paragraphs. Again we will focus on song development in nightingales to provide a comparison to characteristics of its song acquisition.

4.1 *Trajectories of song development*

The subsong of birds consists of soft and rambling vocalizations which are phonologically amorphous and rather difficult to analyze. Therefore, the stage of plastic song is the matter of choice for investigators who search for rules of pattern development. In nightingales who have a particularly extended period of

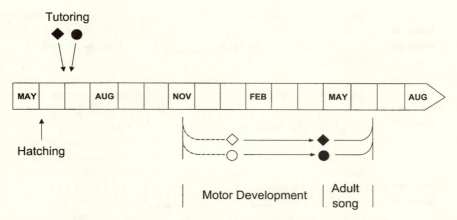

Filled symbols refer to master songs or crystallized imitations, respectively. Precursors of imitations are given by open symbols. Dashed lines during motor development indicate the period of subsong (cf. Figure 5).

Figure 4. *Time schedule of song learning and development in nightingales*

vocal ontogeny, plastic singing starts at an age of about eight months, i.e. in January. Then, first precursors of acquired imitations can be discerned and along with time an increasingly larger number of song-type precursors can be identified. The completion of the repertoire of song-type precursors takes a period of several weeks. During this process, imitations of master songs that the birds heard early in life do not emerge earlier than imitations of others that they had experienced later during the tutoring. In other words, the temporal order of song-type production does not reflect the temporal order of auditory acquisition.

Ontogenetic trajectories are found on both hierarchy levels, that is within or between songs. Trajectories expressed at the intra-song level concern the following traits (Figures 5 & 6). During early stages of ontogeny, birds often sing incomplete songs; i.e. some song constituents may be missing. In addition, the serial succession of song sections may be inverted, which results for instance in the final trill-section of a song being produced ahead of the normally preceding note complex (cf. Figure 5). Thus the intra-song syntax is not initially stereotyped. At the same time, however, the phonetic morphology of patterns is sufficiently elaborated to allow for an easy identification of song-type precursors. In other words, pattern phonetics takes its adult form ahead of the intra-song syntax, which 'crystallizes' only at about 10 months of age. Interestingly, the phonetic or syntactic quality of imitations first produced relatively late in

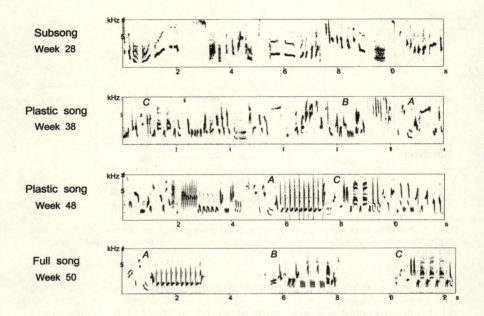

Figure 5. *Frequency spectrograms of vocalizations produced by a young nightingale during four stages of song development*

ontogeny is not inferior to the quality of imitations already produced earlier in age (Figure 6). This suggests a developmental trajectory which does not build on vocal 'experience' with a particular output, but concerns a general progression in motor competence or skill (Hultsch 1991b).

Besides trajectories concerning the pattern structure of vocalizations, ontogenetic progression also proceeds in the time domain of singing. As both the duration of vocal compounds as well as their temporal segregation have to be shaped, trajectories in the time domain are highly interrelated and follow complex rules (Kopp 1996). The adult time structure of singing (songs alternating with silent intervals of about the same duration) is the last performance feature to crystallize; its adult form is achieved only at an age of about 11 months.

On a higher level of song organization, the following rules could be characterized. Imitations which, in the adult performance, are identified as members of the same package emerge, quite consistently, together in time. In addition, throughout ontogeny these precursors are sequentially associated in the same way as in the adult singing (Figure 7; Hultsch 1989). The association of different

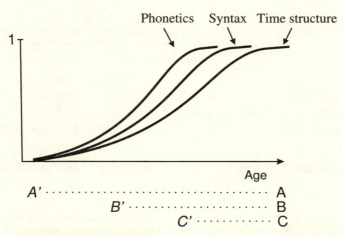

The first feature to become stereotyped is the phonetics of the vocalisations. And only after the syntactical organisation has taken its final form, songs are separated by the typical silent intersong intervals. Capitals in the lower part of the figure illustrate that throughout motor development, new precursors (e.g. A', B', C') of the adult song-types (e.g. A, B, C) can be identified. The ontogenetic trajectories of newly emerging precursors (e.g. C') are not 'delayed', i.e. the time of their crystallization is in phase with the early patterns.

Figure 6. *Illustration of ontogenetic trajectories of the developing song material*

packages, i.e. the development of context groups, on the other hand, seems 'delayed' and in their fully-grown form these can only be assessed close to the time of song crystallization. However, the time structure of singing gives some indication that they are significant levels of performance organization already during ontogeny. During the phase of continuous vocal production, for example, the intervals between imitations acquired from the same master string or context group were significantly shorter than those intervals occuring when the birds switched to imitations of another context group (Hultsch 1993b). This effect suggests that access to the stored representations of song-types may be quick or delayed, depending on whether retrieval is from within a given context group or from a different context group.

In conclusion, on the inter-song level, the ontogeny of song material indeed reflects properties of the song-type association groups referred to earlier (p. 316). Here, trajectories do not only substantiate the view that these groups are memorized and encoded as higher levels units of song organization. It is, in addition, suggestive to think of retrieval following hierarchical mechanisms of action selection.

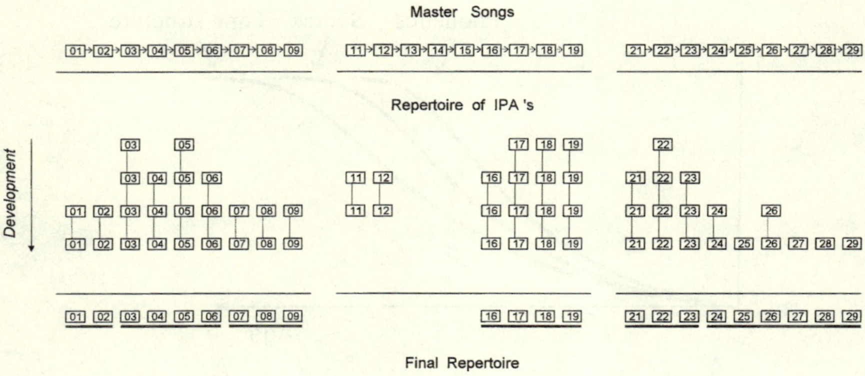

Figure 7. *Song development in nightingales*

Top: Illustration of 3 tutored strings of master songs (songs = cells with ID numbers). Middle: Ontogenetic ordering observed for precursors of imitations observed in one male's repertoire (IPA = identified patterns). Bottom: Final repertoire of that bird. Here, lines below cells indicate which imitations were associated to a song type package. Note: This bird did not learn three of the tutored master songs and discarded two other imitations from his final repertoire.

4.2 *Repertoire modification: Open versus closed processes*

Motor development of song is not simply a process through which a bird improves the quality of acquired song material by vocal rehearsal. At least two further maneuvers merit a short consideration. One of them enlarges the repertoire of a bird, whereas the other one has the opposite effect. In nightingales, increasing the repertoire size is much more pronounced than decreasing it (Freyschmidt et al. 1984; Wistel-Wozniak & Hultsch 1993). Repertoire enlargement is achieved by either acquiring additional song-types, or by developing new recombinations or, finally, inventing novel songs.

In bird species called 'age-independent learners' (Marler & Peters 1987), further learning can occur during the phase of plastic singing or even later in life. When at an age of 9 months, for example, nightingales are exposed to a master string with two parts, a familiar portion (heard by the birds during the first period of song acquisition) and a novel portion (containing new song-types), one can observe two effects: First, the renewed exposure to the familiar song-types raises the performance frequency of imitations that the birds had acquired earlier. A similar finding is reported for white crowned sparrows (*Zonothrichia leucophrys*;

Nelson 1992), pointing to a process coined as 'action based learning' (Marler & Nelson 1993). Second, the birds acquire the novel song-types and perform them as an integral part of that context group from which the familiar song-type sequence was taken (Hultsch 1991b). These effects are in line with observations obtained for birds who, instead of being housed in isolation, are housed together, thus allowing them to vocally interact with each other. Here the composition of song repertoires and also the performance preference of shared song-types clearly converge. Thus, additional learning coupled with a shaping of the performance towards convergence can lead to a sharing of at least parts of repertoires among conspecific neighbors (Hultsch & Todt 1981; Payne 1981; Slater 1989; Lemon et al. 1994).

A different strategy of repertoire enlargement that, in contrast, enhances the vocal individuality of a songster, is the development of new recombinations or novel inventions of songs. Nightingales, for instance, are able to generate individual specific song-types by recombining parts of imitated songs in a novel way. Interestingly, such recombinations are limited to material of song-types associated within the same package group (Hultsch 1993b). In addition, nightingales may develop song-types that do not contain material from the learning experiments, and so are completely new. Both during ontogeny and the adult singing, genuine inventions occur as coherent subsets in the singing, which results in an alternation of performance phases containing acquired imitations or novel inventions. Males classified as poor learners (acquisition success, related to presented master song-types $< 40\%$) develop a larger proportion of inventions than those classified as good learners (acquisition success $> 60\%$). Thus one may speculate that, at least in handraised nightingales, invented songs reflect a predisposition to develop a vocal repertoire of a certain size.

Upon reaching the final stage of song development (crystallization) birds may reduce their song-type repertoire. This phenomenon is especially marked in species that as adults use only small song-type repertoires (Marler & Peters 1982b; Nelson et al. 1995). In nightingales, repertoire constriction is much less conspicuous; only about five to eight percent of imitations identified in the course of song development (Hultsch 1991c) are discarded from the final repertoire. Nevertheless, the ontogenetic 'history' of eventually discarded song-types makes repertoire constriction a quite interesting issue in nightingales, too. During the phase of plastic singing, these song-types are produced with a rather poor copy quality. Such correlational finding has to be closer characterized by further analyses.

5. Conclusions and perspectives

We have shown that the singing behavior of birds reflects a structural hierarchy that, in a bottom-up order, is given by the units that compose a song pattern (intra-song level), by the songs and finally by sequences that are composed by songs (inter-song level). Either of these levels reveals a differentiated organization and dynamics and when this is examined, one arrives at another kind of hierarchy, termed procedural. It is given, for instance, by the rules of unit succession and, for the versatile songster, these may reflect hierarchical mechanisms for decision making during their singing.

Bird song is a learned behavior, and this fact allows to use this signal system for asking questions on the role that individual experience plays in the implementation of these rules. Our findings from learning experiments and studies of song development revealed a close linkage between both hierarchy domains and confirmed that either of them plays a biologically relevant role. Song-type associations, for example, do not only reflect a hierarchical representation of the memorized information (Figure 8). Their characteristics do also allow to trace the properties of the underlying memory mechanisms.

5.1 *Song development and memory mechanisms*

Song acquisition in birds who, like nightingales, develop a large vocal repertoire has been explained as a coordinated operation of three mechanisms: a 'short term memory', a 'recognition memory' and a battery of 'submemories' (Hultsch & Todt 1989c). Properties of the short term memory cause a segmentation of serially coherent master strings into different packages of information. There is evidence that this segmentation results from two constraints, a limited capacity and a time constraint memory span (Hultsch 1992). Sorting into recognition memory codes stimulus patterns as novel or familiar and categorizes information of the familiar patterns by song-type, package type, and context group. Acquired song material is then further processed in a battery of submemories, each of which stores information about a given string segment (a package). Parallel data processing in a battery of submemories would explain why long master strings are learned as effectively as short ones, even when heard only 10 to 20 times. However, since each submemory is supposed to hold information from a given string segment only, an additional process has to be postulated that somehow associates those packages that were developed from a given context group.

The proposed acquisition system predicts that the first exposure to a master string would play a key role in the acquisition of serial information on song-type

COMPLEX SIGNAL SYSTEMS IN ANIMALS 325

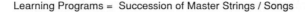

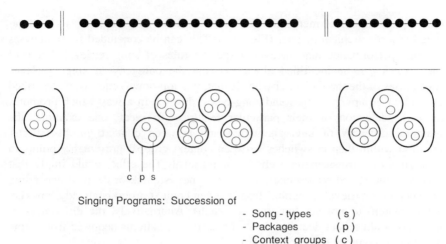

Top: A bird had been tutored with 3 master strings that were composed by different song-types (small circles). Bottom: Schematic documentation of results. Songs developed from different master strings are performed as members of different context groups (large brackets), and the size of these groups depends on the length of the tutored strings. The number of song-type packages (large circles) developed from a master string depends on this length, too, whereas their sizes do not. There is evidence suggesting that these hierarchy levels have a representation in a bird's song memory.

Figure 8. *Illustration of hierarchy levels found in the singing of trained birds (packages, context groups) above the level of songs*

sequencing. This prediction was recently confirmed by experiments in which the serial succession of song-types in a master string was altered upon subsequent exposures during the tutoring. When analyzing the song-type sequencing in the singing of the adult birds, we also found that a single exposure is sufficient for subjects to acquire such serial information. In addition, it turned out that acquisition, nevertheless, improves with increasing exposure frequency to master strings. With respect to the particular salience of the first exposure for sequence memorization, the phenomenon was termed 'primer effect' (Hultsch & Todt 1996). The findings suggest that stimulus acquisition in the song learning of birds operates in a discontinuous, 'all or none' manner and, at the same time, is enhanced gradually, i.e. through an incremental process.

5.2 *Hierarchical representation format and retrieval rules*

The representation of memorized information about songs appears to be organized in a hierarchical manner (Figure 8). This can be concluded from analyses of song performance that uncovered specific rules of song retrieval. Some of these rules can be identified already during the ontogeny of singing. Thus, trajectories of the three hierarchy levels that, in a top-down order, were described as context groups, packages and song-types, develop in a way which promotes an early detection of their particular features. To recall one example, the temporal diversity of intervals within and between context groups (shorter duration within than at switches between context groups) presumably points to properties of intrinsic pattern choice or retrieval. The effect could imply that access to the stored representation of song-types is quick or delayed depending on whether a retrieval 'program' from a given context group is already 'on' (i.e. a non-switch) or not yet 'on' (i.e. a switch). Alternatively, the differences in intervals could reflect decision times for retrieving patterns acquired from same or different contexts (Hultsch 1993b).

A hierarchically prestructured repertoire is a candidate mechanism that would facilitate retrieval in situations demanding rapid vocal responses, e.g. during interactive counter-singing. Especially in the adult, territorial birds centrally or auditorily mediated decisions on 'what to sing next' would not have to be made among the whole pool of developed song-types. Rather, both decision steps and decision time would be reduced by using a search routine that subsequently addresses a particular subset of patterns only.

The adaptive value of a hierarchically organized representation format of song data is quite conclusive in birds who, like the nightingale, have to administer large repertoires. During vocal interactions, the versatile songsters may respond to each other by sophisticated rules, i.e. by pattern specific and time specific relationships between the mutually exchanged songs. For example, in a reply category termed 'rapid matching', a male has to identify a neighbors song and at the time also to select and retrieve a song of the same type from his own repertoire within a latency of approximately one second only (Hultsch & Todt 1982; Wolffgramm & Todt 1982).

5.3 *Resumé and comparative aspects*

The vocal development of birds invites to search for parallels in the language development of humans. Such parallels were postulated for the role of interactional variables (Pepperberg 1993), and for predispositions or sensitive phases guiding the acquisition process (Marler & Peters 1981). Our inquiries into the mechanisms of learning allow to add further facets to such a comparative framework. One of them is given by the hierarchical organization of memory, allowing to administer and use large amounts of learned information. Another facet lies in the domain of acquisition mechanisms, where the formation of song-type packages shows striking similarities to the chunking of information in human serial learning (Bower 1970; Simon 1974). In humans, chunking is related to cognitive processes, that allow to define a chunk as a unit of sense, given for example by a term, or a sentence, or more. In the song acquisition of birds, on the other hand, a chunk equivalent would be a song (strophe), and a song can be regarded as a unit of sense as well. This can be concluded from the fact that songs are units of interaction, which play a particular role e.g. during vocal communication between neighbors.

On formal grounds 'songs' have been contrasted to 'sentences' (Todt & Hultsch 1996). The rules of intra-song organization, for instance, appear comparable to our syntactical rules, since changes of unit positions are meaningful in both cases (Todt 1974). At the same time, however, there are striking differences between these rules. Such differences become evident when we compare the repertoires of vocal units to the repertoires of higher level compounds. To recall, the element-type repertoire of an individual bird is clearly larger in size than his song-type repertoire. In human language, however, a small number of basic units (e.g. phonemes) serves as a pool to compose an almost unlimited amount of verbal patterns, e.g. words or sentences. The limited flexibility of element sequencing in the songs of birds is explained as a consequence of evolutionary adaptation. That is, a high flexibility could jeopardize or impair the prime function of communication by song — species recognition. Although the pattern of a song may encode individual variables, like state and status, the information on species identity of a songsters is most crucial, and this function has a strong impact on the structure of a song.

There are good reasons to suggest that cognitive accomplishments are involved in the development and use of bird song (see also Pepperberg 1993). An interesting case is given, for instance, when the birds' performance is organized according to categorical cues acquired during exposure to stimuli. Such cues may be temporal, spatial or social ones. The exposure induced song-type associations developed by our nightingales, the context groups, highlight such accomplishments on higher levels of behavioral organization. A further example is the particular performance mode of invented songs, that might reflect to the category 'individual specific song patterns'. Finally, there are other studies demonstrating that e.g. warbler species do learn the situations in which to use their songs (Kroodsma 1988; Spector et al. 1989). Currently, however, it remains open on which particular cues such categorization is based and by which mechanisms a categorical representation would be achieved. This leaves us with a challenge to explicitly address this issue in the forthcoming research on repertoire birds.

Acknowledgments

We appreciate the skillful help in handraising our birds, performing experiments or conducting data analyses provided by many people, namely H. Brumm, C. Fichtel, N. Geberzahn, M. Hoffmann, F. Schleuß, G. Schwarz-Mittelstädt and A. Wistel-Wozniak. We also are grateful to the BBAW (AG RULE, project A1) and the DFG (Az: To 13/30-1) for financial support of our studies.

References

Bondesen, P. 1979. "The Hierarchy of Bioacoustic Units Expressed by a Phrase Formula." *Biophon* 6: 2–6.
Bower, G. H. 1970. "Organizational Factors in Memory." *Cognitive Psychology* 1: 18–46.
Catchpole, C. K. 1983. "Variation in the Song of the Great Reed Warbler *Acrocephalus arundinaceus* in Relation to Mate Attraction and Territorial Defense." *Animal Behaviour* 31: 1217–1225.
Catchpole, C. K. & Slater, P. J. B. 1995. *Bird Song — Biological Themes and Variations*. Cambridge: Cambridge Univ. Press.
Chaiken, M., Böhner, J. & Marler, P. 1993. "Song Acquisition in European Starlings, *Sturnus vulgaris*: A Comparison of the Songs of Live-Tutored, Tape-Tutored and Wild-Caught Males." *Animal Behaviour* 46: 1079–1090.
Crowder, R. G. 1976. *Principles Of Learning And Memory*. Hillsdale, N.J.: Lawrence Erlbaum.
Falls, J. B. & D'Agincourt, L. G. 1982. "Why Do Meadowlarks Switch Song-Types?" *Canadian Journal of Zoology* 60: 3400–3408.
Freyschmidt, J., Kopp, M. L. & Hultsch, H. 1984. "Individuelle Entwicklung von gelernten Gesangsmustern bei Nachtigallen." *Verhandlungen Deutsche Zoologische Gesellschaft* 77: 244.
Horn, A. & Falls, J. B. 1988. "Repertoires and Countersinging in Western Meadowlarks (*Sturnella neglecta*)." *Ethology* 77: 337–343.
Hultsch, H. 1980. "Beziehungen zwischen Struktur, zeitlicher Variabilität und sozialem Einsatz im Gesang der Nachtigall, *Luscinia megarhynchos*." PhD Thesis, Faculty of Biology, Freie Universität Berlin.

Hultsch, H. 1989. "Ontogeny of Song Patterns and Their Performance Mode in Nightingales." In *Neural Mechanisms of Behaviour*, J. Erber, R. Menzel, H. J. Pflüger & D. Todt (eds.). Stuttgart: Thieme.
Hultsch, H. 1991a. "Early Experience Can Modify Singing Styles — Evidence From Experiments With Nightingales, *Luscinia megarhynchos*." *Animal Behaviour* 42: 883–889.
Hultsch, H. 1991b. "Song Ontogeny in Birds: Closed or Open Developmental Programs?" In *Synapse, Transmission, Modulation*, N. Elsner & H. Penzlin (eds.). Stuttgart: Thieme.
Hultsch, H. 1991c. "Correlates Of Repertoire Constriction in the Song Ontogeny of Nightingales (*Luscinia megarhynchos*)." *Verhandlungen Deutsche Zoologische Gesellschaft* 84: 474.
Hultsch, H. 1992. "Time Window and Unit Capacity: Dual Constraints on the Acquisition of Serial Information in Songbirds." *Journal Comparative Physiology A* 170: 275–280.
Hultsch, H. 1993a. "Ecological Versus Psychobiological Aspects of Song Learning in Birds." *Etologia* 3: 309–323.
Hultsch, H. 1993b. "Tracing the Memory Mechanisms in the Song Acquisition of Birds." *Netherlands Journal of Zoology* 43: 155–171.
Hultsch, H. & Todt, D. 1981. "Repertoire Sharing and Song Post Distance in Nightingales." *Behavioural Ecology and Sociobiology* 8: 182–188.
Hultsch, H. & Todt, D. 1982. "Temporal Performance Roles During Vocal Interactions in Nightingales." *Behavioural Ecology and Sociobiology* 11: 253–260.
Hultsch, H. & Todt, D. 1989a. "Song Acquisition and Acquisition Constraints in the Nightingale (*Luscinia megarhynchos*)." *Naturwissenschaften* 76: 83–86.
Hultsch, H. & Todt, D. 1989b. "Memorization and Reproduction of Songs in Nightingales (*Luscinia megarhynchos*): Evidence for Package Formation." *Journal Comparative Physiology A*, 165: 197–203.
Hultsch, H. & Todt, D. 1989c. "Context Memorization in the Learning of Birds." *Naturwissenschaften* 76: 584–586.
Hultsch, H. & Todt, D. 1992. "The Serial Order Effect in the Song Acquisition of Birds." *Animal Behaviour* 44: 590–592.
Hultsch, H. & Todt, D. 1996. "Discontinuous and Incremental Processes in the Song Learning of Birds: Evidence for a Primer Effect." *Journal Comparative Physiology A*: 291–299.
Hultsch, H., Lange, R. & Todt, D. 1984. "Pattern-Type Labeled Tutoring: a Method for Studying Song-Type Memories in Repertoire Birds." *Verhandlungen Deutsche Zoologische Gesellschaft* 77: 249.
Kopp, M. L. 1996. *Ontogenetische Veränderungen in der Zeitstruktur des Gesangs der Nachtigall, Luscinia megarhynchos*. PHD Thesis, Faculty of Biology, Freie Universität Berlin.
Kroodsma, D. E. 1977. "Correlates of Song Organization Among North American Wrens." *American Naturalist* 11: 995- 1008.

Kroodsma, D. E. 1979. "Vocal Dueling Among Male Marsh Wrens: Evidence for Ritualized Expressions of Dominance/Subordinance." *Auk* 98: 506–15.

Kroodsma, D. E. 1982. "Song Repertoires: Problems in their Definition and Use." In *Acoustic Communication in Birds*, Vol. 2, D. E. Kroodsma & E. H. Miller (eds.). New York: Academic Press.

Kroodsma, D. E. 1988. "Song-Types and their Use: Developmental Flexibility of The Male Blue-Winged Warbler." *Ethology* 79: 235–47.

Lemon, R. E. & Chatfield, C. 1971. "Organization of Song in Cardinals." *Animal Behaviour* 19: 1–17.

Lemon, R. E., Perrault, S. & Weary, D. M. 1994. "Dual Strategies of Song Development in American Redstarts." *Setophaga ruticilla. Animal Behaviour* 47: 317–329.

Marler, P. 1976. "Sensory Templates in Species-Specific Behavior." In *Simpler Networks and Behavior*, J. C. Fentress (ed.). Sunderland, MA: Sinauer Associates.

Marler, P. 1991. "Differences in Behavioural Development in Closely Related Species: Bird Song." In *The Development and Integration of Behaviour*, P. Bateson (ed.). Cambridge: Cambridge Univ. Press.

Marler, P. & Peters, S. 1981. "Birdsong and Speech: Evidence for Special Processing." In *Perspectives on the Study of Speech,* P. Eimas & J. Miller (eds.). Hillsdale, N.J.: Lawrence Erlbaum.

Marler, P. & Peters, S. 1982a. "Structural Changes in Song Ontogeny in the Swamp Sparrow, *Melospiza georgiana*." *Auk* 99: 446–58.

Marler, P. & Peters, S. 1982b. "Developmental Overproduction and Selective Attrition: New Processes in the Epigenesis of Birdsong." *Developmental Psychobiology* 15: 369–78.

Marler, P. & Peters, S. 1987. "A Sensitive Period for Song Acquisition in the Song Sparrow, *Melospiza melodia*: a Case of Age Limited Learning." *Ethology* 76: 89–100.

Marler, P. & Nelson, D. 1993. "Action-Based Learning: a New Form of Devlopmental Plasticity in Bird Song." *Netherlands Journal Zoology* 43: 91–101.

Müller-Bröse, M. & Todt, D. 1991. "Lokomotorische Aktivität von Nachtigallen (*Luscinia megarhynchos*) während auditorischer Stimulation mit Artgesang, präsentiert in ihrer lernsensiblen Altersphase." *Verhandlungen Deutsche Zoologische Gesellschaft* 84: 476- 477.

Naguib, M., Kolb, H. & Hultsch, H. 1991. "Hierarchische Verzweigungsstruktur in den Gesansgstrophen der Vögel.*" Verhandlungen Deutsche Zoologische Gesellschaft* 48: 477.

Naguib, M. & Kolb, H. 1992. "Vergleich des Strophenaufbaus und der Strophenabfolgen an den Gesängen von Sposser (*Luscinia luscinia*) und Blaukehlchen (*Luscinia svecica*)." *Journal für Ornithologie* 133: 133–145.

Nelson, D. A. 1992. "Song Overproduction, Song Matching and Selective Attrition During Development." In *Playback and Studies of Animal Communication,* P. K. McGregor (ed.). New York: Plenum Press.

Nelson, D. A., Marler, P. & Palleroni, A. 1995. "A Comparative Approach to Vocal Learning: Intraspecific Variation in the Learning Process." *Animal Behaviour* 50: 83–97.
Nottebohm, F., Nottebohm, M. & Crane, L. 1986. "Developmental and Seasonal Changes in Canary Song and their Relation to Changes in the Anatomy of the Song Control System." *Behavioural Neural Biology* 46: 445–471.
Payne, R. B. 1981. "Song Learning and Social Interaction in Indigo Buntings." *Animal Behaviour 29*: 688–697.
Pepperberg, I. M. 1993. "A Review of the Effects of Social Interaction on Vocal Learning in African Grey Parrots *(Psittacus erithacus)*." *Netherlands Journal of Zoology* 43: 104–124.
Pöppel, E. 1978. "Time Perception." In *Handbook of Sensory Physiology, Vol VIII*. Heidelberg: Springer.
Simon, H. A. 1974. "How Big is a Chunk?" *Science* 183: 482–468.
Slater, P. J. B. 1989. "Bird Song Learning Causes and Consequences." *Ethology Ecology and Evolution* 1: 19–46.
Spector, D. A., McKim L. K. & Kroodsma, D. E. 1989. "Yellow Warblers are Able to Learn Songs and the Situations in Which to Use Them." *Animal Behaviour* 38: 723–725.
Thompson, N, S., LeDoux, K. & Moody, K. 1994. "A System for Describing Bird Song Units." *Bioacoustics* 5: 267–279.
Todt, D. 1968. "Zur Steuerung unregelmässiger Verhaltensabläufe." In *Kybernetik*, H. Mittelstaedt (ed.). München.
Todt, D. 1970. "Zur Ordnung im Gesang der Nachtigall (Luscinia megarhynchos)." *Verhandlungen Deutsche Zoologische Gesellschaft* 64: 249–252.
Todt, D. 1974. "Strophen-Syntax bei der Amsel *(Turdus merula)*." *Zeitschrift für Naturforschung* 23: 178–185.
Todt, D. & Hultsch, H. 1980. "Functional Aspects of Sequences and Hierarchy in Bird Song." *Acta XVII Congressus Internationalis Ornithologici Berlin*: 663–670.
Todt, D. & Böhner, J. 1994. "Former Experience Can Modify Social Selectivity During Song Learning in the Nightingale *(Luscinia megarhynchos)*." *Ethology 97*: 169–176.
Todt, D., Hultsch, H. & Heike, D. 1979. "Conditions Affecting Song Acquisition in Nightingales *(Luscinia megarhynchos)*." *Zeitschrift für Tierpsychologie* 51: 23–25.
Todt, D. & Hultsch, H. 1994. "Biologische Grundlagen des Dialogs." In *Kommunikation und Humanontogenese*, K. F. Wessel & F. Naumann (eds.). Bielefeld: Kleine Verlag.
Todt, D. & Hultsch, H. 1996. "Acquisition and Performance of Repertoires: Ways of Coping With Diversity and Versatility." In *Ecology and Evolution of Communication*, D. E. Kroodsma & E. H. Miller (eds.). Ithaka, NY: Cornell University Press.
Wistel-Wozniak, A. & Hultsch, H. 1993. "Konstante und altersabhängig veränderte Gesangsmerkmale bei handaufgezogenen Nachtigallen." *Verhandlungen Deutsche Zoologische Gesellschaft* 86: 281.
Wolffgramm, J. & Todt, D. 1982. "Pattern and Time Specificity in Vocal Responses of Blackbirds, *Turdus merula*." *Behaviour* 81: 264–286.

Index

A

acquisition 24, 25, 31, 36, 41, 42, 45, 46, 48–51, 53–56, 59, 60, 62, 63, 68, 70, 72, 76–78, 80–82, 87, 99, 121, 123, 146, 159, 167, 173–175, 197, 198, 208, 221, 242, 251, 263, 270, 276, 281, 282, 285, 299, 300, 302, 314–316, 318, 319, 322–325, 327
adult input 165–168, 176
articulatory form (AF) 284–286, 288–290, 293, 297–299, 301, 304
amalgams 122, 124, 126, 128, 129, 131–135, 137, 145, 146, 149, 155
ambiguity 122, 157, 167–170, 172, 175, 303
argument structure (AS) 294, 296, 304
association groups 317, 321
auditory learning 318
auxiliaries 12, 92, 99, 103, 121–126, 128, 130–132, 137, 145, 146, 149, 150, 152, 153, 154, 251

B

bird song 309–311, 324, 327
brain activity 233, 235, 247–249, 252, 254, 255, 269
Broca's area 232, 243

C

categorization 285, 287, 288, 293, 297, 298, 303, 304, 318, 328
catenatives 122–126, 128, 130–132, 137, 139, 153, 154

CDI 248, 249, 251
childhood aphasia 232, 233, 236
chunking 327
clitics 11, 23, 32, 34, 36, 157
closed class words 251, 252, 254, 255
coda 32, 45–50, 53–56, 59
coda fricatives 47–51, 53–56
compounds 35, 59–61, 72–79, 81
consonant clusters 59, 60, 77
constituency 36
constraint-based approach to language acquisition 4, 18
context effect 317
crosslinguistic 158, 159, 163, 165, 174
cue 60, 70, 71, 80, 157, 166, 175, 176, 182, 183, 185, 186, 188, 190–192, 195–197, 209, 212, 214, 267, 268, 310, 316, 318, 327, 328

D

development of song 322
developmental neuropsychology 197
developmental pattern 60, 64–67, 76, 78, 170, 248
Dutch 4, 5, 7, 9–11, 17, 18, 24, 49, 59–62, 65, 68, 80–82, 163, 266

E

early speech 3, 4, 111, 114
ELAN 233, 235, 240–242
English 4, 5, 7, 9–12, 15–19, 24, 25, 41, 43, 81, 82, 93, 103, 122, 123, 126, 154, 155, 160, 163, 194, 243, 264–267, 270, 274, 304

event-related potentials (ERPs) 181–186, 190–192, 194–197, 201–203, 205–207, 210–219, 233, 237, 239, 247, 248, 252, 255, 265, 269
EXHAUSTIVITY 37–41, 43

F
filler syllables 24, 30, 122, 124, 126, 132, 154, 171
focal brain lesions 254, 255
foot (F) 3, 5, 6, 8–11, 13–16, 24, 29, 32–34, 37–43, 60–62, 64, 65, 67–73, 75–82
formal features 282, 293, 295, 297, 299
frame-and-slot grammars 121
function words 12, 24, 34, 37, 38, 54, 157, 158, 163, 165–171, 173–176, 237, 251
functional categories 42, 122, 155, 298

G
German 23–34, 37–43, 163, 238, 239, 243, 264, 271, 272, 303
grammatical form (GF) 124, 153, 288
grammatical morphemes 3, 4, 7, 11, 12, 14–17, 122, 159, 175
grammatical morphology 3, 4, 11, 13, 15, 17–19

H
hierarchy 291, 310, 311, 317, 319, 324, 326

I
I-language 283–285, 287, 289, 291, 301
Icelandic 157–163, 173, 175, 176
imitation 133, 143, 144, 148, 315–317, 319–323
infancy 174, 175, 182, 183, 192, 195
input 37, 55, 60, 62, 67, 70, 71, 75, 77, 79–81, 157–163, 165–168, 171, 173–176, 182, 263, 264, 267, 268, 271, 276, 277, 289, 318
input frequency 159, 167, 174

K
kernel structures 88, 103–105, 108, 112–116

L
LAN 233, 243
language ability 248, 254–256
language acquisition 87, 94, 121, 181, 197, 209, 231, 242, 263, 264, 269, 272, 273, 281, 287, 289, 300, 302
language-brain relationship 231, 232, 236
language development 18, 153, 160, 163, 171, 173, 174, 181, 182, 212, 213, 221, 223, 247, 248, 255, 257, 264, 268, 269, 273, 309, 326
language impairment 231, 248
late talkers 248, 254–257
lexical development 269
longitudinal case studies 157–159

M
mapping 39, 40, 87, 115, 158, 167, 168, 283, 299
maximal alignment 87, 95, 97, 99, 101–103, 115, 116
memory mechanisms 315, 324
minimal word 5–7, 9, 10, 81, 82
mismatch 41, 67, 70, 80, 204, 205, 211, 295
mismatch negativity (MMN) 192, 194, 195
modals 121–126, 128, 130–132, 137, 141, 153, 154
monosyllabic 5–8, 14, 24, 32, 39–41, 62, 64, 65, 67, 68, 70, 71, 81, 82, 165, 170, 176
morphological development 3

morphological features 293–299, 303, 304
morphosyntax 45

N
N200 185, 206, 207, 209, 248, 252, 254–256
N400 233, 237–242, 254
N450 252, 254
nativism 266
network architecture 266, 276
nightingale 311, 314–318, 322–324, 326, 327

O
ontogenetic trajectories 318–321
open class words 127, 251, 252, 254, 255
Optimality Theory (OT) 23, 36, 80, 301
output 37, 66, 68, 70–72, 79, 80, 102, 105–107, 110–114, 232, 236, 265, 274, 276, 277, 282, 300, 320

P
P100 206, 255–257
P600 233–235, 240–242
package effect 317
parameters 46, 49, 56, 60, 61, 67–72, 78–82, 242, 316
partial analysis and partial acquisition 121
past tense 126, 137, 140, 141, 145, 153, 270, 294
phonetic features 281–283, 286, 287, 289
phonetic form (PF) 286–291, 301–303
phonological phrases (PP) 4–7, 9, 11–18, 24, 89–91, 99, 101, 109, 113
phonological words (PW) 4–16, 31–33, 36

phonology 30, 40, 68, 87, 89, 91, 93, 94, 99, 101–105, 108–111, 113, 114, 116, 154, 181, 301
plural 16, 45, 48, 50, 51, 54–56, 147, 263, 270–272, 285, 297
Portuguese 45, 46, 48, 49, 51, 56, 82
predisposition 316, 323, 326
prepositions 4, 12, 13, 34, 159–162, 165, 171, 173–175, 251, 297
procedural knowledge 232
prosodic clitics 11–14
prosodic constraints 4, 10–18, 37
prosodic development 7, 45
prosodic hierarchy 5, 37, 41
prosodic structure 4, 6–8, 10–12, 15–18, 23, 24, 31, 36–40, 42, 45, 50, 54–56, 59, 60, 62, 66, 73, 79, 80, 90, 95
prosodic words (PW) 23, 24, 37–42, 61, 74, 75, 78
prosody 56, 96, 111, 113, 123, 159, 232
prosody-syntax mapping 39
proto-articles 23–30, 41–43
protomorpheme 130

R
repertoire modification 322
representation 14, 31–33, 40, 71, 80, 87, 89, 94–96, 98, 99, 105, 106, 108, 110, 111, 113, 115, 116, 160, 165, 263, 264, 266, 269–272, 274, 277, 281, 282, 284, 292, 293, 299, 300, 304, 321, 324, 326, 328
retrieval rules 326
rhythmic production constraints 3, 4, 9, 10, 14, 18

S
segmental structure 64, 66, 167
segmentation 152, 158, 167, 175, 267, 316, 324

semantic components 281, 282, 296, 299
semantic form (SF) 284, 285, 288–295, 297–299, 302–304
sensitive phases 326
sign language 287–289, 301
song-type 310, 311, 313–319, 321–327
Spanish 4, 7–12, 15, 17, 18, 23–31, 34–43, 264, 266
speech perception 17, 181, 182, 185, 186, 196, 197, 201, 212, 214, 222, 223, 263, 265, 301
stress 4, 5, 7–9, 11, 18, 34, 35, 50, 53, 54, 56, 61–82, 157–160, 162, 166, 167, 173, 174–176, 266–268, 304
Swedish 157–164, 168, 170, 171, 174–176
syllable 3–5, 7–10, 13, 14, 17, 18, 24, 26–29, 32, 34, 37, 39, 43, 45, 46, 48–50, 53–56, 59–65, 67–73, 75–82, 170, 184, 185, 188, 190, 191, 203, 204, 217, 218, 265, 267, 301, 310
syllable structure 7, 50, 60, 62, 78, 80, 82, 301
syntactic features 293, 294, 296–299

T
telegraphic speech 87, 94, 95, 97, 103, 111, 115
template 67–71, 76, 81, 160, 167, 168, 173, 174, 315
transition 63, 66, 72, 82, 157, 174, 175, 188, 190–192, 221
trochaic foot 3, 8–11, 61, 65, 68, 70, 80

U
unfooted syllables 10, 18, 24, 31, 32, 37, 38, 40, 43
Universal Grammar (UG) 68, 282, 284, 285, 287–290, 292, 293, 299–303

V
verb particles 160, 163, 171, 175
vocabulary size 213, 248, 249, 254, 256
vocabulary spurt 248, 249, 268–270, 276
vocal repertoire 323, 324

W
Wernicke's area 232

In the series LANGUAGE ACQUISITION AND LANGUAGE DISORDERS (LALD) the following titles have been published thus far or are scheduled for publication:

1. WHITE, Lydia: *Universal Grammar and Second Language Acquisition.* 1989.
2. HUEBNER, Thom and Charles A. FERGUSON (eds): *Cross Currents in Second Language Acquisition and Linguistic Theory.* 1991.
3. EUBANK, Lynn (ed.): *Point Counterpoint. Universal Grammar in the second language.* 1991.
4. ECKMAN, Fred R. (ed.): *Confluence. Linguistics, L2 acquisition and speech pathology.* 1993.
5. GASS, Susan and Larry SELINKER (eds): *Language Transfer in Language Learning.* Revised edition. 1992.
6. THOMAS, Margaret: *Knowledge of Reflexives in a Second Language.* 1993.
7. MEISEL, Jürgen M. (ed.): *Bilingual First Language Acquisition. French and German grammatical development.* 1994.
8. HOEKSTRA, Teun and Bonnie SCHWARTZ (eds): *Language Acquisition Studies in Generative Grammar.* 1994.
9. ADONE, Dany: *The Acquisition of Mauritian Creole.* 1994.
10. LAKSHMANAN, Usha: *Universal Grammar in Child Second Language Acquisition. Null subjects and morphological uniformity.* 1994.
11. YIP, Virginia: *Interlanguage and Learnability. From Chinese to English.* 1995.
12. JUFFS, Alan: *Learnability and the Lexicon. Theories and second language acquisition research.* 1996.
13. ALLEN, Shanley: *Aspects of Argument Structure Acquisition in Inuktitut.* 1996.
14. CLAHSEN, Harald (ed.): *Generative Perspectives on Language Acquisition. Empirical findings, theoretical considerations and crosslinguistic comparisons.* 1996.
15. BRINKMANN, Ursula: *The Locative Alternation in German. Its structure and acquisition.* 1997.
16. HANNAHS, S.J. and Martha YOUNG-SCHOLTEN (eds): *Focus on Phonological Acquisition.* 1997.
17. ARCHIBALD, John: *Second Language Phonology.* 1998.
18. KLEIN, Elaine C. and Gita MARTOHARDJONO (eds): *The Development of Second Language Grammars. A generative approach.* 1999.
19. BECK, Maria-Luise (ed.): *Morphology and its Interfaces in Second Language Knowledge.* 1998.
20. KANNO, Kazue (ed.): *The Acquisition of Japanese as a Second Language.* 1999.
21. HERSCHENSOHN, Julia: *The Second Time Around – Minimalism and L2 Acquisition.* 2000.
22. SCHAEFFER, Jeanette C.: *The Acquisition of Direct Object Scrambling and Clitic Placement. Syntax and pragmatics.* 2000.
23. WEISSENBORN, Jürgen and Barbara HÖHLE (eds): *Approaches to Bootstrapping. Phonological, lexical, syntactic and neurophysiological aspects of early language acquisition. Volume 1.* 2001.
24. WEISSENBORN, Jürgen and Barbara HÖHLE (eds): *Approaches to Bootstrapping. Phonological, lexical, syntactic and neurophysiological aspects of early language acquisition. Volume 2.* 2001.
25. CARROLL, Susanne E.: *Input and Evidence. The raw material of second language acquisition.* n.y.p.
26. SLABAKOVA, Roumyana: *Telicity in the Second Language.* 2001.